A Staffordshire Pot Lid:
The Red Bull Inn.
Sold for £4,600.

A Fairing: Every Vehicle
Driven by a Horse, Mule or
Ass 2d. Sold for £600.

POT LIDS & FAIRINGS
Goss & Crested China, Fairings & Baxter Prints

A Royal Worcester
vase, 340mm high.
Sold for £1,800.

Tsar Nicholas I:
A glass tumbler, c1850.
Sold for £700.

A George III
beaker, c1793.
Sold for £2,800.

A Prattware Plaque,
245mm high.
Sold for £3,800.

1813 French Defeat
by the Russians.
Sold for £700.

A Winston Churchill
Toby Jug, by Wilkinson.
Sold for £1,600.

For catalogues and information whether buying or selling please contact:

SPECIAL AUCTION SERVICES
Kennetholme, Midgham, Near Reading RG7 5UX

(North side of the A4 exactly eight miles west of junction 12 on M4/A4)

www.antiquestradegazette.com/sas   commemorative@aol.com

Fax: 0118 971 2420   **Tel: 0118 971 2949**

ENTRIES ARE NOW INVITED FOR OUR FORTHCOMING AUCTIONS IN 2006
4th & 5th March, 3rd & 4th June, 9th & 10th September, 25th & 26th November

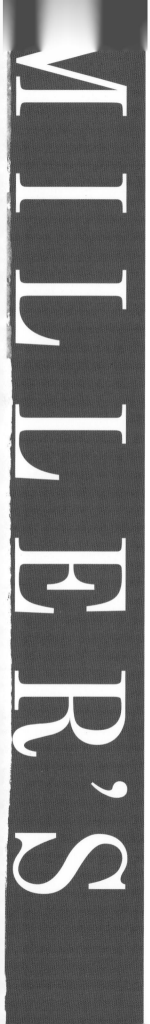

MILLER'S

ceramics

ceramics

John Sandon *GENERAL EDITOR*

MILLER'S CERAMICS BUYER'S GUIDE

Created and designed by
Miller's Publications
The Cellars, High Street
Tenterden, Kent, TN30 6BN
Tel: +44 (0) 1580 766411
Fax: +44 (0) 1580 766100

First published in Great Britain in 2006
by Miller's, a division of Mitchell Beazley,
imprints of Octopus Publishing Group Ltd,
2–4 Heron Quays, London E14 4JP
Miller's is a registered trademark of
Octopus Publishing Group Ltd

Some images have appeared in previous editions of
Miller's Antiques Price Guide, Miller's Collectables Price Guide
and Miller's Collecting Pottery & Porcelain

ISBN: 1 84533 0625

A CIP catalogue record for this book is
available from the British Library

Set in Frutiger

Colour origination by One Thirteen Ltd, Whitstable, Kent
Additional colour origination by Ian Williamson, Pevensey Scanning
Printed and bound in China by Toppan Printing Company Limited

General Editor: John Sandon
Managing Editor: Valerie Lewis
Production Co-ordinator: Philip Hannath
Editorial Co-ordinator: Deborah Wanstall
Designer: Nick Harris
Editorial Assistants: Melissa Hall, Joanna Hill, Maureen Horner
Production Assistants: Charlotte Smith, Mel Smith, Ethne Tragett
Advertising Executives: Emma Gillingham, Michael Webb, Carol Woodcock
Advertising Co-ordinator & Administrator: Melinda Williams
Advertisement Designer: Kari Moody
Indexer: Hilary Bird
Production: Jane Rogers
Jacket Design: Rhonda Summerbell
Additional Photographers: Emma Gillingham, Paul Harding, Dennis O'Reilly, Robin Saker

Front cover illustration:
A Burmantofts Persian-style faïence vase, painted with stylized flowers,
impressed and painted marks, 1892–1904, 6¾in (17cm) high.
£240–280 / €340–400 / $450–530 ✗ SWO

Contents

6 Acknowledgments
7 How to use this book
8 General Infomation

**10 Collecting By Type,
Period & Style**
12 Tin-Glazed Earthenware
24 English Pottery
30 Early English Porcelain
39 Blue Printed Pottery
47 Staffordshire Figures
56 Majolica
62 Armorial & Crested China
66 Art Pottery
81 Art Deco
87 Post-War Design and
Contemporary Ceramics

98 Collecting By Maker
100 Belleek
103 Clarice Cliff
111 Derby
114 Doulton
125 Mason's Ironstone
129 Minton
134 Meissen
146 Moorcroft
155 Sèvres & Sèvres Style
159 Wedgwood
163 Worcester

174 Collecting By Country
176 American
184 Scandinavian
190 Scottish
196 Welsh

204 Collecting By Shape
206 Animals
211 Baskets & Centrepieces
215 Bowls
217 Boxes
220 Candlesticks & Extinguishers
225 Clocks & Mirrors
227 Cups & Saucers
231 Figures & Busts
235 Inkwells & Desk Sets
239 Jardinières
245 Jugs & Ewers
250 Mugs & Tankards
255 Plates & Dishes
260 Plaques
264 Pot Lids
268 Sauce Boats & Cream Boats
270 Scent Bottles
271 Services
276 Tea Canisters
278 Teapots & Coffee Pots
284 Tiles
289 Toby Jugs & Character Jugs
294 Tureens
298 Vases

305 Index to Advertisers
306 Glossary
308 Directory of Restorers
309 Directory of Specialists
311 Key to Illustrations
315 Index

Acknowledgments

The publishers would like to acknowledge the great assistance given by our consultants.
We would also like to extend our thanks to all auction houses and their press offices, as well as
dealers and collectors, who have assisted us in the production of this book.

TIN-GLAZED EARTHENWARE:

Jonathan Horne,
66c Kensington Church Street,
London W8 4BY

EARLY ENGLISH POTTERY,
STAFFORDSHIRE FIGURES:

John Howard, 6 Market Place,
Woodstock,
Oxon OX20 1TE

EARLY ENGLISH PORCELAIN, MEISSEN,
WEDGWOOD, WORCESTER:

John Sandon, Bonhams,
101 New Bond Street,
London W1Y 0AS

BLUE-PRINTED POTTERY:

Gillian Neale Antiques,
P O Box 247,
Aylesbury, Bucks HP20 1JZ

ARMORIAL & CRESTED CHINA:

Linda Pine,
Goss & Crested China Club,
62 Murray Road,
Horndean, Hants PO8 9JL

DERBY, MINTON AND SEVRES:

Mark Law,
Ash Cottage,
Ashmore Green Road,
Ashmore Green,
Newbury, Berks RG18 9ER

POST-WAR DESIGN AND
CONTEMPORARY CERAMICS:

Beverley,
30 Church Street,
Marylebone, London NW8 8EP

ART POTTERY, ART DECO, DOULTON,
SCANDINAVIAN:

Mark Oliver, Bonhams,
101 New Bond Street,
London W1Y 0AS

WELSH:

Islwyn Watkins,
Offa's Dyke Antiques Centre,
4 High Street, Knighton,
Powys, Wales LD7 1AT

SCOTTISH:

Campbell Armour,
Lyon & Turnbull,
Edinburgh,
Scotland EH1 3RR

How to use this book

In order to find a particular item, consult the contents list on page 5 to find the main heading – for example, Collecting by Maker. Having located your area of interest, you will find that larger sections have been sub-divided. If you are looking for a particular factory, designer or craftsman, consult the index which starts on page 315.

163

Worcester

A Worcester teapot, painted in underglaze blue with Prunus Root pattern, c1753, 5in (12.5cm) wide.
£2,500–2,800 / €3,700–4,100
$4,700–5,300 ⊞ JUP

Eighteenth-century Worcester
The Worcester factory was one of the most successful porcelain manufacturers of the 18th century and is famous, primarily, for the vast amount of tea and coffee wares it produced. Together with Chelsea, Worcester remains perhaps the most popular of the 18th-century factories with collectors. The porcelain made by Worcester contained soapstone which made it very stable and able to withstand boiling water. As a result, vast quantities of hollow wares have survived. So daunting is the range available that collectors often concentrate their efforts on a particular area such as early wares, transfer-printed designs, teapots or coffee cups. Prices for Worcester pieces are generally lower than for Chelsea ones. Among the most readily available blue printed patterns are the Three Flowers pattern, Fence pattern and Fisherman and Cormorant pattern.

Information box
covers relevant collecting information on factories, makers, care and restoration, fakes and alterations.

A Worcester coffee cup, painted with a Chinese lady and other figures, c1753, 2¼in (5.5cm) high.
£2,000–2,250 / €2,950–3,300
$3,750–4,250 ⊞ JUP

A Worcester bowl, painted in underglaze blue with Cormorant pattern, slight damage, 1755–56, 6in (15cm) diam.
£540–600 / €790–880
$1,000–1,150 ⊞ JUP

Caption
provides a brief description of the item including the maker's name, medium, year it was made and in some cases condition.

Further reading
Miller's Collecting Pottery & Porcelain: The Facts At Your Fingertips, Miller's Publications, 2001

A Worcester sauce boat, printed with a smoky primitive depicting a squirrel, pheasant and herdsman, c1755, 8in (20.5cm) wide.
£1,100–1,250 / €1,600–1,800
$2,050–2,350 ⊞ JUP
The earliest transfer prints at Worcester are known as 'smoky primitives' because of their characteristic smoky appearance, caused by imperfect printing.

▶ A Worcester pickle dish, moulded in the form of a shell, painted with Two Peony Rock Bird pattern, c1758, 3in (7.5cm) diam.
£630–700 / €930–1,050
$1,200–1,350 ⊞ JUP

Further reading
directs the reader towards additional sources of information.

Source code
refers to the Key to Illustrations on page 311 that lists the details of where the item was photographed. The ✗ icon indicates the item was sold at auction. The ⊞ icon indicates the item originated from a dealer.

Price guide
this is based on actual prices realized. Remember that Miller's is a price guide not a price list and prices are affected by many variables such as location, condition, desirability and so on. Don't forget that if you are selling it is quite likely you will be offered less than the price range. Price ranges for items sold at auction tend to include the buyer's premium and VAT if applicable. The exchange rate used in this edition is 1.47 for € and 1.88 for $.

General Information

The term 'ceramics' refers to anything that is shaped from wet clay and then fired in a kiln to make it hard. Different consistencies and colours of clay, mixed with a variety of other ingredients, produce different types of finished ceramic body, from coarse-grained, porous earthenware and the harder stoneware, both referred to as pottery, to the finest porcelain.

The Body

Earthenware: To make it waterproof, earthenware has to be coated with a glaze. Earthenware clays come in many colours, which can often only be seen if the object has a chip, and the colour can give a clue as to its origins. For example, Torquay and Watcombe earthenwares contain the rusty orange of the iron-rich Devon clays. Creamware, a form of earthenware, was developed in Staffordshire in the mid-18th century using good-quality white Devon clay, and was a cheap alternative to porcelain. It can be fired at a higher temperature than other earthenwares, and has been used consistently for everyday crockery.

Stoneware: Harder than earthenware, stoneware is also finer-textured and non-porous even if left unglazed, and could be fired at a higher temperature. Fine white stoneware was developed by Staffordshire potters in the early 18th century to compete with imported Chinese porcelain. The white, strong clay could be potted very thinly to produce a cream-coloured body. Other fine stonewares include black basalt and jasper ware.

Porcelain: First developed in China over a thousand years ago, porcelain can be white, grey or cream. Objects are strong but delicate and often translucent – hollow pieces usually resonate when tapped. Its development came from experiments in adding materials such as ground glass, quartz, flint and bones to the clay base. Soft-paste porcelain was made in Europe from the 16th century onwards, and was fired at a lower temperature than hard-paste porcelain. Hard-paste porcelain originated in China and is watertight even if left unglazed. It consisted of a mixture of china clay, or kaolin, and a ground felspar mineral called china stone, or petuntse, and the resulting shiny surface is difficult to scratch. A true porcelain similar to this but creamier was made at Meissen in Germany by Böttger c1708, and was first produced in Britain in 1768, using china clay and china stone from Cornwall.

The Glaze

Glaze is a glassy film, usually made from powered minerals mixed with water, washed over the ceramic body to which it fuses during firing. Glazes are used either to make a piece waterproof, as in the case of earthenware, or for decoration. They can be matt or shiny, soft or hard, coloured or colourless. Earthenware glazes were commonly based on either tin or lead, while European hard-paste porcelain used glazes based on ground felspar. A colourless lead glaze was used on early soft-paste porcelain, but later a mixture of crushed flint and/or glass was used, known as frit. The three principal glazes are:

Lead glaze – transparent, glassy, used on most European earthenware. It can also be coloured by adding metal oxides. Creamware, developed by Josiah Wedgwood in the 18th century, is covered in a thin, lead glaze.

Tin glaze – contains tin oxide, giving the glaze an opaque white finish that could be left plain or decorated with colours.

Salt-glaze – formed by throwing salt into the kiln at about 1,300ºC during the firing of stoneware. The sodium in the salt combined with silicates in the body to form a thick glassy glaze. English salt-glaze from the mid-18th century is light buff in colour with a dimpled 'orange peel' surface.

The Surface

The surface of pottery often features distinctive characteristics:

Crackling – the surface of lead-glazed wares often features a network pattern, owing to the fact that the glaze does not form a natural bond with the body and also has cooled at a different rate, thus causing a cracking of the surface.

Iridescence – the structure of lead glaze is prone to break down over time into layers, giving an iridescent or 'rainbow' effect.

Pinholes – minute air bubbles sometimes produce small holes in the glaze. This effect can also be caused by variations in the thickness of the glaze.

Decoration

It is sometimes hard to distinguish between transfer-printing and painting on ceramics, but after close examination and a little experience it becomes easier to recognise the difference. For instance, shading that has been painted on to an object will be colour-washed, while on a transfer-print taken from a copperplate engraving it will be crosshatched. Vertical lines on a printed image are consistently straight, whereas an artist will create a different impression with freehand brushstrokes. Although few pieces would be signed by an artist, some factories added a code to their own mark to indicate who painted the item. If a signature of a renowned artist appears on a piece, it indicates a transfer-print as they would not have painted commercial porcelain themselves.

Underglaze colours, known as high temperature colours, are able to withstand a temperature of 1,300°C. The colours are usually antimony (yellow), iron (brown), manganese (purple) and copper (green).

Overglaze enamels, fired at a lower temperature of up to 950°C, give a much greater range. Enamel colours were made by adding metallic oxides to molten glass and reducing the cooled mixture to a fine power. This was then mixed with an oily base, painted on to the surface and fused by firing.

Slip decoration:
1. Sgraffito: a sharp pointed tool is used to cut through a layer of slip (liquid clay with a creamy consistency, applied using a nozzle), to the pottery body underneath. Used throughout Europe on earthenware and stoneware, this technique was also used in the United States.
2. Slip combing: two colours of slip are combed over one another to give a feathered effect.
3. Slip trailing: the body is trailed with slip in a colour contrasting to the ground colour of the piece.
4. Sprigging: relief decoration moulded from slip is added to the surface of a piece before firing.
5. Stamping: a pad of contrasting clay is applied to the body and a design stamped on to it. The excess clay is removed when dry.
6. Piercing: the unfired body is marked with a design that is then cut out using a knife.
7. Metallic lustre: shiny, metallic decoration with the appearance of copper or silver.
8. Sponging: the piece is daubed with a sponge giving a mottled effect after firing. Popular in the United States from about 1825 to 1850, pottery with this type of decoration was known as spatterware.
9. Low relief: decoration that is slightly raised from the surface of the object.
10. Incised decoration: made by cutting or engraving into the body.

Moulding & Casting

Most ceramic figures were reproduced in quantities ranging from tens to thousands, using moulds made from an original model. Clay pressed into the mould was left to harden before the figure was freed and fired. To make more complex forms with bold or undercut detail, parts of the figure or vessel would be made in separate moulds and then stuck together with slip. Heavy, almost solid pieces were produced by this method.

Many factories used moulds made from plaster of Paris from c1720. Liquid clay was poured into these moulds and left to stand; the water was absorbed into the plaster leaving a layer of clay to harden on the mould's inner surface. Excess slip was poured off and after drying the hardened clay could be removed. Called slip-casting, this method allowed finer detail to be used.

Handling Ceramics

An essential part of learning about ceramics is handling them. Damage can occur very easily, and with a little care pitfuls can be avoided. Firstly, when picking up an object that has a lid, always remove the lid first, preferably not by the knop which may be insecure. Secondly, lift hollow objects by supporting the body gently with two hands. Handles are often weakened by use, so it is best not to use these to hold an item. After examining an object, replace it carefully, well away from any other objects on the surface. Try to avoid touching gilding as it is easily rubbed and worn through handling.

Care & Restoration

The investment value of old pottery and porcelain will be reduced considerably by damage, except in the case of very early and rare earthenware where a certain amount of damage is inevitable. However, a buyer may wish to build up a dinner service from a certain pattern and may find items with some damage that will not affect its practical use.

Different types of ceramic bodies need to be cleaned in various ways. Despite its fragile appearance, hard-paste porcelain and high-fired stoneware can safely be washed by hand in warm water with a little detergent added. Unglazed ceramics are porous and washing them may cause the dirt to soak into the body causing discolouration. Soft-paste porcelain and low-fired earthenwares may also be discoloured and damaged by washing, but can usually be wiped gently with a damp cloth. If in doubt about how to deal with a certain type of ceramic do not be afraid to consult a specialist dealer or restorer for advice.

As the main problem with handling ceramics is breakage, it is advisable to have repairs carried out by a specialist. Everyday crockery of little or no monetary value can be mended at home using special resin, but it is essential that the surfaces to be joined are clean and dry before the glue is applied. Any excess adhesive that seeps out from the join must be wiped off immediately before it sets, otherwise it will be impossible to remove when it dries. Broken parts of figures etc can be remodelled with plastic resins or ceramic pastes, but this would be a job for a qualified restorer who will also know how to retouch the paint and glaze to disguise the repair.

Always check for rivets and signs of poor repair when purchasing an old piece pottery. If the object is inexpensive and attractive, you can have the rivets removed and any poor restoration can probably be improved upon by a professional restorer.

COLLECTING BY TYPE, PERIOD & STYLE

When you walk round a general auction sale, a vast assortment of different styles are laid out in random mayhem. This reflects the contents of the typical home. As a result of inheritance the accumulation of generations usually fights for space in crowded rooms and bulging china cabinets. Most households acquire antiques and ornaments one by one, as gifts are received or objects are bought simply because they appeal to the purchaser at the time. When forming a collection, however, items are chosen because they go with objects already owned. A collection has to have a common theme running through it, a theme that entirely depends on the taste of the collector.

One of the most common influences is the age of the home where a collector lives, for it is natural to acquire furnishings and objects that match the age of your house. This can, when taken to extemes, result in the creation of a living museum. The effect can certainly be stunning, but living so firmly in the past may not be particularly comfortable. Today, collectors are far more likely to live in a 1930s or more modern house and as a result many more artefacts of the 20th century are purchased.

The taste of most home-owners falls into one of three categories – traditional, country or modern. Within a traditional interior, it is possible to mix and match Georgian and Victorian dark wood furniture with Turkish rugs, French bronzes, Dresden porcelain and

A London delft plate, painted with a gentleman in a garden, c1760, 7¾in (19.5cm) diam.
£190–220 / €280–320
$360–410 ✠ G(L)

old Wedgwood. In a country home, 17th-century oak or Arts and Crafts-style vernacular furniture suits exposed brickwork and beams, Delft dishes and blue-printed earthenware. Meanwhile, a modern house or flat will blend with Scandinavian design, Clarice Cliff and contemporary studio pottery. What you cannot easily do is mix up these three different lifestyles without creating a bit of a jumble. For this reason you really do have to think about storage and display before you become too serious about collecting any specific kind of ceramics. A collection has to be lived with and must be practical.

To avoid a mixture of items, it is important to specialize early on in your collecting career. This section of the book highlights a few popular areas where collecting is determined by design and decoration, irrespective of maker. The colour and the look are what matters. Very few collectors of blue and white printed earthenware limit their buying to just a single maker; instead the shelves of a dresser or an entire wall can be covered with plates and dishes, and it doesn't actually matter if the pieces are not all of the same period. In order to prevent a large blue and white collection becoming unmanageable, though, it is advisable to choose themes – Indian views or animal subjects, for example.

A creamware teapot and cover, with a moulded handle and spout, one side printed with Harlequin, Columbine and Pierrot, the reverse with five sheep and a cottage, c1765, 7¼in (18.5cm) wide.
£500–600 / €740–880
$940–1,150 ✠ WW

If you like early pottery or porcelain, it is perfectly possible to mix different types together. Delft, faïence and maiolica from Holland, France, Italy and England can live hand-in-hand. Quality, though, needs to be consistent, as late Victorian or 20th-century copies don't really belong with 17th- and 18th-century originals. Many more delft plates survive than any other shape in tin-glazed pottery, and collectors generally like variety. Surprisingly few collectors of early English porcelain are attracted to more than one maker, and this is a shame. While collecting just a single factory has obvious appeal – Worcester or Derby for example – a different viewpoint of the porcelain market in the middle of the 18th century can be gained by bringing together comparable pieces from rival makers.

Within the massive field of Staffordshire figures, the individual maker can rarely be identified. Collectors instead specialize according to subjects such as theatrical, royalty or animals. Model houses or cottage pastille burners have obvious appeal, as have Toby jugs, but the proliferation of reproductions has discouraged new collectors.

A **Staffordshire pottery pastille burner,** in the form of a country house, early 19thC, 5¼in (13.5cm) high.
£140–165 / €210–250
$260–310 ✗ GIL

As a result, there are far fewer collectors of Staffordshire figures today than there used to be 30 years ago. This means lower prices and consequently a lot of opportunity, as long as you keep an eye on quality, rarity and condition.

A number of collectors' markets have fluctuated in value over the years. Since the 1980s, high prices have brought a huge amount of majolica onto the marketplace. Many sizeable collections have been formed, for the rich and colourful majolica glazes are stunningly decorative. Collectors don't always pay enough attention to the difference in quality between the best makers and anonymous also-rans. The value of relatively ordinary majolica has fallen in recent years, while at the same time some Minton, George Jones and Wedgwood pieces, while certainly not cheap, are perhaps undervalued today in terms of the quality of workmanship that they represent.

Whatever subject you collect, it is important to observe quality above all else. Similarly, a good design is more important than the maker alone. When collecting 20th-century ceramics, it is vital to judge the power of the design. A good piece of Art Deco by a minor maker is usually better value than an unexciting or untypical design by the famous Clarice Cliff.

Although some artist-potters have been collected for many years, the fashion for collecting post-war design is relatively new. Not everything made in the 1950s and '60s is good, and collectors have to be selective. With a keen eye, though, it is possible to buy a really fine 20th-century ceramic design before it is widely recognized.

A **Minton majolica vase,** c1860, 9in (23cm) high.
£2,100–2,400 / €3,100–3,550
$3,950–4,500 ⊞ BRT

Tin-Glazed Earthenware
Dutch & English Delft

A Bristol delft charger, painted with tulips and chrysanthemums, 17thC, 13½in (34.5cm) diam.
£3,600–4,300 / €5,300–6,300
$6,800–8,100 ✷ SWO

A London delft Sack wine bottle, inscribed and dated 1662, 4¾in (12cm) high.
£6,300–7,500 / €9,300–11,000
$11,800–14,100 ✷ SWO

Delft & delft

Delft or tin-glazed earthenware made in Holland since the 16th century, is named after the town where so much of it was produced. Tin-glazed earthenware was also made in England using similar techniques and styles. To differentiate them it has become customary for dealers and auction houses to use 'Delft' for the Dutch wares and 'delft' or 'delftware' for the English.

◀ **A pair of Dutch Delft enamelled earthenware plates,** one marked 'PK', the other 'GK', rim chips, 17thC, 13¾in (35cm) diam.
£1,050–1,250 / €1,550–1,850
$1,950–2,350 ✷ BERN

A delft flask, inscribed 'Boy', Continental, 1680–1700, 6in (15cm) high.
£1,300–1,450 / €1,900–2,150
$2,450–2,750 ⊞ KEY

◀ **A London delft jar,** with a C-scroll handle, painted with a Chinese figure in a rocky landscape, minor restoration, c1685, 2in (5cm) high.
£2,600–3,100
€3,800–4,550
$4,900–5,800
✷ WW

A Dutch Delft commemorative pipkin, on a flared foot, monogram of William II, minor damage, late 17thC, 3in (7.5cm) high.
£360–430 / €530–630
$680–810 ✷ WW

A Dutch Delft dish, commemorating William III, restored section to rim, late 17thC, 8½in (21.5cm) diam.
**£910–1,050 / €1,350–1,550
$1,700–1,950 ⚒ DN**

A Dutch Delft De Paeuw commemorative plate, inscribed 'IR' for James II, restored, dated 1698, 10¼in (26cm) diam.
**£2,350–2,800 / €3,450–4,400
$4,100–5,300 ⚒ DN**

A Dutch Delft chinoiserie dish, decorated with an Oriental and a warrior on horseback, minor chips and wear, haircrack to rim, c1700, 13in (33cm) diam.
**£410–490 / €600–720
$770–920 ⚒ S(Am)**

A Dutch Delft fluted dish, painted with a stylized hare or dog within a floral border, foot rim chipped, c1700, 13¾in (35cm) diam.
**£540–640 / €790–940
$1,000–1,200 ⚒ WW**

▶ **A pair of Dutch Delft vases,** with flared rims and tapered necks, c1700, 16¼in (41.5cm) high.
**£1,900–2,250 / €2,800–3,300
$3,550–4,250 ⚒ G(L)**

A Dutch Delft lobed dish, painted with a dog within a floral border, restored, c1700, 14in (35.5cm) diam.
**£740–820 / €1,100–1,050
$1,400–1,550 ⊞ G&G**

A Dutch Delft dish, with a lobed rim, reeded border and raised central boss, early 18thC, 13½in (34.5cm) diam.
**£130–155 / €195–230
$240–290 ⚒ G(L)**

▶ **A Lambeth delft wet drug jar,** inscribed 'S: Caryoph' beneath a shell and flanked by angels, early 18thC, 7¼in (18.5cm) high.
**£1,050–1,250 / €1,550–1,850
$1,950–2,350 ⚒ SWO**
The full inscription would be *syrupus caryophullata (herba Benedicta)* or *caryophilli*, meaning syrup of cloves.

A Dutch Delft onion-necked vase, the body decorated with panels of flowers, rim chips, early 18thC, 12¾in (32.5cm) high.
**£550–620 / €810–910
$1,000–1,150 ⊞ G&G**

A Dutch Delft plate, painted with flowers and corn sheaves, 18thC, 8¾in (22cm) diam.
£260–310 / €380–450
$490–580 ⚲ WW

An English delft charger, possibly Liverpool, painted with cockerels under a blossoming tree, 18thC, 14in (35.5cm) diam.
£310–370 / €460–540
$580–700 ⚲ AH

An English delft dish, painted with flowers, 18thC, 10½in (26.5cm) diam.
£180–200 / €260–290
$340–380 ⊞ G&G

A Dutch Delft bowl, painted with a masted ship, restored, 18thC, 9¾in (25cm) diam.
£400–480 / €590–710
$750–900 ⚲ WW

A London delft plate, painted with Chinese riverscapes, cracked, 18thC, 9in (23.5cm) diam.
£110–130 / €160–190
$210–250 ⚲ G(L)

▶ **A Bristol delft posset pot and cover,** damaged, 18thC, 9½in (24cm) diam.
£1,150–1,350 / €1,700–2,000
$2,150–2,550 ⚲ WW

A Dutch Delft plate, with floral decoration, 18thC, 9in (23cm) diam.
£400–450 / €590–660
$750–850 ⊞ SEA

◀ **A Bristol delft plate,** decorated with a bird, tree and floral sprays, c1710, 9in (23cm) diam.
£300–360
€440–530
$560–670 ⚲ Mit

A Bristol delft two-handled posset pot, painted with stylized leaf motifs, slight damage, c1720, 6½in (16.5cm) diam.
£720–860 / €1,050–1,250
$1,350–1,600 ⚲ WW

Eighteenth-century British delftware
From c1720, British deltware becomes increasingly distinctive – the decoration is less complex and looser in style. A large variety of wares was produced, including punchbowls, plates, flower bricks, wine bottles, fuddling cups, puzzle jugs and posset pots. Many examples were decorated with British landscapes, buildings and figures, but chinoiserie decoration, such as pagodas and Chinese figures, birds and flowers, was also popular. By the end of the 18th century, production had virtually ceased due to the rise in the popularity of creamware.

▶ **A London delft plate,** c1730, 9in (23cm) diam.
£700–780 / €1,000–1,150
$1,300–1,450 ⊞ JHo

A delft plate, London or Bristol, c1725, 10in (25.5cm) diam.
£390–440 / €570–650
$730–830 ⊞ JHo

▶ **A Bristol delft blue dash charger,** depicting Adam and Eve, c1730, 12¼in (31cm) diam.
£4,200–5,000 / €6,200–7,400
$7,900–9,400 ⚲ WW

A Dutch Delft dish, painted with Oriental flowers within a floral and leaf border, rim chips, 18thC, 12in (30.5cm) diam.
£120–140 / €175–210
$220–260 ⚲ TMA

A London delft flower brick, glaze chips, c1720, 8¼in (21cm) wide.
£7,500–9,000 / €11,000–13,200
$14,100–16,900 ⚲ S(O)
The decoration on this flower brick is particularly unusual.

A delft plate, probably Liverpool, painted with a seated figure of a woman in a Chinese river landscape, c1740, 9in (23cm) diam.
£320–380 / €470–560
$600–710 ✦ SWO

A delft plate, probably Bristol, decorated with chinoiserie figures, c1740, 8in (20.5cm) diam.
£700–780 / €1,050–1,150
$1,300–1,450 ⊞ JHo

A Bristol delft charger, painted with an Oriental landscape, c1740, 14in (35.5cm) diam.
£1,400–1,600 / €2,050–2,350
$2,650–3,000 ⊞ KEY

A delft plate, probably Bristol, painted with a songbird perched on flower stems, mid-18thC, 9in (23cm) diam.
£360–430 / €530–630
$680–810 ✦ WW

A Dutch Delft dish, decorated with a deer, some wear and rim chips, c1750, 13½in (34.5cm) diam.
£790–880 / €1,150–1,300
$1,500–1,650 ⊞ G&G

A pair of Bristol delft plates, painted with stylized flowers, rim chips, mid-18thC, 8¾in (22cm) diam.
£540–640 / €790–940
$1,000–1,200 ✦ WW

Cross Reference
Plates & Dishes see
pages 255–259

▶ **An English delft plate,** minor damage, mid-18thC, 14¼in (36cm) diam.
£250–300 / €370–440
$470–560 ✦ SWO

An English delft apothecary jar, the strapwork label inscribed 'S:Spin:Cerv', c1750, 7½in (19cm) high.
£1,450–1,650 / €2,150–2,450
$2,750–3,100 ⊞ G&G
The label is an abbreviation of *Spina cervina* – the buckthorn plant.

An London delft plate, decorated with a tree in a pot, mid-18thC, 9in (23cm) diam.
£700–840 / €1,050–1,250
$1,300–1,550 ♪ WW

A London delft tile, depicting a bowl of flowers, c1750, 5in (12.5cm) square.
£85–95 / €125–140
$165–185 ⊞ JHo

A delft dish, painted with a Chinese pagoda, c1750, 6in (15cm) diam.
£280–320 / €410–470
$530–600 ⊞ KEY

An English delft plate, c1750, 12in (30.5cm) diam.
£670–750 / €980–1,100
$1,250–1,400 ⊞ SEA

A Liverpool delft puzzle jug, c1750, 7½in (19cm) high.
£1,050-1,200 / €1,550–1,750
$1,950–2,250 ⊞ KEY

A Liverpool delft dish, painted with two cockerels beneath a prunus branch, damaged, c1760, 14½in (36cm) diam.
£320–380 / €470–560
$600–710 ♪ WW

A Bristol delft charger, damaged, c1760, 13½in (34.5cm) diam.
£220–250 / €320–370
$410–470 ⊞ G&G

A Bristol delft charger, painted with a bird on a rocky pinnacle, c1760, 12in (30.5cm) diam.
£1,000–1,150 / €1,450–1,700
$1,900–2,150 ⊞ KEY

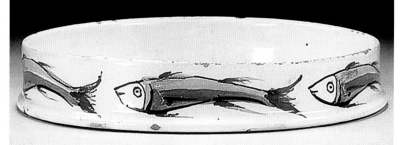

◀ **A Liverpool delft char dish,** painted with fish, minor damage, c1760, 8¾in (22cm) diam.
£1,300–1,550
€1,900–2,250
$2,450–2,900 ♪ S(O)
A char is a fish of the *salmonidae* family and is rarely seen today. They were made into a paste and served in dishes such as these.

A delft bowl, probably London, c1760, 8¾in (22cm) diam.
£450–500 / €660–740
$850–940 ⊞ AUC

A pair of London delft pancake dishes, 1760, 9in (23cm) diam.
£240–270 / €350–400
$450–510 ⊞ MER

▶ **An English delft flower brick,** decorated with flowers and foliage, rim chips, c1760, 6¼in (16cm) wide.
£530–630
€780–930
$1,000–1,200
⚒ WW

An English delft flower brick, painted with insects among flowers and foliage, restored, 1760–70, 6in (15cm) wide.
£550–660 / €810–970
$1,050–1,250 ⚒ WW

▶ **An London delft plate,** painted with a gentleman in a garden, c1760, 7¾in (19.5cm) diam.
£190–220 / €280–320
$360–410 ⚒ G(L)

A Liverpool delft plate, c1760, 8¾in (22cm) diam.
£360–400 / €530–590
$680–750 ⊞ KEY

A Dutch Delft model of a cow, restored, c1760, 5¾in (14.5cm) high.
£430–480 / €630–710
$810–900 ⊞ G&G

A Dutch Delft plate, painted with a floral design, c1760, 9¼in (23.5cm) diam.
£360–400 / €530–590
$680–750 ⊞ KEY

A Liverpool delft tile, c1770, 5in (12.5cm) square.
£55–65 / €80–95
$105–125 ⊞ JHo

A London delft bowl, with polychrome decoration, c1770, 9in (23cm) diam.
£320–380 / €470–560
$600–710 ↗ WW

A London delft armorial pill slab, decorated with the arms of the Apothecaries' Company, pierced with two holes, c1770, 10¼in (26cm) wide.
£3,600–4,300 / €5,300–6,300
$6,800–8,100 ↗ SWO
Pill slabs were used to roll pills and mix ointments and also as signs. The motto of the Apothecaries' arms (granted in 1617) is from Ovid's poem 'Apollo and Daphne', and in full translates as 'The art of medicine is my discovery, and I am called help-bringer throughout the world, and the potency of herbs is given unto me.'

A Liverpool delft dish, painted with birds, a figure and buildings in a landscape, damaged, c1780, 11½in (29cm) diam.
£300–360 / €440–530
$560–670 ↗ SWO

An London delft documentary barrel, initialled 'B:P', dated 1793, 6¼in (16cm) long.
£4,000–4,800 / €5,900–7,100
$7,500–9,000 ↗ G(L)

A delft wall pocket, in the form of a violin painted with river scenes and foliage, finger board and bridge restored, 19thC, 18½in (47cm) long.
£150–180 / €220–260
$280–340 ↗ G(L)

◄ A Dutch Delft character jug, in the form of Mr Punch, with tassel hat cover, damaged, 19thC, 12½in (32cm) high.
£110–130
€160–190
$210–240 ↗ NSal

► A delft wall tile, painted with a fish, mid-19thC, 5¼in (13.5cm) diam.
£85–95
€125–140
$165–185 ⊞ RdV

French Faïence

Faïence
The name faïence derives from the Italian town of Faenza, and applies to the tin-glazed earthenware that developed from Italian maiolica. The term is also used for tin-glazed earthenware products from Germany and Scandinavia. Faïence was first produced in France in Rouen during the 16th century, mainly by Italians and in Italian style, but from the 17th century designs were influenced by Chinese porcelain and Baroque style, with the main centres of production being Nevers, Rouen and Moustiers. During the 18th century the decorating and firing process was transformed, and the colours used became more subtle and refined. Other important centres at this time were Sceaux, Strasbourg and Marseilles. However, by the end of the 18th century demand for faïence had significantly decreased owing to the development of creamware for everyday use and porcelain for finer products.

A faïence plate, painted with peasants playing boules, the reverse signed 'Fait par Moy Gilot, 1773', 18thC, 9in (23cm) diam.
£45–50 / €65–75
$85–95 ✱ G(L)

A Strasbourg faïence dish, with a pierced border, the centre with a floral spray, signed 'Joseph Hannong', minor damage, 1762–81, 11¾in (30cm) diam.
£670–750 / €990–1,100
$1,250–1,400 ⊞ G&G

A Strasbourg faïence plate, painted with a flower spray and scattered blooms, minor damage, monogrammed, painter's mark, c1765, 9¾in (25cm) diam.
£900–1,050 / €1,300–1,550
$1,700–1,950 ✱ S(O)

◀ **A pair of Gien faïence pedestal vases,** with serpent handles, 19thC, 14¼in (11cm) high.
£420–500 / €620–740
$790–940 ✱ DN(EH)

A Gien faïence ewer and stand, painted with figures and foliage, 19thC, ewer 12in (30.5cm) high.
£100–120 / €145–175
$190–220 ✱ G(L)

◀ **A faïence dish,** painted with a dove, cornucopia and foliage, on turned feet, painted marks, 19thC, 9in (23cm) diam.
£45–50 / €65–75
$85–95 ✱ G(L)

A pair of Quimper faïence bowls, painted with figures, monogrammed, 19thC, 11in (28cm) diam.
£150–180 / €220–260
$280–330 ⚒ G(L)

A faïence jardinière, one side painted with a seated lady playing a guitar and a gentleman singing, the reverse with boats sailing on a lake, 19thC, 8½in (21.5cm) diam.
£60–70 / €85–100
$115–135 ⚒ TMA

A faïence cup, c1874, 5in (12.5cm) high.
£165–185 / €240–270
$300–350 ⊞ SER

◄ **A faïence porcelain coffee pot and cover,** by Emile Gallé, printed marks, c1808, 10¾in (27.5cm) high.
£200–240 / €290–350
$380–450 ⚒ SWO

A faïence lantern, with a swing handle and glazed doors and sides, decorated with floral and trellis designs, late 19thC, 7¾in (19.5cm) high.
£110–130 / 160–190
$210–240 ⚒ WW

A Desvres faïence wall pocket, c1900, 13in (33cm) long.
£135–150 / €200–220
$250–280 ⊞ SER

A faïence cat, by Emile Gallé, with glass eyes, signed, extensively damaged, c1900, 12¾in (32.5cm) high.
£500–600 / €740–880
$940–1,100 ⚒ SWO

Italian Maiolica

A Pesaro maiolica *crespina*,
depicting Paris and Mercury, restored,
c1540, 9¾in (24.5cm) diam.
£3,600–4,300 / €5,300–6,300
$6,800–8,100 ⚒ S(O)

A maiolica *albarello*, probably
Castelli, painted with a shield enclosing
a fleur-de-lys within scrollwork, the
reverse inscribed 'GAT 1701', cracked,
4¾in (12cm) high.
£380–450 / €560–660
$710–850 ⚒ SWO

A maiolica *albarello*, possibly Deruta,
painted with the inscription 'P Liri' and
a pair of grotesques above an armorial
device, damaged, 1500–50,
8¼in (21cm) high.
£1,550–1,850 / €2,300–2,700
$2,900–3,500 ⚒ S(O)

◄ **A Montelupo maiolica dish,**
painted with a soldier carrying a long-
handled axe, damaged, 17thC,
12¼in (31cm) diam.
£1,100–1,300 / €1,600–1,900
$2,050–2,450 ⚒ SWO

A maiolica wet drug jar, painted
with a reserve of berries and leaves,
the label marked 'Ollo Lavrino', the
handle painted with a winged angel,
17thC, 5½in (14cm) high.
£500–600 / €740–880
$940–1,100 ⚒ TMA

Italian maiolica

Tin-glazed earthenware, or maiolica, was made in Italy from at least
the 13th century in the form of simple household items such as
bowls, dishes, basins or jugs. By the 15th century wares had become
increasingly sophisticated in both form and design, and important
centres of production grew up in Faenza, Florence, Orvieto, Naples
and Deruta. The high point was reached with the *istoriato* wares of
the 16th century. This is the term for narrative Italian maiolica wares –
that is, pieces that tell a story. The most common themes are biblical,
mythological or historical. Examples are high-fired in a brilliant
palette, usually with orange and blue the predominant colours.
The most important centres of prodcution were Urbino,
Casteldurante and Gubbio. In Montelupo in northern Italy high-
quality wares decorated with saints or single figures were produced.

◄ **A Montelupo
maiolica dish,**
painted with a
young woman
holding a heart
pierced with an
arrow, damaged,
17thC, 11½in
(29cm) diam.
£1,250–1,500
€1,850–2,200
$2,350–2,800
⚒ SWO

A maiolica *albarello*, painted with a
boy in a landscape, holding a banner
inscribed 'Dianisum', Italian, 17thC,
8in (20.5cm) high.
£1,500–1,800 / €2,200–2,650
$2,800–3,350 ⚒ WW

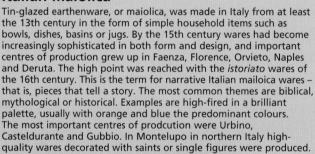

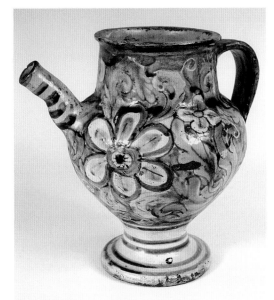

A Sicilian maiolica wet drug jar, the body decorated with floral motifs, some wear, mid-17thC, 8¾in (22cm) high.
£420–500 / €620–740
$790–940 ➢ SWO

A maiolica apothecary jar, inscribed 'Inennfar', repaired, 17th–18thC, 8in (20.5cm) high.
£280–330 / €410–490
$530–620 ➢ G(L)

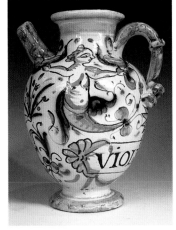

A Sicilian maiolica wet drug jar, decorated with unusual mermaid subjects among foliage flanking an angel, 1708, 8¼in (21cm) high.
£600–720 / €880–1,050
$1,150–1,350 ➢ SWO

LOCATE THE SOURCE
The source of each illustration in Miller's can be found by checking the code letters below each caption with the Key to Illustrations, pages 311–314.

A maiolica saucer, decorated with the Virgin and Child, damaged, 18thC, 5¼in (13.5cm) diam.
£670–800 / €980–1,150
$1,250–1,500 ➢ S(Mi)

A Siena maiolica plate, probably after Antonia Tempesta, decorated with figures in a landscape, 18thC, 10in (25.5cm) diam.
£470–560 / €690–820
$880–1,050 ➢ WW

A Castelli maiolica plate, painted with figures among ruins, 18thC, 7in (18cm) diam.
£730–870 / €1,100–1,300
$1,400–1,650 ➢ Bea

A Milan maiolica dish, by Felice Clerici and Giuseppe Maria Clerici, small chips, 1756–80, 9in (23cm) diam.
£6,600–7,900 / €9,700–11,600
$12,400–14,900 ➢ S(Mi)
The Clerici Pottery was set up in Milan in 1745 by Felice Clerici and continued in production until 1780.

◄ **A Gerace maiolica drug jar,** painted with the head of a helmeted warrior, mid-19thC, 9½in (24cm) high.
£320–380 / €470–560
$600–710 ➢ SWO

Early English Pottery

A creamware teapot, printed with a portrait of John Wesley, the cover with winged angel heads, damaged, 18thC, 5in (12.5cm) high.
£240–280 / €350–410
$450–530 ⚒ G(L)

A Whieldon-style cow creamer and cover, restored, 18thC, 7½in (19cm) long.
£550–650 / €810–970
$1,050–1,250 ⚒ WW

A creamware dish, printed with a rural scene and a monogram, rim chips, 18thC, 18¼in (46.5cm) diam.
£240–280 / €350–410
$450–530 ⚒ WW

Whieldon pottery

Thomas Whieldon (1719–95) was one of the principal 18th-century Staffordshire potters. In 1740 he began making a wide range of wares and partnered Josiah Wedgwood between 1754 and 1759. The wares, which are often unmarked, take the form of domestic items such as teapots and plates, or decorative objects such as figural groups and animals. All the pieces have mottled lead underglaze colours, typically brown, green, grey, blue and yellow, as well as the 'tortoiseshell ware' with sponged manganese decoration.

A Whieldon teapot, with a branch handle and spout, the cover with a poppy-head finial, 18thC, 7in (18cm) wide.
£290–340 €430–500
$550–640 ⚒ SJH

A salt-glazed miniature teapot, c1740, 3in (7.5cm) wide.
£940–1,050 / €1,400–1,550
$1,750–1,950 ⊞ KEY

◀ **A Staffordshire coffee pot,** cover missing, c1745, 6in (15cm) high.
£1,300–1,450
€1,900–2,150
$2,450–2,750
⊞ JHo

▶ **An agate salt-glazed stoneware model of a pug dog,** 1745–50, 2¾in (7cm) long.
£3,100–3,700
€4,550–5,400
$5,800–7,000
⚒ WW

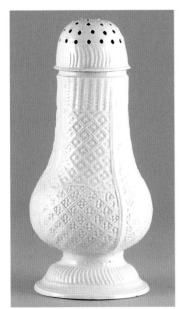

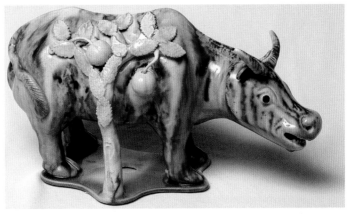

◄ **A Staffordshire salt-glazed stoneware sugar sifter,** moulded with diaper-work panels, c1760, 5¼in (13.5cm) high.
£620–740 / €910–1,100
$1,150–1,350 ➶ WW

A Staffordshire water buffalo, possibly Whieldon, c1755, 6in (15cm) long.
£5,800–6,500 / €8,500–9,600
$10,900–12,200 ⊞ JHo

▶ **A salt-glazed plate,** with printed decoration by Sadler & Green, Liverpool, c1765, 9in (23cm) diam.
£700–780
€1,000–1,150
$1,300–1,450
⊞ JHo

A Staffordshire salt-glazed stoneware bear-baiting jug and cover, with applied clay chippings to simulate fur, c1760, 9½in (24cm) long.
£3,200–3,800 / €4,700–5,600
$6,000–7,100 ➶ WW

◄ **A Staffordshire salt-glazed teapot and cover,** spout repaired, finial replaced, c1770, 4½in (11.5cm) high.
£630–700
€930–1,050
$1,150–1,300
⊞ G&G

A creamware milk jug and cover, possibly Wedgwood, one side printed with Harlequin, Columbine and Pierrot, the reverse with five sheep beneath a tree, spout restored, c1765, 6in (15cm) high.
£260–310 / €380–450
$490–580 ➶ WW

A creamware teapot and cover, printed with a tea party scene, the reverse with a shepherd, with a twist handle and floral knop, 1770–80, 6¾in (17cm) wide.
£280–330 / €410–490
$530–620 ➶ WW

◄ **A salt-glazed stoneware shop pot,** c1780, 9in (23cm) high.
£65–75 / €95–105
$125–145 ⊞ OD

Salt-glazed pottery

In the late 17th century John Dwight of London began experiments to produce a pottery body that would rival the whiteness and delicacy of porcelain. By 1719, the Staffordshire potters were also making stoneware whitened with calcined flint. White clay from Dorset and Devon was the preferred clay and remained the staple ingredient for all white-bodied pottery. It is extremely difficult to attribute salt-glazed pottery to any particular area as there is an absence of potters' marks. Although traditionally associated with and certainly made in some quantity in Staffordshire, there were potteries producing salt-glazed wares in other centres including Yorkshire and Liverpool until the end of the 1770s, when finer ceramics such as creamware took over in popularity.

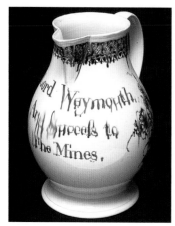

A creamware jug, c1780,
6½in (16.5cm) high.
£1,450–1,650 / €2,150–2,450
$2,750–3,100 ⊞ AUC

A creamware jug, inscribed 'Lord Weymouth Success to the Mines', c1780, 12in (30.5cm) high.
£1,500–1,700 / €2,200–2,500
$2,800–3,200 ⊞ AUC

A Leeds Pottery coffee pot, with enamelled decoration, c1780, 10in (25.5cm) high.
£580–650 / €850–960
$1,100–1,250 ⊞ KEY

Creamware

The creamware pottery manufactured by Josiah Wedgwood in the 1760s replaced the use of tin-glazed and salt-glazed pottery in the late 18th century. Wedgwood's creamware, sometimes referrred to as Queen's ware, was a truly significant step as it brought together beauty with lightness and strength. Other major producers of creamware were the Leeds Pottery, Staffordshire and Swansea.
The designs used often replicated silver items and the classic shapes, often with intricate and finely executed moulding and attention to detail, have never been surpassed.

A creamware teapot, c1780, 4in (10cm) high.
£670–750 / €980–1,100
$1,250–1,400 ⊞ HOW

A pair of creamware leaf dishes, c1780, 6½in (16.5cm) long.
£360–400 / €530–590
$680–750 ⊞ AUC

Fourteen creamware pierced dessert plates, Yorkshire or Staffordshire, minor wear, 1780–90, 9½in (24cm) diam.
£2,500–2,800 / €3,700–4,100
$4,700–5,300 ⊞ KEY

◀ **A Leeds Pottery creamware water cistern and cover,** c1790, 32½in (82.5cm) high.
£4,800–5,400 / €7,100–7,900
$9,000–10,200 ⊞ KEY
There were several designs of water cisterns made by the Leeds Pottery and it is believed that they were made for a local market. Although they were frequently referred to as filters, this is erroneous as there is no arrangement in them for filtering. The water supply in Leeds when these cisterns were made was of extremely poor quality and there was a great demand for Holbeck Spa Water, particularly for the very fashionable occupation of tea drinking. These immensely elaborate and refined cisterns would no doubt take pride of place in the wealthier homes in Leeds.

▶ **A creamware model of a bear,** with sponged decoration, c1790, 3in (7.5cm) high.
£1,050–1,200
€1,550–1,750
$1,950–2,250
⊞ TYE

A Prattware model of a cockerel, c1790, 4in (10cm) high.
£400–440 / €590–650
$750–830 ⊞ DAN

A Prattware pearlware jug, with underglaze decoration, c1790, 8in (20.5cm) high.
£1,350–1,550 / €2,000–2,300
$2,550–2,900 ⊞ RdV

◄ **A creamware coffee pot and cover,** with bat-printed decoration and strap handle, 1790, 10in (25.5cm) high.
£430–480
€630–710
$810–900 ⊞ **TYE**

► **A Liverpool creamware mug,** printed with the east view of Liverpool light-house and signals on Bidston Hill, late 18thC, 6in (15cm) high.
£1,650–1,850
€2,450–2,700
$3,100–3,500
⊞ **KEY**

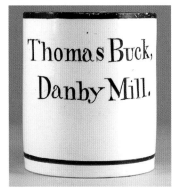

A slipware inkwell, the top with five holes and a central aperture, inscribed 'James Whitaker 1793', losses to glaze, 18thC, 4¼in (11cm) diam.
£660–790 / €970–1,150
$1,250–1,500 ↗ **S(O)**

A Leeds creamware teapot, decorated with a sailor's farewell, the reverse with a floral spray, late 18thC, 6in (15cm) high.
£4,250–5,100 / €6,200–7,500
$8,000–9,600 ↗ **Mit**

► **A slipware dish,** late 18thC, 16in (40.5cm) wide.
£1,800–2,000 / €2,650–2,950
$3,400–3,750 ⊞ **KEY**

A Leeds Pottery creamware mug, with a strap handle, double impressed marks, restored hair crack, late 18thC, 3¾in (9.5cm) high.
£280–330 / €410–490
$530–620 ↗ **WW**

► **A creamware mug,** printed and painted with the Arkwright arms, entitled 'Within The Ark, Safe Forever', late 18thC, 4¾in (12cm) high.
£190–220 / €280–320
$360–410 ↗ **WW**

A creamware Masonic mug, painted with scientific instruments beneath an all-seeing eye, inscribed 'Love the Brotherhood', chipped and cracked, late 18thC, 5½in (14cm) high.
£480–570 / €710–840
$900–1,050 ↗ **WW**

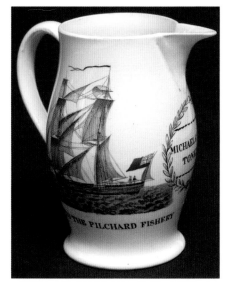

A creamware jug, inscribed 'Success to the Pilchard Fishery', late 18thC, 5¾in (14.5cm) high.
£1,450–1,650 / €2,150–2,450
$2,750–3,100 ⊞ KEY

A Prattware plaque, in the form of a female term, slight damage, c1800, 7¾in (19.5cm) high.
£150–180 / €220–260
$280–330 ⚹ WW

A creamware botanical dish, painted with a botanical specimen of Cape Aitonia, hairline crack, 1800–10, 10¾in (27.5cm) long.
£130–150 / €190–230
$240–290 ⚹ WW

▶ **A Castleford creamware ink-stand and cover,** with four sections for bottles and a candle sconce, the cover with a gun dog finial, cracks, impressed marks, c1800, 8in (20.5cm) wide.
£1,400–1,650
€2,050–2,450
$2,600–3,100
⚹ DN

A Prattware commemorative jug, relief-moulded with portraits of Admiral Lord Nelson and Captain Berry, flanked by frigates in full sail, spout chipped, early 19thC, 6in (15cm) high.
£600–720 / €880–1,050
$1,150–1,350 ⚹ G(L)

A creamware nightlight holder, early 19thC, 4in (10cm) high.
£160–180 / €230–260
$300–340 ⊞ HUM

▶ **A Prattware model of a longcase clock,** the pediment flanked by two birds, restored, early 19thC, 8½in (21.5cm) high.
£340–400 / €500–590
$640–750 ⚹ WW

A Yorkshire creamware jug, inscribed 'Samuel Webster his Pitcher 1803', 6½in (16.5cm) high.
£580–650 / €850–960
$1,100–1,250 ⊞ KEY

Early English Porcelain

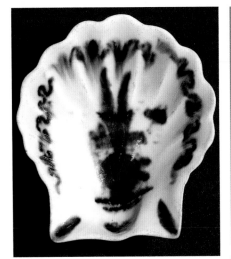

A Limehouse pickle dish, modelled as a shell, painted with a Chinese vase and scroll, c1747, 3in (7.5cm) diam.
£1,600–1,800 / €2,350–2,650
$3,000–3,400 ⊞ JUP

A Bow coffee can, painted with Chinese figures, minor glaze cracks, c1750, 2in (5cm) high.
£420–500 / €620–740
$790–940 ⚒ WW

A Bow baluster vase, painted with a Chinese scene, hairline crack to reverse, restored, incised 'R' mark, c1750, 6¼in (16cm) high.
£1,500–1,800 / €2,200–2,650
$2,800–3,350 ⚒ WW

A Bow dish, painted with peonies, bamboo and rockwork, c1750, 10¾in (27.5cm) wide.
£450–540 / €660–790
$850–1,000 ⚒ WW

Some smaller English porcelain factories

- **Limehouse (1745–48):** recent research has established that wares previously attributed to William Reid of Liverpool were made at this factory
- **Vauxhall (1751–64):** Chinese-style marks only rarely found
- **Lowestoft (1757–99):** made soft paste porcelain similar to Bow. Decoration inspired by Worcester and Chinese models in underglaze blue or transfer-printed. Marked with painted numbers and occasionally copies of Meissen or Worcester marks
- **Caughley (c1775–99):** the most prolific of the minor factories, produced printed wares as well as hand-decorated pieces Marked with a 'C', an 'S', or the word 'Salopian'
- **Longton Hall (1750–60):** typically produced pieces with moulded patterns using floral and vegetable motifs. No marks were used
- **Richard Chaffers (c1755–65)**
- **Samuel Gilbody (1758–61)**
- **William Reid (1756–61)**
- **Philip Christian (1765–78)**
- **Three separate factories of different members of the Pennington family: John, James and Seth.**

A Chelsea strawberry leaf sauce boat, raised anchor mark overpainted in red, 1751–52, 7¼in (18.5cm) long.
£1,600–1,800
€2,350–2,650
$3,000–3,400
⊞ AUC

A Bow sauce boat, with a serpent handle, with *famille rose* decoration, 1752–55, 5in (12.5cm) wide.
£760–850 / €1,100–1,250
$1,450–1,600 ⊞ GIR

A Chelsea strawberry leaf sauce boat, painted with flowers, repaired crack, c1754, 7in (18cm) wide.
£1,250–1,400 / €1,850–2,050
$2,350–2,650 ⊞ JUP

▶ **A pair of Longton Hall figures of Harlequin and Columbine,** 1754–57, 5in (12.5cm) high.
£4,000–4,450
€5,900–6,500
$7,500–8,400
⊞ DMa

How to date Chelsea

Production at the Chelsea factory falls into five periods, four of which are named after marks used at the time:

Triangle Period (c1744–49)
Mark usually incised or painted in underglaze blue. White, glassy, translucent body, often left uncoloured, the shape based on British silverware shapes.

Raised anchor period (1749–52)
Mark embossed on a raised pad. Milky white, silky body, containing impurity specks. Decoration based on Japanese porcelain, Vincennes and Meissen.

Red anchor period (1752–56)
Very small mark in red enamel on the backs of figures and bases of plates and cups. Creamy white body with dribbling glaze, often decorated with Meissen-style flowers. When held up to a strong light, so-called Chelsea 'moons' can be seen – bubbles trapped in the paste, that appear as lighter spots in the body.

Gold anchor period (1756–69)
Mark painted in gold. Creamy body, prone to staining. Clear, thickly applied glaze that tends to craze. Rococo decoration, influenced by Sèvres. Use of gilding significantly increased.

Chelsea-Derby period (1770–84)
Mark of a D with an anchor conjoined, usually in gold. Gold anchor mark also continued to be used. Chelsea factory bought and run by William Duesbury & Co, owners of the Derby porcelain factory, until it was closed in 1784. Predominantly neo-classical decoration with a new French look.

A pair of Longton Hall pickle dishes, 1754–57, 5½in (14cm) long.
£1,200–1,400 / €1,750–2,050
$2,250–2,650 ⊞ AUC

A pair of Bow coffee cans, decorated with moulded prunus sprays, c1755.
£360–430 / €530–630
$680–810 ⏶ SWO

◀ **A Bow *blanc de Chine* egg cup,** decorated with three raised rose sprays, c1755, 3in (7.5cm) high.
£2,350–2,650 / €3,450–3,900
$4,400–5,000 ⊞ GIR

▶ **A Chelsea rose box and cover,** restored, c1755, 3½in (9cm) high.
£1,550–1,850 / €2,300–2,700
$2,900–3,500 ⏶ S

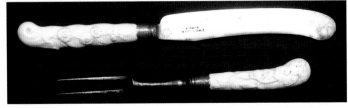

A Chelsea porcelain-handled knife and fork, c1755, knife 11in (28cm) long.
£340–380 / €500–560
$640–710 ⊞ AUC

A Chelsea sweetmeat dish, held by a figure of a Levantine woman, c1755, 5in (12.5cm) high.
£2,150–2,400 / €3,150–3,550
$4,050–4,500 ⊞ DMa

◀ **A Bow coffee cup,** 1755–58, 2½in (6.5cm) high.
£340–380 / €500–560
$640–710 ⊞ DSA

A Longton Hall coffee cup, decorated in the *famille rose* style, 1755–58, cup 2in (5cm) diam.
£1,100–1,250 / €1,600–1,850
$2,050–2,350 ⊞ GIR

A Vauxhall mug, decorated in the Chinese Imari palette, 1755–60, 4in (10cm) high.
£1,350–1,500 / €2,000–2,200
$2,550–2,850 ⊞ GIR

A Chelsea peony dish, moulded as a flowerhead and leaves with a stalk handle, painted with flower sprays, red anchor mark, restored, c1755, 9in (23cm) wide.
£460–550 / €680–810
$860–1,050 ⚒ WW

The history of Chelsea

Nicholas Sprimont, a Flemish silversmith, founded the Chelsea factory in about 1744, and the wares were based on original silver shapes. Chelsea's products were aimed at the top end of the market, so they were made in limited numbers and were expensive to buy. In 1749 the factory moved to larger premises and Sprimont employed a Belgian sculptor, Joseph Willems, who modelled distinctive figures and possibly a series of birds based on the engravings of George Edwards. Wares depicting scenes from Aesop's fables were also produced, the painting of which has been attributed to Jefferyes Hammett O'Neale. Later the famous 'Hans Sloane' pieces featuring botanical studies, and a wide range of figures that are mostly copies of Meissen originals, were produced.

From c1756 Chelsea added bone ash to their paste to strengthen it, making it possible to produce larger, more elaborate wares. These were decorated with high-quality gilding and a richly coloured ground that was inspired by Sèvres. The factory closed in 1769 after Sprimont's health failed. It was bought the following year by the owner of the Derby factory, William Duesbury, who ran the two companies together until 1784, when production ceased completely.

A Bow tea canister and cover, enamel-painted with flowers and insects, cover damaged, 1755–60, 5½in (14cm) high.
£600–720 / €880–1,050
$1,150–1,350 ⚒ WW

A Chelsea leaf-shaped dish, painted with flowers in the Meissen style, 1755–56, 10¾in (27.5cm) wide.
£610–680 / €900–1,000
$1,150–1,300 ⊞ AUC

A pair of Chelsea leaf dishes, 1755–56, 9½in (24cm) wide.
£1,350–1,500 / €2,000–2,200
$2,550–2,850 ⊞ AUC

A Chelsea plate, 1754–55, 9¼in (23.5cm) diam.
£520–580 / €760–850
$980–1,100 ⊞ AUC

► **A Chelsea dish,** moulded as a strawberry leaf, rim chipped and worn, 1755–80, 8½in (21.5cm) wide.
£300–360 / €440–530
$560–670 ✇ WW

A Chelsea sunflower dish, damaged, c1755, 8in (20.5cm) diam.
£760–850 / €1,100–1,250
$1,450–1,600 ⊞ AUC

A Bow bottle vase, painted in the Meissen style, 1756–58, 6in (15cm) high.
£1,550–1,750 / €2,300–2,550
$2,900–3,300 ⊞ GIR

A Chelsea saucer, red anchor mark, c1755–56, 5¼in (13.5cm) diam.
£450–510 / €660–750
$850–960 ⊞ AUC

A Bow figure of a woman, representing Sight, c1760, 7½in (19cm) high.
£2,400–2,700 / €3,500–4,000
$4,500–5,100 ⊞ DMa

Bow marks

Various incised marks were used but wares are often unmarked. The most common mark on figures is a red anchor and dagger.

◄ **A Chaffer's Liverpool dish,** painted in the Imari palette with lotus and bamboo in a watery landscape, c1760, 8in (20.5cm) diam.
£380–450 / €560–660
$710–850 ⚒ WW

A Chaffer's Liverpool mask jug, painted with garden and riverside scenes, 1760–62, 5½in (14cm) high.
£1,050–1,200 / €1,550–1,750
$1,950–2,250 ⊞ DSA

A Chelsea bust of Winter, modelled as a bearded man wearing a cape, on a plinth moulded with garrya husks, c1760, 4in (10cm) high.
£680–810 / €1,000–1,200
$1,300–1,500 ⚒ WW

A Bow figure of Faustina, c1765. 12in (30.5cm) high.
£1,050–1,200 / €1,550–1,750
$1,950–2,250 ⊞ DMa

A Bow mug, painted with flowers, c1765, 3½in (9cm) high.
£580–650 / €850–960
$1,100–1,200 ⊞ DSA

A Bow figure of Air, from the Elements, c1762–65, 8in (20.5cm) high.
£700–780 / €1,000–1,150 $1,300–1,450 ⊞ DMa

A Bow figure of Flora, c1762–65, 10in (25.5cm) high.
£850–950 / €1,250–1,400 $1,600–1,800 ⊞ DMa

The history of Bow

The Bow factory was founded in 1744 by Thomas Frye and Edward Heylyn in Stratford-le-Bow, Essex, and shares with Chelsea the distinction of being one of the earliest porcelain factories in England. The soft paste porcelain contained bone ash, giving it strength but it was coarser than some other porcelains and more liable to staining.

Bow produced huge quantities of Chinese-style porcelain. These pieces were typically decorated with an underglaze powder blue ground, *blanc de Chine* sprigged prunus blossom and, most popular of all, the 'Quail' pattern which is a Japanese design in the Kakiemon palette. The factory's output also included a range of figures based on those of Meissen. Early pieces are unmarked, but after c1756 a red enamel anchor and dagger mark can be found on some colourful pieces that were possibly decorated outside the factory.

The factory closed in 1776 after the figures which had made them famous became unfashionable.

A Bow moulded dish, c1765, 7¾in (19.5cm) wide.
£490–550 / €720–810 $920–1,050 ⊞ AUC

◄ **A pair of Chelsea porcelain figures of a shepherd and shepherdess,** restored, c1765, 11in (28cm) high.
£2,250–2,500 €3,300–3,700 $4,250–4,700 ⊞ AUC

◄ **A pair of Chelsea figural candlesticks,** depicting two of the Four Seasons, gold anchor marks, c1765, 11in (28cm) high.
£5,300–5,900 €7,800–8,700 $10,000–11,100 ⊞ DMa

A Christian's Liverpool coffee can, painted with floral decoration, c1767, 2½in (6.5cm) high.
£450–500 / €660–740 $850–940 ⊞ JUP

A pair of Bow models of goldfinches, perched on stumps among leaves and flowers, restored, 1760–70, 3½in (9cm) high.
£450–500 / €620–740 $790–940 ⌁ WW

A pair of Bow figures, with flowering bocage, c1768, 9in (23cm) high.
£2,100–2,350 / €3,050–3,450 $3,950–4,400 ⊞ DMa

A pair of Worcester leaf dishes, decorated with flower sprays, 1765–68, 9in (23cm) wide.
£800–960 / €1,200–1,400
$1,500–1,800 ⚶ G(L)

A Chelsea Derby basket, 1769–75, 7½in (19cm) diam.
£630–700 / €930–1,050
$1,150–1,300 ⊞ AUC

A Chelsea Derby vase, decorated with a floral spray to each side, gold anchor and D mark, c1770, 7in (18cm) high.
£160–190 / €240–280
$300–360 ⚶ SWO

A pair of Bow plates, painted with birds among foliage, the borders with insects, slight damage to one rim, red anchor and dagger marks, c1770, 8in (20.5cm) diam.
£1,000–1,200 / €1,450–1,750
$1,900–2,250 ⚶ WW

◄ **A Christian's Liverpool teapot and cover,** painted in the Imari palette with flowers and leaves, hair crack, c1770, 8in (20.5cm) wide.
£180–210
€260–310
$340–390 ⚶ WW

A Lowestoft sauce boat, moulded with flowers, printed with flowers and foliage, c1770, 5½in (14cm) wide.
£190–220 / €280–320
$360–410 ⚶ WW

A Bristol saucer dish, printed and painted with a rural scene and two finches on the branches of a tree, some wear, c1770, 8¼in (21cm) diam.
£1,400–1,650 €2,050–2,450
$2,650–3,100 ⚶ F&C

A Lowestoft sauce boat, painted with foliage within leaf-moulded reserves, cracked, 1770–75, 6in (15cm) wide.
£120–140 / €175–200
$220–260 ⚶ G(L)

A Lowestoft jug, with a 'sparrow beak' lip, painted with Oriental figures, 1770–75, 3¼in (8.5cm) high.
£670–750 / €980–1,100
$1,250–1,400 ⊞ DSA

A Lowestoft pickle dish, painted with a vine, c1775, 4in (10cm) long.
£530–600 / €780–880
$1,000–1,150 ⊞ JUP

A Lowestoft jug, after the Worcester original, with a moulded mask spout, printed with flowers and butterflies, internal cracks, c1775, 9in (23cm) high.
£540–640 / €790–940
$1,000–1,200 ↗ SWO

A Chelsea Derby chocolate cup, cover and saucer, c1775, cup 4in (10cm) high.
£760–850 / €1,100–1,250
$1,450–1,600 ⊞ JUP

A Lowestoft jug, with a 'sparrow beak' lip, painted in *famille rose* colours, c1775, 3in (7.5cm) high.
£630–700 / €930–1,050
$1,150–1,300 ⊞ JUP

A Lowestoft tea bowl and saucer, printed with Fisherman Crossing the Bridge pattern, 1775–80, 3in (7.5cm) diam.
£430–480 / €630–710
$810–900 ⊞ DSA

▶ **A Caughley butter boat,** printed with Fisherman pattern, 1780–90, 2¾in (7cm) long.
£110–130 / €160–190
$210–240 ↗ WW

A Chelsea Derby tea bowl, with moulded wrythen decoration, rim chips and some rubbing, gold anchor mark, c1780, 3¼in (8.5cm) diam.
£90–100 / €130–145
$170–190 ↗ SWO

◀ **A Caughley dessert dish,** painted with a flower spray within a border, 1780–85, 10in (25.5cm) wide.
£460–520
€680–760
$860–980
⊞ DSA

A John Pennington Liverpool spoon tray, with a Tudor rose and other flowers within a crow's foot border, c1785, 6½in (16.5cm) wide.
£540–600 / €790–880
$1,000–1,150 ⊞ JUP

A Caughley teapot and cover, transfer-printed with Pagoda pattern, 1785–90, 5in (12.5cm) high.
£180–200 / €260–290
$340–380 ⊞ WAC

A Caughley bowl, painted with Lady with the Parasol pattern, chip to foot, rim repaired, c1785, 5in (12.5cm) diam.
£720–800 / €1,050–1,200
$1,350–1,500 ⊞ JUP

A Lowestoft bowl, cracks, c1785, 6in (15cm) diam.
£250–290 / €370–430
$470–550 ⊞ JUP

◄ **A Caughley sugar bowl and cover,** transfer-printed with Pagoda pattern, 1785–90, 4½in (11.5cm) high.
£175–195 / €260–290
$330–370 ⊞ WAC

A Caughley ladle, the bowl and handle with gilded decoration, c1785, 7in (18cm) long.
£360–400 / €530–590
$680–750 ⊞ JUP

A Caughley junket bowl, printed with Fisherman pattern, c1785, 10in (25.5cm) diam.
£900–1,000 / €1,300–1,450
$1,700–1,900 ⊞ JUP

A Caughley tea bowl and saucer, painted with Target pattern, 1793–95, 2in (5cm) high.
£290–330 / €430–490
$550–620 ⊞ DSA

Blue-Printed Pottery

A Turner dish, transfer-printed with Elephant pattern, c1795,
12in (30.5cm) wide.
£160–180 / €230–260
$300–340 ⊞ DAN

A pair of Riley pickle dishes, transfer-printed with Eastern Street
Scene pattern, some staining, 19thC, 8¼in (21cm) wide.
£190–220 / €280–320
$360–410 ⚒ SWO

A dish, transfer-printed with Fisherman and Castle pattern, c1810,
10in (25.5cm) wide.
£80–90 / €115–130
$155–175 ⚒ SWO

▶ A Joseph Heath
jug and bowl,
with transfer-
printed decoration,
1810, jug 8in
(20.5cm) high.
£540–600
€790–880
$1,000–1,150
⊞ SCO

A Staffordshire jar and cover, with transfer-
printed decoration, 19thC, 7in (18cm) high.
£45–50 / €65–75
$85–95 ⊞ MCC

A fruit bowl, by Jacob Marsh, with moulded
decoration, transfer-printed with a rural scene,
1804–18, 10in (25.5cm) diam.
£360–400 / €530–590
$680–750 ⊞ GN

A meat dish, transfer-printed with an English
country house scene, early 19thC,
20in (51cm) wide.
£290–340 / €430–500
$550–640 ⚒ DA

A Rogers dish, transfer-printed with Camel or Gate Leading to Musjed at Chunar Ghun pattern, impressed mark, c1810, 10in (25.5cm) wide.
£100–120 / €145–175
$195–230 ✗ SWO

A Turner segmented dish, transfer-printed with Stag pattern, Prince of Wales mark, c1810, 9¼in (23.5cm) wide.
£220–250 / €320–360
$410–470 ⊞ GN

A Leeds Pottery butter dish, transfer-printed with The Wanderer pattern, c1810, 6½in (16.5cm) wide.
£250–280 / €370–410
$470–530 ⊞ SCO

Brief history

Transfer-printed pottery was originally produced to satisfy the demands of less wealthy families who could not afford porcelain imported from China. Early pieces were often decorated with chinoiserie patterns – the famous Willow pattern was introduced by Spode around 1790.

A William Adams breakfast set, decorated with Tendril pattern, comprising four covered dishes and a central bowl, on a later mahogany stand, some dishes with impressed numbers, one cover damaged, 1810–15, 21in (53cm) wide.
£500–600 / €740–880
$940–1,100 ✗ SWO

A Ridgway soup plate, transfer-printed with Pembroke Hall, Cambridgeshire, from Oxford and Cambridge College Series, damaged, 1814–30, 9¾in (25cm) diam.
£150–170 / €220–250
$280–320 ⊞ GRe

▶ **A Herculaneum dish,** transfer-printed with the View in Fort Madura pattern, c1815, 9in (23cm) wide.
£150–180
€220–260
$280–330
✗ SWO

A meat dish, transfer-printed with The Winemakers pattern, impressed marks, 1815–25, 15in (38cm) wide.
£1,500–1,700 / €2,200–2,500
$2,800–3,200 ⊞ GRe

A cheese cradle, decorated with Group pattern, chipped, hairline cracks, 1815–20, 12in (30.5cm) wide.
£400–480 / €590–710
$750–900 ↗ SWO

A Rogers meat dish, transfer-printed with the Boston State House pattern, impressed maker's marks, 1820, 18¾in (47.5cm) long.
£900–1,000 / €1,300–1,450
$1,700–1,900 ↗ TMA
This dish was made for the American export market.

A bowl, transfer-printed with Gun Dogs pattern, 1815–25, 7½in (19cm) diam.
£200–230 / €290–340
$380–430 ⊞ GRe

▶ **A Hicks & Meigh pickle dish,** transfer-printed with Exotic Birds pattern, c1820, 6in (15cm) long.
£100–120 / €145–175
$190–220 ⊞ SCO

Boston State House pattern

The Boston State House pattern was produced by the Rogers factory at Longport, Burslem, Staffordshire. Possibly intended for the overseas market, it is the only North American view made by the company. The design is a rural landscape view of Boston State House with cattle in the foreground, surrounded by a floral decorative border. This pattern is rarer in Britain as most pieces have been exported.

Five C. J. Mason pearlware dishes, transfer-printed with Fountain pattern, 1820, largest 7in (18cm) wide.
£220–260 / €320–380
$410–490 ↗ SWO

▶ **A pair of Spode dishes,** transfer-printed with Flower Cross pattern, c1820, 9¾in (25cm) wide.
£80–90 / €115–130
$155–175 ↗ SWO

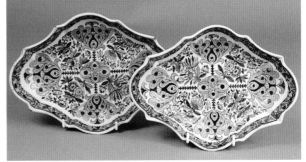

A Davenport hot water plate, transfer-printed with The Villagers pattern, 1815–30, 11in (28cm) wide.
£270–300 / €400–440
$500–560 ⊞ GRe

An Andrew Stevenson pearlware tea bowl and saucer, transfer-printed with a rural scene, impressed mark, c1820, saucer 5in (12.5cm) diam.
£170–190 / €250–280
$320–360 ⊞ DSA

A pearlware soup bowl, transfer-printed with a figure holding a scroll inscribed with the names of Scottish families, c1820, 11in (28cm) diam.
£140–165 / €210–240
$260–300 ⚒ SAS

Transfer printing

The process of transfer printing involves a design being drawn onto paper, which is then traced and engraved in dots on a copper plate. A mixture of ink and oils is applied to the copper plate, and both are then passed through heavy steel rollers to force every detail of the pattern onto tissue paper. The pattern (now in reverse) is placed on the object to be decorated and rubbed all over with a stiff brush to transfer the pattern. Borders are applied separately. The tissue is then soaked away using cold soapy water and the article is biscuit-fired in a kiln at approximately 680–700 degrees centigrade to evaporate the oils and set the colour. The object is then dipped into a glaze, and the excess glaze shaken off to leave a fine coating over the transfer – hence the process is often referred to as 'underglaze transfer printing'. After drying, the transfer-printed items are put into the kiln for refiring at very high temperatures to melt the glaze and form a tough, even, transparent coating. Sometimes, due to a fault in the glazing process, the blue colour flows over the edges of the pattern, giving what is commonly known as a 'flow blue' design. Owing to the popularity of flow blue in the last part of the 19th century, this effect was produced artificially by adding a flow powder to the glaze at the time of firing.

A jug, transfer-printed with Fishermen with Nets pattern, spout damaged, c1820, 4¼in (11cm) high.
£110–130 / €160–190
$210–240 ⚒ SWO

A jug, transfer-printed with a hunting scene, c1820, 7in (18cm) high.
£440–490 / €650–720
$830–920 ⊞ SCO

◄ **A slop bowl,** transfer-printed with Fortune Teller pattern, hairline crack, 1820, 6¼in (16cm) diam.
£110–130 / €160–190
$210–240 ⚒ SWO

A Spode water jug, transfer-printed with Chinamen of rank, c1820, 8in (20.5cm) high.
£1,550–1,750 / €2,300–2,550 $2,900–3,300 ⊞ GN

A Hackwood cup and saucer, transfer-printed with a boy shearing a sheep, 1820, saucer 6in (15cm) diam.
£270–300 / €400–440 $500–560 ⊞ GN

◄ **A pickle dish,** transfer-printed with a chinoiserie pattern, c1820, 5in (12.5cm) long.
£140–160 €210–240 $260–300 ⊞ CoCo

► **A cream jug,** transfer-printed with a fish curing scene, c1820, 6in (15cm) long.
£310–350 €460–510 $580–660 ⊞ GN

A Keeling dog bowl, transfer-printed with Lakeside Meeting pattern, c1820, 9½in (24cm) high.
£1,300–1,450 / €1,900–2,150
$2,450–2,750 ⊞ GN

A meat platter, transfer-printed with Piping Shepherd pattern, c1820, 22in (56cm) wide.
£630–700 / €930–1,050
$1,200–1,300 ⊞ SCO

A Davenport dish, transfer-printed with The Villagers pattern, impressed mark, 1820–30, 17¾in (45cm) wide.
£870–970 / €1,300–1,450
$1,650–1,800 ⊞ GRe

A Ridgway footbath jug, transfer-printed with Sicilian pattern, the handle in the form of a mythical beast, 1825, 12½in (32cm) high.
£1,400–1,600 / €2,050–2,350
$2,650–3,000 ⊞ GN

A baby's bottle, transfer-printed with a romantic scene, c1825, 7in (18cm) high.
£670–750 / €980–1,100
$1,250–1,400 ⊞ GN

◄ **A meat dish,** transfer-printed with a view of Lancaster, from the Antique Scenery series, 1825–35, 21½in (54.5cm) wide.
£790–880 / €1,150–1,300
$1,500–1,650 ⊞ GRe

A bowl and saucer, possibly by William Smith, Stockton, transfer-printed with Tea Party pattern, 1825–30, cup 3in (7.5cm) diam.
£150–165 / €220–250
$280–320 ⊞ GRe

► **A Copeland & Garrett drainer,** with transfer-printed decoration, c1830, 15in (38cm) wide.
£420–470 / €620–690
$790–880 ⊞ CoS

A **Rogers serving dish,** transfer-printed with Elephant pattern, impressed mark, c1830, 10in (25.5cm) wide.
£150–180 / €220–260
$280–330 ⚲ **G(L)**

A **Stevenson soup bowl,** transfer-printed with a picture of Windsor Castle, from the Lace Border series, c1830, 10in (25.5cm) diam.
£145–165 / €210–250
$270–310 ⊞ **GN**

A **dish,** transfer-printed with a sailing boat before a mill, from the English Scenery series, printed crowned Semi China mark, c1830, 15in (38cm) wide.
£140–165 / €210–250
$260–310 ⚲ **WW**

A **pearlware jug,** attributed to Ralph Stevenson, transfer-printed with British scenes, c1830, 5in (12.5cm) high.
£200–220 / €290–320
$370–410 ⊞ **DSA**

◀ **An Elkin Knight & Co plate,** transfer-printed with an Irish scene, c1835, 20in (51cm) wide.
£270–300
€400–440
$500–560 ⊞ **STA**

▶ **A Patterson & Co sugar bowl,** transfer-printed with Bacchanalian Cherubs pattern, with lion-mask handles, cover missing, rim restored, c1837, 3¼in (8.5cm) high.
£75–85
€110–125
$145–165
⚲ **SWO**

A **pilgrim flask,** with flow blue decoration, c1840, 8in (20.5cm) high.
£450–500 / €660–740
$850–940 ⊞ **GN**

A puzzle jug, transfer-printed with flower sprays, c1840, 11½in (29cm) high.
£1,200–1,350 / €1,750–2,000
$2,250–2,550 ⊞ SCO

A jug, transfer-printed with Masonic symbols and union border, inscribed 'E. R. Broom' and dated 1841, 9½in (24cm) high.
£850–950 / €1,250–1,400
$1,600–1,800 ⊞ GN

◄ **A George Jones dish,** transfer-printed with Abbey pattern, c1930, 7¼in (18.5cm) wide.
£25–30 / €40–45
$50–55 ⊞ CHAC

Abbey pattern

The Abbey pattern produced by George Jones in the early part of the twentieth century is very popular in all parts of the world. It is marked 'Abbey 1790' which is the date the pattern was registered rather than the date of the item. It is quite dark in colour and usually of good quality. The most famous objects produced in the pattern are the Shredded Wheat dishes, which came in two sizes and were acquired by collecting tokens from cereal boxes in the 1930s. The pattern was obviously the pattern of choice for token collectors and a tea service could also be brought using coupons saved from cigarette packets.

A mug, commemorating the marriage of the Duke of York to Princess May, c1893, 2¾in (7cm) high.
£40–45 / €60–70
$75–85 ⚒ SAS

A Staffordshire quart measure, c1905, 6in (15cm) high.
£80–90 / €115–130
$155–175 ⊞ OD

A cheese dish, transfer-printed with a landscape, c1914, 7in (18cm) long.
£105–120 / €155–175
$195–230 ⊞ CoCo

Staffordshire Figures

A **Staffordshire tithe pig figural group,** c1780, 5½in (14cm) high.
£260–310 / €380–450
$490–580 ✗ G(L)
This type of figural group was also produced in porcelain by the Derby factory in the 18th century.

A **Staffordshire figure,** 'Winter', c1790, 5in (12.5cm) high.
£220–250 / €320–370
$410–470 ⊞ LBr

A **Staffordshire figure of a lady gardener,** repaired, late 18thC, 8¾in (22cm) high.
£80–90 / €115–130
$155–175 ✗ G(L)

◀ A **Staffordshire creamware cow creamer,** c1790, 7in (18cm) long.
£860–950 / €1,250–1,400
$1,600–1,800 ⊞ DAN

Bocage figures

Bocage is a French term for a grove or copse, and it is a mystery why the French rather than the English term was adopted. The bocage are press-moulded leaves applied to the backs of figural groups. Bocage figures were produced by several factories in Staffordshire, such as Walton, Sherratt and Salt. The figures often depict a romantic rural theme such as a ewe and ram with lambs or a shepherd and lady gardener. Rarer examples are often quite complex and expensive, sometimes showing an entire flock of sheep or depicting jungle animals. Bocage items are decorated in bright enamel colours in pearlware glaze that can be identified by its pale blue colour. The production of bocage figures ceased c1840, probably as a result of the time-consuming nature of their production.

A **Staffordshire figure of a boy reaching towards a squirrel,** late 18thC, 6¼in (16cm) high.
£280–330 / €410–490
$520–620 ✗ G(L)

A Staffordshire figural group, entitled 'The Vicar and Moses', probably by Ralph Wood, Burslem, repaired, impressed number, late 18thC, 9½in (24cm) high.
£950–1,100 / €1,400–1,600
$1,800–2,100 ⚒ G(L)

A Staffordshire pearlware figure of Jupiter with an eagle, c1795, 12in (30.5cm) high.
£800–890 / €1,150–1,300
$1,500–1,650 ⊞ AUC

▶ **A Staffordshire figure of a lady with a watering can,** early 19thC, 5½in (14cm) high.
£195–220 / €290–320
$370–410 ⊞ G&G

A Staffordshire figure of a putto, holding a basket of flowers, slight damage, c1800, 5¼in (13.5cm) high.
£135–150 / €200–220
$250–280 ⊞ G&G

A Staffordshire figure of a girl reading, by Enoch Wood, c1800, 7in (18cm) high.
£610–680 / €900–1,000
$1,150–1,300 ⊞ TYE

A Staffordshire pearlware figure of a country couple, he plays a pipe while she holds the sheet music, repaired, early 19thC, 6¾in (17cm) high.
£90–105 / €130–155
$170–195 ⚒ WW

◀ **A Staffordshire figure of a lady on horseback,** early 19thC, 6½in (16.5cm) high.
£3,250–3,650 / €4,800–5,400
$6,100–6,900 ⊞ JHo

A Staffordshire figure of a girl holding a box, repaired, early 19thC, 8in (20.5cm) high.
£80–90 / €120–135
$150–170 ⚒ WW

A Staffordshire pottery figure, entitled 'Widow', damaged, early 19thC, 8½in (21.5cm) high.
£60–70 / €85–100
$115–135 ⚒ G(L)

A Staffordshire Pottery pastille burner, in the form of a country house, early 19thC, 5¼in (13.5cm) high.
£140–165 / €210–250
$260–310 ⚒ GIL

A Staffordshire tithe pig figural group, early 19thC, 8½in (21.5cm) high.
£280–330 / €410–490
$530–620 ⚒ Mit

A pair of Staffordshire pearlware groups, entitled 'Flight in to Egypt' and 'Return from Egypt', in the style of Obadiah Sherratt, early 19thC, 8in (20.5cm) high.
£2,000–2,400 / €2,950–3,550
$3,750–4,500 ⚒ WW

A Staffordshire money box, in the form of a cottage flanked by a male and a female figure, early–mid-19thC, 5¼in (14cm) high.
£380–450 / €560–660
$720–850 ⚒ AH

A pair of Staffordshire pearlware figures of Tam O'Shanter and Souter Johnny, 1810–20, 6in (15cm) high.
£570–630 / €820–930
$1,050–1,200 ⊞ DAN
These figures are characters in a poem by Robert Burns.

A Staffordshire figure of a French horn player, 1810–15, 10in (25.5cm) high.
£610–680 / €900–1,000
$1,150–1,300 ⊞ DAN

▶ **A Staffordshire pottery group of The Vicar and Moses,** c1820, 9in (23cm) high.
£850–950 / €1,250–1,400
$1,600–1,800 ⊞ DAN

A Staffordshire pearlware figure of a bagpiper, 1810–15, 9in (23cm) high.
£540–600 / €790–880
$1,000–1,150 ⊞ DAN

A Staffordshire pearlware figure of Abraham, Isaac and the Angel, repaired, c1820, 7½in (19cm) high.
£420–500 / €620–740
$790–940 ➹ WW

A Staffordshire watch stand, c1820, 8in (20.5cm) high.
£1,650–1,850 / €2,450–2,700
$3,100–3,500 ⊞ JHo

A Staffordshire figure of the widow of Zarephath, by Walton, 1810–20, 11in (28cm) high.
£440–490 / €640–720
$830–920 ⊞ TYE

▶ **A pair of Staffordshire pearlware figures of musicians,** 1820, 6in (15cm) high.
£720–800 / €1,050–1,200
$1,350–1,500 ⊞ TYE

A **Staffordshire group of Peter raising the lame man,** c1820, 10½in (26.5cm) high.
£3,600–4,000 / €5,300–5,900 $6,800–7,500 ⊞ JHo

A **Staffordshire model of Elijah and the Ravens,** repaired, c1820, 11in (28cm) high.
£220–260 / €320–380 $410–490 ⚒ WW

A **Staffordshire figure of Dr Syntax on horseback,** c1820, 6in (15cm) high.
£3,900–4,400 / €5,700–6,500 $7,300–8,300 ⊞ JHo

A **Staffordshire figure of St Luke,** damaged, c1825, 7½in (19cm) high.
£90–100 / €130–145 $170–190 ⚒ G(L)

A **Staffordshire pepperpot figure of Roger Giles,** c1825, 5in (12.5cm) high.
£540–600 / €790–880 $1,000–1,150 ⊞ DAN

A **Staffordshire model of a cottage,** dated 1846, 7in (18cm) high.
£270–300 / €400–440 $510–560 ⊞ TYE

Royalty

The public have always been interested in events surrounding the Royals. The wedding of Queen Victoria and Prince Albert, the birth of their children and visits from foreign dignitaries were all represented by the Staffordshire potters. Even the iconic Staffordshire spaniels were probably inspired by Queen Victoria's fondness for Dash, her King Charles spaniel.

A **Staffordshire figure of Prince Llewellyn and Gellert,** c1850, 9¼in (23.5cm) high.
£430–510 / €630–750 $810–960 ⚒ SJH

A **Staffordshire model of Euston Station,** c1850, 11in (28cm) high.
£850–950 / €1,250–1,400 $1,600–1,800 ⊞ HOW

◄ **A pair of Staffordshire candlestick figural groups,** of Queen Victoria and Prince Albert, with the Prince of Wales in a boat, c1850, 9½in (24cm) high.
£240–280
€350–410
$450–530
🔨 G(L)

A pair of Staffordshire models of spaniels, c1850, 6in (15cm) high.
£810–900 / $1,150–1,300
$1,500–1,700 ⊞ DAN

A Staffordshire figure of R. Cobden, 1845–50, 8in (20.5cm) high.
£430–480 / €630–710
$810–900 ⊞ DAN

A Staffordshire group of a female and a lion, entitled 'Death of the Lion Queen', repaired, c1850, 14½in (37cm) high.
£750–900 / €1,100–1,300
$1,400–1,650 🔨 G(L)

Political figures
Politicians were more popular in the 19th century than they are today, and ceramic figures such as Benjamin Disraeli and Robert Peel were given pride of place in the home.

◄ **A Staffordshire figure of Sir Robert Peel on horseback,** c1850, 11in (28cm) high.
£1,250–1,400 / €1,850–2,050
$2,350–2,650 ⊞ HOW

A Staffordshire pastille burner, in the form of a cottage, c1850, 6in 915cm) high.
£80–90 / €120–135
$150–170 ⊞ OD

A pair of Staffordshre figures of Victoria and Albert, 1850, 6½in (16.5cm) high.
£230–260 / €340–380
$430–490 ⊞ PICA

A Staffordshire figure of a Scots Guard, emblematic of War, c1854, 5½in (39.5cm) high.
£180–210 / €260–310
$340–400 ⚹ SJH

A Staffordshire figure of Victoria and Albert, c1850, 7½in (19cm) high.
£155–175 / €230–260
$290–330 ⊞ SEA

A Staffordshire biblical group spill vase, c1855, 12in (30.5cm) high.
£50–60 / €75–85
$100–115 ⚹ GAK

A Staffordshire figure of a lady huntress with greyhound and hawk, slight damage, c1855, 14½in (37cm) high.
£340–400 / €500–590
$640–750 ⚹ BWL

A set of Staffordshire figures of the Four Seasons, mid-19thC, 9¾in (25cm) high.
£480–570 / €710–840
$900–1,050 ⚹ GIL

A pair of Staffordshire pottery figures of a man and a woman beside a kennel, each holding a dog, c1855, 9in (23cm) high.
£720–800 / €1,050–1,200
$1,350–1,500 ⊞ HOW

A Staffordshire figure, c1855, 16in (40.5cm) high.
£290–340 / €430–500
$550–640 ⚲ BWL

▶ **A Staffordshire figure of a fish seller,** c1860, 10in (25.5cm) high.
£240–270 / €350–400
$450–510 ⊞ DAN

A Staffordshire pastille burner, in the form of a house with a dog and cats, c1860, 6½in (16.5cm) high.
£90–100 / €130–145
$170–190 ⚲ TMA

A Staffordshire figure of Little Red Riding Hood, c1860, 7in (18cm) high.
£120–135 / €175–200
$220–250 ⊞ DAN

A Staffordshire flatback figural group of Sampson and the Lion, c1860, 9in (23cm) high.
£150–180 / €220–260
$280–330 ⚲ SWO

Military subjects

Many historical naval and military battles such as the Crimean War and Indian Mutiny gave rise to interest in the generals and heroes who took part. Napoleon and Garibaldi are among many famous names that were commemorated by pottery figures.

A Staffordshire figure of Garibaldi, by Thomas Parr, c1860, 9in (23cm) high.
£430–480 / €630–710
$810–900 ⊞ HOW

A pair of Staffordshire greyhounds, c1860, 13in (33cm) high.
£990–1,100 / €1,450–1,600
$1,850–2,050 ⊞ HOW

Two Staffordshire figures of jockeys, c1865, 11½in (29cm) high.
£610–730 / €900–1,100
$1,150–1,350 ⚒ SJH

A pair of Staffordshire figures of the Prince and Princess of Wales, c1862, 9½in (24cm) high.
£340–380 / €500–560
$640–720 ⊞ SER

◀ **A Staffordshire pastille burner,** in the form of a cottage, c1860, 11½in (29cm) high.
£170–200 / €250–290
$320–380 ⚒ G(L)

Animals

Ceramic models of dogs such as spaniels, greyhounds, poodles, pugs, setters and many other breeds were produced by the Staffordshire potteries. Nostalgia for life in the countryside was catered for by models of sheep, rabbits, cows with milkmaids and farm hands. Exotic birds and animals such as lions, giraffes, camels and zebras were a novelty in the mid-19th century as few people had seen these animals before.

A Staffordshire pottery group of a woman and a man beside a milestone, entitled 'London 30 Miles', c1870, 10¾in (27.5cm) high.
£180–210 / €260–310
$340–400 ⚒ SWO

▶ **A pair of Staffordshire figures of male and female musicians,** c1870, 9in (23cm) long.
£130–155 / €190–220
$240–290 ⚒ G(L)

◀ **A Staffordshire tureen and cover,** in the form of an hen on a nest, 1870, 8in (20.5cm) wide.
£450–500 / €660–740
$850–940 ⊞ RdeR

A Staffordshire pastille burner, in the form of a house, c1880, 7in (18cm) high.
£105–120 / €155–175
$195–230 ⊞ NAW

A Staffordshire cow creamer and cover, printed with Willow pattern, slight damage, c1900, 6¼in (16cm) high.
£90–100 / €130–145
$170–190 ⚒ WW

◀ **A Staffordshire tobacco jar,** base damaged, c1880, 13½in (34.5cm) high.
£380–430 / €560–630
$710–810 ⊞ SER

Majolica

A Minton majolica figure of a man with a wheelbarrow, c1851, 13in (33cm) high.
£4,400–4,900 / €6,500–7,200
$8,300–9,200 ⊞ BRT

A Minton majolica dish, in the form a leaf with two rabbits, c1856, 10in (25.5cm) wide.
£3,500–3,900 / €5,100–5,700
$6,600–7,300 ⊞ BRT

A Minton majolica vase, c1860, 9in (23cm) high.
£2,100–2,400 / €3,100–3,550
$3,950–4,500 ⊞ BRT

A majolica model of a lion, his paw on a ball, probably Continental, c1860, 14in (35.5cm) long.
£220–260 / €320–380
$410–490 ✗ AH

A Minton majolica inkwell, c1860, 13in (33cm) wide.
£1,450–1,600 / €2,100–2,350
$2,700–3,000 ⊞ BRT

A Minton majolica cistern, the handles in the form of mythological figures, 1860–70, 22in (56cm) wide.
£1,500–1,800 / €2,200–2,650
$2,800–3,350 ✗ GIL

► Three Minton majolica oyster dishes, marked, c1868, 9in (23cm) diam.
£640–760 / €940–1,100
$1,200–1,450 ✗ SWO

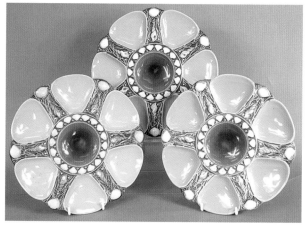

A majolica bread dish, 'Waste Not Want Not', 1860–70, 11½in (29cm) diam.
£130–145 / €190–210
$240–270 ⊞ CHAC

A set of eight majolica plates, one chipped, one marked with an impressed heart, six with '11', 1870–80, 8¾in (22cm) wide.
£550–660 / €810–970
$1,050–1,250 ⚒ SWO

◄ A George Jones majolica cheese bell, c1870, 11in (28cm) diam.
£3,600–3,900
€5,100–5,700
$6,600–7,300
⊞ BRT

A majolica game pie dish, in the form of a basket with a partridge on the cover, c1870, 13in (33cm) diam.
£900–1,050 / €1,300–1,550
$1,700–1,950 ⚒ SWO

A George Jones majolica nut dish, c1870, 9in (23cm) wide.
£1,250–1,400 / €1,850–2,050
$2,350–2,650 ⊞ BRT

A Minton majolica plate, c1872, 10½in (26.5cm) diam.
£350–400 / €510–590
$660–750 ⊞ BGe

◄ A George Jones majolica sardine dish and cover, decorated with panels of fish and foliage, the cover with a crane finial, registration mark for 1875, 6in (15cm) diam.
£780–930 / €1,150–1,350
$1,450–1,750 ⚒ SWO

A majolica planter, with moulded decoration, 1870–80, 17in (43cm) wide.
£320–380 / €470–560
$600–710 ↗ SWO

A George Jones majolica teapot, the handle in the form of a monkey, 1875–80, 9in (23cm) wide.
£3,500–3,900 / €5,100–5,700
$6,600–7,300 ⊞ BRT

▶ **A George Jones majolica cheese bell,** c1875, 11in (28cm) diam.
£3,500–3,900 / €5,100–5,700
$6,600–7,300 ⊞ BRT

A majolica garden seat, the top with a cut-away handle, modelled in relief with cranes among bulrushes, c1875, 19¾in (50cm) high.
£330–390 / €480–570
$620–730 ↗ AH

A George Jones majolica cheese bell, c1875, 12in (30.5cm) diam.
£4,400–4,900 / €6,500–7,200
$8,300–9,200 ⊞ BRT

▶ **A majolica teapot,** in the form of a three-legged sailor sitting on a coiled rope, damaged, 1875–80, 9½in (24cm) high.
£350–420 / €510–610
$660–790 ↗ CHTR

A George Jones majolica butterfly tray, c1875, 11in (28cm) wide.
£1,450–1,650 / €2,150–2,450
$2,750–3,100 ⊞ BRT

A Joseph Holcroft majolica cheese stand and cover, moulded with a fish swimming among aquatic plants, c1875, 9½in (24cm) diam.
£800–960 / €1,200–1,400
$1,500–1,800 ✣ SWO

Victorian majolica

Inspired by 16th-century Italian and French pottery, majolica is a type of earthenware moulded in relief and painted with colourful translucent glazes. Bold shapes predominate, such as jugs modelled as fish and plates as shells. Jardinières, umbrella stands, fountains and tiles were also popular. Manufacturers included Minton, George Jones, Wedgwood and many small factories.

▶ **A Minton majolica teapot,** 1875, 8in (20.5cm) high.
£4,400–4,900
€6,500–7,200
$8,300–9,200
⊞ BRT

◀ **A Minton majolica jug,** c1876, 10in (25.5cm) high.
£140–155
€200–230
$260–290
⊞ BGe

A majolica strawberry dish, 1879–85, 10½in (26.5cm) long.
£75–85 / €110–125
$145–165 ⊞ CHAC

A majolica teapot, possibly by Foresters, in the form of an elephant, cover chipped, trunk reglued, c1880, 5½in (14cm) high.
£460–550 / €680–810
$860–1,000 ➤ SWO

A majolica tea kettle, in the form of a pineapple, c1880, 9in (23cm) high.
£165–185 / €240–270
$300–350 ⊞ BGe

A majolica-type glazed dish, c1880, 11¾in (30cm) long.
£120–135 / €175–200
$220–250 ⊞ CHAC

A majolica cheese dish and cover, moulded with a band of raspberries and leaves, the cover with a bud and leaf finial, minor damage, 1880–90, 9½in (24cm) high.
£240–280 / €350–410
$450–530 ➤ TMA

► **A Wedgwood majolica strawberry set,** c1880, 9in (23cm) long.
£590–660 / €870–970
$1,100–1,250 ⊞ BGe

Two Staffordshire majolica 'guggle' jugs, c1880, 8in (20.5cm) high.
£180–200 / €260–290
$340–380 each ⊞ BRT

► **A majolica teapot,** c1880, 9in (23cm) wide.
£45–50 / €65–75
$85–95 ⊞ BGe

A **Palissy-style charger,** by Mafra, relief-decorated with a lizard, beetle, butterfly and snake, Portuguese, Caldas de Rainha, c1880, 10½in (26.5cm) diam.
£380–450 / €560–660
$710–850 ⚒ SWO

Condition
Condition is absolutely vital when assessing the value of an antique. Damaged pieces on the whole appreciate much less than perfect examples. However, a rare desirable piece may command a high price even when damaged.

A **Palissy-style charger,** by Mafra, relief-decorated with lizards, a snake and beetle, Portuguese, Caldas de Rainha, c1880, 12½in (32cm) diam.
£380–450 / €560–660
$710–850 ⚒ SWO

A **Wedgwood majolica salad bowl and servers,** c1882, 10in (25.5cm) diam.
£250–280 / €370–410
$470–530 ⊞ BGe

An **Orchies majolica jardinière,** French, c1890, 11in (28cm) wide.
£260–290 / €380–430
$490–530 ⊞ MLL

A **majolica plate,** with a figure of Joan of Arc, inscribed 'Glorie, Honneur, Liberté, Patrie', French, c1890, 8in (20.5cm) diam.
£45–50 / €65–75
$85–95 ⚒ BWL

A **majolica-type model of a duck,** Continental, c1900, 9in (23cm) long.
£150–175 / €220–260
$280–330 ⊞ MLL

Armorial & Crested China

◀ **A tin-glazed armorial dish,** printed with the arms of the cardinal, Spanish, 17thC, 10¼in (26cm) diam.
£320–380
€470–560
$600–710
⚒ WW

A Meissen plate, from the Podewils Service, painted with the arms of Podewils and scattered sprigs of *indianische Blumen*, minor damage, German, c1742, 10in (25.5cm) diam.
£2,500–2,800 / €3,650–4,100
$4,700–5,300 ⊞ G&G
This plate is part of the service made for Graf Heinrich von Podewils, 1695–1760, Minister to Frederick the Great of Russia and Knight of the Prussian Order of the Eagle. He may have received the service as a diplomatic gift in connection with the second Silesian War of 1740–42, during which Saxony was allied with Prussia. The form of the service followed the design of that executed by Johann Joachim Kändler in 1741 for the Jagd Service of Clemens August, Elector of Cologne.

A Worcester Flight & Barr teacup and saucer, enamelled with a peacock crest within a roundel, saucer repaired, script mark 'Manufacturers to their Majesties and Royal Family', 1792–1807.
£280–330 / €410–490
$530–620 ⚒ G(L)

◀ **A Caughley mug,** decorated with the arms of William Earl of Essex, 1790–95, 5¼in (13.5cm) high.
£1,350–1,500
€2,000–2,200
$2,550–2,850 ⊞ AUC

A silver lustre jug, with armorial, c1820, 5in (12.5cm) high.
£630–700 / €930–1,050
$1,150–1,300 ⊞ HOW

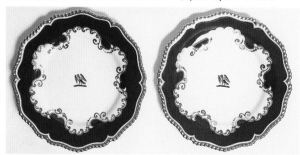

A pair of Worcester Flight, Barr & Barr plates, with a crest, c1825, 10½in (26.5cm) diam.
£720–800 / €1,050–1,200
$1,350–1,500 ⊞ TYE

▶ **A J. & R. Riley pickle dish,** decorated with the arms of the Coventry Drapers Service, 1828, 6in (15cm) long.
£430–480 / €630–710
$810–900 ⊞ GN

A Staffordshire porcelain armorial plate, with painted vignettes, possibly the arms of an Irish count, c1830, 10in (25.5cm) diam.
£180–200 / €260–290
$340–380 ⊞ ReN

A Ridgway porcelain armorial plate, made for the Westhead family, c1830, 10in (25.5cm) diam.
£270–300 / €400–440
$500–560 ⊞ ReN

A Copeland plate, decorated with the arms of the City of London and Prince of Wales feathers, with a pierced border, 1836, 8¾in (22cm) diam.
£500–600 / €740–880
$940–1,100 ⚘ SAS

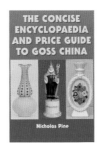

A Goss model of a Letchworth Celtic cinerary urn, with Maidenhead crest, 1881–1929, 3¾in (9.5cm) high.
£70–80 / €100–115
$135–155 ⊞ G&CC

A Willow Art model of a whisky bottle, with Gretna Green and agent crest, 1905–30, 4in (10cm) high.
£15–20 / €22–29
$29–38 ⊞ JMC

◀ **A Goss model of a Swiss cow bell and clapper,** with the arms of Paisley, 1900–28, 3in (7.5cm) high.
£20–25 / €30–35
$40–50 ⊞ G&CC

An Arcadian model of a Sussex pig, with City of London crest, 1903–33, 2in (5cm) high.
£10–15 / €15–20
$20–30 ⊞ JMC

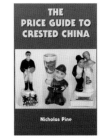

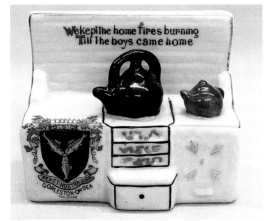

A Carlton model of a range, inscribed 'We Kept the Home Fires Burning Till the Boys Came Home', with Gorleston-on-Sea crest, 1914–18, 2¾in (7cm) high.
£20–25 / €30–35
$40–50 ⊞ G&CC

A Shelley model of a bulldog and kennel, inscribed 'The Black Watch', with Prestatyn crest, 1910–23, 4in (10cm) high.
£25–30 / €40–45
$50–55 ⊞ TWO

A Caledonia model of a curling stone, with Ayr crest, 1910–33, 2½in (6.5cm) high.
£20–25 / €30–35
$40–50 ⊞ G&CC

An Arcadian model of a sailor winding a capstan, with New Milton crest, 1914–18, 4½in (11cm) high.
£120–135 / €175–200
$220–250 ⊞ G&CC

◄ **An Arcadian model of a WWI Red Cross van,** with Salisbury crest, c1914–18, 4in (10cm) long.
£50–60 / €75–85
$110–115 ⊞ BtoB

A Shelley model of a hand grenade, with Eastbourne crest, 1914–18, 3in (7.5cm) high.
£30–35 / €45–50
$55–65 ⊞ TWO

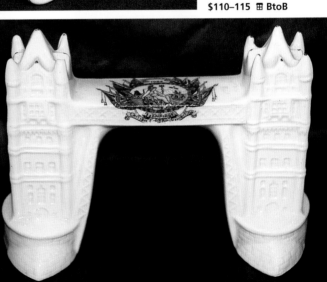

An Arcadian model of Tower Bridge, with Wembley 1924 Exhibition crest, 1924, 4in (10cm) high.
£55–65 / €80–95
$105–125 ⊞ JMC

◄ **A Carlton figure,** with Scarborough crest, 1902–30, 5in (12.5cm) high.
£40–45 / €60–70
$75–85 ⊞ HeA

► **A china model of a bulldog,** with arms of Blackpool, 1910–35, 4in (10cm) long.
£25–30 / €40–45
$50–55 ⊞ HeA

A Goss model of a font, inscribed 'Model of Font in which Shakespeare was Baptized', 1920s, 4in (10cm) diam.
£50–60 / €75–85
$100–115 ⊞ HeA

A Goss pin tray, with Skegness crest, 1900–29, 6in (15cm) long.
£15–20 / €22–29
$29–38 ⊞ HeA

A Goss model of the Longships lighthouse, with Walton-on-the-Naze crest, 1900–29, 5in (12.5cm) high.
£30–35 / €45–50
$55–65 ⊞ HeA

A Goss Limpet Shell bowl, with Blackgang crest, 1900–29, 3in (7.5cm) wide.
£30–35 / €45–50
$55–65 ⊞ HeA

An Arcadian model of a caddy on a golf ball, with arms of Norwich, 1903–33, 3in (7.5cm) high.
£50–60 / €75–85
$100–115 ⊞ JMC

A Goss beaker, inscribed 'Arms for Burns', 1900–29, 4½in (11.5cm) high.
£50–60 / €75–85
$100–115 ⊞ JMC

◄ **A Goss model of a whisky bottle and soda siphon on a thistle-shaped tray,** with Land's End crest, 1929–39, 2in (5cm) high.
£40–45 / €60–70
$75–85 ⊞ G&CC

► **A pair of White Star Line pickle dishes,** by Stony & Co, Liverpool, transfer-printed with the company's crest, 1930s, 8in (20.5cm) long.
£350–420 / €510–610
$660–790 ⚒ CHTR

Art Pottery

A Minton Studio plaque, by W. S. Coleman, depicting a girl, signed, impressed and printed marks, No. 369, 1872, 19¼in (49cm) diam.
£5,000–6,000 / €7,400–8,800
$9,400–11,300 ✗ TEN
Minton opened a studio in Kensington Gore, London in 1870, specifically for producing art pottery. It was only in production for three years before the studio burnt down. Their leading artist, W. S. Coleman, often depicted naked or scantily-clad children as well as fantastic or mythical worlds, typically in a palette of vivid enamels with subtle flesh tones. Pieces should be signed by Coleman and stamped 'Minton'.to the reverse.

▶ **A William de Morgan Isnik tile panel,** with floral decoration, impressed Merton Abbey factory mark, c1880, 24⅛in (61.5cm) square.
£3,400–4,000 / €5,000–5,900
$6,400–7,500 ✗ TEN

A William de Morgan tile, decorated with a pelican and a fish, framed, c1880, 6in (15cm) square.
£4,500–5,000 / €6,600–7,400
$8,500–9,400 ⊞ POW

▶ **A William de Morgan tile,** decorated with a dodo, framed, c1880, 6in (15cm) square.
£4,500–5,000 / €6,600–7,400
$8,500–9,400 ⊞ POW

William de Morgan (1839-1917)

William de Morgan is probably the most famous pottery tile designer of the Arts and Crafts Movement. He started out as a designer of stained glass, ceramic tiles and painted furniture, and only later became a potter, experimenting with glazes and rediscovering methods of making the intense greens and blues used in majolica wares, and using these tints in new designs. He supplied William Morris from his kiln at his home in Chelsea, London, before moving his pottery works to Merton in c1881 and then to Fulham in 1886. He received several commissions, including one from Lord Leighton to match the deep blue Islamic tiles used in the Arab Hall at Leighton House and to supply tiles for many P&O liners. He was also commissioned to design the tiles for the Tsar of Russia's yacht *Lividia*.

De Morgan married Evelyn Pickering, a painter who was influenced by the pre-Raphaelites, in 1887.

A Burmantofts faïence vase, painted and incised with viking boats, No. 2200, impressed mark, 1880–90, 13¼in (33.5cm) high.
£1,400–1,650 / €2,050–2,450
$2,650–3,100 ✗ AH

◀ **A pair of Linthorpe vases,** with moulded decoration, c1884, 7in (18cm) high.
£850–950 €1,250–1,400
$1,600–1,800 ⊞ HUN

A pair of Linthorpe miniature vases, restored, c1885, 7in (18cm) high.
£180–200 / €260–290
$340–380 ⊞ HUN

◄ **A Linthorpe two-handled vase,** restored, c1884, 18½in (47cm) high.
£260–290 / €380–430
$490–550 ⊞ HUN

A Linthorpe jug, c1885, 11½in (29cm) high.
£300–330 / €440–490
$560–620 ⊞ HUN

A Linthorpe hanging basket, with three handles, c1886, 4in (10cm) high.
£240–270 / €350–400
$450–510 ⊞ HUN

A Linthorpe jardinière, attributed to Christopher Dresser, c1885, 8in (20.5cm) high.
£350–390 / €510–570
$660–730 ⊞ HUN

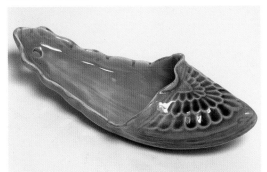

A Linthorpe wall pocket, by Clive Hart, in the form of a slipper, c1886, 7in (18cm) long.
£270–300 / €400–440
$500–560 ⊞ HUN

A pair of Linthorpe terracotta vases, painted with flowers, restored, c1887, 4in (10cm) high.
£180–200 / €260–290
$340–380 ⊞ HUN

A Foley miniature jardinière, with *intarsio* decoration, c1890, 4in (10cm) high.
£490–550 / €720–810
$920–1,050 ⊞ RH
Intarsio is a dramatic form of underglaze decoration often featured on wares designed and decorated by Frederick Rhead.

A Burmantofts two-handled vase, c1890, 6in (15cm) high.
£135–150 / €200–220
$250–280 ⊞ DSG

A Burmantofts faïence vase, c1890, 6½in (16.5cm) diam.
£520–580 / €750–840
$950–1,050 ⊞ SHa

A pair of Bretby vases, decorated with flowers, one signed 'A. T.', the other dated 1891, 9¾in (25cm) high.
£360–400 / €530–590
$680–750 ⊞ HUN

A Bretby vase, in the form of an acorn, c1895, 3¾in (9.5cm) high.
£130–145 / €190–210
$240–270 ⊞ HUN

A Della Robbia plate, signed 'Violet', 1894–1906, 8in (20.5cm) diam.
£200–230 / €530–590
$680–750 ⊞ HABA

◄ **A Lauder vase,** applied with a grotesque creature, c1895, 13in (33cm) high.
**£990–1,100 / €1,450–1,600
$1,850–2,050 ⊞ MMc**
Lauder ware is very similar in style to Brannam ware. Alexander Lauder was headmaster of the Barnstaple School of Art when Charles Brannam was a pupil there in the mid-1870s. In 1876 he established the Lauder pottery and produced a range of sgraffito wares as well as producing tiles and architectural ornaments. Until recent years, collectors often considered Lauder to be inferior to Brannam ware, but since the 1990s there has been growing interest in Lauder and today his pieces are regarded as having equal merit. This is reflected in the high prices they can now command.

A Carlo Manzoni bottle vase, with incised decoration, No. 64, inscribed mark, 19thC, 7in (18cm) high.
**£100–120 / €145–170
$200–230 ➶ SWO**

A Bretby redware two-handled pot, mark and number rubbed, c1896, 9½in (24cm) high.
**£560–630 / €820–930
$1,050–1,200 ⊞ HUN**

A Bretby vase, c1899, 5in (12.5cm) high.
**£145–165 / €210–240
$270–310 ⊞ HUN**

LOCATE THE SOURCE

The source of each illustration in Miller's can be found by checking the code letters below each caption with the Key to Illustrations, pages 311–314.

A Brown-Westhead, Moore & Co charger, painted with a bird, slight damage, late 19thC, 24½in (62cm) diam.
£200–240 / €290–350
$380–450 ✗ MAR

An Arnhem two-handled Astra vase, c1900, 4½in (11.5cm) diam.
£135–150 / €200–220
$250–280 ⊞ DSG

A Brannam two-handled vase, probably by William Baron, decorated with fish, signed and dated 1900, 13¼in (33.5cm) high.
£500–600 / €740–880
$940–1,100 ⊞ CHTR

An Ashworth vase, c1900, 9½in (24cm) high.
£360–400 / €530–590
$680–750 ⊞ DSG

An Arnhem vase, c1900, 5in (12.5cm) high.
£45–50 / €65–75
$85–95 ⊞ DSG

▶ **A pair of Bretby spill vases,** two eyes replaced, c1900, 10½in (26.5cm) high.
£810–900
€1,200–1,350
$1,500–1,700
⊞ HUN

A Brannam Pottery pitcher, moulded with a grotesque face, slight damage, c1900, 5½in (14cm) high.
£670–750 / €980–1,100
$1,250–1,400 ⊞ MMc

An Alexandra Porcelain amphora vase, Austrian, Vienna, c1900, 9in (23cm) high.
£450–500 / €660–740
$850–940 ⊞ ANO

A pair of Ault Pottery vases, c1900, 8¼in (21cm) high.
£240–280 / €350–410
$450–530 ⊞ SHa

◀ **A Brannam Pottery three-handled vase,** incised with fish and aquatic plants, slight damage, marked, dated 1902, 9¾in (25cm) high.
£420–500 / €620–740
$790–940 ⚒ F&C

Brannam ware

Charles Brannam established his pottery in Barnstaple, north Devon in 1879. It is often referred to as Barum ware after the Roman name for Barnstaple. Much of it is sgraffito decorated, meaning that coloured slips were laid over the red clay and carved through by the artist. Popular Brannam subjects include fish and bird designs, often by key designers such as James Dewdney, Frederick Braddon and William Baron. They were also responsible for a number of animal and political caricature models, much sought after by collectors today. The brittle nature of Devon clay means that the wares are subject to damage and collectors should be wary of restoration.

◀ **A Brannum Pottery vase,** the handles in the form of dragons, incised mark, c1903, 4¼in (11cm) high.
£200–240 / €290–350
$380–450 ⚒ SWO

▶ **A Carter & Co lustre vase,** c1904, 15½in (39.5cm) high.
£1,350–1,500 / €2,000–2,200
$2,500–2,800 ⊞ MMc

A Della Robbia plate, with floral decoration, c1902, 8in (20.5cm) diam.
£270–310 / €350–410
$450–530 ⊞ HABA

A Brannam Pottery match striker, early 1900s, 5in (12.5cm) high.
£200–230 / €290–340
$380–430 ⊞ MMc

A Brannam tyg, incised with fish, signed, dated 1906, 5in (12.5cm) high.
£110–125 / €160–185
$210–240 ✗ **BWL**

A vase, attributed to Bretby, c1905, 11½in (29cm) high.
£240–270 / €350–400
$450–510 ⊞ **HUN**

A vase, c1905, 13in (33cm) high.
£360–400 / €530–590
$680–750 ⊞ **HUN**

A Bretby copperette vase, the rim moulded with a figure, neck repaired, c1907, 13¼in (33.5cm) high.
£290–330 / €430–490
$550–620 ⊞ **HUN**

A pair of Bretby copperette vases, c1907, 6½in (16.5cm) high.
£240–270 / €350–400
$450–510 ⊞ **HUN**

▶ **A Pilkington flask,** by William S. Mycock, decorated with a Latin motto, No. 2715, impressed and painted marks, c1908, 10½in (26.5cm) high.
£2,000–2,400
€2,950–3,550
$3,750–4,500 ✗ **G(L)**

A Bretby two-handled vase, c1908, 14½in (37cm) high.
£620–700 / €910–1,050
$1,150–1,300 ⊞ **HUN**

◀ **A stoneware jug,** applied with three roundels, incised 'Made for Liberty & Co', early 20thC, 6¾in (17cm) high.
£190–220
€280–330
$360–420
⚒ TMA

A vase, moulded with a face, slight damage, French, early 20thC, 25in (63.5cm) high.
£190–220 / €280–330
$360–420 ⚒ G(L)

▶ **A Vienna porcelain chamberstick,** in the form of a girl on a lilypad, c1910, 7½in (19cm) wide.
£720–800
€1,050–1,200
$1,350–1,500
⊞ ASP

◀ **A Vienna porcelain centrepiece,** in the form of a girl on a lilypad, c1910, 8in (20.5cm) high.
£900–1,000
€1,300–1,450
$1,700–1,900
⊞ ASP

A Wiener Keramik-style figure of Pan, slight damage, c1910, 25¼in (64cm) high.
£190–220 / €280–330
$360–420 ⚒ SWO

A Pilkington's Royal Lancastrian vase and cover, by Richard Joyce, 1913, 10cm (25.5cm) high.
£6,600–7,400 / €9,700–10,900
$12,400–13,900 ⊞ POW

A Pilkington's Royal Lancastrian lustre vase, by Richard Joyce, decorated with tropical fish and seaweed, c1914, 6in (15cm) high.
£1,000–1,200 / €1,450–1,750
$1,900–2,250 ⚒ G(L)

Insurance values

Always insure your valuables for the cost of replacing them with similar items, regardless of the original price paid. Both dealers and auctioneers can provide a valuation service for a fee.

A Pilkington's Royal Lancastrian vase,
1914–23, 4in (10cm) high.
£95–110 / €140–160
$180–210 ⊞ SAT

A Pilkington's Royal Lancastrian lustre vase, by William S. Mycock,
decorated with a Latin motto, No. 3178, impressed and painted marks,
c1920, 7½in (19cm) high.
£1,100–1,300 / €1,600–1,900
$2,050–2,450 ⚒ G(L)

A Vallauris vase, c1920, 4in (10cm) high.
£60–70 / €85–100
$115–135 ⊞ DSG

A Gray's Pottery lustre plate,
by Gordon Forsyth, c1927,
11in (28cm) diam.
£140–155 / €200–230
$260–290 ⊞ JFME

◀ **A jug,** Belgian, c1925,
13in (33cm) high.
£40–45 / €60–70
$75–85 ⊞ WAC

A Shelley Harmony ginger jar, c1930, 5in
(12.5cm) high.
£135–150 / €200–220
$250–280 ⊞ BEV

A Radford jug, with hand-painted decoration, c1930, 4½in (11.5cm) high.
£80–90 / €120–135
$150–170 ⊞ BEV

A St Ives redware mug, by Michael Cardew, with inscription, slight damage, impressed marks, c1925, 4¼in (11cm) high.
£200–240 / €290–350
$380–450 ⚒ SWO

A bowl and cover, by Jessie Marion King, Scottish, 1930s, 5½in (14cm) diam.
£580–650 / €850–960
$1,100–1,250 ⊞ SDD

An Ault propeller vase, by Christopher Dresser, 1930s, 8in (20.5cm) high.
£2,200–2,500 / €3,250–3,700
$4,150–4,700 ⊞ MMc

▶ **An Oxshott Pottery pitcher,** c1935, 9in (23cm) high.
£140–160 / €210–240
$260–300 ⊞ DSG

◀ **An Upchurch two-handled dish,** c1930, 6in (15cm) wide.
£45–50 / €65–75
$85–95 ⊞ DSG

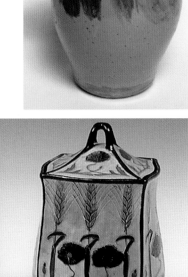

A Salvini Brevettato vase, painted with a portrait of a woman, Italian, early 20thC, 7in (18cm) high.
£880–1,050 / €1,300–1,550
$1,650–1,950 ⚒ G(L)

◀ **A Pair of S. Hancock & Sons Morris ware biscuit jars,** by George Cartlidge, c1900, 7¾in (19.5cm) high.
£4,200–5,000 / €6,200–7,400
$7,900–9,400 ⚒ SWO
First designed by George Cartlidge, Morris ware was one of the main decorative ranges produced by S. Hancock & Sons. The range is actively collected today and the tube-lined patterns resemble Moorcroft designs.

A Wileman & Co *intarsio* coffee pot, in the form of Joseph Chamberlain, c1910, 7½in (19cm) high.
£990–1,100 / €1,450–1,600
$1,850–2,050 ⊞ GaL

A Wileman & Co *intarsio* teapot, in the form of President Kruger of Transvaal, c1910, 5in (12.5cm) high.
£580–650 / €850–960
$1,100–1,250 ⊞ GaL

◀ **An S. Hancock & Sons Morris ware bowl,** by George Cartlidge, c1920, 10in (25.5cm) high.
£1,600–1,800
€2,350–2,650
$3,000–3,400
⊞ GaL

A Wiener Keramik jar and cover, finial repaired, impressed mark and No. 310, Austrian, 1910–12, 4¼in (11cm) high.
£640–760 / €940–1,100
$1,200–1,450 ↗ DORO

A pair of Ram earthenware vases, by T. A. C. Colenbrander, painted by W. Elstrodt, stamped marks, Dutch, 1923, 3¼in (8.5cm) high.
£2,250–2,700 / €3,300–3,950
$4,250–5,100 ↗ S(Am)

◀ **An S. Hancock & Sons Morris ware vase,** by George Cartlidge, c1920, 10in (25.5cm) high.
£1,900–2,200
€2,800–3,250
$3,550–4,150 ⊞ GaL

▶ **A Hollinshead & Kirkham jug,** c1930, 5in (12.5cm) high.
£30–35 / €45–50
$55–65 ⊞ HeA

Martin Brothers

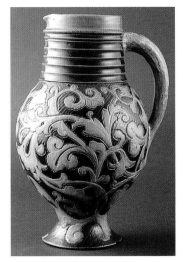

A Martin Brothers stoneware ewer, incised with foliage, damaged, marked, c1881, 8¾in (22cm) high.
£180–210 / €260–310
$340–390 ⚒ WW

A Martin Brothers plate, decorated with scrolling flowers and foliage, 1886, 10in (25.5cm) diam.
£3,000–3,400 / €4,400–5,000
$5,700–6,400 ⊞ POW

A Martin Brothers vase, decorated with fish, 1889, 6½in (16.5cm) diam.
£5,400–6,000 / €7,900–8,800
$10,200–11,300 ⊞ POW

A Martin Brothers jardinière, incised with grotesque birds, 1893, 10in (25.5cm) diam.
£15,700–17,500 / €23,100–25,700
$29,500–33,000 ⊞ POW

◀ **A Martin Brothers jardinière,** painted with pomegranates, incised mark, dated 1896, 9in (23cm) diam.
£620–740
€910–1,100
$1,200–1,400
⚒ BWL

A Martin Brothers stoneware vase, incised with four dragons, incised marks, 1897, 9½in (24cm) high.
£750–900 / €1,150–1,300
$1,400–1,650 ⚒ SWO

▶ **A Martin Brothers two-handled loving cup,** moulded with a grotesque face, 1895, 10½in (26.5cm) high.
£6,300–7,000
€9,300–10,700
$11,800–13,200
⊞ POW

Martin Brothers

The Martin Brothers Pottery was founded by the eldest of three brothers, Robert Wallace Martin, in the late 1860s. In 1873 he set up a new pottery with his brothers, Charles, Walter and Edwin Martin in Fulham, London. In 1877 they moved to Southall, where they made salt-glazed stoneware with Gothic revival influences. The Martin Brothers became famous for their eccentric, grotesquely modelled 'Wally birds' – named after their creator Robert Wallace – and their wheel-thrown sculpted face jugs, vases and other items inspired by the art and architecture of the Middle Ages. In addition to the Wally birds, they also produced a line of more functional pottery, painted with relief decoration. After various difficulties, including a serious fire in 1910 and deaths in the family, the company closed in 1915.

A Martin Brothers ewer, moulded on each side with a grotesque smiling face, inscribed marks, 1903, 6in (15cm) high.
£2,400–2,800 / €3,550–4,100 $4,500–5,300 ➶ **GAK**

A Martin Brothers vase, decorated with Wally birds, 1903, 7in (18cm) high.
£5,400–6,000 / €7,900–8,800 $10,200–11,300 ⊞ **POW**

◄ **A Martin Brothers Wally bird,** 1899, 9½in (24cm) high.
£15,700–17,500 €23,100–25,700 $29,500–33,000 ⊞ **POW**

Condition
The condition is absolutely vital when assessing the value of an antique. Damaged pieces on the whole appreciate much less than perfect examples. However, a rare desirable piece may command a high price even when damaged.

A Martin Brothers tobacco jar, in the form of a Wally bird, damaged and repaired, marked, dated 1903, 10in (25.5cm) high.
£5,500–6,600 €8,100–9,700 $10,300–12,400 ➶ **GAK**

A Martin Brothers grotesque ink pot, 1911, 5¼in (13.5cm) wide.
£6,700–7,500 / €9,800–11,000 $12,600–14,100 ⊞ **POW**

A Martin Brothers stoneware vase, decorated with fish, signed 'Edwin Martin', c1903, 10¼in (26cm) high.
£1,200–1,400 / €1,750–2,050 $2,250–2,650 ➶ **SWO**

► **A Martin Brothers figure of Mr Pickwick,** 1914, 2in (5cm) high.
£2,000–2,300 €2,950–3,400 $3,750–4,300 ⊞ **POW**

Ruskin Pottery

A Ruskin Pottery vase, 1900s, 13in (33cm) high.
£230–270 / €340–400
$430–510 ⊞ JFME

A Ruskin Pottery ginger jar and cover, decorated with vines and tendrils, impressed mark, dated 1910, 7in (18cm) high.
£340–400 / €500–590
$640–750 🔨 GIL

A Ruskin Pottery high-fired vase, 1914, 12in (30.5cm) high.
£6,600–7,400 / €9,700–10,900
$12,400–13,900 ⊞ POW

Ruskin Pottery

Founded in 1898 in West Smethwick, Birmingham, by William Howson Taylor who, a few years later, named it Ruskin Pottery in honour of the artist John Ruskin. The range included high-fired stoneware, which is particularly sought-after today, as well as lustre-decorated or mottled monochrome 'soufflé' earthenwares and crystalline glazed wares in eggshell-thin bone china.

A Ruskin Pottery high-fired flambé vase, c1920, 7in (18cm) high.
£1,250–1,400 / €1,850–2,050
$2,350–2,650 ⊞ DSG

A Ruskin Pottery high-fired vase, c1922, 6in (15cm) high.
£810–900 / €1,200–1,350
$1,500–1,700 ⊞ WAC

A Ruskin Pottery high-fired vase, marked and dated 1923, 7¼in (18.5cm) high.
£700–840 / €1,050–1,250
$1,300–1,550 🔨 L

▶ A Ruskin Pottery jar and cover, 1926, 8in (20.5cm) high.
£1,300–1,450 / €1,900–2,150
$2,450–2,750 ⊞ MMc

A Ruskin Pottery soufflé jar and cover, 1926, 10in (25.5cm) high.
£610–680 / €900–1,000
$1,150–1,300 ⊞ AFD

◄ **A Ruskin Pottery silver-mounted brooch,** with iridescent glaze, 1920s, 1½in (4cm) diam.
£110–125 / €160–185
$210–240 ⊞ ANO

A Ruskin Pottery vase, impressed mark, dated 1930, 6¼in (16cm) high.
£105–125 / €155–185
$200–240 ⚒ MED

◄ **A Ruskin Pottery crystalline table lamp,** stamped marks, dated 1927, 12in (30.5cm) high.
£280–330 / €410–490
$530–620 ⚒ CHTR

A Ruskin Pottery crystalline vase, impressed marks, 1932, 6in (15cm) high.
£110–130 / €160–190
$210–240 ⚒ FHF

A Ruskin soufflé bowl, with three feet, 1928–29, 3½in (9cm) diam.
£190–220 / €280–320
$360–410 ⊞ SAT

A Ruskin Pottery crystalline lamp, 1920s, 14in (35.5cm) high.
£340–380 / €500–560
$640–710 ⊞ MMc

A Ruskin Pottery vase, by William Howson Taylor, signed, impressed marks, dated 1930, 11¾in (30cm) high.
£210–250 / €310–370
$390–470 ⚒ SWO

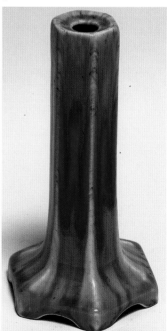

A Ruskin Pottery crystalline lamp, c1930, 8in (20.5cm) high.
£200–230 / €290–340
$380–430 ⊞ RUSK

Art Deco

A Wedgwood Fairyland lustre plate, by Daisy Makeig-Jones, decorated with Imps on Bridge pattern, c1920, 10½in (26.5cm) diam.
£3,900–4,400 / €5,700–6,500
$7,300–8,300 ⊞ POW

A jug and bowl, decorated with flowers, inscribed 'An Idle Brain is the Devil's workshop', and 'Small Cheer and Great Welcome make a Merry Feast', c1926, jug 6in (15cm) high.
£170–200 / €250–290
$320–380 ⚒ SWO

A Carlton Ware vase, decorated with Rainbow Fan pattern, 1920, 8½in (21.5cm) high.
£3,000–3,500 / €4,400–5,100
$5,600–6,600 ⊞ TDG

Carlton Ware

The Carlton Works were set up in 1890 by Wiltshaw & Robinson in Stoke-on-Trent, Staffordshire. During the 1920s, the company became renowned for its Art Deco lustre ware, which is highly sought after today. The imaginative patterns often consisted of geometric and stylized floral designs, some using Egyptian and Oriental influences.

A Carlton Ware ginger jar, decorated with Floral Comets pattern, damaged, c1925, 5½in (14cm) high.
£400–450 / €590–660
$750–850 ⊞ TDG

A Carlton Ware vase, decorated with Scimitar pattern, 1920s, 8in (20.5cm) high.
£1,800–2,000 / €2,650–2,950
$3,400–3,750 ⊞ TDG

A Royal Worcester Crown ware vase, 1927, 11in (28cm) high.
£580–650 / €850–960
$1,100–1,250 ⊞ MMc

A Carlton Ware vase, decorated with a dragon, slight damage, 1920–30, 12in (30.5cm) high.
£80–90 / €120–135
$150–170 ⚒ CHTR

A Crown Devon jug, decorated with Fairy Castles pattern, 1920s, 6in (15cm) high.
£810–900 / €1,200–1,350
$1,500–1,700 ⊞ TDG

A Gouda vase, decorated with Kurba pattern, Dutch, c1929, 9½in (23.5cm) high.
£180–200 / €260–290
$340–380 ⊞ DSG

◄ **A Llmenau porcelain figure,** by Schliepstein, German, 1920s, 8in (20.5cm) high.
£360–400 / €530–590
$680–750 ⊞ LLD

An Ashstead figure, by Pheobe Stabler, entitled 'Buster Boy', 1930, 5½in (14cm) high.
£710–790 / €1,050–1,200
$1,350–1,500 ⊞ MMc

A Beswick vase, c1930, 11in (28cm) high.
£75–85 / €110–125
$145–165 ⊞ HeA

A Boch Frères vase, by Charles Catteau, decorated with a band of penguins, marked, French, c1930, 14½in (35cm) high.
£5,000–6,000 / €7,400–8,800
$9,400–11,300 ➚ SK

Charlotte Rhead

Charlotte Rhead was employed by several Staffordshire pottery factories before joining her father, Frederick Rhead, at Wood & Sons of Burslem in 1912. In 1926 she moved to Burgess & Leigh who produced Burleigh Ware and by 1937 had moved again to A. G. Richardson, makers of Crown Ducal pottery. Finally, in 1941 she worked once more for the Woods at H. J. Wood in Burslem.

A Burleigh Ware charger, by Charlotte Rhead, with tube-lined decoration of a pheasant and pomegranates, pattern No. 4012, c1930, 14in (35.5cm) diam.
£3,100–3,700 / €4,550–5,400
$5,800–7,000 ➚ AH

A Bursley ware dish, by Charlotte Rhead, decorated with stylized flowers, printed marks, c1930, 11¾in (30cm) diam.
£140–165 / €210–240
$260–310 ➚ SWO

A **Susie Cooper teacup and saucer,** decorated with Sea Anemone pattern, c1930, cup 2¼in (5.5cm) high.
£70–80 / €100–115
$135–155 ⊞ RH

A **Crown Ducal two-handled vase,** hand-painted with Firefly pattern, c1930, 8in (20.5cm) diam.
£270–300 / €400–440
$500–560 ⊞ BEV

◄ A **Falcon ware cruet set,** hand-painted with waterlilies, c1930, 5in (12.5cm) wide.
£75–85 / €110–125
$145–165 ⊞ BEV

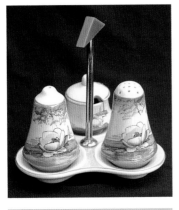

A **Gouda bowl,** decorated with Rhodian pattern, c1930, 7½in (19cm) diam.
£95–110 / €140–160
$180–210 ⊞ PrB

A **vase,** by Emile Lenoble, French, c1930, 9½in (23.5cm) high.
£1,100–1,300
€1,600–1,900
$2,100–2,500 ⚒ SK

A **Gray's Pottery cream jug,** with hand-painted decoration, c1930, 4in (10cm) high.
£100–115 / €145–170
$190–220 ⊞ BEV

A **René Herbst earthenware decanter and plate,** painted marks, French, c1930, decanter 11in (28cm) high.
£3,200–3,850 / €4,700–5,700
$6,000–7,200 ⚒ S(NY)

A **Royal Winton Grimwades plate,** decorated with pixies, c1930, 10in (25.5cm) diam.
£85–95 / €125–140
$160–180 ⊞ HEW

A **Robj figure of a dancer,** 1930, 19in (48.5cm) high.
£540–600 / €790–880
$1,000–1,150 ⊞ JSG

A **Sadler teapot,** modelled as a car, c1930, 9in (23cm) wide.
£200–230 / €290–340
$380–430 ⊞ BEV

A Shelley Harmony Volcano vase, c1930, 5in (12.5cm) high.
£80–90 / €115–130
$155–175 ⊞ HeA

A Shelley Eve tea service, comprising 36 pieces, slop bowl damaged, c1930.
£300–340 / €440–500
$560–640 ↗ L&E

A Wedgwood Veronese lamp base, with silver lustre decoration, impressed marks, c1930, 8¾in (22cm) high.
£80–90 / €120–135
$150–170 ↗ SWO

A cruet set, in the form of elephants, c1930, 5in (12.5cm) wide.
£120–135 / €175–200
$220–250 ⊞ BEV

A lustre egg timer, in the form of a chef, German, c1930, 3in (7.5cm) high.
£45–50 / €65–75
$85–95 ⊞ BEV

A figure, signed 'G. Conde', French, c1930, 10in (25.5cm) high.
£460–510 / €600–750
$770–960 ⊞ MI

A model of a gazelle, c1930, 20in (51cm) wide.
£60–70 / €85–100
$115–135 ⊞ ASP

▶ **A Carlton Ware creamware coffee set,** comprising 15 pieces, pattern No. 4083, printed and painted marks, 1930s, teapot 7¾in (19.5cm) high.
£320–380 / €470–560
$600–710 ↗ SWO

An Amphora vase, Austrian, 1930s, 11½in (29cm) high.
£30–35 / €45–50
$55–65 ↗ TMA
Amphora pottery was made in Austria from 1892 through to the early 1930s. The age of a piece can be identified by the numbers on the bottom. This pottery is made of ivory porcelain, and is surprisingly light.

A Susie Cooper jug, with hand-painted decoration, 1930s, 8in (20.5cm) high.
£990–1,100 / €1,450–1,600
$1,800–2,050 ⊞ GaL

A Crown Ducal cheese dish, decorated with Orange Tree pattern, 1930s, 8in (20.5cm) wide.
£125–140 / €185–210
$230–260 ⊞ JOA

► **A T. G. Green jug,** decorated with Clive pattern, No. C221, 1930s, 6½in (16.5cm) high.
£270–300 / €400–440
$510–560 ⊞ CAL

A Goldscheider figural group, entitled 'The Dolly Sisters', 1930s, 16in (40.5cm) high.
£3,150–3,500 / €4,650–5,200
$5,900–6,600 ⊞ GaL

A Crown Devon bowl, with hand-painted decoration, 1930s, 6in (15cm) diam.
£45–50 / €65–75
$85–95 ⊞ HOM

◄ **A Crown Devon ginger jar,** decorated with Golden Eagle pattern, 1930s, 14½in (37cm) high.
£1,250–1,400
€1,850–2,050
$2,350–2,650 ⊞ GaL

A Goldscheider wall mask, Austrian, 1930s, 13in (33cm) high.
£580–650 / €850–960
$1,100–1,250 ⊞ LLD
Wall masks, popular in the Art Deco period, were made by many companies, those by Goldscheider being the most desirable. This Viennese firm was founded in 1885 for the manufacture of porcelain, faïence and terracotta. Their ouptut was prolific, and they mass-produced a whole range of figures in mainstream Art Deco style.

◄ **A Katzhütte figure of a woman,** German, 1930s, 20in (51cm) high.
£890–1,000 / €1,300–1,450
$1,650–1,900 ⊞ LLD

A **Markmerry mug,** by Catherine Blair, 1930s, 4½in (11.5cm) high.
£240–280 / €350–410
$450–530 ⊞ SDD

◀ A **Myott vase,** 1930s, 10in (25.5cm) high.
£490–550 / €720–800
$920–1,000 ⊞ GaL

◀ A **Wedgwood Moonstone part coffee service,** by Keith Murray, comprising five coffee cans and nine saucers, slight damage, 1930s, can 3in (7.5cm) high.
£120–140 / €175–210
$230–260 ✗ CAu

A **Poole Pottery charger,** by Ruth Paveley, entitled 'Sea Adventure', 1933, 15in (38cm) diam.
£1,000–1,150 / €1,450–1,700
$1,900–2,150 ⊞ MMc

Keith Murray

Keith Murray (1892–1981) trained as an architect but became a designer, not only of ceramics, but also of glass and silver. He is probably best known for his work at Wedgwood, where his output included commemorative ware, tableware and small items such as ashtrays and beakers. All his designs emphasized form rather than decoration, and the most sought-after pieces are the Modernist vases and bowls, some with engine-turned bodies, decorated only with monochrome matt, semi-matt or celadon glazes. Wares are marked with Murray's signature and the Wedgwood mark in black or blue, or rubber-stamped 'KM'.

A **Wedgwood vase,** by Keith Murray, printed marks, 1930s, 11½in (29cm) high.
£400–480 / €590–710
$750–900 ✗ G(L)

◀ A **Radford jug,** 1940s, 11in (28cm) high.
£135–150 / €200–220
$250–280 ⊞ BEV

A **Wedgwood earthenware mug,** by Eric Ravilious, commemorating the coronation of Edward VIII, 1936–37, 4in (10cm) diam.
£850–950 / €1,250–1,400
$1,600–1,800 ⊞ H&G

◀ A **Sadler Kleenware teapot and stand,** 1940s, 6in (15cm) high.
£50–60 / €75–85
$100–115 ⊞ SCH

A **Burleigh Ware jug,** moulded with a cricketer, 1960s, 8in (20.5cm) high.
£620–750 / €910–1,100
$1,200–1,400 ✗ VS

Post-War Design and Contemporary Ceramics

A Gamboni bowl, Italian, 1940–50, 4½in (11.5cm) diam.
£400–450 / €590–660
$750–850 ⊞ EMH

An Iden Pottery plate, c1950, 4¼in (11cm) diam.
£15–20 / €22–29
$29–38 ⊞ PrB

A Leach Pottery, St Ives, coffee pot, c1950, 9in (23cm) high.
£75–85 / €110–125
$145–165 ⊞ RUSK

Bernard Leach

Bernard Leach was born in 1887 in the Far East but was educated in England, although he returned to Japan in 1909. It was there that he first became interested in ceramics and formed his friendship with Shoji Hamada, a Japanese ceramicist. In 1920 Leach returned to England, accompanied by Hamada, and together they set up the Leach Pottery in St Ives, Cornwall. Their work became a fusion of Arts & Crafts principles and a desire to make pots of classic, simple beauty. Although the early years were largely unsuccessful, exhibitions were held in St Ives and London and their wares were also well received in Japan when Hamada returned there in 1928. The Pottery became home to a succession of students and apprentices, of whom Michael Cardew was among the first, and the post-war years were more successful, mainly thanks to Leach's acclaimed writing. Bernard Leach continued potting, with the help of his sons David and John, who left in 1955 to set up their own potteries, and old apprentice, William Marshall, until his death in 1979.

A set of six Piero Fornasetti porcelain plates, with printed decoration of a female face, marked, Italian, 1950–60, 10in (25.5cm) diam.
£400–480 / €590–710
$750–900 ⋟ BUK
Piero Fornasetti (1913–88) worked from his house in Milan, where his son continues the studio today. His whimsical, dramatic decorations were based on the trompe l'oeil techniques of stage scene painters. They were used to cover every surface of his designs for furniture, ceramics and a host of other household objects.

◄ **A set of six tiles,** designed by Salvador Dali, each painted with a different geometric or figural motif, c1954, 7¾in (19.5cm) wide.
£320–380 / €470–560
$600–710 ⋟ L&E

A James Tower earthenware bowl, with cross-hatched decoration, signed 'Tower' and dated '54' on base, 13in (33cm) wide.
£400–480 / €590–710
$750–900 ⋟ DN

A Wedgwood earthenware mug, based on a design by Eric Ravilious, commemorating the coronation of Elizabeth II, 1953, 4in (10cm) diam.
£220–250 / €320–370
$410–470 ⊞ H&G

A Midwinter Riviera covered sugar bowl, by Hugh Casson, c1954, 5in (12.5cm) diam.
£40–45 / €60–70
$75–85 ⊞ CHI

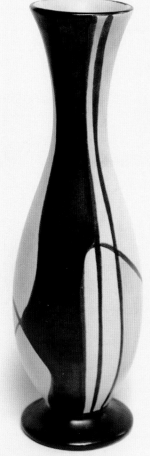

A Florenz vase, German, 1955, 10in (25.5cm) high.
£35–40 / €50–60
$65–75 ⊞ GRo

A Royal Albert sugar bowl and cream jug, decorated with Oriental pattern, 1950s, jug 4in (10cm) high.
£40–45 / €60–70
$75–85 ⊞ CHI

▶ **A Midwinter bowl,** by Jessie Tait, decorated with Savanna pattern, 1950s, 9in (23cm) diam.
£85–100
€125–145
$160–190 ⊞ BEV

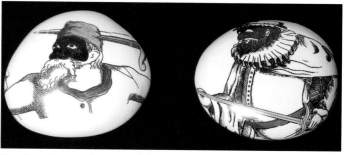

Two Piero Fornasetti paperweights, 1950s, 4in (10cm) wide.
£85–95 / €125–140
$160–180 each ⊞ MARK

◀ **A Britt-Louise Sundell stoneware bowl,** Scandinavian, 1950s, 3½in (9cm) diam.
£40–45 / €60–70
$75–85 ⊞ MARK

◄ **A Hornsea Pottery Studiocraft vase,** 1959, 5¼in (13.5cm) high.
£60–70 / €85–100
$115–135 ⊞ PrB

A Ranleigh vase, decorated with Sandown pattern, 1950s, 18½in (47cm) high.
£35–40 / €50–60
$65–75 ⤢ WilP

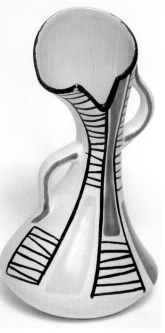

A Piero Fornasetti paperweight, 1950s, 4in (10cm) wide.
£85–95 / €125–140
$160–180 ⊞ MARK

► **A ceramic vase,** Italian, c1960, 11in (28cm) high.
£75–85 / €110–125
$145–165 ⊞ PLB

A Glyn Colledge plate, c1960, 10in (25.5cm) wide.
£10–15 / €15–22
$18–27 ⊞ HeA

A Bitossi Pottery lamp base, by Aldo Mondi, c1960, 22in (56cm) high.
£55–65 / €80–95
$105–125 ⊞ FRD

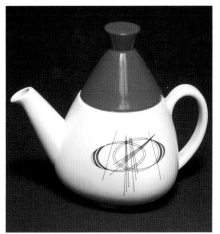

► **A Beswick vase,** No. 1351, c1960, 10in (25.5cm) high.
£45–50 / €65–75
$85–95 ⊞ LUNA

A Carlton Ware teapot, decorated with Orbit pattern, c1960, 6in (15cm) high.
£50–60 / €75–85
$100–15 ⊞ BET

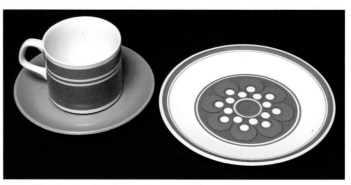

A Meakin Elite Studio trio, c1960, plate 7in (18cm) diam.
£15–20 / €22–29
$29–38 ⊞ CHI

◀ **An Iden Pottery vase,** c1960, 3½in (9cm) high.
£8–12 / €12–18
$16–23 ⊞ PrB

A David Leach porcelain bowl, with a celadon glaze, marked, 1960, 4½in (11.5cm) diam.
£110–125 / €160–185
$210–240 ⊞ RUSK

An Aldermaston Pottery earthenware teapot, by Alan Caiger-Smith, with ribbed strap handle and thumb rest, decorated with calligraphic designs, painted monogram and date code for 1961, 10in (25.5cm) high.
£250–300 / €370–440
$470–560 ⚱ Bea

Portmeirion

In 1960, Susan Williams-Ellis, daughter of Sir Clough Williams-Ellis who built the village of Portmeirion in Wales, acquired the small pottery-decorating company of A. E. Gray Ltd in Stoke-on-Trent. A year later she and her husband, Euan Cooper-Willis, purchased a pottery manufacturing firm, Kirkhams Ltd, thus enabling Susan to create pottery shapes as well as patterns. Her work was produced exclusively for the gift shop at Portmeirion Village. Susan's early designs were for distinctive tableware, often with gold lustre decoration. In the mid-1960s, the company made a range of shapes and designs that have now become well known, including Totem and Greek Key. Probably the best-known pattern is Botanic Garden, which Susan designed in 1972 and is still in production today.

A Portmeirion Cypher coffee service, comprising a coffee pot, milk jug, sugar bowl and six cups and saucers, c1962, coffee pot 12½in (32cm) high.
£125–140 / €185–210
$230–260 ⊞ PrB

Cross Reference
Teapots & Coffee Pots
see pages 278–283

◀ **A Portmeirion Phoenix coffee pot,** 1960s, 13in (33cm) high.
£45–50 / €65–75
$85–95 ⊞ CHI

▶ **A Barker Bros Fiesta coffee service,** 1960s, coffee pot 9in (23cm) high.
£65–75
€95–105
$125–145 ⊞ FRD

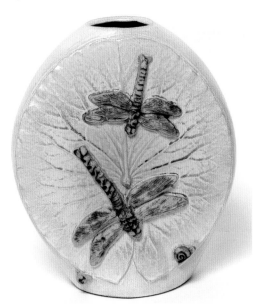

A Bernard Rooke stoneware Dragonfly vase, with raised decoration, 1960s, 14in (35.5cm) high.
£200–230 / €290–340
$380–430 ⊞ MARK

A leather-backed dish, Italian, 1960s, 6½in (16.5cm) wide.
£25–30 / €40–45
$50–55 ⊞ GRo

A Franciscan Reflections coffee pot, 1960s, 10in (25.5cm) high.
£45–50 / €65–75
$85–95 ⊞ CHI

A Carlton Ware coffee service, 1960s, coffee pot 13in (33cm) high.
£40–45 / €60–70
$75–85 ⊞ CCO

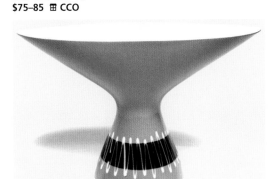

A Hornsea Pottery vase, 1960s, 6in (15cm) high.
£40–45 / €60–70
$75–85 ⊞ LUNA

▶ **A vase,** possibly German, 1965–75, 3in (7.5cm) high.
£1–5 / €2–7
$3–9 ⊞ CRT

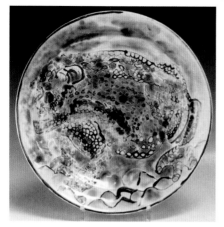

A Poole Pottery Studio ware charger, painted with a stylized frog sitting on rocks, printed factory mark to base, 1964–66, 12in (30.5cm) diam.
£320–380 / €470–560
$600–710 ↗ RTo

Poole Pottery

Poole Pottery was established in 1873 in Poole, Dorset, as Carter & Co. By 1921, the company was known as Carter, Stabler & Adams and in 1963 the name changed to Poole Pottery. During the 1920s and '30s the factory produced a range of hand-thrown ornamental stoneware decorated with floral and geometric patterns under a matt glaze. After WWII Poole became pioneers in developing a range of contemporary designs using bright colours that are now sought after by collectors. The artists who worked for Poole usually initialled their work and many, such as Guy Sydenham and Tony Morris, now have their own collectors.

A Poole Pottery Delphis vase, 1960s, 16in (40.5cm) high.
£310–350 / €450–510
$580–660 ⊞ CHI

A Poole Pottery Delphis bowl, shape No. 58, painted by Irene Kerton, printed factory marks, monogram, c1968, 13½in (34.5cm) diam.
£940–1,050 / €1,400–1,550
$1,750–1,950 ⊞ MI

A Poole Pottery Aegean fruit bowl, 1968, 13in (33cm) diam.
£95–110 / €140–160
$180–210 ⊞ FRD

A Poole Pottery Delphis bowl, base marked, 1960s, 11in (28cm) diam.
£40–45 / €60–70
$75–85 ↗ TMA

An Iden Pottery vase, c1970, 4in (10cm) high.
£15–20 / €22–29
$28–38 ⊞ PrB

◀ **A Celtic Pottery Folk vase,** c1970, 6in (15cm) high.
£10–15 / €15–22
$19–28 ⊞ PrB

A Denby Tall Trees coffee pot, c1970, 9in (23cm) high.
£50–60 / €75–85
$100–115 ⊞ CHI

An Isle of Wight Pottery plate, c1970,
4½in (11.5cm) diam.
£6–10 / €9–15
$12–19 ⊞ PrB

A stoneware boulder vase, by Marea Gazzard,
Australian, c1972, 18½in (47cm) diam.
£6,300–7,600 / €9,300–11,200
$11,800–14,300 ↗ SHSY
Marea Gazzard studied ceramics at the
National Art School, East Sydney and then at
the Central School of Arts and Crafts in
London. After a period of travelling, she
returned to Australia in 1960 to set up her
own workshop. Working in both clay and
metal, her designs are influenced by
Aboriginal culture.

Denby

Founded in the early 19th century, Denby Pottery originally
produced salt-glazed and utilitarian wares, however from
the end of the century until the 1920s its output was
influenced by the Arts & Crafts movement. In 1923,
designer and decorator Albert Colledge took charge of the
factory's decorating department, and for the next 40 years
he made an outstanding contribution by keeping abreast
of changing fashion and style and helping other designers
to bring their work to fruitition. Albert was joined in the
business by his son Glyn, who continued to develop new
ranges and styles until his retirement in 1983.

A Denby Falstaff coffee pot, c1971,
12in (30.5cm) high.
£60–70 / €85–100
$115–135 ⊞ CHI

**An Aldermaston Pottery jug and
cover,** by Alan Caiger-Smith, painted
pottery marks and date code for 1974,
10in (25.5cm) high.
£85–115 / €125–140
$165–185 ↗ DN
Alan Caiger-Smith was the founder
of the Aldermaston Pottery.

A Briglin Pottery vase, 1970s,
7in (18cm) high.
£40–45 / €60–70
$75–85 ⊞ GRo

**A Briglin Pottery Sunflower studio
vase,** 1974, 8in (20.5cm) high.
£35–40 / €50–60
$65–75 ⊞ FRD

A **Hornsea Pottery vase,** 1970s, 9in (23cm) high.
£30–35 / €45–50
$55–65 ⊞ LUNA

A **Midwinter Country Blue plate,** 1970s, 10in (25.5cm) diam.
£15–20 / €22–29
$29–38 ⊞ CHI

A **Midwinter Riverside coffee cup and saucer,** Stonehenge Range,
by Eve Midwinter, 1970s, cup 2½in (6.5cm) high.
£15–20 / €22–29
$29–38 ⊞ CHI

◀ A **Midwinter
Wild Cherry
plate,** Stonehenge
Range, by Eve
Midwinter, 1970s,
7in (18cm) diam.
£6–10 / €9–15
$12–19 ⊞ CHI

A **Poole Pottery Sea Urchin
vase,** by Guy Sydenham,
impressed marks to base,
1970s, 4in (10cm) diam.
£240–280 / €350–410
$450–530 ⚲ SWO

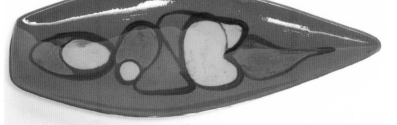

◀ A **Poole Pottery dish,**
1970s, 18in (45.5cm) long.
£60–70 / €85–100
$115–135 ⊞ LUNA

A Poole Pottery vase, commemorating the Silver Jubilee of Elizabeth II, 1977, 11in (28cm) high.
£115–130 / €170–190
$220–240 ⊞ H&G

A Poole Pottery Atlantis helmet lamp, by Guy Sydenham,1970s, 11in (28cm) high.
£2,300–2,600 / €3,400–3,800
$4,300–4,900 ⊞ MMc

A Lucie Rie stoneware vase, with pitted glaze, monogrammed, c1980, 12¼in (31cm) high.
£3,150–3,750 / €4,650–5,500
$5,900–7,000 ✗ S(NY)

A set of three ceramic cups and saucers, Italian, c1980, saucers 6in (15cm) diam.
£120–140 / €175–210
$230–260 ⊞ PLB

A Spode bone china plate, commemorating the christening of Prince William, limited edition of 5000, 1982, 9in (23cm) diam.
£65–75 / €95–105
$125–145 ⊞ H&G

A ceramic teapot, by Mateo Thun for Memphis, Italian, 1980s, 12in (30.5cm) high.
£190–220 / €280–320
$360–410 ⊞ PLB

A ceramic model of the Pink Panther, 1980s, 4in (10cm) high.
£35–40 / €50–60
$65–75 ⊞ HYP

Troika

A Troika vase, painted marks, 1960s–70s, 6½in (16.5cm) high.
£220–260 / €320–380
$410–490 ➣ SJH

Troika

Troika was founded in St Ives, Cornwall, in 1963 by Benny Sirota, a potter, Leslie Illsley, a sculptor, and Jan Thompson, an architect. They began by producing small decorative pieces such as tiles and small bottles. As the company expanded it produced larger items, and shapes and decoration echoed the rugged Cornish landscape. By 1964, Troika was producing wares for Liberty and Heal's, and in 1970 the factory moved to larger premises in Newlyn. Despite their success, however, sales declined during the mid-1970s as fashions changed and the company closed in 1983.

A Troika vase, decorated with a circle and a band on each face, slight damage, marked 'SV' for Sylvia Valance, 1967–69, 13in (33cm) high.
£340–400 / €500–590
$640–750 ➣ SWO

A Troika vase, scratch-decorated with geometric forms on an unglazed ground, 1960s, 12½in (32cm) high.
£200–240 / €290–350
$380–450 ➣ L&E

A Troika vase, of double form, 1960s, 5½in (14cm) high.
£650–780 / €960–1,150
$1,200–1,450 ➣ BWL

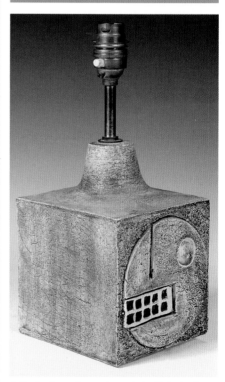

A Troika lamp base, decorated with incised geometric designs, marked 'Troika AB Cornwall', 1960s–70s, 10¾in (27.5cm) high.
£200–240 / €290–350
$380–450 ➣ SWO

A Troika vase, 1960–70, 7¾in (19.5cm) high.
£250–280 / €370–410
$470–530 ⊞ PrB

A Troika planter, decorated with incised designs, printed mark, c1970, 6in (15cm) high.
£200–240 / €290–350
$380–450 ⚒ SWO

A Troika planter, decorated with incised motifs, painted marks to base, c1970, 5¾in (14.5cm) high.
£200–240 / €290–350
$380–450 ⚒ SWO

A Troika slab vase, decorated with embossed motifs, c1970, 6¾in (17cm) high.
£450–540 / €660–790
$850–1,000 ⚒ AH

A Troika pot and cover, decorated with stylized petal motifs, printed 'Troika, St. Ives, England', c1970, 5¼in (13.5cm) high.
£440–520 / €650–760
$830–980 ⚒ SWO

◄ **A Troika model of an Aztec mask,** decorated with an abstract mask to the reverse, marked 'Troika AB', 1976–83, 10in (25.5cm) high.
£2,200–2,600
€3,200–3,800
$4,150–4,900 ⚒ G(B)

A Troika vase, decorated with star motifs, painted marks, c1970, 7¾in (19.5cm) high.
£120–140 / €175–210
$220–260 ⚒ SWO

COLLECTING BY MAKER

Collecting the products of a single ceramics factory makes a lot of sense. There are, of course, clear display advantages, for pieces from a single factory are usually similar in style and this means they will live happily together in a collector's home. Sticking to just one maker requires discipline and a certain amount of specialist knowledge, but the opportunity to learn is probably the greatest advantage of this kind of collecting.

Some factories were short-lived and their products are rare and expensive, while others lasted for a century or more and collectors are literally spoilt for choice. If you collect Wedgwood or Worcester, for instance, you simply have to restrict your purchasing within the realms of common sense. So much Wedgwood survives that at any one time several thousand pieces are available for sale from dealers, on internet sites and at auctions. By contrast, if you fancied collecting pottery by Josiah Wedgwood's 18th-century rivals such as William Greatbatch or James Neale, you would have to wait weeks or even months for the chance of buying any pieces at all.

Rarity alone doesn't make a factory's products valuable. Plenty of artist potters were obscure in their day and have remained so. Choosing a maker that nobody else collects can be rewarding, as even unusual examples are likely to be affordable. The opportunity may be there to research and study a little-known Staffordshire maker but, if there are too few other enthusiasts, values are unlikely to rise. More significantly, if you can't converse with like-minded collectors, the satisfaction and enjoyment of discovering a rare piece is somewhat diluted. The fun of collecting is being able to share your obsession with others.

Most collectors love to show off. A large number of collectors' societies have been formed and if you are keen about a specific maker it is worth finding out if there is a club or society you can join, if only to show your obsession is not unique. Collectors' clubs organize meetings and lectures and produce newsletters where the latest research is published, including information not available in reference books. Many clubs have active websites which provide a forum for members to share new discoveries, and even a chance to swap pieces as well as information.

A Wedgwood Fairyland lustre plate, by Daisy Makeig-Jones, decorated with Imps on Bridge pattern, c1920, 10½in (26.5cm) diam.
£3,900–4,400 / €5,700–6,500
$7,300–8,300 ⊞ POW

I have recently catalogued for sale two exceptional single-factory collections and they could not have been more different. Joyce Mountain spent her life collecting every product of the Davenport factory. She wanted a totally comprehensive collection, so if Davenport made it, she bought it. The ultimate problem was space. Joyce collected more than 2,000 pieces and her home wasn't big enough to house them. For 15 or 20 years, much of the collection was packed up in boxes, and so couldn't be enjoyed. The greatest collection of Davenport ever formed could only be appreciated after Joyce Mountain's death when Bonhams catalogued it for a memorable sale.

A Worcester cream boat, printed with the Obelisk Fisherman pattern, slight damage, disguised numeral mark, c1780, 4¼in (11cm) wide.
£700–840 / €1,050–1,250
$1,350–1,600 ➶ WW

The Zorensky collection of Worcester porcelain was also massive, but far more focused. Because Worcester was founded in 1751 and is still producing today, collectors tend to specialize in specific periods. Milton and Jeanne Zorensky chose to collect pieces made before 1790, the so-called First period. After 30 years, their collection amounted to more than 1,300 pieces but, unlike Joyce Mountain, the Zorenskys had room to display every piece. They also shared it with others by commissioning a major book illustrating most of their rare pieces. Because of its size, it has taken me three years to sell the Zorensky collection in a series of sales at Bonhams. Their items have been bought by a new generation of Worcester buyers, mostly collecting on a much more modest scale.

This is the key to collecting single makers. If you collect Pinxton or Rockingham, Ludwigsburg or Fulda, a limited supply and high prices determine the scale of your acquisitions.

A David Leach porcelain bowl, with a celadon glaze, marked, 1960, 4½in (11.5cm) diam.
£110–125 / €160–185
$210–240 ⊞ RUSK

To learn about your subject you need key reference books and some of these are just as difficult to find as rare pieces of porcelain. Whatever you collect, though, it is essential to read as much as you can about the subject, and to follow international auctions. Try to identify any dealers who specialize in your chosen factory and befriend them, as they can seek out rare pieces for you. Don't just buy ordinary pieces. Common examples belong in any collection, but you must also be prepared to wait for unusual pieces and dig deep into your pockets when you find them, as these will usually prove to be your best buys in the end.

Similar discipline is necessary if you collect a bigger pottery or porcelain factory. With Meissen there is a huge amount of choice, but if you only buy the best pieces you need a very deep pocket indeed. Dating Meissen is difficult and fakes are commonplace, so you cannot collect early Meissen unless you have studied your subject thoroughly. For reasons of price and knowledge, new Meissen collectors tend to favour 19th-century productions but, as this guide shows, these too have become expensive in recent years.

Firms like Wedgwood, Doulton and Minton were enormously versatile. Some dedicated collectors in America and Australia used to buy almost everything these factories made, but nowadays specialization is the norm. A collector of Wedgwood Fairyland lustre or 20th-century design will not collect early jasper or 18th-century Wedgwood creamware. Someone, somewhere, collects every single facet of these great factories' productions. It is better to choose a smaller part of a factory's output and collect it in earnest, buying the very best examples, rather than trying to collect too wide a range of different pieces.

A Royal Doulton two-handled vase, by Maud Bowden and Minnie Forster, c1906, 4in (10cm) high.
£130–145 / €190–210
$240–270 ⊞ CANI

Belleek

A Belleek Artichoke pattern cup and saucer, Irish, First Period, 1863–90, 2½in (6.5cm) high.
£800–900 / €1,200–1,350
$1,500–1,700 ⊞ MLa

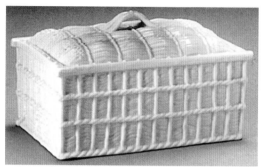

A Belleek biscuit box and cover, modelled as a crate bound by string, cover with retouched chip, impressed and printed marks, Irish, First Period, 1863–90, 7¾in (19.5cm) wide.
£420–500 / €620–740
$790–940 ⚲ S(O)

The history of Belleek

The Belleek factory was established in 1863 by John Caldwell Bloomfield, David McBirney and Robert Williams Armstrong in County Fermanagh, Northern Ireland. Initially the pottery concentrated on producing high-quality domestic ware such as tableware, floor tiles and washstands, and earthenware remained the principal product until 1920. A small amount of Parian was produced after 1863 and porcelain was first featured by Belleek at the Dublin Exposition in 1872. The firm is now famous for its thin, high-quality white porcelain figures, finely-woven baskets, shells decorated with iridescent glazes and tea wares. Several factories were established in the United States copying Belleek products and these are known as American Belleek. The Belleek factory in Ireland is still in production today, producing both traditional and new designs.

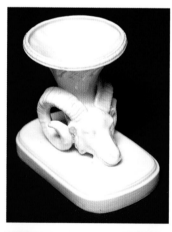

◀ A Belleek ram's head cornucopia spill vase, Irish, First Period, 1863–90, 4in (10cm) wide.
£850–950 / €1,250–1,400
$1,600–1,800 ⊞ MLa

A pair of Belleek figures of Belgian Hawkers, Irish, First Period, 1863–90, 9in (23cm) high.
£900–1,000 / €1,300–1,450
$1,700–1,900 ⊞ MLa

A Belleek Bamboo teapot, Irish, First Period, 1863–90, 6in (15cm) high.
£590–650 / €860–950
$1,050–1,200 ⊞ DeA

◀ A Belleek Florence jug, Irish, First Period, 1863–90, 8in (20.5cm) high.
£720–800 / €1,050–1,200
$1,350–1,500 ⊞ MLa

Standard Belleek marks

First Period: black mark	1863–90
Second Period: black mark	1891–1926
Third Period: black mark	1926–46
Fourth Period: green mark	1946–55
Fifth Period: green mark	1955–65
Sixth Period: green mark	1965–80
Seventh Period: gold mark	1980–92
Eighth Period: blue mark	1993–96
Ninth Period: blue mark	1997–99

A Belleek tea kettle, decorated with Grass pattern, Irish, First Period, 1863–90, 6½in (16.5cm) high.
£740–820 / €1,050–1,200
$1,400–1,550 ⊞ DeA

A Belleek earthenware spongeware bowl and mug, Irish, First Period, 1863–90, 6in (15cm) diam.
£150–170 / €150–170
$280–320 ⊞ Byl

◄ A Belleek jug, with a harp handle, Irish, First Period, 1863–90, 6½in (16.5cm) high.
£1,000–1,150 / €1,450–1,650
$1,900–2,150 ⊞ DeA

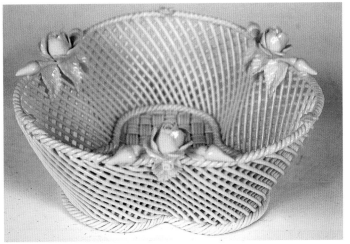

A Belleek Shamrock basket, with a four-strand base, Irish, c1890, 5¼in (13.5cm) wide.
£130–155 / €195–230
$250–290 ➚ SWO

► A Belleek model of a hand holding a fan, Irish, Second Period, 1891–1926, 8in (20.5cm) high.
£1,250–1,400 / €1,850–2,050
$2,350–2,650 ⊞ MLa

A pair of Belleek Bird Tree Stump vases, Irish, Second Period, 1891–1926, 13in (33cm) high.
£1,700–1,900 / €2,500–2,800
$3,200–3,550 ⊞ DeA

A Belleek pot, Irish, Second Period, 1891–1926, 4in (10cm) diam.
£40–45 / €60–70
$75–85 ⊞ WAA

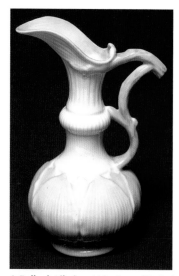

A Belleek Lily jug, Irish, Second Period, 1891–1926, 4½in (11.5cm) high.
£430–480 / €630–710
$810–900 ⊞ MLa

A Belleek cabaret set, comprising 13 pieces, modelled as sea shells with coral-style handles, on shell feet, one bowl and jug with later marks, Irish, Second Period, 1891–1926.
£650–780 / €960–1,150
$1,200–1,450 ⚒ G(L)

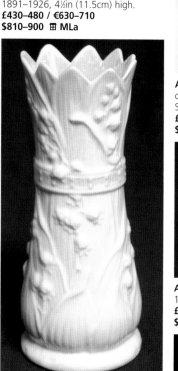

A Belleek Lily of the Valley vase, Irish, Third Period, 1926–46, 6in (15cm) high.
£260–300 / €380–440
$480–560 ⊞ WAA

A Belleek New Shell cream jug and sugar bowl, Irish, Third Period, 1926–1946, 3in (7.5cm) high.
£70–80 / €100–115
$135–155 ⊞ MLa

A pair of Belleek models of dogs, Irish, Sixth period, 1965–80, 4in (10cm) wide.
£220–250 / €330–370
$410–460 ⊞ MLa

A Belleek bust of Sorrow, Irish, Sixth Period, 1965–1980, 11in (28cm) high.
£360–400 / €520–580
$660–730 ⊞ MLa

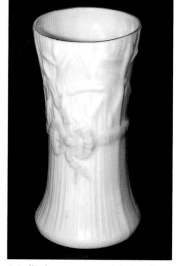

A Belleek posy vase, printed mark, Irish, Seventh Period, 1980–1992, 4in (10cm) high.
£25–30 / €40–45
$50–55 ⊞ TAC

Clarice Cliff

A Clarice Cliff egg cup, decorated with Autumn Crocus pattern, c1928, 2¼in (5.5cm) high.
£175–195 / €260–290
$330–370 ⊞ JFME

Clarice Cliff (1899–1972)

Born in Stoke-on-Trent in 1899, Clarice Cliff started her career as an apprentice at the earthenware manufacturers Ligard, Webster & Co, where she learnt freehand painting, and then moved to Hollingshead & Kirkham where she mastered lithography techniques. In 1916 she moved to A. J. Wilkinson's Middlesport factory, run by Guy and Colley Shorter, and worked in the decorating department. Cliff's career received a boost in 1925 when Colley Shorter provided her with her own studio at the Newport Pottery, which had just been acquired by Wilkinsons. It was here that Cliff was able to develop her own ideas.

The Bizarre range was launched in 1928 with 700 designs and Cliff soon began touring the country with her own apprentices, giving in-store demonstrations of their methods. Early geometric and abstract designs were followed by floral patterns such as Crocus, Lupin, Gayday, Lily, Gardenia and Cowslip, which in turn were succeeded by stylized landscapes and the Fantasque range. Cliff's personal success continued until the outbreak of war in 1939 when the main factory was turned over to the production of undecorated hotel ware. Throughout this time Cliff's relationship with Colley Shorter had continued to develop and, after the death of Shorter's wife, they married in December 1940. Cliff continued to work on the administrative side of the business until Colley's death in 1963 and, grief-stricken and in poor health, she sold the company to Midwinter in 1964.

A Clarice Cliff jug and bowl, decorated with Cherry pattern, c1929, 10in (25.5cm) high.
£1,350–1,500 / €2,000–2,300
$2,800–3,100 ⊞ HEW

A Clarice Cliff Fantasque toilet set, comprising jug, bowl, chamber pot and soap dish, decorated with Broth pattern, c1929.
£1,800–2,150 / €2,650–3,150
$3,400–4,050 ⚒ GAK

A Clarice Cliff honey pot, decorated with Canterbury Bells pattern, c1930, 3in (7.5cm) high.
£450–500 / €660–740
$850–940 ⊞ TDG

A Clarice Cliff Bizarre Lotus jug, decorated with Summer House pattern, c1930, 12in (30.5cm) high.
£4,600–5,100 / €6,700–7,500
$8,600–9,600 ⊞ MI

▶ A Clarice Cliff Conical sugar caster, decorated with Autumn Crocus pattern, c1930, 5½in (14cm) high.
£540–600 / €790–880
$1,000–1,150 ⊞ TDG

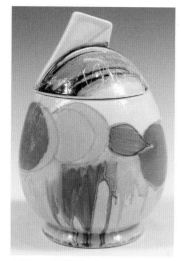

A Clarice Cliff Biarritz preserve pot and cover, decorated with Delecia Citrus pattern, printed mark, c1930, 5in (12.5cm) high.
£320–380 / €470–560
$600–710 ↗ SWO

A Clarice Cliff Biarritz preserve pot and cover, decorated with Rhodanthe pattern, printed marks, c1930, 5in (12.5cm) high.
£120–140 / €175–210
$220–260 ↗ SWO

A Clarice Cliff Bizarre Chick chocolate pot and cover, printed marks, c1930, 6¼in (16cm) high.
£120–140 / €175–210
$230–260 ↗ SWO

A Clarice Cliff preserve pot and cover, decorated with Autumn Crocus pattern, c1930, 3½in (9cm) high.
£150–180 / €220–260
$280–330 ↗ SWO

A Clarice Cliff honey pot, in the form of a beehive, decorated with Liberty pattern, c1930, 4in (10cm) high.
£430–480 / €630–710
$800–900 ⊞ TDG

A Clarice Cliff cream jug, cup and saucer, decorated with Gayday pattern, c1930.
£140–165 / €210–240
$260–310 ↗ G(L)

A Clarice Cliff Bizarre Bon Jour coffee service, comprising 15 pieces, decorated with Capri pattern, c1930.
£1,200–1,400 / €1,750–2,050
$2,250–2,650 ↗ GH

A Clarice Cliff preserve pot and cover, decorated with Celtic Harvest pattern, c1930, 5in (12.5cm) high.
£120–140 / €175–210
$230–260 ⊞ CoCo

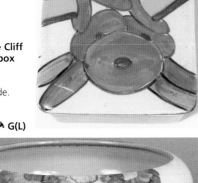

► **A Clarice Cliff Fantasque box and cover,** c1930, 5¾in (14.5cm) wide.
£260–310
€380–450
$490–580 ⚒ G(L)

A Clarice Cliff Bizarre Stamford tea service, comprising eight pieces, decorated with Patina Coastal pattern, restored, printed marks, c1930.
£720–860 / €1,050–1,250
$1,350–1,600 ⚒ SWO

A Clarice Cliff Lotus jug, decorated with Blue Crocus pattern, c1930, 11½in (29cm) high.
£900–1,050 / €1,300–1,550
$1,700–1,950 ⚒ CHTR

◄ **A Clarice Cliff Bizarre bowl,** No. 55, c1930, 9in (23cm) diam.
£150–180 / €220–260
$280–330 ⚒ DA

A set of five Clarice Cliff fruit bowls, decorated with Woodland pattern, printed and impressed marks, c1930.
£400–480 / €590–710
$750–900 ⚒ SWO

A Clarice Cliff Biarritz plate, painted with Aurea pattern, printed marks, c1930, 9in (23cm) wide.
£150–180 / €220–260
$280–330 ⚒ SWO

A Clarice Cliff Bizarre honey pot, decorated with Autumn Crocus pattern, c1930, 3in (7.5cm) high.
£135–150 / €200–220
$250–280 ⊞ HUM

A Clarice Cliff honey pot, c1930, 4½in (11.5cm) high.
£220–250 / €320–370
$410–470 ⊞ HUM

A Clarice Cliff preserve pot, decorated with Latona Bouquet pattern, c1930, 3in (7.5cm) high.
£400–450 / €590–660
$750–850 ⊞ HEW

A Clarice Cliff Fantasque Isis vase, decorated with Melon pattern, 1930–31, 12in (30.5cm) high.
£2,700–3,000 / €3,950–4,400
$5,000–5,600 ⊞ HEW

A Clarice Cliff Bizarre Isis vase, restored, c1930, 9¾in (25cm) high.
£340–400 / €500–590
$640–750 ⚲ SWO

◄ **A Clarice Cliff Bizarre ashtray,** decorated with a geometric pattern, c1930, 4¾in (12cm) diam.
£150–180 / €220–260
$280–330 ⚲ G(L)

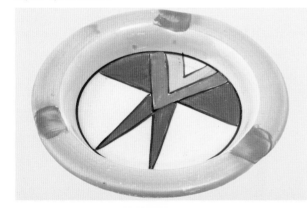

A Clarice Cliff fruit bowl, decorated with Delecia Pansies pattern, c1930, 8½in (21.5cm) diam.
£200–240 / €290–350
$380–450 ⚲ G(L)

◄ **A Clarice Cliff Bizarre teapot,** decorated with Double V pattern, slight damage, printed marks, c1930, 5¾in (14.5cm) high.
£170–200 / €250–290
$320–380 ⚲ CDC

A Clarice Cliff jug, decorated with Fruitburst pattern, c1930.
£310–350 / €460–510
$580–660 ⊞ HEW

▶ A pair of Clarice Cliff jugs, c1930, 6in (15cm) high.
£85–100 / €125–145
$165–190 ⊞ SAT

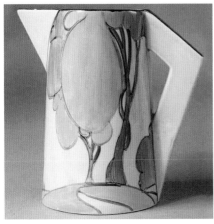

A Clarice Cliff Bizarre Conical jug, decorated with Pastel Autumn pattern, c1930, 6½in (16.5cm) high.
£340–400 / €500–590
$640–750 ⋗ DA

▶ A Clarice Cliff Conical cruet set, decorated with Autumn Crocus pattern, c1930, 3¼in (8.5cm) high.
£420–470 / €620–690
$790–880 ⊞ JFME

A Clarice Cliff Bizarre Conical jug, decorated with Blue Eyed Marigold pattern, c1931, 6½in (16.5cm) high.
£760–850 / €1,100–1,250
$1,450–1,600 ⊞ JFME

A Clarice Cliff tea-for-two set, comprising eight pieces, slight damage, factory marks, c1930.
£280–330 / €410–490
$530–620 ⋗ SWO

A Clarice Cliff teapot, in the form of a rooster, c1930, 7in (18cm) high.
£220–250 / €320–370
$410–470 ⊞ BEV

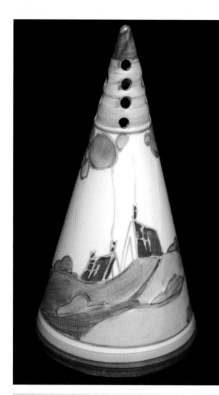

◄ **A Clarice Cliff Conical sugar sifter,** decorated with Secrets pattern, c1932, 5½in (14cm) high.
£810–900 / €1,200–1,350
$1,500–1,700 ⊞ TDG

A Clarice Cliff jug, decorated with Nuage pattern, c1932, 6in (15cm) high.
£580–650 / €850–960
$1,100–1,250 ⊞ HEW

A Clarice Cliff Bizarre tea-for-two set, decorated with Windbells pattern, c1933, teapot 4½in (11.5cm) high.
£3,400–3,800 / €5,000–5,600
$6,400–7,100 ⊞ GaL

A Clarice Cliff biscuit barrel, decorated with Acorn pattern, printed mark, shape No. 335, c1934, 6in (15cm) diam.
£360–430 / €530–630
$680–810 ⋟ GAK

► **A Clarice Cliff plate,** decorated with Rhodanthe pattern, c1934, 9in (23cm) diam.
£360–400 / €530–590
$680–750 ⊞ HEW

A Clarice Cliff preserve pot, decorated with Blue Japan pattern, c1934, 3in (7.5cm) high.
£450–500 / €660–740
$850–940 ⊞ JFME

A Clarice Cliff bowl, decorated with Rhodanthe pattern, c1934, 9in (23cm) diam.
£360–400 / €530–590
$680–750 ⊞ HEW

Two Clarice Cliff plates, unsigned, c1936, larger 9in (23cm) diam.
£15–20 / €22–29
$29–38 ⊞ HeA

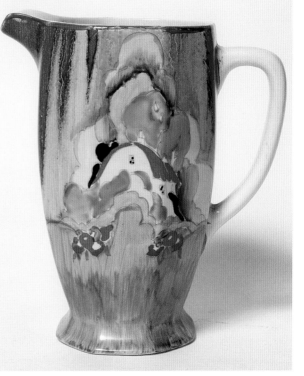

◄ A Clarice Cliff plate, decorated with Capri pattern, c1935, 10in (25.5cm) diam.
£400–450 €590–660
$750–850 ⊞ HEW

A Clarice Cliff jug, decorated with Forest Glen pattern, c1936, 6in (15cm) high.
£810–900 €1,200–1,350
$1,500–1,700 ⊞ HEW

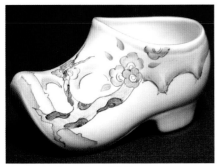

A Clarice Cliff sabot, decorated with Tiger Tree pattern, c1936, 6in (15cm) wide.
£360–400 / €530–590
$680–750 ⊞ JFME

A Clarice Cliff Fantasque fruit bowl, decorated with Trees and House pattern, with a silver-plated mount, marked, 1930s, 8in (20.5cm) diam.
£300–360 / €440–530
$560–670 ⚒ GIL

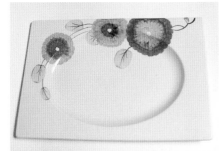

A Clarice Cliff Bizarre platter, No. 6315, 1930s, 16¼in (41.5cm) wide.
£290–330 / €430–490
$550–620 ⊞ NAW

A pair of Clarice Cliff Bizarre coffee cups and saucers, 1930s, cups 3in (7.5cm) high.
£260–300 / €380–440
$490–560 ⊞ NAW

◄ **A pair of Clarice Cliff Celtic Harvest jugs,** printed marks, 1930s, 8½in (21.5cm) high.
£140–165 / €200–240
$260–310 ➹ SWO

A Clarice Cliff Bizarre biscuit barrel, decorated with Secrets pattern, with chrome-plated handle and cover, printed marks, 1930s, 15½in (39.5cm) high.
£300–360 / €440–530
$560–680 ➹ SWO

A Clarice Cliff Bizarre preserve pot, decorated with House and Bridge pattern, 1930s, 3in (7.5cm) high.
£630–700 / €930–1,050
$1,150–1,300 ⊞ GaL

A Clarice Cliff sugar sifter, decorated with My Garden pattern, No. 660, 1930s, 5½in (14cm) high.
£300–360 / €440–530
$560–670 ➹ G(L)

A Clarice Cliff Bizarre preserve pot and cover, decorated with Gayday pattern, 1930s, 3½in (9cm) high.
£70–80 / €100–115
$135–155 ➹ SWO

A Clarice Cliff jardinière, in the form of a waterlily, printed mark, 1930s, 8¾in (22cm) wide.
£60–70 / €85–100
$115–135 ➹ WW

A Clarice Cliff wall plaque, decorated with a swallow, c1947.
£220–250 / €320–370
$410–470 ⊞ HEW

Derby

A Derby leaf-moulded sauceboat, painted with flowers, c1765, 6½in (16.5cm) wide.
£540–600 / €780–870
$980–1,100 ⊞ GIR

A pair of Chelsea Derby dishes, decorated with gold and painted with garlands of flowers, c1770, 9in (23cm) wide.
£1,750–1,950 / €2,550–2,850
$3,300–3,650 ⊞ JUP

Marks

Various marks were used between 1750 and 1770. After 1770, the factory merged with Chelsea, and marking became more consistent – usually crowned Ds or crossed batons.

Derby

Derby was home to a succession of major porcelain factories, including King Street Derby and the Derby Crown Porcelain Co. King Street Derby was managed by George Stephenson and Sampson Hancock between 1862 and 1866 and was continued by Sampson alone until 1935. The Derby Porcelain Co specialized in producing figures in the style of Meissen; most pieces are elaborate and would have been expensive even when made. Its other speciality was decorative wares such as vases and other ornamental pieces. Early wares are of the highest quality, whereas later pieces were often less detailed.

The two factories were rivals and made similar pieces that were based on patterns and shapes made in Derby earlier in the century, which in turn were based on designs by Sèvres. Items decorated with Imari patterns were another speciality of the Derby factory, and these reached their peak from about 1890 to 1915. After WWI production deteriorated and later pieces from the two factories are less sought after today.

A Derby model of a ewe, with bocage, patch marks, c1770, 7in (18cm) high.
£500–550 / €730–810
$900–1,000 ⊞ TYE

A pair of Derby candlesticks, with rabbits and bocage, c1775, 8in (20.5cm) high.
£2,500–2,750 / €3,700–4,100
$4,700–5,200 ⊞ DMa

A pair of Derby sheep, with bocage, c1775, 3¼in (8.5cm) high.
£880–980 / €1,300–1,450
$1,600–1,800 ⊞ AUC

A Derby moulded tea bowl, c1780, 3¼in (8.5cm) diam.
£50–60 / €75–85
$110–115 ⊞ JAY

A Derby model of a cow and calf, with bocage, c1800, 6in (15cm) high.
£700–780 / €1,000–1,150
$1,250–1,400 ⊞ TYE

A Derby ice pail and cover, painted with a Japan pattern, painted mark, early 19thC, 10in (25.2cm) high.
£380–450 / €560–660
$710–850 ➚ G(L)

A Derby mug, enamel-painted with a landscape within gilt floral scrollwork, crowned crossed batons and 'D' mark, titled to base 'View in Cumberland', early 19thC, 4½in (11.5cm) high.
£1,300–1,550 / €1,900–2,250
$2,450–2,900 ➚ PFK

◄ **A Derby two-handled vase,** painted with a continuous band of flowers between gilt foliate borders, c1815, 13in (33cm) high.
£2,700–3,000 / €3,950–4,400
$5,000–5,600 ⊞ JOR

Two Derby Sèvres-style spill vases, decorated with panels of birds, interlaced 'L' marks, c1830, 3¼in (8.5cm) high.
£100–120 / €145–175
$175–210 ➚ WW

A Derby dish, painted with a Yorkshire scene, 1825–35, 11in (28cm) wide.
£360–400 / €520–580
$660–730 ⊞ JAK

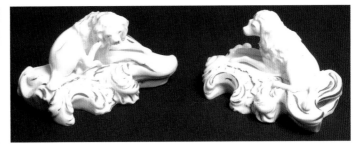

A pair of Derby models of poodles, with gilt decoration, on scrolled bases, c1845, 4in (10cm) wide.
£610–680 / €880–990
$1,100–1,250 ⊞ TYE

A Derby cup and saucer, painted with playing cards, c1830, 5in (12.5cm) diam.
£1,050–1,200 / €1,550–1,750
$1,950–2,200 ⊞ ReN

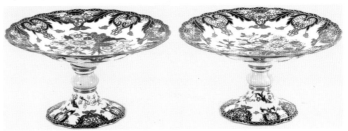

A pair of Derby Crown Porcelain Co comports, decorated in Imari colours with an Imari design, printed marks and date cipher, 1885, 9in (23cm) diameter.
£105–125 / €155–185
$200–240 ⚒ GAK

A Royal Crown Derby miniature vase, with gilt decoration and painted with flowers, 1896, 4½in (11.5cm) high.
£80–90 / €120–135
$150–170 ⚒ SWO

◄ **A Royal Crown Derby plate,** painted with a view of an English country garden, signed J. P. Wale, c1911, 8½in (21.6cm) diam.
£1,600–1,800
€2,350–2,650
$3,000–3,350
⊞ BP

A Royal Crown Derby Vase, painted by Cuthbert Gresley with a landscape entitled 'Lake Menteith, Scotland', on four feet, signed, c1920, 6½in (16.5cm) high.
£1,950–2,200 / €2,850–3,250
$3,650–4,150 ⊞ JUP

A Royal Crown Derby coffee service, comprising 15 pieces, decorated in Imari colours, dated 1927, coffee pot 7in (18cm) high.
£600–680 / €870–990
$1,100–1,250 ⊞ K&M

Doulton

◀ **A pair of Doulton Lambeth cruets,** with plated rims and stand stamped 'HB', together with a sifter spoon and ladle, dated 1878, pots 3¼in (8.5cm) high.
£240–290 / €350–420
$440–530 ⚒ SWO

A Doulton & Watts stoneware reform flask, modelled as Lord John Russell holding a scroll entitled 'The True Spirit of Reform', the reverse impressed 'Lambeth Pottery Doulton & Watts, 16 High Street Lambeth', c1845, 7½in (19cm) high.
£320–380 / €460–550
$600–710 ⚒ SJH

Doulton

The Doulton factory was first established in 1815 in Fulham, south London by John Doulton (1793–1873) and John Watts. Trading as Doulton & Watts it produced stoneware items such as inkwells and ginger beer bottles. In 1826 it moved to larger premises in Lambeth Walk and production expanded to include sanitary ware, drainpipes and laboratory articles, and the famous salt-glazed ware with blue decoration first appeared in 1862. John Doulton's son Henry had joined the firm in 1835 and under his direction many advances had been made. After John Watts retired in 1854 John Doulton ran the company until his death. In 1867 George Tinworth, Doulton's first resident sculptor, was appointed; he had a long career at the Lambeth studio, producing a range of figures, vases, jugs, tankards and reliefs, as well as monumental sculptures. The number of art potters at Lambeth rose to 345 by 1890 and these included such well known names as Frank Butler, Eliza Simmance, Arthur Barlow and his sisters Hannah and Florence Barlow.

In about 1880 a second factory was opened in Burslem, Staffordshire, which manufactured earthenware and bone china, most notably dinner services and tea sets. In 1889, Charles Noke, a modeller, joined the Burslem factory and introduced figures to their range, which became very successful, and invited well-known independent sculptors to submit designs. The figure painting department was put in the charge of Harry Nixon, whose initials gave rise to the numbering system for models which is still used today.

The company was granted a Royal Warrant by Edward VII in 1901 and became known as Royal Doulton. Production at the Lambeth factory ceased in 1956, but Doulton continued at Burslem, where they remain to this day.

A Doulton Lambeth stoneware vase, by Louisa E. Edwards, incised and enamelled with stylized flowers, incised monogram, dated 1876, 8¼in (21cm) high.
£480–580 / €710–850
$900–1,050 ⚒ G(L)

A Doulton Lambeth Faïence ware jar and cover, painted with flowers, stalks and leaves, impressed date 1876, 4½in (11.5cm) high.
£110–130 / €160–190
$200–240 ⚒ G(L)

◀ **A Doulton Lambeth silver-mounted jug,** by Florence Barlow, with leaf scroll decoration and relief-moulded florettes, 1876, 8in (20.5cm).
£360–430 / €520–620
$660–780 ⚒ G(L)

A Doulton Lambeth jug, with geometric relief-moulded decoration, 1878, 9in (23cm) high.
£140–170 / €200–240
$260–310 🪓 G(L)

A Doulton Lambeth silver-mounted tea set, slight damage to teapot,1878, teapot 5in (12.5cm) high.
£380–420 / €550–620
$690–780 ⊞ CANI

Doulton designers and their marks

- George Tinworth specialized in modelling religious plaques and frog and mice groups. His marks were GT and Doulton
- Hannah Barlow specialized in incised decoration and animal subjects. Her marks were BHB and Doulton
- Florence Barlow specialized in incised bird subjects. Her marks were FEB and Doulton
- Frank Butler specialized in bold shapes decorated with natural forms. His marks were FAB and Doulton
- Harry Nixon specialized in Song and Chang and flambé wares. His mark was H. Nixon, generally on the side of his pieces
- Mark V. Marshall specialized in well-modelled stoneware and worked with the Martin Brothers. His mark was MVM
- Eliza Simmance specialized in high-quality Art Nouveau designs. Her mark was ES

A Doulton Lambeth biscuit barrel, by Frank Butler, with leaf scroll design and silver-plated lid and handle, slight damage, c1880, 6¾in (17cm) high.
£360–430 / €520–620
$660–780 🪓 G(L)

A Doulton Lambeth stoneware jug, by Elizabeth Atkins, Florence Bowditch and Miss Felton, for Glasgow Fishmarket, 1880–91, 7in (18cm) high.
£240–265 / €350–390
$440–490 ⊞ CANI

A Doulton Lambeth stoneware spill vase, by George Tinworth, entitled 'The Waning of the Honeymoon', modelled with two rabbits, c1881, 4¾in (12cm) high.
£1,000–1,200 / €1,450–1,750
$1,800–2,250 🪓 SWO

A pair of Doulton Lambeth vases, decorated in *pâte-sur-pâte* by Eliza Simmance, with assistant artists Rosina Brown and Alice E Groom, 1883, 11in (28cm) high.
£880–975 / €1,300–1,450
$1,600–1,800 ⊞ CANI

A Doulton Lambeth tea set, by Hannah Barlow, decorated with a hunting scene, c1881, teapot 4½in (11.5cm) high.
£3,500–3,900 / €5,100–5,700
$6,600–7,300 ⊞ POW

A pair of Doulton Lambeth vases, by Frank A. Butler, No. 964, with sgraffito foliate scrolling decoration and raised floral medallions, slight damage, impressed marks, rosette mark for 1884, 9¼in (23.5cm) high.
£680–820 / €1,000–1,200
$1,250–1,500 ⚲ SWO

A Doulton Lambeth oil lamp, modelled as an owl, 1883, 26½in (67.5cm) high.
£4,400–4,900
€6,500–7,200
$8,300–9,200 ⊞ POW

A Doulton Lambeth oil lamp, designed by Florence Barlow, borders by Lucy Barlow, c1884, 20in (51cm) high.
£3,300–3,650
€4,850–5,400
$6,200–6,900 ⊞ JE

▶ **A Doulton Lambeth Silicon Ware amphora vase,** by Edith Lupton, incised and enamelled with three panels of flowers, incised signature and initials 'RW' and 'MD', with a metal tripod, dated 1885, vase 10¾in (27.5cm) high.
£200–240 / €290–350
$360–430 ⚲ G(L)

A Doulton Lambeth planter, designed by John Broad, c1885, 6in (15cm) high.
£810–895 / €1,150–1,300
$1,450–1,600 ⊞ CANI

Marks

All wares bear impressed, printed or painted marks, either 'Doulton, Lambeth', 'Doulton Burslem' or 'Royal Doulton England'. Figures are usually named and have an HN number.

A Doulton Lambeth stoneware jug, commemorating Fred Archer, the body with a portrait medallion, the spout in the form of a cap, the handle moulded with horse's harness, inscribed, stamped factory and retailer marks, c1886, 6¾in (17cm) high.
£260–310 / €390–460
$490–580 ⚲ SWO
Fred Archer was a champion jockey between 1869 and 1886.

▶ **A Doulton Lambeth vase,** by Hannah Barlow and Eliza Simmance, c1888, 14½in (37cm) high.
£1,300–1,450 / €1,900–2,150
$2,450–2,750 ⊞ JE

A Doulton Lambeth Faïence ware vase, by Margaret M. Challis, c1889, 10in (25.5cm) high.
£410–460 / €600–680
$770–860 ⊞ CANI

▶ **A pair of Doulton Lambeth vases,** by Eliza Simmance, decorated with parrots, 1892, 16in (40.5cm) high.
£4,300–4,800 / €6,300–7,100
$8,100–9,000 ⊞ POW

A Doulton stoneware jug, in memory of Cardinal Manning, the printed portrait with an inscription, c1892, 9¼in (23.5cm) high.
£220–260 / €320–380
$410–490 ✗ SAS

A Doulton Burslem beaker, printed with a bust of Queen Victoria and an inscription to the reverse, 1897, 4½in (11.5cm) high.
£130–155 / €190–230
$240–290 ⚒ SAS

A Doulton Slater patent silver-mounted tyg, dated 1899, 6in (15cm) high.
£340–380 / €500–560
$640–710 ⊞ SAT
Slater patent was a decorative process in which lace and other materials were impressed into the ware.

A Doulton Lambeth tankard, by Louisa J. Davis, with a silver cover, the body with geometric leaf and floral decoration, late 19thC, 10¾in (27.5cm) high.
£260–310 / €380–460
$490–580 ⚒ G(L)

A Doulton Lambeth pipe stand, moulded with masks and foliate swags, with a surmount for a matchbox, the sides with holes for pipes, impressed mark, c1900, 4¾in (12cm) high.
£75–85 / €110–125
$140–160 ⚒ L&E

A Doulton Burslem ewer, c1900, 7in (18cm) high.
£100–115 / €145–170
$190–220 ⊞ BET

A pair of Doulton vases, by Mark Marshall, c1900, 9¾in (25cm) high.
£1,650–1,850 / €2,450–2,700
$3,100–3,500 ⊞ JE

A pair of Doulton Lambeth vases, by Eliza Simmance, incised with floral motifs, one with slight damage, impressed and incised marks, c1900, 8¾in (22cm) high.
£200–240 / €290–350
$360–430 ⚒ SWO

◄ **A pair of Doulton Lambeth Faïence ware vases,** decorated with poppies, monogrammed 'HK' and 'MW', printed mark, No. 99, c1900, 11½in (29cm) high.
**£600–720 / €880–1,050
$1,150–1,350 ⚒ SWO**

A Royal Doulton Lambeth mug, depicting golfers, c1900, 6in (15cm) high.
**£450–500 / €660–740
$850–940 ⊞ SHER**

◄ **A Doulton toilet set,** comprising seven pieces, decorated with Kelmscott pattern, c1900, ewer 12in (30.5cm) high.
**£810–900 / €1,200–1,300
$1,500–1,700 ⊞ ASP**

A Doulton Lambeth stoneware vase, with incised decoration, the base incised 'For Eliza Simmance' and 'FG', early 20thC, 6¾in (17cm) high.
£220–260 / €320–380
$410–490 ♪ TMA

A pair of Royal Doulton vases, by Florence and Lucy Barlow, decorated with birds, c1902, 7½in (19cm) high.
£2,250–2,500 / €3,300–3,700
$4,250–4,700 ⊞ POW

A Royal Doulton vase, by Frank Butler, with tube-lined decoration, 1902, 12in (30.5cm) high.
£1,950–2,200
€2,900–3,250
$3,650–4,150 ⊞ POW

A Royal Doulton silver-mounted tea service, comprising 11 pieces, silver by W. Comyns, c1904.
£190–220 / €280–330
$350–410 ♪ G(L)

A Royal Doulton vase, by Frank Butler, Bessie Newberry and Helen Pennant, 1904, 16in (40.5cm) high.
£1,750–1,950
€2,550–2,850
$3,300–3,650 ⊞ CANI

A Royal Doulton Silicon ware ewer, c1905, 6in (15cm) high.
£175–195 / €260–290
$330–370 ⊞ PGO

◀ **A Royal Doulton jug,** commemorating Admiral Lord Nelson, inscribed 'England expects every man to do his duty', with a moulded relief portrait and two views of the Battle of Trafalgar, rope-twist handle, c1905, 8in (20.5cm) high.
£320–380 / €470–560
$600–710 ♪ SWO

A Royal Doulton vase, by David Dewsberry, painted with orchids, 1906, 18in (45.5cm) high.
£36,000–40,000 / €53,000–59,000
$68,000–75,000 ⊞ JE
This vase was made for the Christchurch Exhibition in New Zealand in 1906. Subsequently it was the centrepiece of an exhibition in the factory in 1913 when visited by George V and Queen Mary. It was then sold for £500 / €740 / $940 (the highest price ever achieved for a single vase at the time), to an Australian collector. It was exhibited in the Canterbury Museum, New Zealand, in 1993.

A Royal Doulton vase, by Mark V. Marshall, c1907, 14in (35.5cm) high.
£2,600–2,900 / €3,800–4,250
$4,900–5,500 ⊞ POW

◄ **A Royal Doulton two-handled vase,** by Maud Bowden and Minnie Forster, c1906, 4in (10cm) high.
£130–145 / €190–210
$240–270 ⊞ CANI

A pair of Royal Doulton stoneware jugs, with stiff leaf petal decoration, impressed marks, No. 1700, c1910, 7¾in (19.5cm) high.
£100–120 / €145–175
$190–230 ⋏ SWO

A Royal Doulton Silicon ware vase, c1910, 3½in (9cm) high.
£70–80 / €105–120
$130–150 ⊞ PGO

◄ **A Royal Doulton vase,** by Eliza Simmance, restored, c1910, 15in (38cm) high.
£200–240 / €290–350
$380–450 ⋏ SWO

► **A Royal Doulton stoneware ice cream drum,** the inner compartment with a lid and wooden cover, the base also with a wooden cover, impressed mark, c1910, 10¾in (27.5cm) high.
£110–130 / €160–190
$210–250 ⋏ SWO

A Doulton Lambeth salt-glazed spirit flask, modelled as Lloyd George, impressed marks, c1910, 8in (20.5cm) high.
£150–180 / €220–260
$280–340 ➢ G(L)

A pair of Royal Doulton plates, by Percy Curnock, c1915, 8¾in (22cm) diam.
£850–950 / €1,250–1,400
$1,600–1,800 ⊞ JE

A Royal Doulton figure, by Charles Noke, entitled 'The Scribe', inscription to base, No. HN305, 1918–36, 6in (15cm) high.
£980–1,150 / €1,450–1,750
$1,850–2,200 ➢ BWL

A Royal Doulton figure, entitled 'Lady with Rose', decorated in lilac and yellow with white spots, No. HN52A, slight damage, printed and inscribed marks, 1921–36, 10in (25.5cm) high.
£1,200–1,400 / €1,750–2,050
$2,250–2,650 ➢ SWO

A Royal Doulton Chang vase, by Fred Moore, c1925, 9in (23cm) diam.
£3,400–3,800 / €5,000–5,600
$6,400–7,100 ⊞ POW

HN numbers

The HN numbers on Royal Doulton figures refer to Harry Nixon, the first manager of the factory's Figure Painting Department. HN1 is 'Darling', first issued in 1912.

A Royal Doulton stoneware vase, by Harry Simeon, c1928, 3½in (9cm) high.
£200–230 / €290–340
$380–430 ⊞ CANI

◀ **A Royal Doulton double-sided figure,** entitled 'Mephistopheles and Marguerite', printed, No. HN755, painted and impressed marks, 1925–45, 7¾in (19.5cm) high, with associated bevel-edged mirror and mahogany stand.
£750–900 / €1,100–1,300
$1,400–1,650 ➢ CDC

A Royal Doulton stoneware vase,
No. X8864/2876, impressed marks,
c1930, 7in (18cm) high.
£90–105 / €130–155
$170–195 ✚ SWO

A Royal Doulton Burslem jug,
decorated with magnolia, c1930,
9in (23cm) high.
£90–105 / €130–155
$170–200 ⊞ WAC

A Royal Doulton studio vase,
by Vera Huggins and Florrie Jones,
c1930, 16in (40.5cm) high.
£1,150–1,300 / €1,700–1,900
$2,150–2,450 ⊞ CANI

A Royal Doulton Burslem bowl,
decorated with Arcady pattern, c1930,
10in (25.5cm) diam.
£135–150 / €200–220
$250–280 ⊞ HUM

A Royal Doulton figure, by Leslie
Harradine, entitled 'Miss Demure', No.
HN1440, 1930–49, 7in (18cm) high.
£150–180/ €220–260
$280–330 ✚ BWL

A Royal Doulton jug, decorated with
characters from *Treasure Island*, limited
edition No. 390/600, slight damage,
c1934, 7½in (19cm) high.
£260–310 / €380–460
$490–580 ✚ BWL

A Royal Doulton figure, entitled 'Gladys', No. HN1740, 1935–49,
5in (12.5cm) high.
£280–330 / €410–490
$530–620 ✚ SWO

A **Royal Doulton honeycomb box,** stamped marks, c1937, 4in (10cm) high.
£200–230 / €290–340
$380–430 ⊞ EHCS

A **Royal Doulton Series ware jug,**
transfer-decorated with a Native
American and a verse from 'Hiawatha',
1930s, 7¾in (19.5cm) high.
£180–210 / €260–310
$340–400 ⚒ L&E

A **Royal Doulton commemorative
jug,** entitled 'The Regency Coach',
limited edition 158/500, printed mark,
1930s, 11in (28cm) high.
£320–380 / €470–560
$600–710 ⚒ G(B)

A **Royal Doulton commemorative
loving cup,** moulded with Royal
portraits, limited edition No.
689/2,000, c1937, 6½in (16.5cm) high.
£250–300 / €370–440
$470–560 ⚒ SAS

A **Royal Doulton two-handled loving
cup,** decorated with The Three
Musketeers, 1930s, 12in (30.5cm) high.
£460–550 / €680–810
$860–1,050 ⚒ CAu

A **Royal Doulton brooch,** modelled
as a spaniel's head, 1930s,
1½in (4cm) wide.
£190–220 / €280–330
$350–410 ⚒ Pott

A **Royal Doulton De Luxe coffee service,** comprising eight pieces, printed and
painted marks, No. RA959V1284, 1940s, coffee pot 8¼in (21cm) high.
£140–165 / €210–250
$260–310 ⚒ SWO

A **Royal Doulton Etude sugar pot
and cover,** 1960s, 4in (10cm) wide.
£35–40 / €50–60
$65–75 ⊞ CHI

Mason's Ironstone

A **Mason's Ironstone jug,** with gilded decoration, c1820, 12in (30.5cm) high.
£2,550–2,850 / €3,750–4,200
$4,800–5,400 ⊞ HA

A **Mason's Ironstone mug,** decorated with Schoolhouse pattern, impressed mark, c1820, 4½in (11.5cm) high.
£690–770 / €1,000–1,150
$1,300–1,450 ⊞ RdV

A **Mason's Ironstone fruit comport,** with hand-painted decoration, marked 'Felt Spar', 1815–20, 6in (15cm) high.
£670–750 / €980–1,100
$1,250–1,400 ⊞ JP

A **Mason's Ironstone mug,** marked, c1820, 6in (15cm) diam.
£360–400 / €530–590
$680–750 ⊞ ANAn

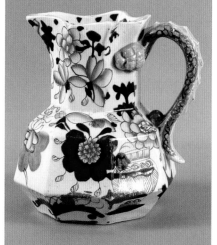

A **Mason's Ironstone jug,** decorated with Japan pattern, impressed mark, 1820–40, 7¾in (19.5cm) high.
£200–240 / €290–350
$380–450 ➚ SWO

◄ A **Mason's Ironstone chamber pot,** decorated with Japan pattern, impressed mark, c1820, 6in (15cm) high.
£1,550–1,750 / €2,250–2,550
$2,900–3,300 ⊞ RdV

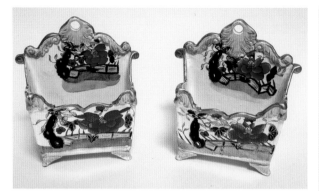

A pair of Mason's Ironstone card racks, c1820, 7in (18cm) high.
£1,650–1,850 / €2,450–2,700
$3,100–3,500 ⊞ ReN

▶ A Mason's Ironstone meat plate and drainer, decorated with Japan pattern, c1820, 16½in (42cm) wide.
£1,150–1,300 / €1,700–1,900
$2,150–2,450 ⊞ RdV

A Mason's Ironstone jug, painted with floral decoration, with 'Hydra' handle, printed mark, 1820–30, 9½in (24cm) high.
£140–165 / €210–240
$260–310 ⏶ G(L)

A Mason's Ironstone footbath jug, 1825–30, 13in (33cm) high.
£780–930 / €1,150–1,350
$1,450–1,750 ⏶ SWO

A pair of Mason's Ironstone mugs, transfer-printed and hand-painted with chinoiserie scenes, c1825, 4in (10cm) high.
£1,350–1,500 / €2,000–2,400
$2,550–2,850 ⊞ ReN

Mason's Ironstone

George Miles Mason and Charles James Mason took out their patent for Ironstone China in 1813 and went into production in the Staffordshire factory founded by their father, Miles Mason. This early Ironstone was a hard, dense greyish-white material, usually without crazing, and was immediately successful, particularly in America. The company became famous for its robust, heavy earthenware that could be decorated to imitate the porcelain of the day and had a similar ring when struck, but was cheaper to produce. The Ironstone was very durable and therefore ideal for domestic use. Approximately 120 patterns a year were being introduced, and by 1840 Mason's tableware was available in over 3,000 patterns. Decoration was bright and bold, often with a Japanese influence – Imari patterns are among the most popular. Several new types of ware were introduced after 1840, but proved to be unpopular. In 1848, Charles Mason was declared bankrupt and the golden age of Mason's Ironstone came to an end.

A pair of Ironstone vases and covers, possibly Mason's, with wolf masks and floral decoration, restored, c1825, 22in (56cm) high.
£4,100–4,900 / €6,000–7,200
$7,700–9,200   ⚘ G(L)

A Mason's Ironstone jug, painted with flowers, leaves and a butterfly, impressed mark, 1830–40, 6¼in (16cm) high.
£150–180 / €220–260
$280–340   ⚘ G(L)

A Mason's pearlware dish, decorated with a view of Lynmouth, Devon, c1830, 11¼in (28.5cm) wide.
£430–490 / €630–720
$810–920   ⊞ RdV

▶ **A Mason's Ironstone vase,** printed mark, 1830–40, 12¼in (31cm) high.
£175–210 / €260–310
$330–390   ⚘ SWO

A Mason's Ironstone part dinner service, comprising 31 pieces, decorated with panels of Oriental landscapes, slight damage, printed marks, c1830–40.
£2,450–2,950 / €3,600–4,350
$4,600–5,500   ⚘ WW

A Masons's Ironstone tureen and cover, transfer-printed and painted with a chinoiserie landscape, maker's and retailer's marks, 1830–40, 14½in (37cm) wide.
£100–120 / €145–175
$185–220   ⚘ PFK

Two Mason's Ironstone jugs, printed with griffins, printed marks, pattern No. B9479, mid-19thC, larger 6½in (16.5cm) high.
£180–210 / €260–310
$340–390 ⚒ SWO

◄ **A Mason's Ironstone lustre ginger jar,** decorated with Fruit Basket pattern, 1935–39, 8in (20.5cm) high.
£145–165 / €210–240
$270–310 ⊞ TAC

A set of three Mason's Ironstone jugs, late 19thC, largest 9in (23cm) high.
£1,050–1,200 / €1,550–1,750
$1,950–2,250 ⊞ ANAn

A Mason's Ironstone vase, decorated with ducks, lotus flowers and a landscape, printed mark, c1840, 15in (38cm) high.
£610–730 / €900–1,050
$1,150–1,350 ⚒ WW

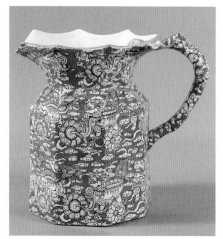

Two Mason's Ironstone jugs, decorated with Imari pattern, printed marks, pattern No. B8839, late 19thC, larger 6in (15cm) high.
£210–250 / €310–370
$390–470 ⚒ SWO

A Mason's Ironstone jug, printed with dragons, printed mark, No. 99440, c1900, 6½in (16.5cm) high.
£180–210 / €260–310
$340–390 ⚒ SWO

Minton

A Minton bone china cup and saucer, painted with landscapes, pattern No. 306, c1810.
£260–310 / €380–460
$490–580 ⚒ WW

Minton

Established in 1793 by Thomas Minton, the factory produced a wide range of ceramics from earthenware and fine bone china to majolica. Minton's peak period was from the mid- to late 19th century. Its finest wares included pieces made using the *pâte-sur-pâte* technique, a process developed on the Continent. Items in the Japanese style were also produced, using patterns based on those found on Japanese porcelain, using brilliant turquoise enamels, and including cloisonné. The company's success was partly due to the new majolica glazes. In 1835, Minton produced the first pattern book of encaustic tiles which was highly praised by Augustus Pugin. Pugin designed encaustic and majolica tiles for the company from around 1840 until the early 1850s.

A Minton bone china bowl, decorated with a leaf pattern, 1812–15, 9¼in (23.5cm) diam.
£100–120 / €145–170
$200–230 ⚒ BWL

A Minton pearlware footed bowl, printed with a camel and giraffe, c1820, 11¾in (30cm) wide.
£160–190 / €240–280
$300–360 ⚒ SWO

◄ A Minton cup and saucer, by Joseph Bancroft, painted with feathers, the handle in the form of a butterfly, c1830.
£1,450–1,650 / €2,150–2,450
$2,750–3,100 ⊞ JOR

A Minton pottery footed bowl, printed with Chinese Marine pattern, slight damage, printed mark, c1830, 10¾in (27.5cm) wide.
£150–180 / €220–260
$280–340 ⚒ SWO

◄ A Minton cabinet cup and saucer, the cup on paw feet, decorated with raised paste gilding, c1830.
£550–620 / €810–910
$1,050–1,150 ⊞ JOR

A **Minton footbath,** printed and painted with vases of flowering shrubs, impressed 'BB' and 'New Stone', c1840, 19in (48.5cm) wide.
£250–300 / €370–440
$470–560 ➚ SWO

A **Minton encaustic bread plate,** by A. W. N. Pugin, inscribed 'Waste Not Want Not', c1850, 13½in (34.5cm) diam.
£720–860 / €1,050–1,250
$1,350–1,600 ➚ SWO

A **Minton Parian model of a spaniel,** c1845, 4in (10cm) wide.
£250–280 / €370–430
$470–550 ⊞ TYE

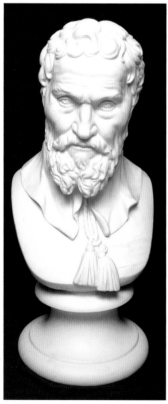

A **Minton jug,** moulded with cherubs, c1855, 8½in (21.5cm) high.
£150–170 / €220–250
$280–320 ⊞ JAK

A **Minton majolica jug,** decorated with medieval characters, c1860, 14in (35.5cm) high.
£1,700–1,900 / €2,500–2,800
$3,200–3,550 ⊞ BRT

A **Minton Parian bust of Michelangelo,** 1851, 24½in (62cm) high.
£1,350–1,500 / €2,000–2,200
$2,550–2,800 ⊞ JAK

► A **Minton part dessert service,** comprising 11 pieces, one plate damaged, c1860, 9in (23cm) diam.
£360–430
€530–630
$680–810
➚ SWO

A Minton plate, by James Rouse, signed, c1860, 9in (23cm) diam.
£450–500 / €660–740
$850–940 ⊞ JAK

A Minton majolica jardinière, c1860, 21in (53.5cm) wide.
£3,500–3,900 / €5,100–5,700
$6,600–7,300 ⊞ BRT

◄ A Minton bust of Albert Edward, Prince of Wales, 1863, 13in (33cm) high.
£360–400 / €530–590
$680–750 ⊞ JAK

A Minton Parian figure, by John Bell, entitled 'Miranda', signed, dated 1865, 15½in (39.5cm) high.
£280–330 / €410–490
$530–620 ⚒ AH

A Minton Argyle plate, painted with a view entitled 'Strawberry Hill', 1861, 9in (23cm) diam.
£70–80 / €100–115
$135–155 ⊞ LGr

A pair of Minton cabinet plates, painted with butterflies, c1871, 9¼in (23.5cm) diam.
£270–300 / €400–440
$510–560 ⊞ LGr

A Minton figure of Whistler's Mother, 1872, 11in (28cm) high.
£630–700 / €930–1,050
$1,200–1,300 ⊞ JAK

► A Minton two-handled vase, by Antonin Boullemier, painted with panels representing Summer and Winter, on a gilt foot, c1873, 11in (28cm) high.
£1,650–1,850
€2,450–2,700
$3,100–3,500 ⊞ JOR

A Minton majolica urn, impressed marks, No. 1009, 1874, 17in (43cm) high.
£500–600 / €740–880
$940–1,150 ⚒ BWL

A Minton dessert service, comprising nine pieces, printed and enamelled with fans, birds and bamboo shoots, 1878, 9½in (24cm) diam.
£140–165 / €210–240
$260–310 ⚒ G(L)

A Minton reticulated plate, painted by Antonin Boullemier with figures in a classical landscape, c1880, 10in (25.5cm) diam.
£1,900–2,150 / €2,800–3,150
$3,550–4,050 ⊞ JOR

A Minton plate, painted with flowers and a butterfly, c1880, 9½in (24cm) diam.
£180–200 / €260–290
$340–380 ⊞ JAK

A Minton cabinet plate, painted with an Arabian butcher, signed 'F. Bellanger', impressed marks, dated 1887, 9¾in (25cm) diam.
£160–190 / €240–280
$300–360 ⚒ SWO

A Minton vase, decorated by Alboin Birks with a *pâte-sur-pâte* panel, c1890, 14in (35.5cm) high.
£4,500–5,000 / €6,600–7,400
$8,500–9,400 ⊞ HKW

A Minton Secessionist vase, No. 42, 1900–05, 5in (12.5cm) high.
£165–185 / €240–270
$310–350 ⊞ MMc

▶ **A Minton *pâte-sur-pâte* ewer,** decorated by Lawrence Birks with two panels of putti and a further panel with a classical portrait, on a ground filled with urns, cornucopiae of fruit, leaves and swags, the handle with a gilt satyr-mask terminal, on a fluted socle, impressed and printed marks, c1892, 11in (28cm) high.
£11,400–13,700 / €16,800–20,200
$21,500–25,800 ⚒ DA

A Minton Secessionist jardinière, decorated with stylized flowers, printed marks, c1900, 8¾in (22cm) high.
£200–240 / €290–350
$380–450 ➶ SWO

Cross Reference
Majolica see pages 56–61

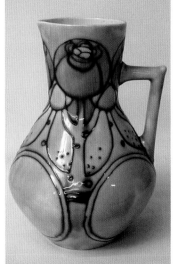

A Minton secessionist vase, decorated with stylized flowers, printed mark, 1905, 8in (20.5cm) high.
£200–240 / €290–350
$380–450 ➶ TMA

A Minton Secessionist vase, decorated with stylized flowers, restored, c1905, 9¾in (25cm) high.
£140–165 / €210–240
$260–310 ➶ SWO

Three Minton pedestal bowls, decorated with fruits and foliage, printed marks and incised numbers, 1910–20, largest 3½in (9cm) high.
£270–320 / €400–470
$510–600 ➶ SWO

A Minton lustre bowl, printed and painted with a cockerel, printed mark, c1930, 7½in (19cm) diam.
£100–120 / €145–170
$200–230 ➶ SWO

A Minton pottery mug, inscribed 'MCC', '1787' and '1937', 1937, 4in (12.5cm) high.
£20–25 / €30–35
$40–50 ➶ SAS

A Minton loving cup and cover, commemorating the coronation of Queen Elizabeth II, 1953, 4in (10cm) high.
£310–350 / €460–510
$580–660 ⊞ H&G

Meissen

A Meissen silver-gilt-mounted sugar box and cover, painted in the manner of J. G. Höroldt, silversmith's mark and crossed swords mark, German, 1723–24, 4¾in (12cm) wide.
£8,400–10,100 / €12,300–14,800
$15,800–19,000 ⚒ S

Meissen

The Meissen factory opened near Dresden around 1710. Some early wares were direct copies of Oriental prototypes, although most productions were original. Every piece of 18th-century Meissen was decorated to the highest standards. The brilliant painter J. G. Höroldt specialized in chinoiserie subjects, and other enamellers painted landscapes, detailed figure subjects or the finely executed flowers known as *deutsche Blumen*. Their principal figure modeller was J. J. Kändler, who is best known for his harlequins and figures of street vendors.

During the early 19th century Meissen produced elaborately decorated and gilded pieces, often with topographical views or Classical subjects. During the century Meissen's output was increasingly repetitions of 18th-century designs, always superb in execution, a trend which continued into the 20th century.

A Meissen *Hausmalerei* bowl, probably painted in Dresden, the cartouche decorated with peasant figures in landscapes, the interior similarly painted, restored, German, c1725, 5¼in (13.5cm) diam.
£700–840 / €1,050–1,250
$1,200–1,450 ⚒ G(L)

A Meissen figure, entitled 'The Pipe Smoker', German, c1747, 5in (12.5cm) high.
£3,600–4,000 / €5,300–5,900
$6,800–7,500 ⊞ BHa

A Meissen figure of an Eastern gentleman, German, c1748, 7in (18cm) high.
£3,400–3,800 / €5,000–5,600
$6,400–7,100 ⊞ BHa

A Meissen figure of a boy, German, c1750, 5in (12.5cm) high.
£1,300–1,450 / €1,900–2,150
$2,450–2,750 ⊞ MAA

A Meissen figural group of child musicians, by J. J. Kändler, German, c1755, 7in (18cm) high.
£7,100–7,900 / €10,400–11,600
$13,300–14,900 ⊞ BHa

A Meissen sucrier and cover,
painted with flowers and sprigs, the
cover with a floral finial, slight damage,
German, c1750, 4½in (11cm) diam.
£760–850 / €1,100–1,250
$1,450–1,600 ⊞ G&G

Marks

Almost every piece of Meissen is clearly marked with crossed swords.
In the 18th century each sword was painted as a neat, straight line.
During the 'Academic' period (1763–74), a dot was placed between
the sword hilts, and during the 'Marcolini' period (1774–1813) a star
or asterisk was painted above the hilts. Rather scruffy marks were
used until the 1840s and then, until the early 20th century, the
swords were carefully painted, both gently curved, and a 'pommel'
(dark spot) placed at the tip of each hilt. From 1926 to 1939 a dot
was placed between the blades of the swords. Post-war pieces have
thin, curved swords, with no dots or pommels.
  Meissen is the most widely copied porcelain and the marks are
extensively faked, especially by other Dresden factories. It is
therefore essential to distinguish between original pieces and
Dresden-style porcelain, which is always inferior.

A Meissen figure of The Marquis,
designed by C. Huet and modelled by
P. Reinicke, German, c1757,
5in (12.5cm) high.
£2,550–2,850 / €3,750–4,200
$4,800–5,400 ⊞ BHa

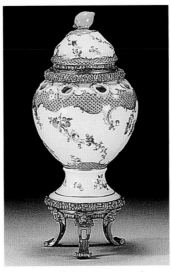

**A Meissen gilt-metal-mounted
potpourri vase and cover,** the cover
with a lemon finial, decorated with
gilding, repaired, German, c1760,
11in (28cm) high.
£600–720 / €880–1,050
$1,150–1,350 ⤢ S(O)

**A Meissen figural potpourri and
cover,** German, c1760, 9in (23cm) high.
£4,200–4,700 / €6,200–6,900
$7,900–8,800 ⊞ BHa

A Meissen butter box and cover,
in the shape of a lemon, chipped
and restored, German, c1760,
6in (15cm) wide.
£780–940 / €1,150–1,400
$1,450–1,750 ⤢ S(O)

**A Meissen figure of Cupid in
disguise as a lady,** German, c1770,
4in (10cm) high.
£850–950 / €1,250–1,400
$1,600–1,800 ⊞ MAA

A Meissen figure of a girl, German,
c1772, 5in (12.5cm) high.
£1,300–1,450 / €1,900–2,150
$2,450–2,750 ⊞ MAA

A Meissen figure of Cupid disguised as a hurdy gurdy player, German, c1775, 4in (10cm) high.
£850–950 / €1,250–1,400
$1,600–1,800 ⊞ MAA

A Meissen figural group, entitled 'Winter', c1800, 4½in (11.5cm) high.
£1,450–1,650 / €2,150–2,450
$2,750–3,100 ⊞ MAA

Meissen in the early 19th century

The Meissen factory was in decline at the beginning of the 19th century, due to competition from other European porcelain factories and the effects of the Napoleonic Wars (1799–1815). Mass production was growing steadily, however, reducing costs and ensuring that demands could be met, and from the 1820s the factory began using circular kilns which resulted in a fourfold increase in production. In the late 1820s an inexpensive method of decoration using gold mixed in a solution, known as gloss-gilding, was introduced for use on cheaper figures.

A Meissen figure of a young woman holding grapes, German, c1800, 5½in (14cm) high.
£1,450–1,650 / €2,150–2,450
$2,750–3,100 ⊞ MAA

A Meissen figure of Sight, from the series by Schöneit, German, c1840, 6in (15cm) high.
£1,100–1,250 / €1,600–1,800
$2,100–2,350 ⊞ MAA

A pair of Meissen bowls, both depicting a view of Dresden, German, c1840, 13in (33cm) wide.
£1,350–1,500 / €2,000–2,200
$2,500–2,800 ⊞ DAV

A Meissen cup and saucer, with a deep base for hot water, German, c1850, 5in (12.5cm) high.
£990–1,100 / €1,450–1,600
$1,850–2,050 ⊞ BROW

A Meissen figure of a man reading, German, 1840–50, 5in (12.5cm) high.
£220–250 / €320–370
$410–470 ⊞ SER

A Meissen figural water group, first modelled by Acier, No. D81, c1850, 10in (25.5cm) high.
£2,250–2,500 / €3,300–3,700
$4,250–4,700 ⊞ DAV

A Meissen figural group of Aeneas carrying his father Anchises with his son Ascanius, first modelled by J.J. Kändler, No. 2030, German, c1850, 10in (25.5cm) high.
£1,400–1,600 / €2,100–2,350
$2,700–3,000 ⊞ DAV

A Meissen figure of a girl with a cat, first modelled by Acier, No. B94, crossed swords mark, German, c1850, 5½in (14cm) high.
£1,050–1,200 / €1,550–1,750
$1,950–2,200 ⊞ DAV

A Meissen figural group, entitled 'Autumn', from the Four Seasons series, first modelled by Acier, No. F92, c1850, 6½in (16.5cm) high.
£1,700–1,900 / €2,500–2,800
$3,200–3,550 ⊞ DAV

◄ **A Meissen figural group of Mars God of War and three putti,** first modelled by Acier, No. D80, crossed swords mark, German, c1850, 9in (23cm) high.
£2,900–3,250
€4,250–4,800
$5,500–6,100 ⊞ DAV

► **A Meissen figural group,** entitled 'Broken Bridge', first modelled by Acier No. F63, crossed swords mark, German, c1850, 10in (25.5cm) high.
£2,450–2,750
€3,600–4,050
$4,600–5,200 ⊞ DAV

A Meissen figural group, entitled 'Spanish Lovers', first modelled by Acier, No. F98, crossed swords mark, German, c1850, 10in (25.5cm) high.
£2,450–2,750 / €3,600–4,050
$4,600–5,200 ⊞ DAV

A pair of Meissen figures, depicting a boy with a dog and a girl with a cat, German, c1850, 5in (12.5cm) high.
£3,300–3,700 / €4,850–5,400
$6,200–7,000 ⊞ MAA

A Meissen model of a Bolognese hound, German, mid-19thC, 9¼in (23.5cm) high.
£520–620 / €760–910
$980–1,150 ➶ SJH

A Meissen figural group, entitled 'The Good Mother', first modelled by Michel Victor Acier, German, c1850, 8¼in (21cm) high.
£950–1,100 / €1,400–1,650
$1,800–2,150 ➶ SWO

A pair of Meissen models of golden oriels, restored, German, c1850, 10in (25.5cm) high.
£1,100–1,300 / €1,600–1,900
$2,050–2,450 ➶ WW

A Meissen figural inkstand, on a gilt-brass dish, minor damage, marked, German, c1850, 5¼in (13.5cm) high.
£610–730 / €900–1,050
$1,150–1,350 ➶ TEN

A Meissen figure of a boy on a
hobby-horse, German, c1860,
6½in (16.5cm) high.
£1,350–1,500 / €2,000–2,200
$2,500–2,800 ⊞ BROW

Meissen figures

The factory's fortunes, which had been ailing at the beginning of
the 19th century, had begun to improve by the 1820s and were
further revived when the rococo style became fashionable again in
the early 1830s. The factory began reusing their 18th-century figure
moulds and these, as well as other rococo revival wares, became
greatly in demand and formed the bulk of the output during the
second half of the 19th century. Produced under the supervision
of the chief modeller, Ernst August Leuteritz, the figures were
always carefully moulded and painted to the highest standards.
They represent typically 18th-century subjects such as shepherds and
shepherdesses, the aristocracy and allegorical figures of the Seasons
and the four Continents.

A pair of Meissen figures of a shepherd and shepherdess, German, c1860,
10in (25.5cm) high.
£3,150–3,500 / €4,600–5,100
$5,900–6,600 ⊞ MAA

A Meissen figural group of a
courting couple, German, c1860,
8in (20.5cm) high.
£2,300–2,600 / €3,400–3,800
$4,300–4,900 ⊞ BROW

A Meissen figural group, entitled
'Bird in a Hoop', German, c1860,
5in (12.5cm) high.
£1,300–1,450 / €1,900–2,150
$2,450–2,750 ⊞ MAA

◄ A Meissen group of two cherubs
with a goat, German, c1860,
4in (10cm) high.
£850–950 / €1,250–1,400
$1,600–1,800 ⊞ MAA

A Meissen figure, entitled 'Sight',
German, c1860, 10¾in (27.5cm) high.
£480–570 / €700–840
$900–1,050 ⚒ SWO

A Meissen figural group of two lovers with birds, first modelled by Acier, No. E65, German, c1860, 7½in (19cm) high.
£1,600–1,800 / €2,350–2,650 $3,00–3,400 ⊞ DAV

A pair of Meissen candlesticks, German, c1860, 5½in (14cm) high.
£1,450–1,650 / €2,150–2,450 $2,750–3,100 ⊞ MAA

A Meissen figure of Cupid in disguise, German, c1860, 8½in (21.5cm) high.
£1,300–1,450 / €1,900–2,150 $2,450–2,750 ⊞ MAA

A Meissen figure of Healing, from the series by Schönheit, German, c1860, 4½in (11.5cm) high.
£950–1,100 / €1,400–1,600 $1,800–2,050 ⊞ SWO

A Meissen figural group of three cherubs, German, c1860, 5in (12.5cm) high.
£1,300–1,450 / €1,900–2,150 $2,450–2,750 ⊞ MAA

A Meissen figure of a cherub making a cup of chocolate, restored, crossed swords mark, German, c1860, 4¼in (11cm) high.
£240–280 / €350–410 $450–530 ⚒ SWO

A Meissen figural group of two cherubs and a dog by an urn, German, c1870, 8½in (21.5cm) high.
£2,300–2,600 / €3,400–3,800 $4,300–4,900 ⊞ MAA

A pair of Meissen figures of a lady and gentleman, German, c1870, 7in (18cm) high.
£2,250–2,500 / €3,300–3,700 $4,250–4,700 ⊞ MAA

A Meissen figural group, entitled 'The Good Father', German, c1870, 8in (20.5cm) high.
£3,950–4,400 / €5,700–6,500
$7,300–8,300 ⊞ BROW

A pair of Meissen figures of a lady and gentleman, German, c1870, 7in (18cm) high.
£2,250–2,500 / €3,300–3,700
$4,250–4,700 ⊞ MAA

A pair of Meissen figures of cherubs, entitled 'Night' and 'Day', German, c1870, 7in (18cm) high.
£2,600–2,900 / €3,800–4,250
$4,900–5,500 ⊞ MAA

A Meissen figural group, entitled 'Summer', from the Four Seasons series, first modelled by Schönheit, No. G92, German, c1870, 6½in (16.5cm) high.
£1,700–1,900 / €2,500–2,800
$3,200–3,550 ⊞ DAV

A Meissen figure of a cherub, entitled 'Balance', from a series of 16, first modelled by Acier, No. F2, German, 1870, 6in (15cm) high.
£900–1,000 / €1,300–1,450
$1,700–1,900 ⊞ DAV

▶ A Meissen figure of a cherub, German, c1870, 4½in (11.5cm) high.
£670–750 / €980–1,100
$1,250–1,400 ⊞ MAA

A Meissen figure of Cupid in disguise, German, c1870, 9in (23cm) high.
£1,100–1,250 / €1,600–1,850
$2,050–2,350 ⊞ MAA

A Meissen figure of a child playing with a doll, German, c1870, 5½in (14cm) high.
£1,300–1,450 / €1,900–2,150
$2,450–2,750 ⊞ MAA

▶ **A Meissen figural group,** entitled 'The Broken Bridge', German, c1870, 9½in (24cm) high.
£3,500–3,900 / €5,100–5,700
$6,600–7,300 ⊞ BHa

A Meissen figure of a young boy with a lamb, German, c1870, 5in (12.5cm) high.
£1,100–1,250 / €1,600–1,800
$2,100–2,350 ⊞ BHa

A Meissen figure of Venus in a chariot, German, c1870, 7in (18cm) high.
£3,150–3,500 / €4,600–5,100
$5,900–6,600 ⊞ MAA

A Meissen figure, entitled ' Flower Seller', German, c1870, 5½in (14cm) high.
£1,200–1,350 / €1,750–2,000
$2,250–2,550 ⊞ BHa

A pair of Meissen figures of a boy and girl holding chickens, German, c1870, 6in (15cm) high.
£2,350–2,650 / €3,450–3,900
$4,400–5,000 ⊞ BROW

A Meissen figural group of cherubs, depicting Sculpture, from the Arts series, German, c1870, 8in (20.5cm) high.
£3,100–3,450 / €4,550–5,100
$5,800–6,500 ⊞ BROW

A Meissen coffee pot, decorated with painted panels of flowers within gilt scrolls, the cover with a rose finial, damaged, German, c1870, 10in (25.5cm) high.
£210–250 / €310–370
$390–470 ↗ G(L)

A Meissen model of a bullfinch, German, c1880, 3½in (9cm) high.
£300–340 / €440–500
$560–640 ⊞ BROW

A Meissen cup and saucer, with flower-encrusted decoration, German, c1880, cup 4in (10cm) diam.
£520–580 / €760–850
$980–1,100 ⊞ BROW

A Meissen figure of a cherub, German, c1880, 5in (12.5cm) high.
£670–750 / €980–1,100
$1,250–1,400 ⊞ MAA

A pair of Meissen candelabra, both moulded with figures, German, c1880, 19½in (49.5cm) high.
£4,500–5,000 / €6,600–7,400
$8,500–9,400 ⊞ BROW

A Meissen figural group of cherubs, entitled 'Astronomy', German, c1880, 5in (12.5cm) high.
£1,300–1,450 / €1,900–2,150
$2,450–2,750 ⊞ MAA

◄ **A Meissen stand,** the sides decorated with lattice work, the top encrusted with flowers, German, c1880, 5in (12.5cm) diam.
£1,100–1,250 / €1,600–1,800
$2,100–2,350 ⊞ BROW

A Meissen figural group of cherubs carrying a fox and a bird, German, c1880, 5¾in (14.5cm) high.
£1,100–1,250 / €1,600–1,800
$2,100–2,350 ⊞ MAA

▶ **A Meissen model of a parrot,** first modelled by J. J. Kändler, No. 63, German, c1880, 13in (33cm) high.
£2,150–2,400 / €3,150–3,550
$4,050–4,500 ⊞ DAV

A Meissen desk set, decorated with *Fels und Vogel* pattern, slight damage, No. 7, German, 1870–90.
£600–720 / €880–1,050
$1,150–1,350 ⚒ S(Am)

A pair of Meissen figures of gallants, German, c1880, 7in (18cm) high.
£3,150–3,500 / €4,600–5,100
$5,900–6,600 ⊞ BHa

▶ **A Meissen figural group of a woman and two cherubs under a tree,** German, c1890, 11in (28cm) high.
£2,000–2,250 / €2,950–3,300
$3,750–4,250 ⊞ MAA

A Meissen figural group of three cherubs, German, c1900, 6½in (16.5cm) high.
£1,650–1,850 / €2,450–2,700
$3,100–3,500 ⊞ MAA

A Meissen figural group of two young grape pickers, incised numeral, German, c1880, 6in (15cm) high.
£650–780 / €960–1,150
$1,200–1,450 ⚒ G(L)

▶ A Meissen model of a badger, by Max Esser, No. H244, from a series of 75 models entitled 'Reineke Fuchs', German, c1923, 11in (28cm) high.
£2,450–2,750 / €3,600–4,050
$4,600–5,200 ⊞ DAV

A Meissen figure of a girl with a basket of vegetables and a dog, first modelled by Jakob Ungerer, No. T62, German, c1908, 9in (23cm) high.
£1,950–2,200 / €2,850–3,200
$3,650–4,150 ⊞ DAV

A Meissen figure of a girl with cherries, first modelled by A. Konig, No. Y149, c1910, 7in (18cm) high.
£1,100–1,250 / €1,600–1,800
$2,100–2,350 ⊞ DAV

▶ A Meissen head of a Balinese woman, first modelled by Willi Munch-Khe, No. A1133, German, 1953, 11in (28cm) high.
£1,550–1,750 / €2,300–2,550
$2,900–3,300 ⊞ DAV

Moorcroft

A Moorcroft MacIntyre Flamminian ware vase, restored, Liberty mark, early 20thC, 8in (20.5cm) high.
£200–240 / €290–350
$380–450 ➤ BWL

◄ **A Moorcroft MacIntyre Florian ware vase,** decorated with butterflies, c1900, 8in (20.5cm) high.
£990–1,100 / €1,450–1,600
$1,850–2,050 ⊞ HABA

A Moorcroft MacIntyre lustre vase, marked 'For Liberty & Co', signed, 1902, 6¾in (17cm) high.
£950–1,100 / €1,400–1,650
$1,800–2,100 ➤ GIL

◄ **A Moorcroft two-handled vase,** with incised medallions, signed, early 20thC, 7in (18cm) high.
£115–135 / €170–200
$210–250 ➤ BWL

◄ **A Moorcroft MacIntyre Florian ware bowl,** c1903, 3½in (9cm) high.
£990–1,100
€1,450–1,600
$1,850–2,050
⊞ GOv

A pair of Moorcroft MacIntyre Aurelian ware vases, decorated with floral panels and gilt highlights, printed mark, c1904, 10in (25.5cm) high.
£1,100–1,300 / €1,600–1,900
$2,050–2,450 ➤ G(L)

A Moorcroft MacIntyre **Aurelian ware two-handled vase,** decorated with floral panels, with gilt highlights, printed mark, c1904, 6½in (16.5cm) high.
£520–620 / €760–910
$980–1,150 ➤ **G(L)**

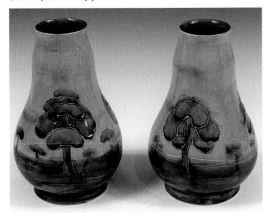

History of Moorcroft

William Moorcroft (1872–1945) began his career as a designer with the established pottery James MacIntyre & Co, Burslem, Staffordshire in 1898. At MacIntyre he was in charge of the art pottery department and responsible for the production and decoration of the wares. The range that established Moorcroft as a designer was Florian ware, launched in 1898. Around 1902 a long association with Liberty & Co was begun and many pieces were marked with a Liberty backstamp. Designs developed during this period include Flamminian ware, Aurelian ware, Claremont and Hazeldene.

When the art pottery department at MacIntyre was closed in 1913, Moorcroft set up on his own at Cobridge, on the outskirts of Burslem, and employed some of the redundant potters and decorators. The Pansy and Pomegranate patterns had been developed c1910 and these designs were transferred to the new factory where they remained in production until the 1930s. The Flambé glazes were developed c1919, using a specially built kiln and Moorcroft became a master of the process; he only revealed its secrets to his son Walter, who developed his own Flambé ware after William's death.

In 1928 the firm received a Royal Warrant – Queen Mary was a keen collector – and subsequently all pieces made until 1978 were marked 'Potter to HM the Queen'. William's son, Walter, had joined the firm in 1937 and continued to run the business after his father's death. Walter retired in 1987 but the business continues to this day.

◄ **A pair of Moorcroft MacIntyre vases,** decorated with Hazeldene pattern, printed mark 'Made for Liberty & Co', painted signature, c1910, 6¼in (16cm) high.
£2,100–2,500 / €3,100–3,700
$3,950–4,700 ➤ **SWO**

A Moorcroft MacIntyre **vase,** decorated with peacock feathers, impressed marks, signed, c1910, 9in (23cm) high.
£900–1,050 / €1,300–1,550
$1,700–1,950 ➤ **SWO**

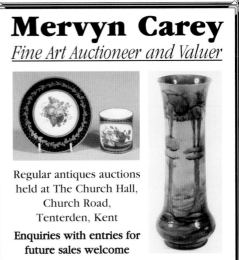

A pair of Moorcroft MacIntyre vases, decorated with Hazledene pattern, printed 'Made for Liberty & Co', painted signature, c1910, 4¾in (12cm) high.
£3,900–4,650 / €5,700–6,800
$7,300–8,700 ⚘ SWO

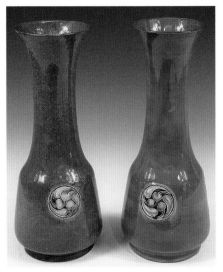

A pair of Moorcroft MacIntyre Flamminian ware vases, inscribed 'Made for Liberty & Co', incised signature, c1910, 12in (30.5cm) high.
£400–480 / €590–710
$750–900 ⚘ SWO

◀ **A Moorcroft Macintyre vase,** decorated with Cornflower pattern, printed and painted marks, 1912–13, 9in (23cm) high.
£1,900–2,250 / €2,800–3,300
$3,550–4,250 ⚘ S(O)

A Moorcroft vase, decorated with Wisteria pattern, impressed and painted marks, 1914–16, 12½in (32cm) high.
£1,000–1,200 / €1,450–1,750
$1,900–2,250 ⚘ RTo

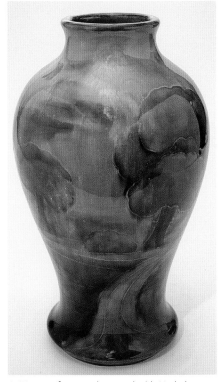

A Moorcroft vase, decorated with Hazledene pattern, impressed mark, signed, c1914, 9in (23cm) high.
£2,700–3,000 / €3,950–4,400
$5,000–5,600 ⊞ PGO

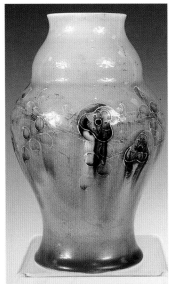

◀ **A Moorcroft vase,** printed 'Liberty & Co', signed, c1915, 6¼in (16cm) high.
£200–240 / €290–350
$380–450 ⚘ SWO

Marks

All MacIntyre wares that were made under William Moorcroft's control and in his department carry his painted signature or initials together with the printed factory mark: 'James MacIntyre & Co, Burslem'. Items made to Moorcroft's designs but not in his department, such as Aurelian wares and Dura table wares were rarely signed.

After the move to Cobridge in 1913 pieces were impressed with the Cobridge factory mark and have Williams's painted initials or signature. From 1928–49 all wares were additionally impressed 'Potter to HM the Queen', and a printed paper Royal Warrant label was in use from 1928–78 when the warrant expired. Walter Moorcroft's pieces have a painted signature and impressed factory marks.

A pair of Moorcroft vases, decorated with Orchid pattern, c1919, 10½in (26.5cm) high.
£4,500–5,000 / €6,600–7,400
$8,500–9,400 ⊞ GaL

A Moorcroft bowl, by William Moorcroft, decorated with Big Poppy pattern, c1920, 6¾in (17cm) high.
£450–500 / €660–740
$850–940 ⊞ PGO

A Moorcroft posy vase, by William Moorcroft, decorated with Wisteria pattern, impressed and painted marks, c1920, 3½in (9cm) high.
£220–260 / €320–380
$410–490 ⚒ G(L)

A Moorcroft two-handled bowl, decorated with Pomegranate pattern, printed signature, c1920, 6½in (16.5cm) high.
£450–540 / €660–790
$850–1,000 ⚒ G(L)

A Moorcroft preserve pot, decorated with Pomegranate pattern, impressed mark, c1920, 3½in (9cm) high.
£260–310 / €380–450
$490–580 ⚒ G(L)

A Moorcroft ashtray, with silver-plated mount, decorated with Pomegranate pattern, impressed marks, c1920, 4¾in (12cm) high.
£300–360 / €440–530
$560–670 ⚒ G(L)

A Moorcroft vase, decorated with Cornflower pattern, slight damage, painted signature, impressed marks, c1920, 7in (18cm) high.
£160–190 / €240–280
$300–360 🔨 G(L)

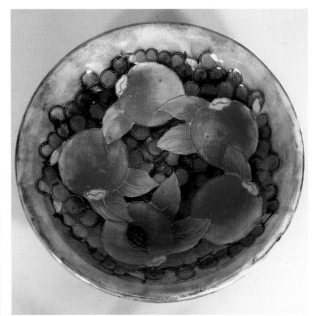

A Moorcroft plate, decorated with Pomegranate pattern, impressed mark, signed, c1920, 8½in (21.5cm) diam.
£220–260 / €320–380
$410–490 🔨 Hal

A Moorcroft Liberty & Co Tudric comport, decorated with Pomegranate pattern, painted and impressed marks, c1925, 5¼in (13.5cm) high.
£750–900 / €1,100–1,300
$1,450–1,700 🔨 G(L)

A Moorcroft vase, by William Moorcroft, decorated with Moonlit Blue pattern, impressed mark, c1925, 10in (25.5cm) high.
£1,700–2,000
€2,500–2,950
$3,200–3,750 🔨 Mit

A Moorcroft humidor, by William Moorcroft, decorated with Pomegranate pattern, c1925, 7in (18cm) high.
£810–900 / €1,200–1,300
$1,500–1,700 ⊞ GOv

◄ **A Moorcroft vase,** decorated in Leaf and Fruit pattern, c1928, 9½in (24cm) high.
£900–1,000 / €1,300–1,450
$1,700–1,900 ⊞ GOv

A Moorcroft bowl, decorated with Pansy pattern, 1920s, 6in (15cm) diam.
£360–400 / €530–590
$680–750 ⊞ PGO

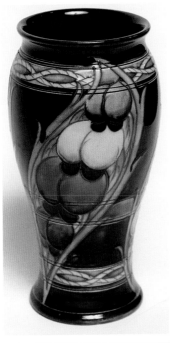

◄ **A Moorcroft plate,** decorated with Leaf and Fruit pattern, impressed marks, c1930, 9¼in (23.5cm) diam.
£240–280 / €350–410
$450–530 ✎ TMA

A Moorcroft vase, decorated with Leaf and Fruit pattern, slight damage with paper label inscribed 'PTHMTQ', with painted and impressed marks, c1930, 5¾in (14.5cm) high.
£340–400 / €500–590
$640–750 ✎ G(L)

◄ **A Moorcroft vase,** decorated with Wisteria pattern, c1930, 8in (20.5cm) high.
£900–1,000 / €1,300–1,450
$1,700–1,900 ⊞ BD

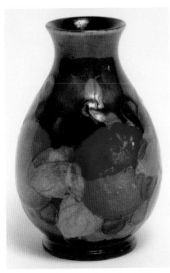

A Moorcroft vase, decorated with Pomegranate pattern, c1930, 5in (12.5cm) high.
£250–300 / €370–440
$470–560 ✎ MED

► **A Moorcroft bowl,** by William Moorcroft, decorated with Hazeldene pattern, c1930, 4in (10cm) diam.
£810–900 / €1,200–1,350
$1,500–1,700 ⊞ WAC

A Moorcroft vase, decorated with Pomegranate Deco Bands pattern, c1930, 12in (30.5cm) high.
£1,600–1,800 / €2,350–2,650
$3,000–3,400 ⊞ BD

◄ **A Moorcroft bowl,** No. 01333, decorated with Pomegranate pattern, with a Liberty & Co Tudric pewter cover, impressed marks, painted signature, c1930, 6cm (15cm) diam.
£400–480
€590–710
$750–900
✎ SWO

A Moorcroft vase, decorated with Leaf and Fruit pattern, impressed signature, c1930, 9in (23cm) high.
£270–320 / €400–470
$510–600 ➚ **Hal**

A Moorcroft dish, decorated with Fish pattern, c1930, 4¼in (11cm) diam.
£290–330 / €430–490
$550–620 ⊞ **JFME**

◄ **A Moorcroft vase,** decorated with Leaf and Fruit pattern, c1930, 4in (10cm) high.
£380–430 / €560–630
$710–810 ⊞ **PGO**

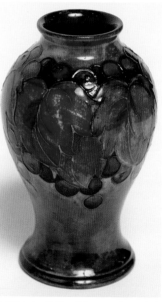

A Moorcroft Flambé vase, decorated with Leaf and Berry pattern, c1930, 6in (15cm) high.
£850–950 / €1,250–1,400
$1,600–1,800 ⊞ **BD**

A Moorcroft vase, with a hammered pewter neck, decorated with Wisteria pattern, impressed marks, c1930, 7in (18cm) high.
£380–450 / €560–660
$710–850 ➚ **SWO**

A Moorcroft vase, decorated with Big Poppy pattern, c1933, 6¼in (16cm) high.
£670–750 / €980–1,100
$1,250–1,400 ⊞ **GOv**

► **A Moorcroft vase,** decorated with Anemone pattern, c1933, 5½in (14cm) high.
£900–1,000 / €1,300–1,450
$1,700–1,900 ⊞ **GOv**

A Moorcroft Flambé bowl, decorated with Orchid pattern, c1935, 8¾in (22cm) diam.
£250–300 / €370–440
$470–560 ➹ SWO

A Moorcroft bowl, decorated with Claremont and Toadstools pattern, slight damage, impressed signature, 1930s, 4in (10cm) diam.
£200–240 / €290–350
$380–450 ➹ G(L)

A Moorcroft powder bowl and cover, decorated with Pansy pattern, impressed mark, c1935, 5½in (14cm) diam.
£260–310 / €380–450
$490–580 ➹ G(L)

▶ **A Moorcroft Flambé perfume bottle,** decorated with Orchid pattern, c1935, 6in (15cm) high.
£990–1,100 / €1,450–1,600
$1,850–2,050 ⊞ GOv

A Moorcroft bowl, decorated with Orchid pattern, impressed mark, painted signature, c1940, 11in (28cm) diam.
£180–210 / €260–310
$340–390 ➹ SWO

▶ **A Moorcroft bowl,** decorated with Hibiscus pattern, 1940s, 3¾in (9.5cm) diam.
£125–140 / €185–210
$240–260 ⊞ PGO

A Moorcroft jug, decorated with Anemone pattern, slight damage, painted signature, c1949, 7¼in (18.5cm) high.
£160–190 / €240–280
$300–360 ♠ G(L)

▶ **A Moorcroft lamp,** decorated with Hibiscus pattern, impressed mark, remains of paper label, c1950, 11½in (29cm) high.
£130–155 / €190–230
$240–290 ♠ G(L)

A Moorcroft ginger jar, decorated with Anemone pattern, 1940s, 5in (12.5cm) high.
£330–370 / €490–540
$620–700 ⊞ HarC

A Moorcroft table lamp, decorated with Orchid pattern, with gilt-metal mounts, 1940s–50s, 11½in (29cm) high.
£400–480 / €590–710
$750–900 ♠ G(L)

A Moorcroft powder bowl and cover, decorated with Hibiscus pattern, impressed marks, c1960, 4½in (11.5cm) diam.
£150–180 / €220–260
$280–330 ♠ G(L)

A Moorcroft vase, decorated with Spring Flowers pattern, impressed and painted marks, dated 1954, 13in (33cm) high.
£1,000–1,200
€1,450–1,750
$1,900–2,250 ♠ S(O)

A Moorcroft plate, decorated with Hibiscus pattern, painted initials and impressed marks, 1970s, 8½in (21.5cm) diam.
£35–40 / €50–60
$65–75 ♠ G(L)

A Moorcroft year plate, decorated with Bramble pattern, c1998, 8½in (21.5cm) diam.
£70–80 / €105–120
$130–150 ♠ G(B)

Sèvres & Sèvres Style

A Sèvres tray, with entwined floral decoration, French, interlaced 'LL' mark and date code 'e', painter's mark 'O', c1757, 12in (30.5cm) wide.
£750–900 / €1,100–1,300
$1,400–1,650 ⚒ Hal

Sèvres

France's most famous porcelain factory, Sèvres, started life at Vincennes near Fontainebleau, where in 1738 a new factory began to produce soft-paste porcelain. In 1756 the factory moved to Sèvres, near the home of one of its keenest patrons, Louis XV's mistress Madame de Pompadour; soon after, the king became the owner of the factory. After 1769, Sèvres began making hard-paste porcelain (as well as soft paste) and after c1803 stopped making soft paste completely.

Sèvres porcelain is famed for its lavish gilding and brilliantly coloured grounds, which formed a framework for panels decorated with flowers, figures or landscapes. Its illustrious reputation has, however, attracted numerous imitators. Marks and styles were copied throughout Europe and confusion also arises because at the time of the French Revolution the factory was taken over by the state and numerous pieces were sold in white to independent decorators in France and England. Coloured grounds are prone to faking; probably about 90 per cent of all *bleu céleste* pieces (the delicate sky blue for which Sèvres is known) are imitations.

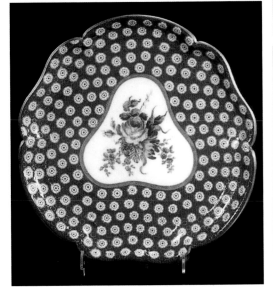

A Sèvres tray, painted with a central flower spray, interlaced 'LL' mark, indistinct date letter and painter's mark, French, c1766, 8½in (21.5cm) diam.
£9,000–10,800 / €13,200–15,900
$16,900–20,300 ⚒ S

A pair of Sèvres glass coolers, by Nicolas Catrice, from the Du Barry service, each decorated with the 'DB' monogram below a border of urns and floral swags, slight damage, one with incised marks, French, c1771, 4¼in (11cm) high.
£13,200–15,800 / €19,400–23,200
$24,800–29,700 ⚒ S

Colours

Vibrant green was one of Sèvres' most distinctive colours. The range of coloured grounds was gradually introduced in the 18th century. Knowledge of these colours can help with dating and spotting fakes, since some pastiches combine late colours with early date marks. Green was introduced in 1756. Other Sèvres colours include: *bleu lapis* (lapis blue), 1749; *bleu céleste* (sky blue), 1752; *jaune jonquille* (pastel yellow), 1753; *violette* (violet), 1757; *rose* (pink), 1758; and *bleu royal* (royal blue), 1763.

▶ **A Sèvres cup and saucer,** by Jean Baptiste Sandart, French, 1789, cup 2¼in (5.5cm) high.
£1,400–1,600 / €2,050–2,350
$2,650–3,000 ⊞ DHu

A Sèvres two-handled cup and saucer, decorated by Fumez with military trophies and agricultural implements within gilt borders, one handle restored, painted 'RF', 'FX' and 'IN', French, c1795, saucer 6½in (16.5cm) diam.
£420–500 / €620–740
$790–940 ⚘ Hal

Marks

The Sèvres interlaced LL mark was centred with a date letter from 1753. This is one of the most commonly faked of all porcelain marks. Look for strong definition on genuine pieces – a weak and attenuated mark is usually suspect.

A Sèvres cabinet cup and saucer, decorated with Greek Key pattern within a palmette and gilt border, marked 'av Ja No. 20', interlaced 'LL' mark, French, early 19thC, cup 2½in (6.5cm) high.
£460–550 / €680–810
$860–1,000 ⚘ SWO

A Sèvres coffee pot, decorated with flowers, French, 1830, 6in (15cm) high.
£1,400–1,600 / €2,050–2,350
$2,650–3,000 ⊞ DHu

A pair of Sèvres monteiths, with incised marks and stamps for 1828 and 1830, French, 14¼in (36cm) wide.
£7,900–9,500 / €11,600–14,000
$14,900–17,900 ⚘ S(P)

A pair of Sèvres-style table salts, with ormolu mounts, marked, French, c1840, 5in (12.5cm) wide.
£540–600 / €790–880
$1,000–1,150 ⊞ JAK

A Sèvres-style sucrier and cover, painted with reserves of children picking fruit and playing musical instruments, with applied ram's-head handles, later mounted with ormolu, inscribed to base 'Vieillard 1756', mid-19thC, French, 5¾in (14.5cm) high.
£400–480 / €590–710
$750–900 ⚘ Hal

◄ A Sèvres-style *vase Hollandais,* decorated with cherub cartouches heightened with gilding, interlaced 'LL' mark, c1860, 5½in (14cm) high.
£360–430 / €530–630
$680–810 ⚒ SWO

► A Sèvres porcelain cup and saucer, French, c1860, saucer 4½in (11.5cm) diam.
£50–60 / €75–90
$100–115 ⊞ JOA

A Sèvres cup and saucer, decorated with flowers, French, c1862, 2½in (6.5cm) high.
£280–320 / €410–470
$530–600 ⊞ DHu

A pair of Sèvres pâte-sur-pâte vases, French, 1869, 14¼in (36cm) high.
£3,150–3,500 / €4,600–5,100
$5,900–6,600 ⊞ JPe

A Sèvres-style cup and saucer, the cup painted with a portrait of Aimable Jean Jacques Pelissier, Duc de Malakoff, the saucer painted with floral panels, slight damage to cup, underside of cup named in gilt, printed marks, French, late 19thC.
£180–210 / €260–310
$340–400 ⚒ SAS

A Sèvres-style plate, signed 'Malpass', with printed marks, French, late 19thC, 9¼in (23.5cm) diam.
£80–95 / €120–140
$150–180 ⚒ SWO

► A Sèvres-style plate, decorated by Leclerc, with a countryman and a lady within a rural landscape, on a gilt-metal stand, printed and incised marks, French, 1870, 9¼in (23.5cm) diam.
£150–180
€220–260
$280–330
⚒ SWO

A pair of Sèvres-style vases, French, 19thC, 9in (23cm) high.
£1,100–1,250 / €1,600–1,800
$2,050–2,350 ⊞ SHa

A pair of Sèvres-style cabinet plates, decorated and gilt with flower garlands, French, c1875, 9½in (24cm) diam.
£320–380 / €470–560
$600–710 ⚒ SWO

A Sèvres-style tea/coffee pot, c1880, 5in (12.5cm) high.
£500–550 / €740–820
$940–1,050 ⊞ MAA

A Sèvres-style vase, c1880, 11½in (29cm) high.
£990–1,100 / €1,450–1,600
$1,850–2,050 ⊞ DHu

A pair of Sèvres-style vases, with gilt-bronze mounts and handles, printed and painted with female figures, signed, c1890, 17in (43cm) high.
£340–400 / €500–590
$640–760 ⚒ SWO

◄ **A Sèvres Parian commemorative medal,** commemorating the visit of the Emperor and Empress of Russia to the Sèvres factory, French, October 8th 1896, 3½in (9cm) diam.
£120–140 / €175–210
$230–270 ⚒ SWO

A Sèvres-style *écuelle*, cover and stand, decorated with classical bands of scrolls, foliage and beasts, printed and incised marks, late 19thC, stand 9in (23cm) diam.
£440–520 / €650–770
$830–980 ⚒ WW

A pair of Sèvres-style plates, both painted with a battle scene, interlaced 'LL' mark, c1900, 9½in (24cm) diam.
£210–250 / €310–370
$390–470 ⚒ SWO

Wedgwood

A Wedgwood jasper ware plaque, depicting the bust of Reverend Willett, impressed mark, title to reverse, late 18thC, 4½in (11.5cm) high.
£200–240 / €290–350
$380–450 ⚒ SJH

Wedgwood

Josiah Wedgwood occupies a pivotal position in the development of ceramics. His factories at Burslem and Etruria were the first to introduce industrial production techniques to pottery. Wedgwood's name is synonymous with several different types of body such as black basalt, *rosso antico*, caneware, jasper ware, agate ware and creamware, all of which became fashionable and were much copied. A master self-publicist, Wedgwood made high-quality wares that were renowned throughout England, Europe and America and his fame has endured two centuries. The factory's 20th century products are known for good design, many of which are keenly sought after by collectors today.

Wedgwood was also the first potter to commission leading artists to create designs for his products. John Flaxman was responsible for many of the jasper ware designs of the 18th and 19th centuries. The range of Wedgwood available is so enormous that many collectors tend to concentrate on particular objects, or specific types of body or on certain designers. Early marked pieces often attract the highest prices.

A pair of Wedgwood pearlware vases and covers, with slip decoration, c1790, 7½in (19cm) high.
£1,450–1,650 / €2,150–2,450
$2,750–3,100 ⊞ AUC

◄ **A Wedgwood & Bentley black basalt twin-handled vase and cover,** decorated with a frieze of scrolling acanthus leaves and figures, cover replaced, c1775–80, 14½in (37cm) high.
£800–960 / €1,200–1,400
$1,500–1,800 ⚒ G(L)

Marks

Although early pieces were unmarked, the vast majority of wares made after 1768 were marked 'Wedgwood & Bentley', or 'Wedgwood' after 1780. From 1860 a system of date coding was used.

◄ **A Wedgwood jasper ware scent bottle,** with portrait busts to either side within floral swag surrounds, with a metal top, c1800, 2½in (6.5cm) high.
£500–600 / €740–880
$940–1,100 ⚒ Hal

A Wedgwood caneware bough pot, with jasper ware decoration, c1800, 7½in (19cm) high.
£720–800 / €1,050–1,200
$1,350–1,500 ⊞ LGr

A Wedgwood dish, decorated with water lilies, c1810, 10in (25.5cm) wide.
£310–350 / €460–510
$580–660 ⊞ SCO

A Wedgwood 'drabware' coffee pot, cover with slight damage, impressed marks, c1820, 9½in (24cm) high.
£130–155 / €190–220
$240–290 ✎ WW

Jasper ware

Inspired by antique cameos and Roman glass and tombs, jasper ware was a form of unglazed stoneware introduced c1767. It became one of the company's most popular products. It was made in a vaiety of colours; green, yellow, lilac, claret, black and white and most commonly blue. Early blue jasper ware was far more distinctive in colour than 20th century versions: either a very deep purplish blue, or a strong slate blue – not the pale shade nowadays called 'Wedgwood' blue.

A pair of Wedgwood jasper ware potpourri vases, decorated with Grecian figures, with pierced inner and outer covers, one with slight damage, 19thC, 16in (40.5cm) high.
£1,750–2,100 / €2,600–3,100
$3,300–3,950 ✎ BWL

A Wedgwood creamware basket and stand, c1830, 8in (20.5cm) diam.
£210–240 / €310–350
$390–440 ⊞ AUC

Beware

During the late 19th century, a rival factory called Wedgewood (note the additional 'e') also marked its products with its name. Wares by this manufacturer are generally of inferior quality and therefore far less valuable. Wedgwood wares were also imitated on the Continent by factories such as Sèvres, but few fakes are marked.

◀ **A Wedgwood jasper model of the Portland vase,** slight damage, impressed marks, 19thC, 10in (25.5cm) high.
£420–500 / €620–740
$790–940 ✎ WW

A Wedgwood candlestick, with floral decoration, c1840, 8½in (21.5cm) high.
£500–550 / €740–810
$940–1,050 ⊞ GN

A Wedgwood jasper ware coffee can and saucer, with relief decoration, the saucer with a stiff leaf band, impressed marks, c1850.
£450–540 / €660–790
$850–1,000 ➚ DN

A Wedgwood majolica dessert service, comprising two comports and eight plates, with basket-weave-moulded borders, one plate damaged, c1870.
£750–900 / €1,100–1,300
$1,450–1,700 ➚ BWL

A Wedgwood jasper ware vase, applied with flowers, panels and pilasters, impressed mark, slight damage, 19thC, 5¼in (13.5cm) high.
£220–260 / €320–380
$410–490 ➚ WW

A pair of Wedgwood majolica wall pockets, both modelled as a bird's nest surmounted by a bird, damaged, marked, date letter for 1872, 9in (23cm) high.
£400–480 / €590–710
$750–900 ➚ G(B)

Black basalt

Black basalt is among Wedgwood's most popular products, and was produced at the Etruria factory and later at Barlaston.

▶ A Wedgwood black basalt plaque, depicting Josiah Wedgwood, late 19thC, 5in (12.5cm) high.
£540–600
€790–880
$1,000–1,150
⊞ TYE

A Wedgwood creamware part service, comprising 28 pieces, decorated with botanical specimens with egg and dart borders, four pieces damaged and some with slight damage, 1879–82, bowl 11¼in (28.5cm) wide.
£3,500–4,200 / €5,200–6,200
$6,600–7,900 ➚ RIT

▶ A Wedgwood bone china cabaret set, transfer-printed with birds and foliage, slight damage, late 19thC.
£140–165 / €210–250
$260–310 ➚ CHTR

A **Wedgwood lustre bowl,** decorated with Dragon pattern, printed gilt Portland vase mark, early 20thC, 10½in (26.5cm) diam.
£800–960 / €1,200–1,450
$1,500–1,800 ✷ SWO

A **Wedgwood Portland vase,** moulded with classical scenes, impressed mark, early 20thC, 8in (20.5cm) high.
£240–280 / €350–410
$450–530 ✷ GAK

A **Wedgwood Fairyland lustre vase,** by Daisy Makeig-Jones, c1920, 12in (30.5cm) high.
£5,800–6,500 / €8,500–9,600
$10,900–12,200 ⊞ POW

A **Wedgwood Fairyland lustre vase and cover,** decorated in Rainbow Cottage pattern, 1920s, 9in (23cm) high.
£2,950–3,300 / €4,350–4,850
$5,500–6,200 ⊞ TDG

A **Wedgwood vase,** by Keith Murray, the body moulded with a ribbed design, facsimile signature, marked, c1932, 11½in (29cm) high.
£360–430 / €530–630
$680–810 ✷ Hal

A **Wedgwood lustre bowl,** decorated with Daventry pattern, the interior decorated with a Chinese garden bridge and pagoda-roofed house, slight damage, c1950, 8¼in (21cm) diam.
£240–280 / €350–410
$450–530 ✷ G(L)

A **Wedgwood lemonade set,** designed by Eric Ravilious, decorated with Garden Implement pattern No. CMH6322, printed marks, one beaker damaged, 1950s.
£1,300–1,550 / €1,900–2,250
$2,450–2,900 ✷ SWO

Worcester

A Worcester teapot, painted in underglaze blue with Prunus Root pattern, c1753, 5in (12.5cm) wide.
£2,500–2,800 / €3,700–4,100
$4,700–5,300 ⊞ JUP

Eighteenth-century Worcester

The Worcester factory was one of the most successful porcelain manufacturers of the 18th century and is famous, primarily, for the vast amount of tea and coffee wares it produced. Together with Chelsea, Worcester remains perhaps the most popular of the 18th-century factories with collectors. The porcelain made by Worcester contained soapstone which made it very stable and able to withstand boiling water. As a result, vast quantities of hollow wares have survived. So daunting is the range available that collectors often concentrate their efforts on a particular area such as early wares, transfer-printed designs, teapots or coffee cups. Prices for Worcester pieces are generally lower than for Chelsea ones. Among the most readily available blue printed patterns are the Three Flowers pattern, Fence pattern and Fisherman and Cormorant pattern.

A Worcester coffee cup, painted with a Chinese lady and other figures, c1753, 2¼in (5.5cm) high.
£2,000–2,250 / €2,950–3,300
$3,750–4,250 ⊞ JUP

◀ **A Worcester pickle dish,** moulded in the form of a shell, with painted decoration, c1754, 3in (7.5cm) wide.
£2,600–3,100
€3,800–4,550
$4,900–5,800
⚒ WW

A Worcester bowl, painted in underglaze blue with Cormorant pattern, slight damage, 1755–56, 6in (15cm) diam.
£540–600 / €790–880
$1,000–1,150 ⊞ JUP

A Worcester sauce boat, printed with a smoky primitive depicting a squirrel, pheasant and herdsman, c1755, 8in (20.5cm) wide.
£1,100–1,250 / €1,600–1,800
$2,050–2,350 ⊞ JUP
The earliest transfer prints at Worcester are known as 'smoky primitives' because of their characteristic smoky appearance, caused by imperfect printing.

▶ **A Worcester pickle dish,** moulded in the form of a shell, painted with Two Peony Rock Bird pattern, c1758, 3in (7.5cm) diam.
£630–700 / €930–1,050
$1,200–1,350 ⊞ JUP

A Worcester butter boat, moulded in the form of leaf, painted in underglaze blue with leaves, workman's mark, c1758, 3¼in (8.5cm) wide.
£300–360 / €440–530
$560–670 ✎ G(L)

▶ **A Worcester guglet,** painted with Willow Bridge Fisherman pattern, rim restored, open crescent mark, c1760, 9¾in (25cm) high.
£320–380 / €470–560
$600–710 ✎ SWO

A Worcester coffee cup, painted with Pu Tai pattern, c1765, 2¼in (5.5cm) high.
£540–600 / €790–880
$1,000–1,150 ⊞ JUP

Marks

The usual Worcester mark is a crescent, either painted or printed. The factory also marked with a square Chinese fret with cross hatching and used pseudo-Chinese or alchemical marks.

A Worcester basket, pierced with interlocking rings, c1765, 5in (12.5cm) diam.
£1,450–1,650 / €2,150–2,450
$2,750–3,100 ⊞ GIR

▶ **A Worcester bowl,** painted with Jabberwocky pattern, c1768, 6¼in (16cm) diam.
£400–480 / €590–710
$750–900 ✎ SWO

A Worcester tea cup and saucer, painted with panels of flowers in Kakiemon palette, painted seal marks, c1770.
£230–270 / €340–400
$430–510 ✎ G(L)

A pair of Worcester tea canisters and covers, painted with Kylin pattern, damaged, square seal marks, c1770, 5½in (14cm) high.
£610–730 / €900–1,050
$1,150–1,350 ✎ WW

◄ **A Worcester tea bowl,** decorated with Mansfield pattern, c1770, 3¼in (8.5cm) diam.
£90–100 / €130–145
$170–190 ⊞ JAY

A Worcester two-handled basket, cover and stand, decorated with applied flowers and enamelled floral bouquets, some losses and damage, underglaze blue seal mark, c1770, 10in (25.5cm) diam.
£950–1,100 / €1,400–1,650
$1,800–2,150 ➹ BWL

A Worcester tea bowl and saucer, decorated with Cannonball pattern, c1772.
£100–120 / €145–175
$190–220 ➹ CHTR

A Worcester plate, painted in underglaze blue with Kangxi Lotus pattern, a Buddhistic symbol on the reverse, c1770, 7½in (19cm) diam.
£260–310 / €380–450
$490–580 ➹ G(L)

◄ **A Worcester sauce boat,** with moulded decoration, the painted flower panels beneath a diaper border, some restoration, marked 'W', c1775, 7¾in (19.5cm) wide.
£175–210 / €260–310
$330–390 ➹ WW

Worcester: What's in a Name?
Worcester is classified according to the factory's owners:

1751–74	Dr Wall or First Period (Dr John Wall, William Davis and other partners)
1774–83	Davis period (William Davis principal manager)
1783–92	Flight period (John and Joseph Flight)
1792–1804	Flight & Barr period (Joseph Flight and Martin Barr senior)
1804–13	Barr, Flight & Barr period (Martin Barr senior, Joseph Flight and Martin Barr junior)
1813–40	Flight, Barr & Barr period (Joseph Flight, Martin Barr junior and George Barr)
1840–52	Chamberlain & Co period, (Chamberlain's and Flight, Barr & Barr amalgamated)
1852–62	Kerr & Binns period (W. H. Kerr and R. W. Binns joint owners)
1862–present	Worcester Royal Porcelain Co Ltd (known as Royal Worcester)

A Worcester mug, printed with La Pêche and La Promenade Chinoiserie patterns, 1775–80, 5¾in (14.5cm) diam.
£580–650 / €850–960
$1,100–1,250 ⊞ DSA

A Worcester coffee pot, decorated in underglaze blue with Three Flowers pattern, finial repaired, crescent mark, 1775–78, 9½in (24cm) high.
£360–430 / €530–630
$680–810 ⚷ G(B)

A Worcester milk jug, transfer-printed with the Three Flowers pattern, 1775–80, 5in (12.5cm) high.
£125–140 / €185–210
$230–260 ⊞ WAC

A Worcester cabbage leaf-moulded mask jug, printed with chrysanthemums and roses, c1775, 9in (23cm) high.
£420–500 / €620–740
$790–940 ⚷ G(B)

Further reading
Miller's Collecting Pottery & Porcelain: The Facts At Your Fingertips, Miller's Publications, 2001

A Worcester jug, with a sparrow beak, painted with a rose spray an inner border, c1780, 3¾in (9.5cm) high.
£400–480 / €590–710
$750–900 ⚷ WW

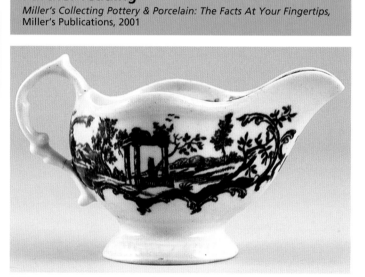

A Worcester cream boat, printed with the Obelisk Fisherman pattern, slight damage, disguised numeral mark, c1780, 4¼in (11cm) wide.
£700–840 / €1,050–1,250
$1,350–1,600 ⚷ WW

A Worcester cabbage leaf-moulded mask jug, decorated with Parrot and Fruit pattern, disguised numeral mark, c1780, 8in (20.5cm) high.
£400–450 / €590–660
$750–850 ⊞ LGr

A Worcester tea bowl, decorated with Fruit pattern, c1780, 3¼in (8.5cm) diam.
£95–110 / €140–160
$180–210 ⊞ JAY

A Worcester reeded coffee cup and saucer, the floral decoration within a gilt border, 1780–85, cup 2½in (6.5cm) high.
£360–400 / €530–590
$680–750 ⊞ DSA

A Worcester tea cup and saucer, with underglaze blue and gilt decoration,c1785, saucer 5¼in (13.5cm) diam.
£220–250 / €320–360
$410–470 ⊞ LGr

A Worcester part coffee service, comprising ten pieces, with spiral-moulded decoration, slight damage, crescent and incised 'B' marks, c1790.
£160–190 / €240–280
$300–360 ✗ WW

▶ **A Worcester Flight Hope Service plate,** painted *en grisaille* by John Pennington, with the figure of Hope gazing out to sea, damaged and repaired, crowned Flight and crescent marks in underglaze blue, 1790–92, 9¾in (25cm) diam.
£450–540 / €660–790
$850–1,000 ✗ F&C
This plate is from the Hope Service, made for the Duke of Clarence, later William IV.

A Worcester milk jug, printed with Temple pattern, disguised numeral mark, 1780–90, 4¾in (12cm) high.
£110–130 / €160–190
$210–250 ✗ WW

A Worcester sucrier, with gilt detail, c1785, 5in (12.5cm) high.
£400–450 / €590–660
$750–850 ⊞ AUC

A Worcester Flight mug, decorated with Royal Lily pattern, c1790, 4½in (11.5cm) high.
£550–620 / €810–910
$1,050–1,200 ⊞ JOR

A Chamberlain's Worcester part dessert service, comprising nine pieces, painted in enamels and gilt with Finger and Thumb pattern, c1800.
£600–720 / €880–1,050
$1,150–1,350 ⚒ G(L)

A Worcester Barr, Flight & Barr two-handled chocolate cup and saucer, the cup painted with birds' feathers, cover missing, script marks, 1807–13, cup 3½in (9cm) high.
£980–1,150 / €1,450–1,700
$1,850–2,200 ⚒ SWO

A Worcester Barr, Flight & Barr chamberstick, painted with shells, impressed and painted marks, restored, 1807–13, 3¼in (8.5cm) wide.
£1,000–1,200 / €1,450–1,750
$1,900–2,250 ⚒ G(L)

A Worcester Barr, Flight & Barr candlestick, the stem painted with feathers against a border of anthemions, the gilt handle in the form of a serpent, impressed marks, slight damage, 1807–13, 3¼in (8.5cm) high.
£1,100–1,300 / €1,600–1,900
$2,050–2,450 ⚒ G(L)

A pair of Worcester Barr, Flight & Barr dishes, decorated with Queen Charlotte pattern, c1810, 8in (20.5cm) diam.
£1,000–1,150 / €1,450–1,700
$1,900–2,150 ⊞ DAN

A Worcester Barr, Flight & Barr teapot and stand, c1810, 6in (15cm) high.
£1,750–1,950 / €2,550–2,850
$3,300–3,650 ⊞ JOR

◄ A Chamberlain's Worcester pen tray, painted with feathers with gilded decoration, c1810, 9in (23cm) wide.
£1,900–2,150 / €2,800–3,150
$3,550–4,050 ⊞ JOR

A Worcester Grainger, Lee & Co teapot and stand, 1812–20, 7in (18cm) high.
£410–450 / €600–660
$770–850 ⊞ TYE

A Worcester Barr, Flight & Barr hot water dish, painted with roses, the cover with an acorn finial, 1812–13, 13in (33cm) diam.
£2,500–2,800 / €3,700–4,100
$4,700–5,300 ⊞ JOR

A Chamberlain's Worcester dessert dish, painted with feathers surrounded by gilded foliage and scrolls, printed script mark, slight damage, c1815, 9½in (24cm) wide.
£500–600 / €740–880
$960–1,150 ⚒ G(L)

A Worcester Flight, Barr & Barr muffin dish, printed with rustic scenes, 1820–25, 8in (20.5cm) diam.
£880–980 / €1,300–1,450
$1,650–1,850 ⊞ JOR

Chamberlain's Worcester

Robert and Humphrey Chamberlain headed the decorating department at Worcester until 1788 when they broke away to set up on their own, in direct competition. Their speciality was fine gilding but the factory was also renowned for its armorial decoration. In the 19th century they produced a fine, white hard porcelain body that they named Regent China in honour of the Prince Regent. Chamberlains employed many fine craftsmen including Humphrey Chamberlain Jr and Thomas Baxter. Landscape painting became a speciality, although cabinet wares painted with shells and feathers are the most valuable. They also produced a range of small animal models.

Humphrey Chamberlain Sr retired in 1827, and the firm suffered declining fortunes. In 1840, Chamberlains amalgamated with old rivals Flight, Barr and Barr to form a new company that traded as Chamberlain & Co.

A Worcester Flight, Barr & Barr sucrier, decorated with vignettes of peasants in a rural landscape, 1820–30, 5½in (14cm) wide.
£600–670 / €880–980
$1,100–1,250 ⊞ MER

A Chamberlain's Worcester model of a poodle, 1820–40, 4in (10cm) wide.
£400–450 / €590–660
$750–850 ⊞ TYE

A Worcester Flight, Barr & Barr cup and saucer, 1815–25, saucer 5in (12.5cm) diam.
£340–380 / €500–560
$640–710 ⊞ DAN

A Worcester Kerr & Binns bust of General Havelock, by W. B. Kirk, 1858, 9in (23cm) high.
£310–350 / €460–510
$580–660 ⊞ JAK

Royal Worcester

The Worcester Royal Porcelain Company was formed in 1862 and later became known as Royal Worcester. The kaleidoscopic range of wares produced by this factory spanned from humble domestic goods to the finest cabinet pieces exquisitely decorated by leading painters.

A set of three Grainger's Worcester jugs, printed with Willow pattern, mark for 1866, largest 8in (20.5cm) high.
£160–190 / €240–280
$300–360 ↗ G(L)

A pair of Royal Worcester two-handled vases, with moulded and painted decoration of birds among flowers and foliage, date mark for 1873, 8in (20.5cm) high.
£650–780 / €960–1,150
$1,200–1,450 ↗ GIL

▶ **A Royal Worcester claret jug,** 1884, 8¼in (21cm) high.
£340–380 / €500–560
$640–710 ⊞ GRI

A Royal Worcester vase, painted with flowers heightened with gilding, printed marks, 1895, 10¾in (27.5cm) high.
£320–380 / €470–560
$600–710 ↗ SWO

A Royal Worcester dish, modelled as a leaf, painted with flowers on a blush ivory ground, 1898, 6½in (16.5cm) diam.
£100–120 / €145–175
$190–230 ↗ G(L)

▶ **A Grainger's Worcester potpourri bowl and cover,** the body moulded with flowers and foliage, on three paw feet, printed mark, c1900, 8in (20.5cm) diam.
£100–120 / €145–175
$190–230 ↗ WW

A Royal Worcester vase, painted by Lucien Boullemier, c1895, 8in (20.5cm) high.
£1,600–1,800 / €2,350–2,650
$3,000–3,400 ⊞ HKW

◀ **A Grainger's Worcester bowl,** modelled as a shell, painted with flowers and gilding on a blush ivory ground, date mark for 1902, 7¼in (18.5cm) wide.
£90–100
€130–145
$170–190 ↗ SAS

A Hadley's Worcester faïence jardinière, painted with panels of blackberries and dragonflies, c1900, 8in (20.5cm) high.
£400–480 / €590–710
$750–900 ↗ G(L)

A Royal Worcester tyg, painted by Frederick Chivers, the body decorated with fruit panels within gilded borders, the handles decorated with beading, on a pedestal foot, dated 1903, 9in (23cm) high.
£2,500–3,000 / €3,700–4,400
$4,700–5,600 ↗ AH

A pair of Royal Worcester vases, painted by James Stinton, with reticulated rims, c1905, 5in (12.5cm) high.
£1,500–1,700 / €2,200–2,500
$2,800–3,200 ⊞ HKW

A Royal Worcester flatback jug,
decorated with sprays of flowers on a
blush ivory ground, c1909,
5in (12.5cm) high.
£270–300 / €400–440
$500–560 ⊞ GRI

**A Royal Worcester Sabrina ware
vase,** c1910, 11in (28cm) diam.
£630–700 / €930–1,050
$1,200–1,350 ⊞ DSG

A Royal Worcester potpourri vase,
by Harry Davis, the domed fluted cover
with a bud finial and stiff leaf banding,
with gilded loop handles, the pierced
neck with moulded swags, painted
with sheep in a Highland setting,
on a gilded foot, 1911, 13½in
(34.5cm) high.
£11,500–13,800 / €16,900–20,300
$21,600–25,900 ➤ AH
Harry Davis painted many
different subjects but is famous
for his Highland sheep in
atmospheric settings.

A Royal Worcester jug, decorated
with flowers on a blush ivory ground,
c1913, 7in (18cm) high.
£500–550 / €740–820
$940–1,050 ⊞ WAC

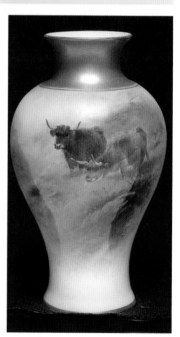

A Royal Worcester vase, painted by
Harry Stinton with Highland cattle,
1917, 6in (15cm) high.
£1,600–1,800 / €2,350–2,650
$3,000–3,400 ⊞ JUP

Four Worcester models of animals and a fish, from the Netsuke series, 1915–25, largest 3in (7.5cm) wide.
£360–400 / €530–590
$680–750 each ⊞ HKW

A set of 12 Royal Worcester plates, by William Powell, each painted with a named British bird perched among wild flowers, within a gilt border, one with slight damage, signed, factory mark and date code for 1918, 4½in (11.5cm) diam.
£1,500–1,800 / €2,200–2,650
$2,850–3,400 ⚒ **F&C**

A Royal Worcester coffee service, comprising ten pieces, printed marks, 1918, coffee pot 7in (18cm) high.
£100–120 / €145–175
$190–230 ⚒ **SWO**

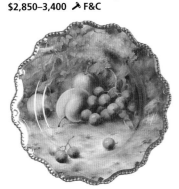

A Royal Worcester dessert plate, painted with fruit by Frank Roberts, c1919, 9in (23cm) diam.
£630–700 / €930–1,050
$1,200–1,350 ⊞ **JUP**

A Royal Worcester wall plaque, by John Stinton, decorated with Highland cattle, signed, c1928, 12in (30.5cm) diam.
£10,800–12,000 / €15,900–17,600
$20,300–22,600 ⊞ **BP**

A Royal Worcester vase, by Kitty Blake, No. G923, painted with cherries and leaves, date code for 1938, 8¾in (22cm) high.
£320–380 / €470–560
$600–710 ⚒ **G(L)**

A pair of Royal Worcester fruit dishes, by Harry Ayrton, painted with apples and blackberries, with shell terminals, signed, printed mark, c1959, 11in (28cm) wide.
£1,400–1,650 / €2,050–2,450
$2,600–3,100 ⚒ **TMA**

COLLECTING BY COUNTRY OF ORIGIN

I am fortunate that my work takes me to many countries to view porcelain collections and in the course of my travels I have learnt that today's collectors are incredibly nationalistic. When I am in Italy I don't see any Wedgwood, or very much Sèvres or Copenhagen for that matter. Instead, china cabinets in apartments in Rome are filled with Neapolitan and Venetian porcelain, maiolica from Liguria or Sicily, and terracotta from local workshops. In Germany I am in seventh heaven viewing the most amazing Meissen porcelain, but when I mention fascinating links with Worcester, or Chelsea copies of Meissen, the German collectors switch off completely. They are not interested in English porcelain which is hardly surprising, I suppose, considering the way Continental porcelain is generally neglected by collectors living in England. The British choose instead to collect ceramics made close to their hearts and to their homes. If you are Scottish, this means figures from Portobello or colourful

A redware pie plate, with slip decoration, New Jersey, c1860, 10in (25.5cm) diam.
£1,000–1,150 / €1,450–1,700
$1,900–2,200 ⊞ RCA

Art Nouveau and Art Deco painted in Glasgow. Living in Wales, you will like either crude Ewenny or fantastically beautiful Nantgarw, depending on your taste and your pocket.

Collecting the wares of your own country adds obvious interest to your hobby, as you can visit local museums to learn about the items you are collecting and the people who made them. In addition, you can usually share your passion with like-minded collectors. This all adds to the fun of collecting. There is an inevitable flipside, though, as collectors end up in competition with each other. When a rare piece of Spanish maiolica comes onto the market, every active collector and interested institution in Spain will get to hear about it and maybe bid against one another. Prices can be surprisingly high as a result.

Collectors in England are the exception, for they are simply spoilt for choice. With so many makers in Staffordshire and elsewhere to choose from, no one can possibly collect them all. Nationalistic concerns only come into effect when there is a finite range of wares to collect. It is a curious anomaly that the countries with the smallest ceramics industries enjoy a proportionately greater number of selective collectors; also the most tolerant in terms of the artistry of their local pottery. Take Australia for example. No one ever discovered any

A Royal Copenhagen vase, by Karri Christensen, Danish, c1967, 11in (28cm) high.
£95–110 / €140–160
$180–210 ⊞ FRD

indigenous porcelain clay, so Australian ceramics are typically handmade pottery with a few modelled gum leaves and are very much an acquired taste.

How else does one justify the extraordinary prices that rare early American stoneware can sell for today? Stoneware potters had made very similar wares in their native Germany before they emigrated to the United States. To the uninitiated, German grey stoneware looks much the same as the early domestic pottery made in parts of America, and yet these German prototypes are worth a fraction of the price early American pottery can command. I dream of finding a piece of Bonnin and Morris's Philadelphia porcelain masquerading as Bow or Derby, for this would be like winning the Lottery. Early American-made ceramics are exceedingly rare and as a result collectors in the United States are just as interested in the wares that were made in China or England specifically for the American market. We have included in the American section of this guide some English pottery depicting American subjects. This is regarded as 'Americana' and, indeed, I rarely encounter any pieces that are not part of collections in the United States.

The collecting of wares from certain nations is not restricted to collectors living in the country of origin. Because of the romantic stories associated with the Romanovs, Russian history enjoys a worldwide fascination. Russian art, including rare porcelain has for a long time

A Methven of Kirkcaldy pottery spongeware bowl, made for the Fife market, c1860, 8½in (21.5cm) diam.
£75–85 / €110–125
$145–165 ⊞ GAU

been collected in America and Britain. More recently, however, new money in Russia itself has led to a revival of interest in reclaiming lost heritage. Many wealthy new collectors have caused a dramatic rise in the price of Russian ceramics. Hungarians living in America and elsewhere collect Herend or Zsolnay ceramics to remind them of their homeland. Families of Dutch descent likewise collect Delft pottery, no matter where in the world they live today.

Some ex-patriot Danes collect Royal Copenhagen, but mostly the collecting of Scandinavian ceramics is not related to national heritage. Good design is the key to the popularity of 20th-century Swedish, Danish and Finnish ceramics and well as glass from these countries. In Millers' various guides to collecting items from the 20th century, a significant number of the ceramic pieces featured originate from Scandinavia. Collectors no longer have to travel to Denmark or Sweden to find good Scandinavian design, however. The internet has made a huge difference to collectors' buying patterns and opportunities exist as never before. Wherever you live you can buy products from around the world at the click of a mouse. Thanks to eBay, Canada's Blue Mountain art pottery from the 1960s and '70s is bought by Canadian collectors from sellers in England where so much of it was originally sold. The collecting world has become a much smaller place, but if you are buying internationally, just remember to allow for postage costs and insist on adequate packing for delicate porcelain.

A Ewenny pottery two-handled mug, commemorating the general election in South Glamorgan, c1895, 6in (15cm) high.
£220–250 / €320–360
$410–470 ⊞ WeW

American

A pearlware plate, decorated with the seal of the United States of America, repaired, c1800, 6in (15cm) diam.
£830–930 / €1,200–1,350
$1,550–1,750 ⊞ KUR
Made in England for the American market.

A Liverpool creamware jug, with transfer-printed decoration, c1800, 8in (20.5cm) high.
£790–880 / €1,150–1,300
$1,500–1,650 ⊞ KUR
Made in England for the American market.

Two redware jars, c1800, larger 11¼in (28.5cm) high.
£180–200 / €260–290
$340–380 ⋟ COBB

A redware pudding mould, with spotted decoration, marked 'No. 9', c1800, 9½in (24cm) diam.
£25–30 / €35–40
$45–50 ⋟ COBB

◀ **A creamware jug,** decorated with American shipping, with a copper lustre rim, 1815–20, 7in (18cm) high.
£1,250–1,400 / €1,850–2,050
$2,300–2,600 ⊞ KUR
Made in England for the American market.

A plate, decorated with an eagle and a shield, repaired, 1800–20, 7¼in (18.5cm) diam.
£760–850 / €1,100–1,250
$1,450–1,600 ⊞ KUR
Made in England for the American market.

A jar, decorated with a fish and berries, northern New Jersey, 1820–30, 6in (15cm) high.
£1,800–2,000 / €2,650–2,950
$3,400–3,800 ⊞ RCA

Condition

The condition is absolutely vital when assessing the value of an antique. Damaged pieces on the whole appreciate much less than perfect examples. However, a rare desirable piece may command a high price even when damaged.

A platter, transfer-printed with a scene of the Landing of Lafayette, c1825, 16in (40.5cm) wide.
£1,350–1,500 / €2,000–2,200
$2,550–2,850 ⊞ KUR
Made in England for the American market.

Anglo-American pottery

During the 19th century quantities of hand-painted and transfer-printed pottery were made in England by the Liverpool and Staffordshire factories specifically for export to the United States. They were decorated with American views or patriotic subjects; the transfer-printed pieces were often of a very dark blue which was popular in America. These wares have become very collectable in the US where they are now highly sought after, which is why they appear in this section.

An Enoch Wood plate, transfer-printed with a view of the City of Albany, New York State, c1825, 9in (23cm) diam.
£380–430 / €560–630
$720–800 ⊞ KUR
Made in England for the American market.

An Enoch Wood sauce boat, transfer-printed with an American ship off the British coast, c1825, 7in (18cm) long.
£660–740 / €970–1,100
$1,250–1,400 ⊞ KUR
Made in England for the American market.

A salt-glazed figural cooler, inscribed 'Betsy Baker is my name, Taunton, Mass 1834', 15in (38cm) high.
£65,000–72,000 / €96,000–106,000
$122,000–135,000 ⊞ RCA
This is an extremely rare item.

A Staffordshire plate, transfer-printed with a winter view of Pittsfield, Massachusetts, c1835, 9½in (24cm) diam.
£280–320 / €400–460
$540–600 ⊞ KUR
Made in England for the American market.

A Joseph Heath plate, transfer-printed with the residence of Richard Jordan, New Jersey, 1835, 9in (23cm) diam.
£155–175 / €220–250
$290–330 ⊞ KUR
Made in England for the American market.

A Jackson plate, transfer-printed with a view of Hartford, Connecticut, c1835, 9in (23cm) diam.
£95–105 / €140–155
$180–200 ⊞ KUR
Made in England for the American market.

A redware jug, with manganese sponged decoration, c1840, 7in (18cm) high.
£690–770 / €1,000–1,150
$1,300–1,450 ⊞ RCA

◄ **A meat platter,** depicting the Ladies' Cabin on a Boston Mail ship, c1840, 15in (38cm) wide.
£430–480 / €630–700
$810–900 ⊞ KUR

A redware pie plate, with slip decoration, New Jersey, c1860, 10in (25.5cm) diam.
£1,000–1,150 / €1,450–1,700
$1,900–2,200 ⊞ RCA

Three redware tart plates, with slip decoration, south-east Pennsylvania, c1850, 3½in (9cm) diam.
£3,200–3,600 / €4,700–5,300
$6,000–6,800 ⊞ RCA

Redware

Red earthenware pottery was made by the earliest settlers at Jamestown, Virginia and Plymouth, Massachusetts. In the south, as the plantation owners prospered, pottery made by slaves was relegated to the kitchen while imported wares were used on the table by their masters. In New England and the Middle States there was also demand for storage and kitchen wares made by local potters. Before the end of the 17th century, potters decorated their wares with simple slip-trailed designs. Inspired by the folk pottery of the Rhine Valley and Switzerland, sgraffito and slip-decorated redware became popular on ornamental pie plates.

A yellow ware jelly mould, in the form of a beaver, 4½in (11.5cm) high.
£210–£240 / €310–350
$400–450 ⊞ MSB

◄ **A pudding mould,** the base impressed with a corn cob, c1860, 7in (18cm) wide.
£210–£240 / €310–350
$400–450 ⊞ RCA

An N. White & Co salt-glazed flagon, depicting a bird on a branch, Pinghampton, New York State, 1860–80, 12in (30.5cm) high.
£880–990 / €1,300–1,450
$1,650–1,850 ⊞ RCA

A Hermann jug, decorated in underglaze blue, Baltimore, c1870, 10in (25.5cm) high.
£1,800–2,000 / €2,650–2,950
$3,400–3,800 ⊞ RCA

A beer mug, inscribed 'Harry', Haddonfield, New Jersey, c1880, 5in (12.5cm) high.
£350–400 / €510–570
$670–750 ⊞ RCA

Stoneware

Stoneware was produced in the United States by such potters as Remmey and Crolius in New York and Norton in Bennington, Vermont. Among a wide range of stoneware objects made were crocks, jugs, jars, chamber pots, colanders and butter tubs, often decorated with incised or painted cobalt blue designs.

Two stoneware flagons, one inscribed '2', the other incised 'Charlestown', 19thC, larger 13in (33cm) high.
£60–70 / €85–100
$115–135 ⚒ COBB

► **A stoneware five-gallon crock,** decorated with a dog with a basket, c1880, 11½in (29cm) high.
£8,600–9,600 / €12,500–14,500
$16,200–18,000 ⊞ RCA

A pottery yeast pot, 1870–1900, 6¼in (16cm) high.
£25–30 / €35–40
$50–60 ⊞ MSB

A pottery jelly mould, with a relief of a lion, 1880–1900, 10¾in (27.5cm) wide.
£210–240 / €310–350
$390–450 ⊞ MSB

A Trent Tile Co tile, by Isaac Broome, signed, c1890, 6in (15cm) square.
£240–270 / €350–400
$450–500 ⊞ KMG

Grueby Pottery

Grueby of Boston was a prominent Art pottery. William Grueby specialized in organic forms decorated with matt glazes in green, yellow, ochre and brown. His most popular works have crisp, applied decorations in the form of leaves and buds.

A Grueby Pottery vase, by Wilhelmina Post, relief-decorated with irises, impressed mark and signature, 1898–1907, 10in (25.5cm) high.
£8,800–10,400 / €12,800–15,200
$16,400–19,600 ✗ SK

A stein, for the League of American Wheelmen, with a lithophane base, inscribed 'Indianapolis 1898', 6in (15cm) high.
£580–650 / €850–960
$1,100–1,250 ⊞ AU

A Rookwood vase, by Sallie Coyne, with silver overlay, restored, 1905, 8½in (21.5cm) high.
£2,250–2,700 / €3,300–3,950
$4,250–5,100 ✗ TREA

Ott & Brewer Belleek

Around 20 American china-makers copied Belleek, and many added the Belleek name to their marks. A new source of clay that made excellent Parian had been discovered in Trenton, New Jersey, and Ott & Brewer (1865–92) was the first maker to produce Belleek ware. This was because William Bromley, a senior workman from the Irish Belleek factory, had, in 1882, assisted Ott & Brewer to perfect its Parian formula. The company made copies of popular Belleek tablewares but, whereas most Irish Belleek was white, Ott & Brewer specialized in floral designs in raised gold and platinum.

▶ **An Ott & Brewer Belleek porcelain Japanesque hot water jug,** slight damage, printed marks, Trenton, New Jersey, early 20thC, 10¾in (27.5cm) high.
£140–165 / €210–240
$260–310 ✗ SWO

A pottery jelly mould, early 20thC, 7¼in (18.5cm) wide.
£90–100 / €130–145
$170–190 ⊞ MSB

A Newcomb College Pottery vase, by Parkenson, decorated by Roberta Kennon, incised with cotton-flower buds, signed, c1904, 12in (30.5cm) high.
£23,800–26,500 / €35,000–39,000
$45,000–50,000 ⊞ CaF

A Newcomb College Pottery vase, by Joseph Meyer, decorated by Desiree Roman with incised oak trees, marked 'Dr JM AZ22', 1906, 3in (7.5cm) high.
£4,050–4,500 / €5,900–6,600
$7,500–8,500 ⊞ CaF

Newcomb College Pottery (1895–1941)

The pottery at Newcomb College, New Orleans, has produced some of the rarest and most valuable American art pottery. The distinctive hand-thrown wares were hand-decorated with incised patterns of local flora and fauna highlighted in polychrome slip. Early pieces have a high glaze, while post-1910 wares usually have a semi-matt finish. Larger items are the most collectable, as well as those featuring landscape decoration or pieces decorated by the better artists such as Mary Sheerer, or the founder, Joseph Meyer.

A Newcomb College Pottery lamp base, by Joseph Meyer, with three handles and incised leaf decoration, impressed potter's mark 'JM', painted No. BS100, numbered paper label, inscribed mark and 'April, 1907', New Orleans, 7in (18cm) diam.
£1,900–2,150 / €2,800–3,150
$3,550–4,050 ➤ SK

◄ **A Rookwood vase,** by E.T. Hurley, decorated with fish, flame mark 'VII/V/ETH', 1907, 6½in (16.5cm) high.
£1,450–1,700 / €2,150–2,500
$2,750–3,200 ➤ LHA

Rookwood Pottery (1880–1960)

The Rookwood Pottery was established by Maria Longworth Nichols in 1880. It was situated in Cincinnati in the Ohio valley and was able to take advantage of the rich clay deposits and easy access to major water routes. The factory employed many artists and expert technicians and imposed very high production standards.

A Teco Art Pottery earthenware vase, by William Day Gates, No. 431, stamped 'TECO', Illinois, c1910, 10¼in (26cm) high.
£8,300–9,900
€12,200–14,500
$15,600–18,600 ➤ S(NY)

A Rookwood vase, by Lorinda Epply, decorated with a band of foliage, flame mark 946, artist's cipher, 1914, 10½in (26.5cm) high.
£530–630 / €780–930
$1,000–1,200 ↗ LHA

A Rookwood floor vase, decorated by Charles Stewart Todd with a grapevine and fruit, No. 139B, impressed marks, c1915, 17¾in (45cm) high.
£1,750–2,100 / €2,600–3,100
$3,300–3,950 ↗ JAA

A Roseville Pottery Donatello pottery jardinière, Ohio, c1916, 10in (25.5cm) diam.
£50–60 / €75–85
$110–115 ↗ DuM

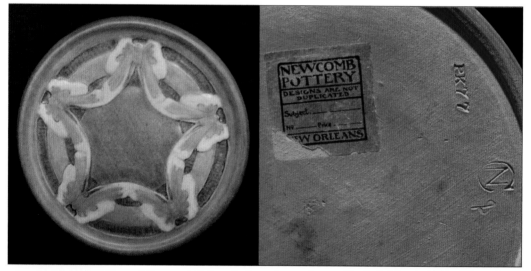

A Newcomb College Pottery plaque, decorated by Sadie Irvine, incised with butterflies, marked 'NCpk77', with paper label, 1926, 5½in (14cm) diam.
£3,300–3,700 / €4,850–5,400
$6,200–7,000 ⊞ CaF

A Muncie Pottery Ruba Rombic vase, by Ruben Haley, No. 301–6, 1927–30, 6in (15cm) high.
£380–430 / €560–630
$710–810 ⊞ CaF

A Roseville Pottery jardinière, decorated with foxgloves, Ohio, 1929, 4½in (11.5cm) high.
£25–30 / €40–45
$50–55 ↗ DuM

A ceramic water jug, possibly made for Norge Refrigerator Company, 1920s–30s, 7½in (19cm) high.
£40–45 / €60–70
$75–85 ⊞ EZC

A Newcomb College Pottery vase, decorated by Anna Frances Simpson with incised egrets, 1930, 7¼in (18.5cm) high.
£7,100–7,900
€10,400–11,600
$13,300–14,900 ⊞ CaF

A ceramic water jug, decorated with stars, 1930s–40s, 6¾in (17cm) high.
£20–25 / €30–35
$40–50 ⊞ EZC

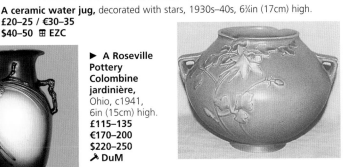

▶ A Roseville Pottery Colombine jardinière, Ohio, c1941, 6in (15cm) high.
£115–135
€170–200
$220–250
⚲ DuM

A Roseville Pottery vase, decorated with wisteria, Ohio, 1933, 8½in (21.5cm) high.
£600–720 / €880–1,050
$1,150–1,350 ⚲ SPG

A Roseville Pottery vase, decorated with pine cones, Ohio, 1930s, 18in (45.5cm) high.
£1,200–1,400
€1,750–2,050
$2,300–2,750 ⚲ SPG

A San Ildefonso plate, by Maria and Santana Martinez, decorated with a stylized snake, signed, 1943–56, 13in (33cm) diam.
£1,850–2,200 / €2,700–3,250
$3,500–4,150 ⚲ JDJ

Scandinavian

A Rörstrand faïence tureen and cover, Swedish, c1758, 16½in (42cm) wide.
£1,700–2,000 / €2,500–2,950
$3,200–3,750 ✱ BUK

A Marieberg faïence snuff box, decorated with figures painted in puce, Swedish, 1758–66, 3½in (9cm) wide.
£600–720 / €880–1,050
$1,150–1,350 ✱ BUK

A pottery tile, by P. Ipsen, Danish, Copenhagen, c1870, 8in (20.5cm) square.
£290–320 / €420–470
$540–600 ⊞ KMG

A Royal Copenhagen porcelain dessert service, comprising ten plates and two bowls, decorated with floral sprigs, with pierced rims, printed marks, Danish, c1900.
£200–240 / €290–350
$380–450 ✱ SWO

Rörstrand

The Rörstrand company was founded in Stockholm in 1726 to manufacture faïence and went on to make flintware. In 1782 it brought Mariebergs Porsalinfabrik and in 1873 Rörstrand opened the Arabia factory in Finland to supply the Russian market. The company moved from Stockholm to Gothenburg in 1926 and then to Lidköping 10 years later. Arabia bought Rörstrand in 1983 and merged four years later with Gustavsberg before being taken over by the Finnish Hackman Group in 1990.

◄ **A Gustavsberg pottery Argenta vase,** designed by Wilhelm Kåge, with leaf decoration, marked, Swedish, c1920, 10¾in (27.5cm) high.
£250–300 / €370–440
$470–560 ✱ G(L)

Gustavsberg

Gustavsberg was founded near Stockholm in 1726. During the 19th century the company had success manufacturing ceramics in the style of English creamware, and at the beginning of the 20th century began producing pottery with floral patterns. In 1917, artist and potter Wilhem Kåge, who studied under Henri Matisse, joined the company, later becoming Artistic Director. He became known for his copper and iron-oxide glazes and for making one-off items in stoneware and porcelain. Kåge remained with Gustavsberg until 1949 and was succeeded by Stig Lindberg who had been a designer with the company for some time. Lindberg set up an experimental studio in 1942 to develop new designs for production.

A Rörstrand vase, by Ilse Claesson, Swedish, c1928, 7in (18cm) high.
£110–125 / €160–185
$210–240 ⊞ MARK

A Royal Copenhagen porcelain model of a dachshund, by Jensen, signed, stamped '856', Danish, c1930, 8in (20.5cm) high.
£160–190 / €240–280
$300–360 ✗ BWL

Royal Copenhagen

The Royal Copenhagen factory was founded c1771 in Copenhagen, Denmark, by F. H. Muller. It is known for its high quality porcelain and the three wavy lines which have formed part of the company's marks since 1775. The subtle underglaze painting of Royal Copenhagen wares was sometimes combined with innovative shapes based on plant designs. The factory came into its own during the Art Nouveau period as a maker of figures – children, dancers and satyrs – all delicately coloured to enhance the sculptural quality of the modelling. During the 1880s the company was taken over by Alumina, who were makers of earthenware, and from that time both porcelain and earthenware ranges have been produced.

A Royal Copenhagen porcelain figure of a herdsman with a dog, Danish, c1945, 8in (20.5cm) high.
£185–210 / €270–310
$350–390 ⊞ PSA

A Bing & Grøndahl porcelain figure of a girl with a cat, Danish, c1948, 4½in (11.5cm) high.
£125–140 / €185–210
$230–260 ⊞ PSA

Bing & Grøndahl

Bing & Grøndahl was the second most important producer of ceramics in Denmark, after Royal Copenhagen. It was started in 1853 by Frederik Vilhelm Grøndahl, a former Royal Copenhagen employee, with Jacob Herman and Meyer Herman Bing. The company is known for its high quality table and artistic wares in porcelain and stoneware.

A Gustavsberg porcelain vase, decorated by Stig Lindberg with a basket of flowers, painted marks and paper label, Swedish, early 1950s, 10½in (26.5cm) high.
£220–260 / €320–380
$410–490 ✗ SWO

A Gustavsberg porcelain cup and saucer, designed by Stig Lindberg, Swedish, c1955, cup 2in (5cm) high.
£10–15 / €15–20
$20–30 ⊞ MARK

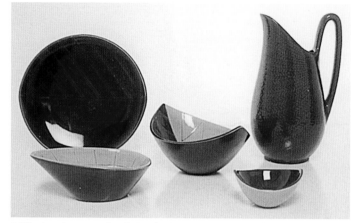

A Rörstrand part service, by Hertha Bengston, comprising five pieces, printed factory marks, Swedish, c1955, jug 9in (23cm) high.
£195–230 / €290–340
$370–430 ➹ SHSY
Hertha Bengston worked for Rörstrand from 1941 to 1964 and then went to Höganäs as a designer from 1965 to 1969. From there she moved to Rosenthal and finally designed for Ideal-Standard from 1976 to 1981.

A Nymolle pottery plaque, by Bjorn Wimblad, Danish, 1950s, 6in (15cm) diam.
£9–13 / €13–19
$18–25 ⊞ GRo

A Gustavsberg stoneware vase, by Stig Lindberg, signed, Swedish, 1950s, 9in (23cm) high.
£3,150–3,750 / €4,650–5,500
$5,900–7,100 ➹ BUK

An Aluminia pottery vase, decorated with a peacock, Danish, 1950s, 5in (12.5cm) high.
£75–85 / €110–125
$145–165 ⊞ MARK

A Rörstrand Chamotte vase, by Gunnar Nylund, Swedish, 1950s, 6in (15cm) high.
£70–80 / €100–115
$135–155 ⊞ MARK

A Rörstrand bowl, by Gunnar Nylund, Swedish, 1950s, 5in (12.5cm) diam.
£85–95 / €125–140
$160–180 ⊞ MARK

A Rörstrand jug, by Gunnar Nylund, Swedish, 1950s, 7in (18cm) high.
£70–80 / €100–115
$135–155 ⊞ MARK

◄ **A Höganäs earthenware bowl,** by Åke Holm, signed, Swedish, 1950s, 21in (53.5cm) diam.
£430–520 / €630–760
$810–980 ✗ BUK

A set of 12 Nymolle pottery plates, designed by Bjorn Wimblad, each representing a month of the year, Danish, 1950s, 6in (15cm) diam.
£5–10 / €5–15
$10–20 each ⊞ MARK

A Gustavsberg bowl, by Stig Lindberg, Swedish, 1950s, 7½in (19cm) wide.
£50–60 / €75–85
$110–115 ⊞ MARK

A Gustavsberg candlestick, by Berndt Friberg, 1950s, 3in (7.6cm) high.
£85–95 / €125–140
$160–180 ⊞ MARK

A Rörstrand dish, by Carl-Harry Stålhane, Swedish, 1950s, 5in (12.5cm) diam.
£50–60 / €75–85
$110–115 ⊞ MARK

► **A Rörstrand footed dish,** by Carl-Harry Stålhane, Swedish, 1950s, 3½in (9cm) diam.
£40–45 / €60–70
$75–85 ⊞ MARK

A Royal Copenhagen Marselis vase, by Nils Thorsson, printed marks, Danish, 1950s, 10¾in (27.5cm) high.
£140–165 / €210–240
$260–310 ✗ SWO

A Gustavsberg pottery model of a hippopotamus, by Lisa Larson, c1965, 7in (18cm) wide.
£75–85 / €10–125
$145–165 ⊞ MARK

A Royal Copenhagen faïence vase, by Nils Thorsson, Danish, 1967, 8in (20.5cm) high.
£55–65 / €80–95
$105–125 ⊞ FRD

A Royal Copenhagen faïence pillow vase, by Nils Thorsson, Danish, 1967, 9in (23cm) wide.
£70–80 / €100–115
$135–155 ⊞ FRD

▶ **A Royal Copenhagen vase,** by Karri Christensen, Danish, c1967, 11in (28cm) high.
£95–110 / €140–160
$180–210 ⊞ FRD

A Höganäs vase, Swedish, 1960s, 6½in (16.5cm) high.
£105–120 / €155–175
$195–230 ⊞ MARK

An Arabia stoneware cup and saucer, Finnish, 1960s, cup 2½in (6.5cm) high.
£10–15 / €15–20
$20–30 ⊞ GRo

▶ **Two Royal Copenhagen pottery models of bear cubs,** by Knud Kyhn, Danish, 1960s, 3in (7.5cm) wide.
£65–75 / €95–110
$120–140 each ⊞ MARK

A Royal Copenhagen faïence bowl,
Danish, 1960s, 3in (7.5cm) high.
£30–35 / €45–50
$55–65 ⊞ MARK

Two Royal Copenhagen pottery models of bear cubs,
by Knud Kyhn, Danish, 1960s, 3in (7.5cm) high.
£65–75 / €95–110
$120–140 each ⊞ MARK

A Royal Copenhagen pottery dish,
Danish, 1960s, 6½in (16.5cm) square.
£35–40 / €50–60
$65–75 ⊞ MARK

A Royal Copenhagen porcelain plate, entitled 'Hare in Winter', Danish, 1971, 7¼in (18.5cm) diam.
£10–15 / €15–20
$20–30 ⊞ HEI

An Arabia stoneware coffee pot, Finnish, 1960s, 7in (18cm) high.
£40–45 / €65–75
$75–85 ⊞ GRo

A Rörstrand pottery vase, Swedish, c1975, 4in (10cm) high.
£20–25 / €30–35
$40–50 ⊞ MARK

An Arabia stoneware dish, by Birger Kaipiainen, signed, Finnish, 1970s–80s, 15¼in (38.5cm) wide.
£1,300–1,550 / €1,950–2,300
$2,450–2,900 ⚒ BUK

Scottish

A **Portobello-style pottery figure of a man riding a horse,** c1820, 5in (12.5cm) wide.
£310–350 / €460–510
$580–660 ⊞ HOW

A **pearlware jug,** painted with a crown flanked by thistles, restored, 1822, 5in (12.5cm) high.
£260–310 / €380–450
$490–580 ⋌ SAS

A **Kirkcaldy Pottery model of a goat,** c1835, 7in (18cm) high.
£1,250–1,400 / €1,850–2,050
$2,350–2,650 ⊞ HOW

A **pottery jug,** commemorating the marriage of Queen Victoria to Prince Albert, printed with portraits flanked by banners, the rim with a cartouche of coronation trophies, flowers of the Union and shaking hands, the underside with a crown entitled 'Union', slight damage, 1840, 7¼in (18cm) high.
£160–190 / €240–280
$300–360 ⋌ SAS

A **pearlware model of a longcase clock,** probably Portobello, c1830, 4½in (11.5cm) high.
£400–450 / €590–660
$750–850 ⊞ RdV

A **pottery gin flask,** modelled as a boot, c1840, 7in (18cm) high.
£180–200 / €260–290
$340–380 ⋌ HOW

▶ A **pottery model of a spaniel,** c1845, 10in (25.5cm) high.
£2,250–2,500 / €3,300–3,650
$4,250–4,700 ⊞ HOW

A **Fife pottery spongeware bowl,** c1850, 9½in (24cm) diam.
£60–70 / €85–100
$115–135 ⊞ GAU

A Methven of Kirkcaldy pottery spongeware bowl, made for the Fife market, c1860, 8½in (21.5cm) diam.
£75–85 / €110–125
$145–165 ⊞ GAU

A Wemyss pottery mug, decorated with goldfinches, c1880, 5½in (14cm) high.
£760–850 / €1,100–1,250
$1,450–1,600 ⊞ SDD

A Dunmore Pottery jug, c1880, 6in (15cm) high.
£130–145 / €190–210
$240–270 ⊞ GLB

A Wemyss pottery honey box, painted with bees and hives, 1880–90, 7in (18cm) square.
£670–750 / €980–1,100
$1,250–1,400 ⊞ HUM

A Seaton pottery money bank, modelled as a hen, Aberdeen, 1860–80, 4in (10cm) wide.
£110–125 / €160–185
$210–240 ⊞ GAU

Dunmore Pottery

This small pottery near Airth in Stirlingshire is known for its distinctive deep-coloured rich lead glazes. Originally a maker of utilitarian wares, it was transformed by Peter Gardner who took over after the death of his father in 1866. Peter was particularly inventive in creating both form and glazes. Queen Victoria was a patron of the factory and in 1876 over 100 pieces were purchased from the pottery for Glasgow Museum and Art Gallery. After Gardner's death in 1902 the pottery was sold and it finally closed during WWI.

A Dunmore Pottery pot, 1880, 5¼in (13.5cm) high.
£430–480 / €630–710
$810–900 ⊞ GLB

Wemyss ware

Wemyss was first produced at the Fife Pottery, Kirkaldy, in 1880. These simple wares were decorated with highly distinctive hand-painted motifs of cabbage roses, fruit, birds and farmyard animals and sold through Thomas Goode in London. The Fife factory closed in 1930 and the moulds were sold to the Bovey Tracey Pottery in Devon.

A Dunmore Pottery two-handled vase, c1885, 5½in (14cm) high.
£115–130 / €170–190
$220–240 ⊞ GLB

A pair of pottery models of cats, with gilt decoration, c1889, 14in (35.5cm) high.
£1,950–2,200 / €2,850–3,250
$3,650–4,150 ⊞ HOW

A Dunmore Pottery vase, c1890, 11in (28cm) high.
£170–190 / €250–280
$320–360 ⊞ GLB

A pair of Dunmore Pottery pilgrim flasks, in the manner of Christopher Dresser, 1890–1900, 9in (23cm) high.
£340–380 / €500–560
$640–710 ⊞ SAAC

A Wemyss pottery bulb bowl, painted by Karel Nekola with roses, impressed marks, 1890–1900, 12in (30.5cm) diam.
£580–650 / €850–960
$1,100–1,250 ⊞ RdeR

A Wemyss pottery preserve pot, painted with oranges, impressed mark, c1900, 5½in (14cm) high.
£270–300 / €400–440
$500–560 ⊞ RdeR

Wemyss marks

Early Wemyss ware has an impressed mark and the words 'Wemyss Ware R. H. & S.' in a semi-circle. The single word 'Wemyss' was used as a mark throughout the 19th and 20th centuries. The words 'Thos Goode' usually indicate an early production. When the factory moved to Bovey Tracey, in Devon in 1930, the words 'Made in England' sometimes appeared with a Wemyss mark.

A Wemyss pottery pin tray, painted with cockerels, c1900, 3½in (9cm) wide.
£220–250 / €320–370
$410–470 ⊞ RdeR

A Wemyss pottery tray, painted with roses, c1900, 12in (30.5cm) wide.
£520–580 / €760–850
$980–1,100 ⊞ GLB

A Wemyss pottery trinket tray, painted with roses, slight damage, c1900, 10in (25.5cm) wide.
£350–390 / €510–570
$660–730 ⊞ GLB

A Wemyss pottery mug, painted by James Sharpe with irises, impressed mark, c1900, 5½in (14cm) high.
£710–790 / €1,050–2,000
$1,350–1,500 ⊞ RdeR

A Wemyss pottery storage jar and cover, painted with strawberries and leaves, c1900, 6in (15cm) high.
£280–330 / €410–490
$530–620 ↗ G(L)

A Wemyss pottery mug, painted with apples, impressed mark, c1900, 5½in (14cm) high.
£610–680 / €900–1,000
$1,150–1,300 ⊞ RdeR

A Wemyss pottery mug, painted with flowering clover, 1900–20, 5½in (14cm) high.
£760–850 / €1,100–1,250
$1,450–1,600 ⊞ RdeR

A Wemyss pottery mug, painted with wild roses, impressed mark, 1900–20, 5½in (14cm) high.
£670–750 / €980–1,100
$1,250–1,400 ⊞ RdeR

▶ **A pottery spongeware porringer,** decorated with the Gordon Highlanders and inscribed 'We'll Fight and We'll Conquer Again and Again', c1915, 7in (18cm) diam.
£140–155 / €200–230
$260–290 ⊞ GAU

A Wemyss pottery inkstand, painted with roses, slight damage, impressed mark, printed mark 'T. Goode & Co, South Audley Street, London W.', early 20thC, 6in (15cm) wide.
£260–310 / €380–460
$490–580 ⚲ TMA

▶ **An agate ware vase,** 1900–20, 5½in (14cm) high.
£110–125 / €160–185
$210–240 ⊞ GAU

A Wemyss pottery tray, in the form of a heart, painted with a chrysanthemum, slight damage, impressed mark, c1900, 12in (30.5cm) wide.
£550–660 / €810–970
$1,050–1,250 ⚲ TMA

A Wemyss pottery preserve pot and cover, decorated with gooseberries, c1905, 4¾in (12cm) high.
£670–750 / €980–1,100
$1,250–1,400 ⊞ GLB

▶ **A Wemyss pottery plate,** decorated with Scottish thistles, c1905, 5½in (14cm) diam.
£230–260 / €340–380
$430–490 ⊞ GLB

A pottery Stump Longniddry storage jar and cover, by William John Watt (Stump), 1927–39, 3½in (9cm) high.
£220–250 / €320–370
$410–470 ⊞ SDD
William John Watt was a disabled veteran of WWI who lived in Longniddry near Edinburgh. He had no hands, one arm being cut off above the elbow, the other at the wrist. He overcame this by painting his pottery holding his brush by means of two strong elastic bands round one forearm, hence his work being marked 'Stump Longniddry'. He worked from 1927 to 1939 and his pieces were widely exported.

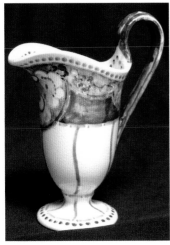

A Mak'Merry pottery jug, painted by Catherine Blair, 1930s, 5in (12.5cm) high.
£195–220 / €290–320
$370–410 ⊞ SDD

A pottery cup and saucer, by Helen Paxton Brown, c1930, cup 2½in (6.5cm) high.
£200–230 / €290–340
$380–430 ⊞ SDD
Helen Paxton Brown shared a studio at the Glasgow School of Art with Jessie Marion King.

A Mak'Merry pottery bowl and cover, painted by Catherine Blair, 1930s, 5in (12.5cm) diam.
£270–310 / €400–460
$510–580 ⊞ SDD

▶ **A pottery jug,** painted by Jessie Marion King, 1930s, 3½in (9cm) high.
£580–650 / €850–960
$1,100–1,200 ⊞ SDD
Jessie Marion King was the wife of Charles Rennie Mackintosh.

Mak'Merry pottery
Mak'Merry pottery grew out of the Scottish Women's Rural Institute, founded in 1917 by Catherine Blair, who opened a pottery studio in a shed on her farm in East Lothian. Institute members from throughout Scotland were encouraged to visit the studio and paint pottery with their own designs. Much of the finished work bore the distinctive mark 'Mak'Merry' (a joke on the name Macmerry, which had been the intended home of the first Institute in Scotland, before it was established at Longniddry.) The studio purchased ready-fired items such as such as jugs, plates, cups, quaichs and bowls from a number of factories including C. W. McNay's of Bo'ness, West Lothian, and David Methven & Sons of Kirkcaldy, Fife, although other factories were used. Designs were painted onto the wares which were then glazed and refired and ranged from fruit, flowers or Chinese dragons to those bearing mottoes such as 'I'm not greedy but I like a lot'.

A Jan Plichta pottery model of a pig, restored, c1930, 4½in (11.5cm) wide.
£80–90 / €120–135
$150–170 ⊞ CCs

Welsh

A Swansea pearlware jug, transfer-printed with shells and flowers, early 19thC, 4in (10cm) high.
£95–110 / €135–160
$165–195 ⚲ SWO

A pottery tea bowl and saucer, decorated with Time Clipping the Wings of Love pattern, 1790–1800, saucer 5¼in (13.5cm) diam.
£145–£165 / €210–240
$250–300 ⊞ GRe

▶ **A pair of Swansea pottery plates, a dish and a shallow bowl,** probably painted by William Weston Young, damaged,1803–06, 9¾in (25cm) diam.
£6,600–7,900 / €9,500–11,400
$11,600–13,800 ⚲ WW

A Swansea pottery meat dish, transfer-printed with Ladies of Llangollen pattern, impressed marks, 19thC, 13½in (34.5cm) wide.
£60–70 / €85–100
$105–125 ⚲ SJH

Nantgarw and Swansea porcelain

Nantgarw produced mainly plates, cups, saucers and a small range of ornaments, whereas Swansea was known for tea and dessert services, cabinet pieces and decorative objects such as tapersticks and inkwells. William Billingsley was one of Britain's most influential porcelain painters of flowers and landscapes and was also a maker of fine porcelain. He was associated with both Nantgarw and Swansea, and is credited with developing the superb Welsh porcelain bodies and glazes produced by these factories. Many of the pieces made were sold in the white and decorated in London, but pieces decorated in Wales are more sought after. Other famous decorators were Thomas Baxter, Thomas Pardoe, David Evans and William Pollard.

A Nantgarw porcelain plate, decorated by William Billingsley, 1813–20, 7½in (19cm) diam.
£980–£1,100 / €1,400–1,600
$1,700–1,950 ⊞ DAP

▶ **A Swansea porcelain cup and saucer,** decorated by William Pollard with Fleur de Lys pattern, restored, 1813–17, 3in (7.5cm) high.
£1,800–£2,000 / €2,600–2,900
$3,150–3,500 ⊞ DAP

A Nantgarw porcelain plate, with moulded borders and painted with flowers, repaired, impressed mark, 1813–20, 10in (25.5cm) diam.
£130–155 / €185–220
$230–270 ⚒ **WW**

Nantgarw porcelain plate, decorated with Three Roses pattern, 1813–22, 9½in (24cm) diam.
£1,400–1,600 / €2,000–2,250
$2,450–2,800 ⊞ **DMa**

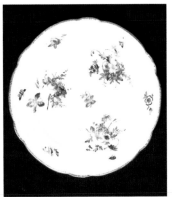

A Nantgarw porcelain plate, 1813–22, 8in (20.5cm) diam.
£2,550–£2,850 / €3,650–4,100
$4,450–5,000 ⊞ **DMa**

A Nantgarw porcelain vase, painted by William Billingsley with flowers, with gilded and bronzed satyr masks, painted mark, 1813–23, 10¾in (27.5cm) high.
£30,000–36,000 / €44,000–53,000
$56,000–67,000 ⚒ **WW**

A Nantgarw porcelain plate, London-decorated with four doves and flowers, impressed mark, 1814–23, 9¾in (25cm) diam.
£7,500–9,000 / €10,800–13,000
$13,100–15,800 ⚒ **WW**

Swansea

Swansea porcelain is special in many ways. The porcelain body has a unique beauty that sets it apart from contemporary English bone china. Elegant shapes are decorated in the French taste with the emphasis on feminine prettiness: delicate painted flowers on pure white porcelain. While much Swansea porcelain was enamelled in London, collectors prefer the work of artists based at the Swansea factory. Attaching the name of a painter adds much to the value. Care must be taken, however, as Staffordshire, Coalport and even Paris porcelain is frequently mistaken for Swansea.

A Swansea porcelain bowl, Paris Flute design, with gilt decoration, 1814–17, 6½in (16.5cm) diam.
£330–£380 / €480–550
$580–660 ⊞ **DAP**

A Swansea porcelain centrepiece, decorated by William Pollard, 1814–22, 13in (33cm) wide.
£4,500–£5,000 / €6,500–7,200
$7,200–8,000 ⊞ **DMa**

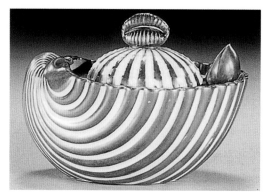

A Swansea porcelain inkwell, cover and liner, modelled as a shell, slight damage, marked, 1814–26, 4in (10cm) wide.
£4,450–5,300 / €6,500–7,800
$8,400–10,000 ⚲ S(O)

A pair of Nantgarw porcelain dishes, London-decorated, c1815, 11in (28cm) wide.
£1,500–1,700 / €2,200–2,500
$2,800–3,200 ⊞ WeW

A Nantgarw porcelain plate, London-decorated, impressed mark, c1815, 9in (23cm) diam.
£850–950 / €1,250–1,400
$1,600–1,800 ⊞ WeW

A Nantgarw porcelain shell dish, from the Marquis of Bute service, Cardiff Castle, c1815, 8in (20.5cm) diam.
£1,550–1,750 / €2,300–2,550
$2,900–3,300 ⊞ WeW

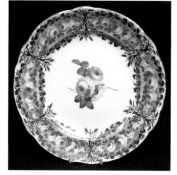

A Nantgarw porcelain plate, decorated with Three Rose pattern, c1815, 9in (23cm) diam.
£1,050–1,200 / €1,550–1,750
$1,950–2,250 ⊞ WeW

A Nantgarw porcelain plate, London decorated, c1815, 9in (23cm) diam.
£2,900–3,250 / €4,250–4,800
$5,500–6,100 ⊞ WeW

A Swansea porcelain dessert tureen, cover and stand, c1815, 6in (15cm) high.
£2,250–2,500 / €3,300–3,700
$4,250–4,700 ⊞ WeW

A Swansea pottery plate, with a pierced rim, painted with a heron, c1815, 8in (20.5cm) diam.
**£1,000–1,150 / €1,450–1,600
1,900–2,100** ⊞ HOW

A Swansea porcelain tea cup and saucer, Paris Flute design, 1815–17, cup 3in (7.5cm) diam.
**£175–195 / €260–290
$330–370** ⊞ DAP

A Swansea porcelain cup and saucer, painted with flower bouquets within gilded borders and rims, painted marks, 1815–17.
**£550–660 / €810–970
$1,000–1,150** ⚒ CAu

A Swansea porcelain cup and saucer, decorated with Osier pattern, red mark, 1815–17, 3½in (9cm) diam.
**£630–700 / €930–1,050
$1,150–1,300** ⊞ DAP

A Swansea porcelain milk jug, red mark, 1815–17, 6in (15cm) wide.
**£880–980 / €1,300–1,450
$1,650–1,850** ⊞ DAP

▶ **A Swansea porcelain bowl,** c1816, 6in (15cm) diam.
**£270–300 / €400–440
$500–560** ⊞ WeW

A Swansea porcelain mug, decorated with Oriental figures, slight damage, c1816, 4in (10cm) diam.
**£720–800 / €1,050–1,200
$1,350–1,500** ⊞ WeW

▶ **A Nantgarw porcelain plate,** London-decorated, with a floral rim and gilt border, impressed mark, 1817–20, 9in (23cm) diam.
**£1,950–2,200 / €2,850–3,250
$3,650–4,150** ⊞ DAP

A Nantgarw porcelain plate,
decorated by Mortlocks Ltd, impressed
mark, 1817–20, 9½in (24cm) diam.
£3,150–3,500 / €4,600–5,100
$5,900–6,600 ⊞ DAP

A Nantgarw porcelain plate, the
floral decoration attributed to Moses
Webster, c1819, 8½in (21.5cm) diam.
£2,150–2,400 / €3,150–3,550
$4,050–4,500 ⊞ DAP

A Nantgarw porcelain plate, the
border moulded with scrolls and
flowers and painted with rose sprays,
the centre with a flower spray, slight
damage, restored, impressed mark,
c1820, 8¾in (22cm) diam.
£750–900 / €1,100–1,300
$1,400–1,650 ⚒ WW

Nantgarw & Swansea porcelain marks

Nantgarw wares were usually marked with an impressed 'Nantgarw
CW' (for china works). Many Swansea pieces were marked in red
with a painted, stencilled or impressed 'Swansea'.

A Nantgarw porcelain plate, decorated
by Thomas Pardoe with a cornflower
design, c1822, 9½in (24cm) diam.
£1,150–1,300 / €1,700–1,900
$2,150–2,450 ⊞ DAP

A Swansea pottery bowl, decorated with Ladies with Baskets pattern, c1830,
10in (25.5cm) diam.
£230–260 / €340–380
$430–490 ⊞ WeW

A Swansea pottery bowl, decorated with Rampant Fern pattern, c1830,
12in (30.5cm) diam.
£200–230 / €290–340
$380–430 ⊞ WeW

**A Pill Pottery earthenware figure of
a woman,** Newport, Gwent, c1830,
9in (23cm) high.
£450–500 / €660–740
$850–940 ⊞ IW

A Swansea pottery jug, c1830, 6in (15cm) high.
£140–160 / €210–250
$250–300 ⊞ WeW

A pair of pottery nursery plates, both entitled 'The Milkmaid', with a raised flower border, c1830, 7in (18cm) diam.
£270–300 / €400–440
$500–560 ⊞ RdeR

A Swansea pottery jug, depicting Father O'Connell, c1830, 7in (18cm) high.
£150–170 / €220–250
$280–320 ⊞ WeW

A Swansea pottery lustre cow creamer, c1835, 7in (18cm) wide.
£175–195 / €260–290
$330–370 ⊞ NAW

A Swansea pottery coronation mug, printed with portraits of Queen Victoria, a crown and dates, restored, 1838, 3¼in (8cm) high.
£940–1,100 / €1,400–1,600
$1,750–2,050 ➹ SAS

A Llanelli porcelain lithophane plaque, depicting a woman in period dress, c1895, 8in (20.5cm) high.
£560–630 / €820–930
$1,050–1,200 ⊞ WeW

A Swansea pottery cow creamer, c1839, 7in (18cm) wide.
£300–340 / €440–500
$560–640 ⊞ WeW

A pottery gaming jug, probably Llanelli, c1840, 7in (18cm) high.
£90–100 / €130–145
$170–190 ⊞ WeW

A Llanelli pottery bowl, decorated with Amherst Japan pattern, c1850, 7in (18cm) diam.
£220–250 / €320–360
$410–470 ⊞ WeW

A Swansea pottery mug, decorated with flowers and scrolls, c1850, 3½in (9cm) high.
£95–105 / €140–155
$180–200 ⊞ WeW

Ewenny ceramics

There has been a thriving ceramics business around the village of Ewenny near Bridgend in South Wales since medieval times, due to the abundance of red clay in the area. Two of the potteries that have survived to the present day are the Claypits Pottery, established in the 18th century and the Ewenny Pottery, founded in 1815. The latter was set up by a Claypits apprentice, Evan Jenkins, and it is still owned by the Jenkins family. The potteries produced simple, traditional pieces for everyday use and in the late 19th century, with the popularity of the Arts & Crafts movement, these wares began to attract wider interest. London designer and dealer Horace Elliott would make annual visits to Ewenny to purchase stock for his showrooms, and a three-handled vase, thrown by David Jenkins and decorated by Elliot, was exhibited at the Arts & Crafts Exhibition in London in 1893. Ewenny wares are usually in the local red earthenware with slip or mottled glaze decoration, although some white-bodied pieces were made using kaolin clay imported from Cornwall.

A Llanelli pottery mug, decorated with Milan pattern, c1880, 4in (10cm) high.
£110–125 / €160–180
$210–240 ⊞ WeW

► **A Ewenny pottery two-handled mug,** commemorating the general election in South Glamorgan, c1895, 6in (15cm) high.
£220–250 / €320–360
$410–470 ⊞ WeW

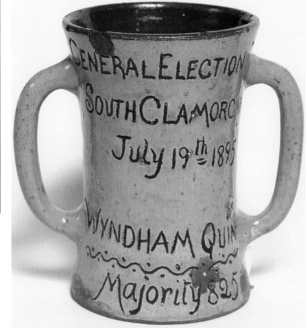

Llanelli Pottery

The Pottery was founded by William Chambers Jnr in 1839 and began by producing high-quality earthenware. Chambers sub-let the business to Messrs Coombes and Holland in 1855 but Holland carried on alone from 1858 and under his stewardship the factory flourished. However, in 1875 a worsening economic situation forced the factory to close, although it reopened in 1877 under the management of David Guest and his nephew Richard Dewsberry. The mainstay of production was transfer-printed and sponge-decorated wares; the latter were much in vogue around 1890 and this helped rescue the factory's ailing fortunes. Popular designs include a naïve cockerel surrounded with a sponged border or alphabet, decorated by Sarah Roberts, known as 'Auntie Sal' by her fellow paintresses. Samuel Walter Shufflebotham, the well-regarded painter from Staffordshire, worked at Llanelli from 1908 to 1915. His main subjects were flowers and fruit but he also painted sailing ships, cottages, chickens and much more. After Shufflebotham's departure the factory's fortunes suffered once more and it eventually closed in 1922.

A Llanelli Pottery plate, painted by Aunt Sal, c1900, 10in (25.5cm) diam.
£580–650 / €850–960
$1,100–1,250 ⊞ WeW

A Llanelli Pottery cow creamer, c1900, 7in (18cm) wide.
£360–400 / €530–590
$680–750 ⊞ WeW

A Llanelli Pottery cabaret set tray, painted by Shufflebotham with Wild Rose pattern, c1910, 12in (30.5cm) wide.
£400–450 / €590–660
$750–850 ⊞ WeW

A Llanelli Pottery plate, painted by Shufflebotham with cockerels, c1910, 7in (18cm) diam.
£990–1,100 / €1,450–1,600
$1,850–2,050 ⊞ WeW

▶ **A Claypits Pottery mug,** with incised Festival of Britain inscription, c1951, 3in (7.5cm) high.
£25–30 / €40–45
$50–55 ⌂ SAS

A Ewenny Pottery tankard, inscribed 'Buller love luck iechyd da', c1930, 5in (12.5cm) high.
£45–50 / €65–75
$85–95 ⊞ IW

COLLECTING BY SHAPE

Collecting a single shape in porcelain or pottery is a most obsessive pastime. Without strict discipline, it can take over your life, your home and your bank balance. One great advantage is availability, for most shapes were made over a long period of time, in every country and in many different styles and materials.

Whatever shape you choose to collect, there is the likelihood of finding more and this is where discipline comes in. Without careful planning, a plate collector can visit a flea market and come home with not just one or two plates, but several stacks. Cups and saucers are everywhere, but few are old and special and for this reason it is essential to be aware of quality and rarity. This usually goes hand-in-hand with price and you should always buy the best you can afford. A small collection of carefully chosen pieces is far better than a much larger one purchased indiscriminately. Collecting has to be fun, so there is no harm in starting out as a collector of ceramic frogs or novelty teapots, just don't get carried away – there are no prizes for having the most of anything. As an auctioneer I am often asked to sell collections of ceramic shapes, and the most frequent reason I am given is a lack of room. 'I'm selling up because my boyfriend can't stand eggcups' or 'my wife says it's them or me!' When you hear these words, it means the obsession has taken over.

Collections don't have to be unmanageable. Choose only what you can cope with and learn to say no to temptation. Space is a crucial factor, so if your home is small, collect single coffee cups, not teapots; thimbles, not vases. Then limit your purchases by careful selection. If somebody tells me they have 150 cream jugs, I know I will probably be disappointed, for most will be ordinary. A collection of 25 really nice ones will give me more pleasure and the owner

A pair of Clarice Cliff Bizarre pottery coffee cups and saucers, 1930s, cups 3in (7.5cm) high.
£270–300 / €400–440
$500–560 ⊞ NAW

much more satisfaction, too. You must buy within your budget, but if you spend £500 / €730 / $940 on one teapot, I guarantee it will be more rewarding in the long term than ten £50 / €75 / $95 teapots. Quality must come first, so don't be afraid to weed out inferior specimens. If you want to end up with a great collection, you must be willing to admit mistakes and sell those learning pieces you bought early on. Upgrading is essential. Every collection benefits from the occasional cull, thus freeing up space and funds for better pieces.

One of the most popular single shapes for ceramic collectors is the humble eggcup, although individual breeds of animals are not

A pair of Royal Worcester bone china coffee cups and *trembleuse* **saucers,** date code for 1904.
£65–75 / €95–105
$125–145 ⚒ G(L)

A Meissen porcelain cream jug, crossed swords mark, German, late 19thC, 3¼in (8.5cm) high.
£130–150 / €190–220
$240–280 ⚒ SWO

A Belleek porcelain teapot, decorated with Grass pattern, Irish, First Period, 1863–90, 4in (10cm) high.
£280–330 / €410–490
$530–620 ⚡ **SWO**

far behind. Lots of people buy plates to hang on their walls, often in large quantities. Collectors' plates are even manufactured on purpose, just to encourage you to complete the whole series. From my experience of really serious collections, people who buy plates, animals or eggcups are rarely discerning. If only they would take some time to learn and pay more for less.

Twenty years ago, I sold a brown teapot for £66,000 / €97,000 / $125,000. It was early Meissen polished red stoneware of the utmost rarity, but the press reported the story: 'little brown teapot sells for record price...' Suddenly everyone thought they had one and I was sent letters with photographs of potentially valuable teapots. Of course none were the same, but it made me appreciate just how many red stoneware teapots are out there, not to mention teapots in other materials. You can learn a great deal by collecting teapots – prior to writing the standard book on teapot shapes, Philip Miller amassed hundreds. He passed most to Norwich Castle museum but, even so, he needed to buy a massive home just to house the rest of his collection. Teapots do take up a lot of space, so if you are going to collect these wonderful shapes, try to specialize in one period, one maker, or even novelties. It is the only way to survive the obsession.

At least plates and dishes can be hung on walls – with the right kind of fixings that cause them no harm. Most collections, though, need to be housed in display cabinets or on sets of shelves. Displayed well, the advantages of a single shape are abundantly clear. I love to visit collectors of Toby jugs, for they always look stunning standing in neat rows. Figures or animal models likewise display very well together. You can mix and match makers and

different periods but it is more difficult to mix different scales. Finely modelled small animals from Staffordshire, Derby or even Meissen can live well together, but large Staffordshire dogs totally dwarf delicate small models. I also think it can look awkward if a collection of shapes mixes up very different styles. Dainty, rococo Dresden will clash with modern Scandinavian design. There is nothing wrong with collecting shapes from very different periods; I just suggest that you display them separately.

This section of *Miller's Ceramics Buyer's Guide* illustrates just some of the different shapes you could collect. Some areas are neglected; for example I know very few collectors of tureens, even though these can be just as representative of antique ceramics as teapots or jugs. Tiles present a huge opportunity as many super examples cost £50 / €75 / $95 or less and storing a tile collection is relatively easy. However, sets and services present enormous problems. I only know of one collector of dinner and tea services, who happens to live in a very large home. Dealers traditionally buy complete services and make a profit by splitting them up, selling them piece by piece to different collectors. Keeping an antique service together may not be very rewarding financially, but there is much satisfaction in owning a complete service that has stayed together and been looked after for centuries.

A Meissen porcelain group of a courting couple, German, c1880, 10in (25.5cm) high.
£4,000–4,500 / €5,900–6,600
$7,500–8,500 ⊞ **BROW**

Animals

A creamware model of a lion, c1790, 3in (7.5cm) high.
£400–450 / €590–660
$750–850 ⊞ TYE

A Wood-style pottery model of a goat, lying on a rocky base, c1785, 6½in (16.5cm) high.
£2,400–2,850 / €3,550–4,200
$4,500–5,400 ⚒ G(L)

A pearlware model of a lion, c1790, 4in (10cm) wide.
£390–440 / €570–650
$730–830 ⊞ TYE

▶ A Staffordshire pottery model of a deer, attributed to Walton, slight damage, early 19thC, 7½in (19cm) high.
£150–180 / €220–260
$280–330 ⚒ G(L)

A Prattware pottery model of a camel, with manganese eyes, c1810–20, 2¾in (7cm) high.
£620–740 / €910–1,100
$1,200–1,400 ⚒ WW

A Staffordshire pottery model of a lamb, c1850, 3in (7.5cm) high.
£165–185 / €240–270
$300–340 ⊞ SER

◀ A pair of Staffordshire pottery models of greyhounds, c1850, 11in (28cm) high.
£1,550–1,700 / €2,300–2,550
$2,900–3,200 ⊞ HOW

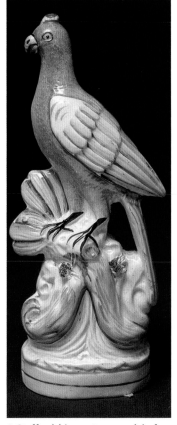

A pair of Staffordshire pottery models of lion dogs, c1855, 8in (20.5cm) high.
£870–975 / €1,300–1,450
$1,650–1,850 ⊞ HOW

A majolica model of a bear holding a barrel, by Joseph Holdcroft, c1870, 4in (10cm) high.
£430–480 / €630–710
$810–900 ⊞ BRT

A Staffordshire pottery model of a parrot, c1855, 9in (23cm) high.
£520–580 / €760–850
$980–1,100 ⊞ DAN

A pair of Staffordshire pottery covered dishes, in the form of swans, c1880, 8in (20.5cm) high.
£520–620 / €760–910
$908–1,150 ✦ SWO

A Meissen porcelain model of a hare, German, c1880, 6in (15cm) high.
£1,050–1,200 / €1,550–1,750
$1,950–2,200 ⊞ K&M

◀ **A Staffordshire pottery model of an elephant,** c1880, 8in (20.5cm) high.
£1,150–1,300 / €1,700–1,900
$2,150–2,450 ⊞ HOW

A Belleek porcelain model of a pig, Irish, Second Period, 1891–1926, 3in (7.5cm) high.
£195–220 / €290–320
$370–410 ⊞ WAA

A pair of Staffordshire pottery models of seated cats, c1900, 8in (20.5cm) high.
£110–130 / €160–190
$210–250 ➤ WW

A faïence model of a cat, in the style of Gallé, with glass eyes, French, c1900, 13¾in (35cm) high.
£220–260 / €320–380
$420–490 ➤ G(L)

A majolica umbrella stand, in the form of a stork, early 20thC, 22¾in (58cm) high.
£190–220 / €280–330
$360–430 ➤ SWO

▶ **A Meissen porcelain model of a cockatoo,** modelled by Paul Walther, crossed swords mark, German, c1925, 12¼in (31cm) high.
£1,800–2,000 / €2,650–2,950
$3,400–3,750 ⊞ DAV

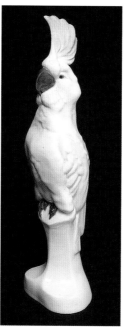

A Meissen porcelain model of an Alsatian dog, No. V188, from a 1927 model by Eric Hosel, crossed swords mark, German, c1928, 7¼in (18.5cm) high.
£1,100–1,250 / €1,600–1,800
$2,050–2,350 ⊞ DAV

A Carter, Stabler & Adams pottery
bookend, in the form of an elephant,
by Harold Brownsword, 1930,
5½in (14cm) high.
£310–350 / €460–510
$580–660 ⊞ MMc

◄ A pair of bisque models of
dachshunds, 1920s, 1in (2.5cm) wide.
£30–35 / €45–50
$55–65 ⊞ CCs

Beswick

- The factory was started by
  James Beswick in 1894 in
  Longton, Staffordshire
  making tablewares, figures,
  flowerpots and other
  domestic ware
- After the death of James
  Beswick in 1921, his son
  John took over the business
  and modernized the designs
- The authenticity of their
  animal models, particularly
  horses, played an important
  part in Beswick's success
- In the 1930s the company's
  Art Deco designs were in
  such demand that over 50
  women were empoyed in
  the factory

◄ A Royal Doulton porcelain
model of a seated fox, No. HN130,
dated 1930, 8½in (21.5cm) high.
£160–195 / €240–290
$300–360 ⋗ G(L)

◄ A Jan Plitcha pottery pig, c1938,
9½in (24cm) high.
£400–450 / €590–660
$750–850 ⊞ CCs

A Beswick pottery model of a
giraffe, No. MN853, 1940–75,
7¼in (18.5cm) high.
£50–60 / €75–115
$100–115 ⋗ Pott

◄ A Beswick pottery model of an
Ayrshire cow, 'Ch Ickham Bessie', No.
1350, 1954–90, 5in (12.5cm) wide.
£95–110 / €140–160
$180–210 ⋗ MED

A Royal Doulton porcelain Chatcull series model of a monkey, No. HN 2657, 1960–69, 4in (10cm) high.
£110–130 / €160–190
$210–250 ⚒ SWO

A Royal Worcester porcelain model of a Jersey cow, by Doris Lindner, No. 370 of edition of 500, black printed mark, certificate, c1975, 6¼in (16cm) high.
£520–620 / €760–910
$980–1,150 ⚒ SAS

A Beswick pottery model of a labrador, No. 2314, 1970–96, 13¾in (35cm) high.
£90–100 / €130–145
$170–190 ⚒ MED

A Royal Worcester porcelain model of a Hereford Bull, by Doris Lindner, No. 150 of edition of 1,000, black printed mark, c1975, 7in (18cm) high.
£600–720 / €880–1,050
$1,150–1,350 ⚒ SAS
This model was first introduced in 1959.

A Royal Doulton porcelain Bunnykins band, commemorating the Jubilee of Queen Elizabeth II, comprising Drummer Bunnykins DB26A, Drum Major Bunnykins DB27, Sousaphone Bunnykins DB23 and Cymbals Bunnykins DB25, 1984, tallest 4in (10cm) high.
£260–310 / €380–450
$490–580 ⚒ G(L)

Baskets & Centrepieces

A Bow porcelain basket, with painted central flower spray, chipped, restored, c1760, 11in (28cm) wide.
£200–240 / €290–350
$380–450 ➴ SWO

A Chelsea-Derby porcelain basket, 1769–75, 7½in (19cm) diam.
£630–700 / €930–1,050
$1,200–1,350 ⊞ AUC

A Wedgwood pottery flower basket and cover, with two leaf handles, impressed mark, c1790, 10in (25.5cm) diam.
£580–690 / €850–1,000
$1,100–1,300 ➴ G(L)

A Meissen porcelain centrepiece, with country figures, damaged, incomplete, German, 19thC, 13in (33cm) high.
£400–480 / €590–710
$750–900 ➴ G(L)

A Chamberlain's Worcester porcelain basket and cover, the cover pierced and encrusted with foliage, c1820, 4in (10cm) high.
£100–120 / €145–175
$190–220 ➴ G(L)

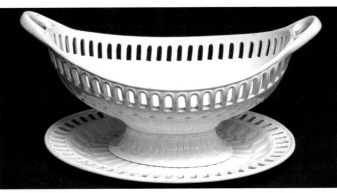

A pearlware dessert basket and stand, 1810–20, 11in (28cm) wide.
£450–500 / €660–740
$850–940 ⊞ TYE

Pearlware

Developed as a variation of creamware by Wedgwood c1790, pearlware was so-called because of its slightly bluish glaze which is produced by the addition of small amounts of cobalt and copper to the transparent lead glaze. The blue tinge is most clearly seen in areas where the glaze 'pools' or gathers more thickly. It has a porcelain-like appearance and was used by all the major potters in England and Wales until the late 19th century; pieces were mainly printed or painted with underglaze blue chinoiseries or floral subjects.

◀ **A Meissen porcelain basket of flowers,** German, c1820, 7in (18cm) wide.
£1,750–1,950 / €2,550–2,850
$3,300–3,650 ⊞ BROW

A Staffordshire pottery two-handled openwork basket, decorated with a river scene and a castle, with matching stand, 1820–30, 11in (28cm) wide.
£600–720 / €880–1,050
$1,150–1,350 ⚒ MCA

◀ **A porcelain basket,** with applied flowers and moulded overlapping leaves, c1840, 3½in (34.5cm) wide.
£160–190 / €240–290
$300–360 ⚒ WW

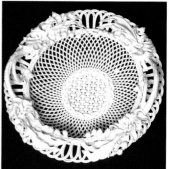

A Belleek porcelain basket, decorated with lily-of-the-valley, Irish, First Period, 1863–90, 10in (25.5cm) diam.
£1,800–2,000 / €2,650–2,950
$3,400–3,750 ⊞ MLa

A Meissen porcelain basket coaster, in the form of a carriage, the pierced sides applied with forget-me-nots, the interior painted with flower sprays, restored, German, mid-19thC, 10in (25.5cm) wide.
£240–280 / €350–410
$450–530 ⚒ TMA

A Minton celadon porcelain centrepiece, in the form of a basket supported by two glazed Parian cherubs, with lovebirds to the centre, 1873, 11in (28cm) wide.
£580–650 / €850–960
$1,100–1,250 ⊞ JAK

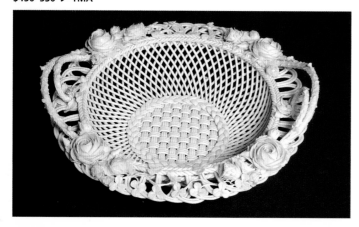

◀ **A Belleek porcelain basket,** with applied roses, thistles and shamrocks, Irish, First Period, 1863–90, 9in (23cm) wide.
£930–1,050 / €1,350–1,550
$1,750–1,950 ⊞ DeA

◄ **A Moore Bros porcelain centrepiece,** in the form of two cherubs flanking a central bowl, encrusted with a blackberry stem, 1875–80, 9¾in (25cm) wide.
£320–380 / €470–560
$600–710 ➹ SWO

A Copeland Parian basket, c1880, 14in (35.5cm) wide.
£135–150 / €200–220
$250–280 ⊞ JAK

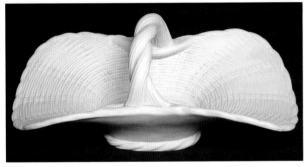

A Parian centrepiece base, in the form of The Three Graces, c1875, 11½in (29cm) high.
£60–70 / €85–100
$115–135 ➹ G(L)

◄ **A Sèvres-style porcelain centrepiece,** French, c1880, 24in (61cm) wide.
£4,050–4,500 / €6,000–6,600
$7,600–8,500 ⊞ MAA

A pair of Moore Bros porcelain centrepieces, in the form of putti carrying bowls, one damaged, 1880s, 8¾in (22cm) high.
£290–340 / €430–500
$550–640 ➹ DN(BR)

◄ **A Belleek porcelain basket,** with applied floral decoration, chip and small crack, Irish, Second Period, 1891–1926, 7in (18cm) wide.
£250–300 / €370–440
$470–560 ➹ BWL

A Belleek porcelain Cardium on Coral centrepiece, Irish, Second Period, 1891–1926, 4½in (11.5cm) high.
£440–490 / €650–720
$830–920 ⊞ MLa

A Dresden-style porcelain centrepiece, the stem with three figures, encrusted with foliage, German, late 19thC, 13¼in (46.5cm) high.
£280–330 / €410–490
$530–620 ⋗ G(L)

A porcelain centrepiece, the floral encrusted bowl supported by three maidens playing lyres, German, c1900, 8in (20.5cm) high.
£45–50 / €60–70
$75–85 ⋗ G(L)

A Belleek porcelain Shamrock basket, Irish, Third Period, 1926–46, 6in (15cm) wide.
£330–370 / €490–540
$620–700 ⊞ WAA

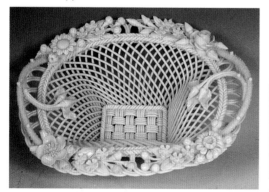

A Belleek porcelain Henshall's Twig basket, pad marks, Irish, Third Period 1926–46, 7¾in (19.5cm) diam.
£420–500 / €620–740
$790–940 ⋗ SWO

A Boehm porcelain centrepiece, commemorating the marriage of the Prince of Wales and Lady Diana Spencer, 1981, 11in (28cm) wide.
£190–220 / €280–330
$360–430 ⋗ Oli

Bowls

An English delft bowl, with powder manganese ground, damaged, c1760, 8in (20.5cm) diam.
£160–190 / €240–280
$300–360 🔨 **WW**

An English delft bowl, c1770, 9in (23cm) diam.
£540–600 / €790–880
$1,000–1,150 ⊞ **HOW**

A Lowestoft porcelain bowl, printed with birds on flowering branches, cracks and small chip, c1770, 8¼in (21cm) diam.
£180–210 / €260–310
$340–390 🔨 **WW**

◀ **A Worcester porcelain bowl,** decorated with Japan pattern, c1775, 5in (12.5cm) diam.
£75–85 / €110–125
$145–165 ⊞ **NAW**

A Sunderland pottery bowl, with lustre decoration, printed with tall ships, mid-19thC, 10¾in (27.5cm) diam.
£190–220 / €280–330
$360–430 🔨 **G(L)**

A Riley pottery bowl, transfer-printed with Feeding the Chickens pattern, c1820, 9in (23cm) diam.
£410–460 / €600–680
$770–860 ⊞ **GN**

◄ **A Scott & Co, Sunderland, pottery fruit bowl,** with lustre decoration, printed with the *Great Eastern* Steam Ship, c1850, 10½in (26.5cm) diam.
£180–210 / €260–310
$340–400 ⚒ G(L)

A Royal Worcester porcelain bowl, from the Cottagers series, the printed outline coloured by Raymond Rushton, c1930, 8½in (21.5cm) diam.
£300–360 / €440–530
$560–670 ⚒ GAK

A Ruskin pottery high-fired bowl, impressed mark, dated 1927, 8in (20.5cm) diam.
£250–300 / €370–440
$470–560 ⚒ G(L)

A Royal Doulton pottery bowl, with silver rim, Birmingham 1921, 5in (12.5cm) diam.
£75–85 / €110–125
$145–165 ⊞ HTE

A Royal Winton lustre bowl, c1938, 12½in (32cm) diam.
£65–75 / €95–105
$125–145 ⊞ BET

A pottery bowl, commemorating the coronation of Queen Elizabeth II, 1953, 7½in (19cm) diam.
£60–70 / €85–100
$115–135 ⚒ SAS

◄ **A Rye Pottery bowl,** 1950s, 9in (23cm) diam.
£135–150 / €200–220
$250–280 ⊞ EMH

Boxes

A Chelsea-Derby porcelain toilet pot and cover, painted with cherubs and musical instruments, 1770–75, 2¾in (7cm) high.
£170–200 / €250–300
$320–380 ⚒ WW

A silver-mounted porcelain pill box, in the form of a mouse, slight damage, Continental, mount London 1797, 2½in (6.5cm) high.
£2,400–2,850 / €3,550–4,200
$4,500–5,400 ⚒ SWO

A pearlware cosmetic box and cover, painted in Pratt colours with leaves and flowers, early 19thC, 5in (12.5cm) diam.
£450–540 / €660–790
$850–1,000 ⚒ WW

A Paris porcelain dressing table box, marks for Eugène Clauss, base restored, 19thC, 6¼in (16cm) wide.
£190–220 / €280–320
$360–420 ⚒ SWO

A pearlware box, decorated in Pratt colours, c1820, 3in (7.5cm) diam.
£540–600 / €790–880
$1,000–1,150 ⊞ HOW

A pottery box, enclosing three compartments, the cover surmounted by a lion, possibly Italian, c1820, 7in (18cm) wide.
£1,050–1,200 / €1,550–1,750
$1,950–2,250 ⊞ ReN

◄ **A Ridgway pottery toilet box,** transfer-printed with the Taj Mahal pattern, from the Parrot Border series, c1820, 7in (18cm) long.
£340–380 / €500–560
$640–710 ⊞ GN

A Bristol pottery thread box, with sliding lid, c1821, 7in (18cm) wide.
£530–590 / €780–870
$1,000–1,100 ⊞ DAN

A pottery box, the cover in the form of two figures on horseback, German, c1880, 7¼in (18.5cm) high.
£65–75 / €95–105
$125–145 ✗ SAS

A Dresden porcelain *bombé* pill box, with gilt-metal mounts, crossed swords mark, German, late 19thC, 2in (5cm) diam.
£100–120 / €145–175
$195–230 ✗ SWO

A porcelain snuff box, decorated with a courting couple and floral sprays, Continental, late 19thC, 4in (10cm) diam.
£130–155 / €190–220
$240–290 ✗ SWO

A Dresden-style porcelain snuff box, with engine-turned gilt-metal mount, marked, German, late 19thC, 3in (7.5cm) wide.
£160–190 / €240–280
$300–360 ✗ G(L)

A porcelain snuff box, Continental, late 19thC, 2in (5cm) wide.
£270–300 / €400–440
$500–560 ⊞ HUM

A metal-mounted porcelain snuff box, painted with vignettes of figures and animals, the inside cover decorated with two gentlemen and a lady playing backgammon, German, 1850–1900, 3¼in (8.5cm) wide.
£840–1,000 / €1,250–1,450
$1,600–1,900 ⚒ S

A porcelain box, painted with cherubs and a goat in a landscape, crossed swords mark, French, c1900, 3¾in (9.5cm) long.
£170–200 / €250–300
$320–380 ⚒ WW

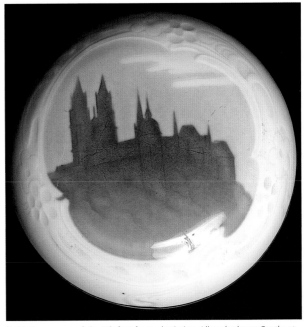

A Meissen porcelain trinket box, depicting Albrechtsburg Castle at Meissen, crossed swords mark, German, c1900, 4in (10cm) diam.
£580–650 / €850–960
$1,100–1,250 ⊞ DAV

◄ **A Carlton Ware pottery powder box,** with lustre decoration, 1920s, 5in (12.5cm) high.
£155–175 / €230–260
$290–330 ⊞ BEV

A Quimper faïence trinket box, c1930, 5in (12.5cm) wide.
£50–60 / €75–85
$100–115 ⊞ MLL

A porcelain box, inscribed 'Father', c1940, 5in (12.5cm) wide.
£55–65 / €80–95
$100–120 ⊞ BET

Candlesticks & Extinguishers

A pair of Chelsea porcelain figural candlesticks, gold anchor mark, c1765, 11in (28cm) high.
£5,300–5,900 / €7,800–8,700
$10,000–11,100 ⊞ DMa

◄ A pair of Derby porcelain figural candlesticks, 1760–65, 9in (23cm) high.
£1,300–1,450 / €1,900–2,150
$2,450–2,750 ⊞ AUC

A Bow porcelain figural candlestick, damaged, c1770, 9¾in (25cm) high.
£280–330 / €410–490
$530–630 ↗ SWO

A pair of Derby porcelain candlesticks, modelled with rabbits, c1775, 8in (20.5cm) high.
£2,450–2,750
€3,600–4,050
$4,600–5,200 ⊞ DMa

► A pair of pearlware candlesticks, c1790, 8in (20.5cm) high.
£900–1,050
€1,300–1,550
$1,700–2,000
⊞ AUC

A pair of Staffordshire pearlware figural candlesticks, c1795, 9½in (24cm) high.
£790–880 / €1,150–1,300
$1,500–1,650 ⊞ AUC

A bone china chamberstick, possibly Coalport, with shell thumbpiece, early 19thC, 2¼in (5.5cm) high.
£950–1,100 / €1,400–1,650
$1,800–2,100 ⚒ G(L)

A pair of Ridgway pottery candlesticks, decorated with Italian Flower Garden pattern, c1830, 9½in (24cm) high.
£900–1,000 / €1,300–1,450
$1,700–1,900 ⊞ GN

◄ **A bone china chamberstick,** with shell thumbpiece, slight damage, early 19thC, 2¾in (7cm) high.
£800–960 / €1,200–1,400
$1,500–1,800 ⚒ G(L)

A Staffordshire porcelain figural candlestick, c1835, 8in (20.5cm) high.
£520–580 / €760–850
$980–1,100 ⊞ DAN

A pair of Minton porcelain figural candlesticks, crossed swords marks, c1840, 11in (28cm) high.
£900–1,000 / €1,300–1,450
$1,700–1,900 ⊞ HKW

A Staffordshire porcelain candle extinguisher, c1850, 3½in (9cm) high.
£165–185 / €240–270
$310–350 ⊞ GGD

A Staffordshire porcelain candle extinguisher, in the form of a sailor on a barrel, 1850–60, 3½in (9cm) high.
£290–330 / €430–490
$550–620 ⊞ TH

A pair of Royal Worcester porcelain figural candlesticks, impressed marks, 1865–70, 6¾in (17cm) high.
£210–250 / €310–370
$390–470 ⚒ FHF

A pair of Doulton Lambeth pottery candlesticks, by Frank Butler, c1885, 8in (20.5cm) high.
£670–750 / €980–1,100
$1,250–1,400 ⊞ HTE

A Royal Worcester porcelain candle extinguisher, Granny Snow, c1890, 3in (7.5cm) high.
£95–110 / €140–160
$185–210 ⊞ WAC

◄ **A pair of Wedgwood jasper ware candlesticks,** impressed mark, late 19thC, 7¼in (18.5cm) high.
£75–85 / €110–125
$145–165 ⚒ G(L)

► **A pair of Worcester porcelain figural candlesticks,** by James Hadley, 1892, 8½in (21.5cm) high.
£1,100–1,300
€1,600–1,900
$2,050–2,450
⚒ AH

A Minton pottery Secessionist candlestick, 1900, 6in (15cm) high.
£165–185 / €240–270
$310–350 ⊞ MMc

A pair of Dutch delft candlesticks, in the form of heraldic lions, blue monogram marks, damaged, French, early 20thC, 7¾in (19.5cm) high.
£200–240 / €290–350
$380–450 ↗ SWO

◄ **A pair of Wemyss pottery candlesticks,** decorated with cockerels, c1900, 11¾in (30cm) high.
£760–850 / €1,100–1,250
$1,450–1,600 ⊞ GLB

A Carter, Stabler & Adams pottery cherub candlestick, by Harold Brownsword, 1928–30, 5in (12.5cm) high.
£270–300 / €400–440
$500–560 ⊞ MMc

Royal Worcester candle extinguishers

Victorian extinguishers were made of Parian, slip-cast in plaster of Paris moulds and decorated by hand. Early examples were plain white, glazed and fully coloured examples appeared later. Blush ivory examples are also known. The designs were so successful that the same master moulds remained in use for almost 120 years. James Hadley designed many of the extinguishers introduced during the 1870s and '80s. Production declined c1900 as demand dropped due to the increasing use of electricity.

In the 20th century extinguishers were made from bone china and intended for decorative use only. Production has continued to this day with reissues of old favourites such as The Monk, French Cook and Old Woman and in 1999 a completely new range, designed by Kevin McGee, was launched.

A Royal Worcester bone china candle extinguisher, The Monk, date code for 1913, 4¾in (12cm) high.
£90–100 / €130–145
$170–190 ↗ G(L)

► **A Clarice Cliff pottery candlestick,** decorated with Viscaria pattern, c1934, 10in (25.5cm) high.
£520–580 / €750–840
$1,000–1,100 ⊞ JFME

A Clarice Cliff pottery candlestick and matchstriker, decorated with Rhodanthe pattern, 1935, 3½in (9cm) diam.
£100–120 / €145–175
$190–220 ⊞ BET

A pair of Clarice Cliff pottery candlesticks, 1930s, 3in (7.5cm) high.
£100–120 / €145–175
$190–220 ⊞ TAC

A pair of Crown Staffordshire porcelain candleholders, 1930s, 4½in (11.5cm) high.
£100–120 / €145–175
$190–220 ⊞ SCH

A pair of Gouda pottery hand-painted candlesticks, Dutch, 1930s, 5½in (14cm) high.
£100–120 / €145–175
$190–230 ⚒ DA

◄ **A Royal Worcester bone china candle extinguisher,** Jenny Lind, the Swedish Nightingale, dated 1953, 4¼in (11cm) high.
£180–210
€260–310
$340–400
⚒ SWO
Jenny Lind (b1820) was a recitalist known for her beautiful voice and natural singing style.

► **A Royal Worcester bone china candle extinguisher,** Old Woman, 1976, 3¼in (8.5cm) high.
£60–70
€85–100
$115–135
⚒ CHTR

Clocks & Mirrors

A porcelain mantel clock and stand, painted and gilded with floral sprays, French, c1840, 14¼in (36cm) high.
£530–630 / €780–930
$1,000–1,200 ↗ DN(BR)

A Jacob Petit porcelain figural clock, modelled with a man and his companion, the urn filled with flowers and painted with cherubs and flowers, highlighted with gilding, minor damage, marked 'J.P.', French, c1850, 16½in (42cm) wide.
£720–860 / €1,050–1,250
$1,350–1,600 ↗ S(O)

A porcelain table clock, dial marked 'Aubert à Paris', slight damage, French, mid-19thC, 13¼in (33.5cm) high.
£930–1,100 / €1,350–1,600
$1,750–2,050 ↗ BUK

◄ **A Dresden-style porcelain clock and stand,** encrusted with flowers and mounted with putti, the pierced stand with scroll feet, restored, French, 1850–1900, 23½in (59.5cm) high.
£900–1,050 / €1,300–1,550
$1,700–2,000 ↗ S(O)

A Meissen porcelain clock, minor losses and restoration, crossed swords mark, painted numeral 59, German, 1850–1900, 24¼in (61.5cm) high.
£5,300–6,400
€7,800–9,400
$10,000–12,000 ↗ S(NY)

Porcelain clocks

Most porcelain clock cases are based on the rococo designs used at Meissen and other 18th-century German factories. It is common to find fake Meissen marks on 19th-century clocks, but examples made by Meissen are always of superior quality. The clock movement is usually of secondary importance, but a good maker will increase value.

A Meissen porcelain clock, German, c1860, 10in (25.5cm) high.
£4,250–4,750 / €6,200–7,000
$8,000–8,900 ⊞ BROW

A bisque porcelain mantel clock, the dial by Dubuisson, the eight-day movement striking on the hour and half-hour, c1870, 15in (38cm) high.
£7,100–7,900 / €10,400–11,600
$13,300–14,900 ⊞ JIL

A Plaue porcelain easel-back mirror, the hand-painted flower-encrusted frame surmounted by two winged cherubs holding a garland of flowers, slight damage, German, c1880, 13in (33cm) high.
£140–165 / €200–240
$260–310 ↗ FHF

◀ **A Martin Brothers clock,** 1875, 16in (40.5cm) high.
£11,200–12,500 / €16,500–18,400
$21,100–23,500 ⊞ POW
This piece was a one-off commission and is therefore unique.

A Meissen porcelain clock and stand, the dial within a floral-encrusted case, surrounded by four cherubs emblematic of the Four Seasons, damaged, crossed swords mark, incised numerals, German, c1880, 23in (58.5cm) high.
£3,100–3,700 / €4,550–5,400
$5,800–7,000 ↗ G(B)

A pair of Volkstadt porcelain easel mirrors, one damaged, German, late 19thC, 10in (25.5cm) high.
£120–140 / €175–210
$220–260 ↗ G(L)

A Dresden-style porcelain girandole, applied with summer flowers and cherubs, the base with three candle holders, German, c1890, 36in (91.5cm) high.
£5,900–6,500 / €8,700–9,600
$11,100–12,300 ⊞ NAW

An Art Deco porcelain timepiece, damaged, French, c1930, 9in (23cm) high.
£95–110 / €140–160
$180–210 ↗ ROSc

A Wedgwood pottery clock plate, depicting a scene from Beatrix Potter's *Peter Rabbit*, 1980s, 8in (20.5cm) diam.
£25–30 / €40–45
$50–55 ⊞ CCH

Cups & Saucers

A creamware cup and saucer, probably Wedgwood, Liverpool-decorated, c1770, saucer 5in (12.5cm) diam.
£190–220 / €280–320
$360–410 ⊞ JHo

A Chamberlain's Worcester porcelain cup and saucer, c1810, cup 4in (10cm) diam.
£270–300 / €400–440
$500–560 ⊞ DAN

A Ridgway porcelain cup and saucer, pattern No. 414, c1810, cup 3½in (9cm) diam.
£270–300 / €400–440
$500–560 ⊞ JOR

Five Staffordshire pottery saucers, with lustre rims, minor damage, 1816–20, largest 5½in (14cm) diam.
£80–90 / €115–130
$155–175 ⚒ SWO

Cabinet porcelain

Although most cups and saucers formed parts of tea services, exceptional pieces were also made as art objects in their own right, intended to be displayed in a china cabinet. Cabinet cups were enamelled with finely painted panels and the richest gilding. The best china painters treated display plates in the same way, and some were given 'jewelled' borders. Nowadays lavish plates from costly dessert services are often sold as cabinet plates, as nobody would dream of eating off them.

A Nantgarw porcelain tea cup and saucer, London-decorated with Dog Rose pattern, Welsh, 1818–20, cup 3½in (9cm) diam.
£900–1,000 / €1,300–1,450
$1,700–1,900 ⊞ DAP

◀ **A Coalport porcelain tea cup and saucer,** c1820, saucer 6in (15cm) diam.
£140–160 / €210–240
$260–300 ⊞ DAN

A Staffordshire pottery cup and saucer, lustre-decorated with a cottage, c1820, 5¾in (14.5cm) high.
£70–80 / €100–115
$135–155 ⊞ RdV

A pair of Rathbone porcelain tea cups and saucers, decorated with scenes featuring Dr Syntax, c1830, cup 4in (10cm) diam.
£520–580 / €760–850
$980–1,100 ⊞ DAN

A bone china lustre tea cup and saucer, c1835, saucer 5½in (14cm) diam.
£25–30 / €40–45
$50–55 ⊞ PSA

A set of 13 harlequin Berlin porcelain cups and 16 saucers, printed marks, German, c1860.
£680–810 / €1,000–1,200
$1,300–1,500 ✶ SWO

A Coalport porcelain cup and saucer, painted by John Randall, 1860–65, saucer 5in (12.5cm) diam.
£580–650 / €850–960
$1,100–1,250 ⊞ JAK

A Belleek porcelain breakfast cup and saucer, decorated with Grass pattern, Irish, First Period, 1863–90, cup 4in (10cm) high.
£180–210 / €260–300
$340–390 ⊞ WAA

A Minton porcelain cup and saucer, c1870, cup 3in (7.5cm) diam.
£320–360 / €470–530
$600–680 ⊞ JOR

A Paris porcelain cabinet cup and saucer, French, c1890, cup 3in (7.5cm) diam.
£65–75 / €95–105
$125–145 ⊞ K&M

A Meissen porcelain cup and saucer, crossed swords mark, German, late 19thC.
£180–210 / €260–310
$340–390 ⚒ G(L)

A Coalport porcelain cabinet cup and saucer, with 'jewelled' decoration, retailer's mark, printed mark, c1900.
£190–220 / €280–320
$360–410 ⚒ SWO

A Copeland Spode porcelain breakfast cup and saucer, inscribed 'The Royal Yacht', 1905.
£260–310 / €380–450
$490–580 ⚒ SAS

A set of four Belleek porcelain tea cups and five saucers, one cup damaged, Irish, late 19thC.
£340–400 / €500–590
$640–750 ⚒ G(L)

A Wemyss pottery cup and saucer, c1900, cup 3½in (9cm) diam.
£400–450 / €590–660
$750–850 ⊞ GLB

A pair of Royal Worcester bone china coffee cups and trembleuse saucers, date code for 1904.
£65–75 / €95–105
$125–145 ⚒ G(L)

A Rosenthal porcelain regimental presentation cup and saucer, German, c1916, cup 3in (7.5cm) diam.
£170–190 / €250–280
$320–360 ⊞ K&M

A Quimper faïence cup and saucer, French, c1920, cup 2in (5cm) high.
£70–80 / €100–115
$135–155 ⊞ MLL

A Shelley Melody trio, c1928, plate 7in (18cm) diam.
£35–40 / €45–50
$55–65 ⊞ WAC

A Royal Crown Derby porcelain cup and saucer, dated 1929, cup 3½in (9cm) diam.
£105–125 / €155–185
$200–240 ⊞ K&M

A Paragon porcelain coffee cup and saucer, commemorating the coronation of King George VI, c1937.
£200–240 / €290–350
$380–450 ⋟ SAS

◄ **A Clarice Cliff pottery cup and saucer,** decorated with Solomon's Seal pattern, 1930s, cup 4in (10cm) diam, and a salt, decorated with Crocus pattern.
£160–190 / €240–280
$300–360 ⋟ G(L)

A pair of Clarice Cliff Bizarre pottery coffee cups and saucers, 1930s, cups 3in (7.5cm) high.
£270–300 / €400–440
$500–560 ⊞ NAW

◄ **A Quimper faïence cup and saucer,** by P. Fouillen, French, 1930s, saucer 6in (15cm) diam.
£20–25 / €30–35
$40–50 ⊞ SER

Figures & Busts

A porcelain bust of a woman, socle repaired, Italian, late 18thC, 2½in (6.5cm) high.
£120–145 / €175–210
$220–260 ➶ WW

A Derby porcelain figure of Mars, c1780, 7in (18cm) high.
£220–250 / €320–370
$410–470 ⊞ SER

A Derby porcelain figure of a musician, c1780, 10½in (26.5cm) high.
£310–350 / €460–510
$580–660 ⊞ SER

A Wedgwood black basalt bust of William Shakespeare, 19thC, 12in (30.5cm) high.
£720–800 / €1,050–1,200
$1,350–1,500 ⊞ LGr

A Derby porcelain figure of a putto, c1810, 4½in (11.5cm) high.
£115–130 / €170–190
$220–250 ⊞ SER

A Berlin porcelain figure of Amphiaraus, German, early 19thC, 9in (23cm) high.
£160–185 / €240–270
$300–350 ⊞ SER

▶ **A Staffordshire porcelain figure of Dr Syntax landing at Calais,** c1830, 6in (15cm) high.
£410–460 / €600–680
$770–860 ⊞ DAN

A Staffordshire pottery figure of **Punch,** with his dog Puck, c1840, 12in (30.5cm) high.
£2,500–2,800 / €3,700–4,100
$4,700–5,300 ⊞ HOW

▶ A Staffordshire pearlware figure of Britannia, c1840, 14in (35.5cm) high.
£1,000–1,150 / €1,450–1,700
$1,900–2,150 ⊞ HOW

A pair of Meissen porcelain portrait busts of a boy and a girl, crossed swords marks, incised marks, German, mid-19thC, 9¼in (23.5cm) high.
£680–810 / €1,000–1,200
$1,300–1,500 ✒ G(L)

LOCATE THE SOURCE
The source of each illustration in Miller's can be found by checking the code letters below each caption with the Key to Illustrations, pages 311–314.

A Copeland Parian bust of Admiral **Lord Nelson,** 1847–50, 11in (28cm) high.
£1,350–1,500 / €2,000–2,200
$2,550–2,850 ⊞ JAK

▶ A bisque bust of Bernard Palissy, by Jean Gille, raised monogram, French, c1855, 13½in (34.5cm) high.
£200–240
€290–350
$380–450
✒ SWO
Bernard Palissy was, among other things, a potter, glassblower, geologist and religious reformer who was imprisoned for his Huguenot beliefs.

A Staffordshire pottery figure, entitled 'Wellington', c1852, 12½in (32cm) high.
£150–180 / €220–260
$280–330 ✒ G(L)

A pair of Staffordshire pottery figures, entitled 'Dick Turpin' and 'Tom King', one repaired, c1860, 11¾in (30in) high.
£120–140 / €175–210
$220–260 ⚹ G(L)

▶ A Copeland porcelain bust of Evangeline, 1861, 12in (30.5cm) high.
£540–600 / €790–880
$1,000–1,150 ⊞ JAK

A Parian bust of Apollo, by Brown-Westhead, Moore & Co, impressed factory marks, c1861, 13in (33cm) high.
£330–390 / €490–570
$620–730 ⚹ SWO

A Staffordshire pottery bust of Homer, damaged, late 19thC, 12½in (32cm) high.
£150–180 / €220–260
$280–330 ⚹ SWO

A Meissen porcelain figure of a boy holding a shuttlecock, German, c1880, 6in (15cm) high.
£1,000–1,150 / €1,450–1,650
$1,900–2,150 ⊞ BROW

◀ A Meissen porcelain group of a courting couple, German, c1880, 10in (25.5cm) high.
£4,000–4,500 / €5,900–6,600
$7,500–8,500 ⊞ BROW

▶ A Meissen porcelain figure of a lady, emblematic of Touch, Five Senses series, German, c1880, 6in (15cm) high.
£1,300–1,450 / €1,900–2,150
$2,450–2,750 ⊞ BROW

▶ **A Meissen porcelain group of a mother and daughter playing with a dog,** German, c1890, 5in (12.5cm) high.
£2,550–2,850 / €3,750–4,200
$4,800–5,400 ⊞ BROW

◀ **A Robinson & Leadbeater Parian portrait bust of Queen Victoria,** by R. J. Morris, impressed 'Jubilee 1887', late 19thC, 13½in (34.5cm) high.
£320–380 / €470–560
$600–710 ⚒ G(L)

Robinson & Leadbeater

Robinson & Leadbeater's entire output was confined to Parian, which they continued to produce long after other factories ceased production. Most wares are unmarked.

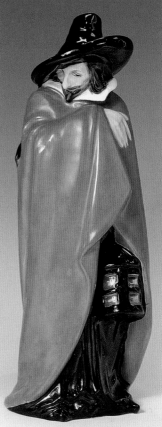

A bisque piano baby, German, c1910, 4in (10cm) long.
£90–100 / €130–145
$170–190 ⊞ JOA

▶ **A Royal Doulton bone china figure of Guy Fawkes,** by C. J. Noke, No. HN98 1918–49, 10½in (26.5cm) high.
£950–1,100 / €1,400–1,600
$1,800–2,050 ⚒ SWO

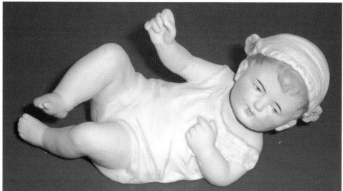

A ceramic salt cellar bust of Winston Churchill, c1950, 3½in (9cm) high.
£55–65 / €80–95
$105–125 ⊞ H&G

▶ **A Zsolnay Pecs porcelain figure of a nude female,** entitled 'Coiffeuse', Hungarian, 1960s, 9in (23cm) high.
£140–165 / €210–240
$260–300 ⚒ TMA

A Royal Doulton porcelain figure, entitled 'A Gentleman from Williamsburg', HN No. 2227, 1960–83, 6¾in (17cm) high.
£75–85 / €110–125
$146–165 ⚒ L&E

Inkwells & Desk Sets

A stoneware inkwell, probably by Wilson, 1810–20, 1¾in (4.5cm) high.
£220–250 / €320–370
$410–470 ⊞ DIA

A salt-glazed stoneware inkwell, in the form of a woman's head, 19thC, 2in (5cm) high.
£220–260 / €320–380
$410–490 ⚒ BBR

A Chamberlain's Worcester porcelain inkwell, decorated with Thumb and Finger pattern, c1810, 3in (7.5cm) high.
£520–580 / €760–850
$980–1,100 ⊞ DIA

A Worcester Barr, Flight & Barr porcelain inkwell, with applied goat's-head masks, on claw feet, impressed mark, c1810, 4in (10cm) wide.
£440–520 / €650–760
$830–980 ⚒ WW

A salt-glazed stoneware inkwell, in the form of a woman's head, 19thC, 2½in (6.5cm) high.
£520–620 / €760–910
$980–1,150 ⚒ BBR

A porcelain inkwell on a stand, decorated in Worcester, painted with a view of Worcester Bridge, cover missing, painted mark, c1815, 4in (10cm) high.
£800–950 / €1,200–1,400
$1,500–1,800 ⚒ G(L)

◀ A Chamberlain's Worcester porcelain inkwell, with everted rim, on three feet, script mark, c1815, 3in (7.5cm) high.
£850–1,000 / €1,250–1,450
$1,600–1,900 ⚒ G(L)

A Derby porcelain inkstand, painted mark, c1820, 11in (28cm) wide.
£600–680 / €880–1,000
$1,150–1,300 ⊞ TYE

A porcelain inkwell, painted with a panel of peasants in a landscape, attributed to William Pollard, c1820, 3in (7.5cm) high.
£1,050–1,200 / €1,550–1,750
$1,950–2,250 ⊞ DIA

◄ **A Sèvres-style porcelain partner's inkstand,** attributed to Coalport, c1830, 11in (28cm) wide.
£2,700–3,000 / €3,950–4,400
$5,100–5,700 ⊞ DIA

A Derby porcelain inkwell, decorated in the Japanese style, early 19thC, 5in (12.5cm) diam.
£160–180 / €230–260
$300–340 ⊞ JOA

A Staffordshire pottery inkwell, in the form of a boy on a dolphin, c1830, 5in (12.5cm) high.
£990–1,100 / €1,450–1,600
$1,850–2,050 ⊞ JHo

A stoneware inkwell, in the form of a pyramid, mid-19thC, 2½in (6.5cm) high.
£50–60 / €75–85
$110–115 ⤢ BBR

A Coalport-style porcelain inkwell, the cover with a flower bud knop, hairline cracks, c1840, 4in (10cm) high.
£95–110 / €140–160
$175–210 ⤢ TMA

A glazed stoneware inkwell, in the form of a beehive, impressed 'Wilson's Beehive Inkwell', numbered, mid-19thC, 4in (10cm) high.
£120–140 / €175–210
$220–260 ⤢ BBR

A salt-glazed stoneware figural inkwell, in the form of a seated Mr Punch, diamond registration mark, mid-19thC, 5in (12.5cm) high.
£270–320 / €400–470
$510–600 ⚒ BBR

A majolica novelty desk stand, by Brown-Westhead, Moore & Co, with a terrier's head flanked by two inkwells, on bun feet, c1870, 11½in (29cm) wide.
£600–720 / €880–1,050
$1,150–1,350 ⚒ G(L)

A Staffordshire pottery quill holder, in the form of a man and his dog, c1845, 6in (15cm) high.
£240–270 / €350–400
$450–510 ⊞ DAN

A pair of Staffordshire pottery inkwells, with models of recumbent greyhounds, 1850–90, 6in (15cm) wide.
£180–210 / €270–310
$350–390 ⚒ WW

A Doulton Lambeth Isobath pottery inkwell, c1885, 7in (18cm) high.
£200–240 / €290–350
$380–450 ⚒ G(B)

A majolica inkwell, in the form of a toad surmounted by a lily pad, well missing, impressed number, French, c1890, 3½in (9cm) high.
£240–280 / €350–410
$450–530 ⚒ SWO

A porcelain inkwell, in the form of a figural group of a mother and child, minor restoration, Continental, 1880–90 7¼in (18.5cm) high.
£90–100 / €130–145
$170–190 ⚒ SAS

A Copeland porcelain letter rack and inkstand, with floral decoration, c1895, 9in (23cm) high.
£720–800 / €1,050–1,200
$1,350–1,500 ⊞ DIA

A faïence inkstand, in the form of a stack of books, the interior with a pewter inkwell, pounce-pot and engraved lining, French, late 19thC, 4½in (11.5cm) wide.
£110–130 / €160–190
$210–240 ↗ G(L)

A Wemyss pottery inkwell, damage and discolouration, impressed marks, early 20thC, 7in (18cm) wide.
£220–260 / €320–380
$410–490 ↗ SWO

A Wemyss pottery inkwell, surmounted by two dolphins, c1900, 8in (20.5cm) wide.
£850–1,000 / €1,250–1,450
$1,600–1,850 ⊞ RdeR

◀ **A Crown Staffordshire porcelain inkwell,** c1910, 3½in (9cm) high.
£260–290 / €380–430
$490–550 ⊞ DIA

Inkwells

By the 18th century, the inkstand was a fashionable addition to the writing desk. It comprised accessories such as an inkpot with holes for spare quills, a 'sand' box for powdering the paper, a 'wafer' box for seals, a taper-holder and a tray for penknife, pencil etc.

A Royal Crown Derby porcelain inkwell, 1919, 3in (7.5cm) high.
£420–470 / €620–690
$790–880 ⊞ DIA

An Art Deco pottery inkwell and pen holder, by W. Goebel, German, c1930, 8in (20.5cm) wide.
£135–150 / €200–220
$250–280 ⊞ HEW

Jardinières

A Nevers faïence jardinière, decorated with shipping scenes, French, c1660, 30in (76cm) diam.
£4,050–4,500 / €5,900–6,600
$7,600–8,450 ⊞ **G&G**

A Coalport porcelain jardinière and stand, with Imari-style panels and gilt dolphin handles, c1800, 6¼in (16cm) high.
£480–570 / €710–840
$900–1,050 ⚒ **SWO**

◀ **A stoneware jardinière and stand,** probably Chetham & Woolley, decorated with panels of figures, c1810, 6¼in (16cm) high.
£240–280
€350–410
$450–520
⚒ **WW**

A pottery jardinière and stand, c1820, 5in (12.5cm) high.
£490–550 / €720–800
$920–1,050 ⊞ **HOW**

◀ **A pair of Sèvres-style Worcester Flight, Barr & Barr porcelain jardinières,** decorated with views of Windsor Castle, c1835, 9in (23cm) wide.
£3,350–3,750 / €4,900–5,500
$6,300–7,000 ⊞ **JOR**

A pair of Sèvres-style porcelain jardinières, the reserves painted with figures and flowers, with gilt-metal mounts, c1850–70, 13¾in (35cm) high.
£5,300–6,300 / €7,800–9,200
$10,000–11,800 ⚒ **GIL**

A Minton majolica jardinière, dated 1856, 11in (28cm) diam.
£450–500 / €660–730
$850–940 ⊞ **BGe**

A Minton majolica jardinière, supported by three doves, dated 1871, 6in (15cm) high.
£1,400–1,650 / €2,050–2,400
$2,650–3,100 ⚒ G(L)

A Minton Chinese-style glazed pottery jardinière, incised with foliage and scroll borders, restored, dated 1878, 12in (30.5cm) high.
£95–110 / €1,400–1,600
$1,800–2,100 ⚒ G(L)

A Doulton Lambeth pottery jardinière and stand, with griffin supports, c1890, 37in (94cm) high.
£1,150–1,300 / €1,650–1,850
$2,000–2,300 ⊞ MMc

▶ **A Burmantofts faïence jardinière,** with moulded geometric decoration, impressed mark, shape No. 2052A, c1890, 5½in (14cm) high.
£55–65 / €80–95
$100–120 ⚒ G(L)

A Wemyss pottery Combe jardinière, c1880, 13in (33cm) diam.
£1,600–1,800 / €2,350–2,650
$3,000–3,400 ⊞ SDD

A George Jones porcelain jardinière, by Frederick Schenck, with *pâte-sur-pâte* decoration, c1890, 5in (12.5cm) high.
£1,400–1,600 / €2,000–2,300
$2,450–2,800 ⊞ WAC

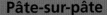

Pâte-sur-pâte

This technique was originally developed by Sèvres but copied by many factories. It involved layers of white slip being built up and carved on a dark-coloured ground before the object was glazed and fired. Most *pâte-sur-pâte* is porcelain; some manufacturers did use the technique on pottery bodies but these were often unglazed and the result is not so fine.

► **A Delphin Massier majolica jardinière and stand,** French, c1895, 36in (91.5cm) high.
£1,800–2,000 €2,600–2,900 $3,150–3,500 ⊞ MLL

A Doulton Lambeth pottery Natural Foliage ware jardinière, by Beatrice M. Durtnall, Emily Randell and Catherine Francis, 1891–1902, 11in (28cm) high.
£175–195 / €250–280
$330–370 ⊞ CANI

A Brannam Pottery jardinière, decorated by Alex Lauder, late 19thC, 14in (35.5cm) high.
£890–1,000 / €1,300–1,450
$1,650–1,900 ⊞ MMc

A Bretby pottery jardinière, with canework decoration, c1892, 8½in (21.5cm) high.
£330–380 / €480–550
$580–670 ⊞ HUN

A Wemyss pottery jardinière, by Karel Nekola, decorated with roses, impressed mark, c1900, 6in (15cm) diam.
£270–300 / €390–430
$470–530 ⊞ RdeR

An Eichwald majolica jardinière, Bohemian, c1900, 8in (20.5cm) high.
£160–180 / €230–260
$280–320 ⊞ ASP

A Burmantofts pottery jardinière, c1900, 13in (33cm) high.
£520–580 / €750–840
$900–1,000 ⊞ AFD

A Leeds pottery jardinière, slight damage, c1900, 9in (23cm) high.
£120–140 / €175–200
$220–250 ⊞ DSG

A Leeds pottery jardinière and stand, stamped '171', marked, c1900, 10¾in (27.5cm) high.
£140–165 / €200–240
$260–310 ↗ SWO

A pair of Wedgwood jasper ware jardinières, slight damage, c1900, 10in (25.5cm) diam.
£490–550 / €710–790
$860–960 ⊞ LGr

▶ A Hadley's Worcester faïence jardinière, painted with panels of blackberries and dragonflies, c1900, 8in (20.5cm) high.
£400–480 / €580–690
$700–840 ↗ G(L)

A Longchamps terracotta jardinière, with enamel decoration, French, c1900, 12in (30.5cm) diam.
£290–330 / €420–480
$510–580 ⊞ **ANO**

A Withnall terracotta jardinière stand, in the form of a bear, with glass eyes, impressed marks, early 20thC, 27½in (70cm) high.
£200–240 / €290–350
$350–420 ⚒ **G(L)**

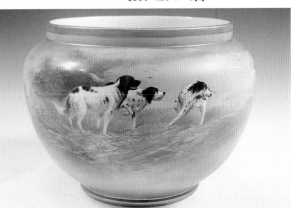

A Fieldings Crown Devon pottery jardinière, decorated with gun dogs, signed 'R. Hinton', printed mark, early 20thC, 7in (18cm) high.
£700–840 / €1,000–1,200
$1,250–1,450 ⚒ **SWO**

A Royal Doulton pottery jardinière and stand, by Eliza Simmance, c1902, 40in (101.5cm) high.
£4,100–4,600 / €5,900–6,600
$7,200–8,100 ⊞ **POW**

A Wemyss pottery jardinière, painted with roses, impressed and painted marks, c1910, 8½in (21.5cm) diam.
£330–390 / €480–580
$580–700 ⚒ **G(L)**

A Wardle Art Pottery jardinière and stand,
with tube-lined decoration, c1910,
27in (68.5cm) high.
£450–500 / €650–720
$790–880 ⊞ ASP

A Wemyss pottery jardinière, painted with oranges, impressed and painted mark, c1910, 8¾in (21.5cm) diam.
£360–400 / €480–580
$580–700 ⚒ G(L)

Wardle Art Pottery

The company was originally founded in the mid-19th century by James Wardle, in Shelton, Stoke-on-Trent and their output included earthenware, Parian and majolica wares. Renamed Wardle Art Pottery Co Ltd in 1910, it was later amalgamated with Cauldon Potteries and ceased trading in 1935.

A Moorcroft pottery jardinière, decorated with Wisteria pattern, c1920, 13in (33cm) high.
£2,250–2,500 / €3,250–3,600
$3,950–4,400 ⊞ JSG

A Royal Doulton stoneware jardinière,
decorated by Maud Bowden, c1920,
8in (20.5cm) high.
£310–350 / €450–500
$540–610 ⊞ RUSK

▶ **A pottery Delecia Iberis jardinière,** probably by Clarice Cliff, c1930, 11in (28cm) diam.
£180–210 / €260–300
$320–370 ⚒ GH

Jugs & Ewers

A glazed stoneware 'Tigerware' jug, German, c1600, 6in (15cm) high.
£340–380 / €500–560
$640–710 ⊞ PeN

A Worcester porcelain milk jug, decorated with the Three Flowers pattern, 1775–80, 5in (12.5cm) high.
£125–140 / €185–210
$230–260 ⊞ WAC

A Gaudy Welsh pottery miniature jug and bowl, decorated with Grape pattern, 19thC, jug 4in (10cm) high.
£170–200 / €250–290
$320–380 ⚒ TMA

A Spode stoneware jug, relief-moulded with hunting scenes, c1810, 7½in (19cm) high.
£210–240 / €310–350
$390–450 ⊞ AUC

A pottery jug, with platinum lustre decoration and Wellington commemorative mottoes, crack and chip to spout, dated 1814, 8½in (21.5cm) high.
£580–650 / €850–960
$1,100–1,250 ⊞ G&G

Gaudy Welsh

First produced in Staffordshire in the 1820s, Gaudy Welsh is the name given to earthenware that was 'gaudily' decorated with stylized flower patterns. Favoured colours included orange, green and cobalt blue; pink, yellow, turquoise and pink or copper lustre was used instead of gold. Although popular in Wales, very little was actually manufactured there. In south Wales, Gaudy Welsh is frequently referred to as Swansea Cottage. Early pieces were not generally marked although later wares were often stamped with the maker's name. Much Gaudy Welsh was exported to the US, where it is very collectable today.

► **A pottery jug,** c1820, 6in (15cm) high.
£370–420
€540–620
$700–790
⊞ AUC

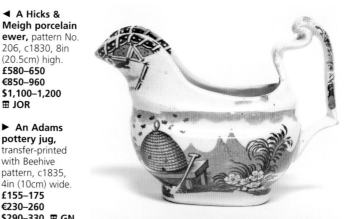

◄ **A Hicks & Meigh porcelain ewer,** pattern No. 206, c1830, 8in (20.5cm) high.
£580–650
€850–960
$1,100–1,200
⊞ JOR

► **An Adams pottery jug,** transfer-printed with Beehive pattern, c1835, 4in (10cm) wide.
£155–175
€230–260
$290–330 ⊞ GN

A Rockingham porcelain milk jug, c1838, 5in (12.5cm) high.
£230–260 / €340–380
$430–490 ⊞ TYE

A pottery trick or puzzle jug, attributed to Elsmore & Forster, mid-19thC, 9½in (24cm) high.
£180–210 / €260–310
$340–390 ↗ SWO

Puzzle jugs

These jugs were made from c1570 to the early 1800s in creamware, delftware, brown saltglaze etc. They had a hollow handle leading to a tube round the rim connecting three or more spouts. One aperture had to be stopped up in order to drink from another. To make drinking more difficult, some jugs had openwork decoration around the rug below the spouts.

A child's pottery jug, with transfer-printed decoration, damaged, c1850, 3in (7.5cm) high.
£155–175 / €230–260
$290–330 ⊞ HUM

A Palissy-style pottery puzzle jug, Portuguese, c1860, 16in (40.5cm) high.
£1,400–1,600
€2,050–2,350
$2,650–3,000 ⊞ BRT

A pottery copper lustre jug, mid-19thC, 5in (12.5cm) high.
£105–120 / €155–175
$200–230 ⊞ DAN

▶ **A Palissy-style pottery jug,** Portuguese, Caldas de Rainha, c1860, 15in (38cm) high.
£990–1,100 / €1,450–1,600
$1,850–2,050 ⊞ BRT

A stoneware jug, commemorating the death of Prince Albert, the reverse with a coat-of-arms, damaged and restored, 1861, 10¾in (27.5cm) high.
£35–40 / €50–60
$65–75 ⚑ SAS

A Minton majolica jug, date code for 1863, 7in (18cm) high.
£100–120 / €145–175
$190–220 ⚑ G(L)

A majolica jug, with boar's head pouring lip, French, late 19thC, 9½in (24cm) high.
£90–100 / €130–145
$170–190 ⚑ G(L)

◀ **A pottery Mocha ware jug,** c1865, 10in (25.5cm) high.
£810–900
€1,200–1,350
$1,500–1,700
⊞ HOW

▶ **A majolica jug,** relief-moulded with birds and leaves, Continental, c1880, 9¼in (23.5cm) high.
£55–65 / €80–95
$105–125
⚑ G(L)

A W. H. Goss porcelain Oxford Ashmolean ewer, with Devon crests, 1880–1920, 5in (12.5cm) high.
£30–35 / €45–50
$55–65 ⊞ G&CC

◀ **A majolica mug,** by William Brownfield, in the form of a bird with a monkey, impressed date mark for 1886, 13½in (34.5cm) high.
£620–740 / €910–1,100
$1,150–1,350 ⚲ SWO

A Royal Worcester porcelain ewer, with bronzed spout and handle, indistinct date code, c1884, 12½in (32cm) high.
£240–280 / €350–410
$450–530 ⚲ G(L)

A stoneware jug, with relief-moulded decoration, c1880, 10¼in (26cm) high.
£100–120 / €145–175
$185–220 ⚲ SWO

A pottery jug, French, c1880, 6in (15cm) high.
£60–70 / €85–100
$115–135 ⊞ MLL

▶ **A Copeland Rugby commemorative jug,** c1890, 5½in (14cm) high.
£680–760 / €1,000–1,100
$1,300–1,450 ⊞ RdV

A Bargeware jug, with a cartouche inscribed 'Mrs Smith, Macclesfield, 1881', slight damage, 7in (18cm) high.
£220–250 / €320–370
$410–470 ⊞ KES

A pottery jug, French, c1890, 5in (12.5cm) high.
£40–45 / €60–70
$75–85 ⊞ MLL

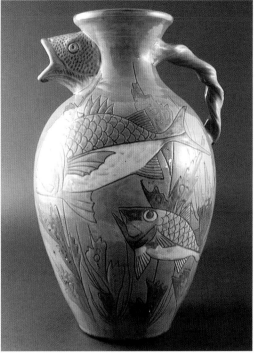

A Brannam Pottery jug, by James Dewdney, incised with fish, incised marks, slight damage, c1890, 14½in (37cm) high.
£220–260 / €320–380
$410–490 ⚲ WW

A graduated set of three majolica jugs, possibly by Joseph Holdcroft, 1875–1925, tallest 11½in (29cm) high.
£120–140 / €175–210
$220–260 ⚲ SWO

A Meissen porcelain cream jug, crossed swords mark, German, late 19thC, 3¼in (8.5cm) high.
£130–150 / €190–220
$240–280 ⚲ SWO

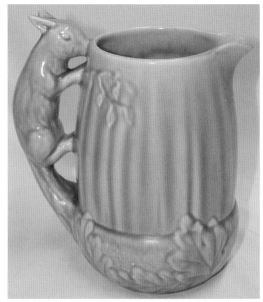

A SylvaC pottery jug, No. 1958, damaged, 1950s, 7½in (19cm) high.
£15–20 / €22–29
$29–38 ⊞ HEI

An Arthur Wood pottery jug, printed with an ice hockey scene, c1955, 4in (10cm) high.
£85–95 / €125–140
$165–185 ⚲ SAS

Mugs & Tankards

A stoneware tankard,
with a pewter cover,
German, dated 1770,
9¾in (25cm) high.
£490–550 / €720–810
$920–1,050 ⊞ G&G

A Worcester porcelain mug,
printed with flowers, marked, c1770,
6in (15cm) high.
£340–400 / €500–590
$640–750 ⚒ G(L)

A Worcester porcelain mug,
transfer-printed with Plantation
pattern, 1760–70, 6in (15cm) high.
£440–520 / €650–760
$830–980 ⚒ G(L)

▶ **A Jackfield pottery
tankard,** c1770,
4½in (11.5cm) high.
£220–250 / €320–370
$410–470 ⊞ IW

**A Staffordshire pottery satyr-head
mug,** decorated with underglaze
colours, c1780, 3½in (9cm) high.
£145–165 / €210–240
$270–300 ⊞ SER

A Staffordshire porcelain mug, with a strap handle, marked 'X17',
c1785, 4¼in (11cm) high.
£440–520 / €650–760
$830–980 ⚒ WW

A creamware mug, printed with Masonic
symbols, c1790, 6in (15cm) high.
£760–850 / €1,100–1,250
$1,450–1,600 ⊞ AUC

◄ **A child's porcelain mug,** decorated with vines and inscribed 'Samuel', early 19thC, 3in (7.5cm) diam.
£155–175
€230–260
$290–330
⊞ HUM

A Sunderland pottery mug, probably by Scott of Southwick, with pink lustre decoration and painted with the 'Sailor's Farewell', c1820, 5in (12.5cm) high.
£450–500 / €660–740
$850–940 ⊞ WAA

Lustreware

Large quantities of lustreware were produced at Sunderland, Staffordshire, Swansea and Leeds during the 19th century. Pink lustre was the most popular colour in the early-mid 19thC, with orange or apricot being introduced around 1855.

The glazed surface is painted with metallic oxides, mixed with fine ochre and refired at a low temperature to produce an iridescent metallic surface.

A Coalport porcelain mug, decorated with mounted Cossacks being addressed by Count Platov, c1812, 5½in (14cm) high.
£110–130 / €160–190
$210–240 ⚒ SAS

A Derby porcelain porter mug, painted with a Japan pattern, c1820, 4½in (11.5cm) high.
£300–360 / €440–530
$560–670 ⚒ G(L)

A Derby porcelain porter mug, crowned crossed batons mark, minor damage, c1820, 4½in (11.5cm) high.
£200–240 / €290–350
$380–450 ⚒ WW

A pottery mug, with silver resist decoration, c1820, 4in (10cm) high.
£490–550 / €720–810
$920–1,050 ⊞ HOW

A pottery Mocha ware tankard, c1820, 6in (15cm) high.
£1,500–1,700 / €2,200–2,500
$2,800–3,200 ⊞ HOW

Mocha ware

The moss-like decoration on Mocha ware was made by dabbing the wet pot with a liquid pigment known as tea, said to contain tobacco juice, urine and manganese, which then fanned out into frond-like patterns when fired.

A porcelain mug, c1830, 5in (12.5cm) diam.
£260–290 / €380–430
$490–550 ⊞ DAN

A child's pearlware mug, c1840, 3in (7.5cm) high.
£110–125 / €160–185
$210–240 ⊞ RdV

A porcelain mug, hand-decorated with flowers and an inscription, c1840, 5in (12.5cm) diam.
£135–150 / €200–220
$250–280 ⊞ HTE

A stoneware mug, commemorating the marriage of Queen Victoria and Prince Albert, decorated with named profiles of Queen Victoria, 1840, 5¼in (13.5cm) high.
£330–390 / €490–570
$620–730 ➚ SAS

A pair of pottery copper lustre mugs, mid-19thC.
£200–230 / €290–340
$380–430 ⊞ DAN

A **Davenport porcelain mug,** inscribed 'F. Thomas Lloyd', c1845, 3in (7.5cm) diam.
£90–105 / €130–145
$170–195 ⊞ DAN

A **child's pottery mug,** with transfer-printed decoration, mid-19thC, 2¾in (7cm) diam.
£135–150 / €200–220
$250–280 ⊞ HUM

A **porcelain mug,** hand-decorated with flowers, 1840–50, 4in (10cm) high.
£80–90 / €115–130
$155–175 ⊞ HTE

An **earthenware mug,** printed with a scene from the Crimean war entitled 'Battle of Inkerman', restored, 1854, 3¼in (8.5cm) high.
£300–360 / €440–530
$560–670 ⚒ SAS

A **pottery spongeware quart tankard,** c1860, 6in (15cm) high.
£270–300 / €400–440
$510–560 ⊞ HUM

A **child's pottery mug,** decorated with an archery scene, c1860, 3in (7.5cm) high.
£100–120 / €145–175
$190–230 ⊞ RdV

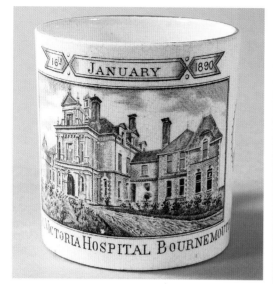

A pottery mug, commemorating a visit to Bournemouth by the Prince of Wales, 1890.
£140–165 / €210–240
$260–300 ⚒ SAS

A Wemyss pottery mug, c1900, 6in (15cm) high.
£410–460 / €600–680
$770–860 ⊞ GLB

A Wemyss pottery mug, painted with thistles by Karel Nekola, marked, early 20thC, 5½in (14cm) high.
£320–360 / €480–530
$600–680 ⚒ DAU

A Royal Crown Derby porcelain miniature loving cup, commemorating the coronation of George V, 1911, 1½in (4cm) high.
£80–90 / €115–130
$155–175 ⚒ SAS

A Glyn Colledge pottery tankard, 1950s, 5in (12.5cm) high.
£45–50 / €65–70
$85–95 ⊞ HeA

A Keele St Pottery mug, decorated with a scene from the Walt Disney production of *Winnie the Pooh*, 1960, 4in (10cm) high.
£25–30 / €40–45
$50–55 ⊞ IQ

Plates & Dishes

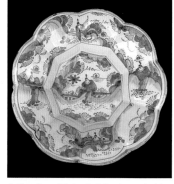

A **tin-glazed lobed dish,** decorated in the Chinese Transitional style, chips and wear to rim, German or Dutch, c1700.
£580–650 / €850–960
$1,100–1,200 ⊞ G&G

A **slipware baking dish,** probably Sussex, 18thC, 18in (45.5cm) wide.
£500–600 / €740–880
$940–1,150 ⚒ G(L)

A **majolica dish,** decorated with a castle in a landscape, Spanish, Aragon, 18thC, 12½in (32cm) diam.
£850–950 / €1,250–1,400
$1,600–1,800 ⊞ G&G

A **Frankfurt delft dish,** painted in the Chinese Transitional style, German, c1720, 13in (33cm) diam.
£680–760 / €1,000–1,100
$1,300–1,450 ⊞ G&G

A **Castelli maiolica plate,** Grue workshop, Italian, c1720, 7in (18cm) diam.
£1,600–1,800 / €2,350–2,650
$3,000–3,400 ⊞ G&G

A **Worcester porcelain dish,** with a scale blue ground, c1775, 7¾in (19.5cm) diam.
£450–500 / €660–740
$850–940 ⊞ AUC

A **Worcester porcelain plate,** c1775, 7½in (19cm) diam.
£350–390 / €510–570
$660–730 ⊞ AUC

A **Spode pottery plate,** transfer-printed with sarcophagi and sepulchres at the harbour at Cacamo, from the Caramanian series, c1810, 10in (25.5cm) diam.
£200–220 / €290–320
$380–420 ⊞ GRe

◄ **A Spode pottery soup plate,** with printed and enamelled decoration, c1820, 10in (25.5cm) diam.
£70–80 / €100–115
$135–155 ⊞ IW

A New Hall porcelain saucer dish, c1820, 9in (23cm) diam.
£230–260 / €340–380
$430–490 ⊞ DAN

A pair of pottery plates, painted with marine scenes, c1825, 10in (25.5cm) diam.
£410–490 / €600–720
$770–920 ✗ G(L)

Six Spode ironstone plates, pattern No. 2147, 1825–30, 8in (20.5cm) diam.
£100–120 / €145–175
$190–220 ✗ SWO

◄ **A Bloor Derby dessert dish,** painted with a view of Windsor Castle, c1825, 11in (28cm) wide.
£490–550 / €720–810
$920–1,050 ⊞ DAN

Bloor Derby

In 1811 the Derby factory was acquired from John Heath and William Duesbury's successors by Robert Bloor who, despite the fact that he suffered from mental illness, continued to manage the ailing business. Owing to indiscriminate marketing of vast quantities of poor-qualtiy goods, the factory finally closed in 1848.

▶ **Six Staffordshire porcelain plates,** each painted with a different floral spray, painted pattern number, 1825–30, 8½in (21.5cm) diam.
£240–280 / €350–410
$450–530 ✗ SWO

A **pottery nursery plate,** the centre printed with a scene entitled 'The Great Performer of the Adelphi', the border moulded with animals, c1829, 6¾in (17cm) diam.
£140–165 / €210–240
$260–310 ➤ SAS

A **pottery nursery plate,** with a hexagonal star outline, moulded with flowers, restored, c1832, 6in (15cm) diam.
£400–480 / €590–710
$750–900 ➤ SAS

A **pottery nursery plate,** the centre printed with a portrait of Earl Grey, the border moulded with flowerheads, c1832, 6in (15cm) diam.
£120–140 / €175–210
$220–260 ➤ SAS

▶ A **pottery plate,** with printed and enamelled decoration, c1840, 10in (25.5cm) diam.
£60–70
€85–100
$115–135 ⊞ IW

Singles or Sets?

Buying individual plates can be a costly business. Although the financial outlay for an entire set or service may seem high, it is possible to recoup much of the cost, if not more, by selling off what is not required. By purchasing plates in this way it is possible to obtain desirable pieces at a lower cost than if purchased individually.

Four pottery plates, moulded with leaves, with ribbed backs, mid-19thC, 8¼in (21cm) diam.
£110–130 / €160–190
$210–240 ➤ SWO

◀ **A porcelain miniature dish,** with a hand-painted scene, c1840, 4in (10cm) wide.
£75–85 / €110–125
$145–165 ⊞ DAN

A pottery plate, with flow blue decoration, c1845, 9½in (24cm) diam.
£40–45 / €60–70
$75–85 ⊞ CHAC

A spongeware pottery soup plate, mid-19thC, 10in (25.5cm) diam.
£150–170 / €220–250
$280–320 ⊞ MFB

Spongeware

The stippled effect is created by dabbing the surface of pottery with a sponge or roll of rags dipped in colour. Sponged decoration was mostly used on tableware.

◀ **A pottery spongeware dish,** c1860, 10in (25.5cm) diam.
£150–170 / €220–250
$280–320 ⊞ MFB

A set of six majolica plates, Continental, 1860–80, 9in (23cm) diam.
£500–600 / €740–880
$940–1,100 ⚒ G(L)

◀ **A pottery spongeware soup plate,** c1860, 10in (25.5cm) diam.
£150–170 / €220–250
$280–320 ⊞ MFB

A Staffordshire pottery sponge-ware dish, c1880, 11in (28cm) diam.
£250–280 / €370–410
$470–530 ⊞ HTE

A set of ten Minton porcelain plates, each painted with different flowers and insects, impressed marks, 1884–85, 9½in (24cm) diam.
£260–310 / €380–450
$490–580 ↗ SWO

A pottery plate, by Wallis Grimson, printed with a portrait of Lord Randolph Churchill, c1886, 10in (25.5cm) diam.
£75–85 / €100–125
$145–165 ↗ SAS

A porcelain plate, printed with portrait ovals including Tsar Nicholas II, French, c1896, 7in (18cm) diam.
£110–130 / €160–190
$200–240 ↗ SAS

A Royal Worcester porcelain plate, commemorating the Jubilee of Queen Victoria, 1887, 10½in (26.5cm) diam.
£30–35 / €45–50
$55–65 ↗ G(L)

A pottery plate, commemorating the Boer War, printed with named portraits of Buller, White and Macdonald, c1900, 9½in (24cm) diam.
£100–120 / €145–175
$190–220 ↗ SAS

▶ A Clarice Cliff pottery side plate, decorated with Honolulu pattern, c1930, 7in (18cm) diam.
£150–180
€220–260
$280–330
↗ G(L)

Plaques

A Prattware pottery plaque, moulded with figures outside an inn, minor damage, c1790, 6 x 9in (15 x 23cm).
**£2,300–2,700 / €3,400–3,950
$4,300–5,100** ⚒ WW

A pottery lustre plaque, printed with a frigate, entitled 'Northumberland 74', impressed 'Dixon', 19thC, 8in (20.5cm) wide.
**£170–200 / €250–290
$320–380** ⚒ SJH

A relief-moulded pottery plaque, depicting St George and the Dragon, the reverse inscribed 'James Wood 1801', 8in (20.5cm) wide.
**£540–600 / €790–880
$1,000–1,150** ⊞ HOW

A porcelain plaque, hand-painted with a young girl wearing national costume, Continental, 19thC, 3¼ x 2½in (8.5 x 6.5cm).
**£170–200 / €250–290
$320–380** ⚒ SWO

A pair of porcelain plaques, depicting Milton and Shakespeare, 1800–25, framed, 8 x 9in (20.5 x 23cm).
**£1,200–1,350 / €1,750–2,000
$2,250–2,550** ⊞ TYE

A Sunderland lustre pottery plaque, indistinct impressed mark, probably 'Dixon', mid-19thC, 8in (20.5cm) wide.
£80–90 / €115–130
$155–175 ⚒ DAU

A porcelain plaque, depicting a country house with figures in the foreground, 1830–40, 6¾ x 8¾in (17 x 22cm).
£300–360 / €440–530
$570–680 ⚒ G(L)

A pottery plaque, printed with a stately home with cattle in the foreground, c1840, 5½in (14cm) high.
£160–190 / €240–280
$300–360 ⚒ SJH

A Meissen porcelain plaque, 'The Chocolate Girl', after the picture by Jean-Etienne Liotard, crossed swords mark, paper label for Sir Edward Reid, contemporary mounts, German, 1850–75, 6 x 4¼in (15 x 11cm).
£1,550–1,850 / €2,300–2,700
$2,900–3,500 ⚒ SWO

A plaque, hand-painted with a detail from the 'Chocolate Girl', Continental, 1850–75, 5 x 3¾in (12.5 x 9.5cm).
£480–570 / €710–840
$900–1,050 ⚒ SWO

◀ **A porcelain plaque,** depicting a girl holding a sprig of flowers, slight rubbing, impressed mark '12/E', German, 1850–1900, 5¼in (13.5cm) high.
£100–120 / €145–175
$190–220 ⚒ SWO

A porcelain plaque, hand-painted with a portrait, reframed, 1850–1900, 3 x 2½in (7.5 x 6.5cm).
£180–210 / €260–310
$330–390 ⚒ SWO

◀ **A pair of maiolica plaques,** decorated with dancing figures and washerwomen, stamped 'Flli Bianchi, Napoli', Italian, late 19thC, 6in (15cm) wide.
£180–210 / €260–310
$340–400 ⚒ G(L)

A pair of porcelain plaques, painted with portraits of young girls, Continental, late 19th/20th century, 3½in (9cm) high.
£140–165 / €200–240
$260–310 ✦ G(B)

A porcelain plaque, hand-painted with a young girl holding roses, Continental, 1850–1900, 4¼ x 3¼in (11 x 8.5cm).
£230–270 / €340–400
$430–510 ✦ SWO

An earthenware plaque, painted with warriors and lions, monogrammed 'EV', 1850–1900, 13½ x 18½in (34.5 x 47cm).
£90–100 / €130–145
$170–190 ✦ G(L)

A Berlin porcelain plaque, painted by Malty with a winged female on a rocky outcrop, impressed KPM and sceptre marks, signed, German, 1850–1900, 12¾ x 10½in (32.5 x 26.5cm).
£6,200–7,400 / €9,100–10,900
$11,600–13,900 ✦ G(L)

A Berlin porcelain plaque, painted with a military portrait of Kaiser Wilhelm I, impressed KPM mark, German, c1875, 10¾in (27.5cm) high.
£680–810 / €1,000–1,200
$1,300–1,500 ✦ SAS

A porcelain plaque, painted with Ruth in the Cornfield, German, late 19thC, 5½in (14cm) high.
£440–520 / €650–760
$830–980 ✦ DN(HAM)

▶ **A Berlin porcelain plaque,** entitled 'Lute Player after Kaulbach', impressed KPM mark, German, 1850–1900, 8¼in (21cm) high.
£640–760 / €940–1,100
$1,200–1,400 ✦ DD

A Dutch Delft-style plaque, painted with an estuary scene after J. H. Wysmuller, late 19thC, in an oak frame, 7½ x 9½in (19 x 24cm).
£240–280 / €350–410
$450–530 ⚒ G(L)

A Royal Doulton earthenware plaque, decorated with a mother and child on a country path, c1900, 9½ x 7½in (24 x 19cm).
£150–180 / €220–260
$280–330 ⚒ G(L)

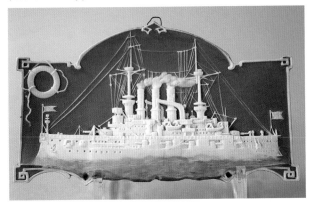

A porcelain plaque, depicting a ship, possibly the *Kaiserin*, German, c1900, 8in (20.5cm) wide.
£35–40 / €50–60
$65–75 ⚒ SAS

A Dutch Delft wall plaque, hand-painted with a rural scene, signed 'Louis Apal', marked, c1905, 21¾in (55.5cm) diam.
£140–160 / €200–240
$260–310 ⚒ SWO

Porcelain plaques

The value of painted porcelain plaques lies primarily in the subject matter depicted. A maker's name, particularly a good one is the next point to be taken into consideration, followed by the quality of the painting.

A Royal Worcester porcelain plaque, painted by Harry Davis with a Highland scene, signed, c1912, 4¼in (11cm) diam, framed.
£4,650–5,200 / €6,800–7,600
$8,700–9,800 ⊞ BP

A Limoges porcelain *pâte-sur-pâte* plaque, signed 'A Barrière', French, c1920, 7¼in (18.5cm) diam.
£110–125 / €160–185
$200–240 ⊞ SER

Potlids

'Bewley & Drapers' Shaving Paste',
19thC, 3in (7.5cm) diam.
£40–45 / €60–70
$75–85 ⚒ BBR

'T. & W. & W. Southall Cold Cream',
19thC, 2½in 6.5cm) diam.
£75–85 / €110–125
$145–165 ⚒ BBR

'French Street Scene', by F. & R.
Pratt, c1850, 4¾in (12cm) diam.
£40–50 / €65–75
$85–95 ⚒ SJH

'Arctic Expedition in Search of Sir John Franklin', No.
19, c1855, 3in (7.5cm)
£200–240 / €290–350
$380–450 ⚒ SAS

'The Queen God Bless Her', No. 319, c1860,
4in (10cm) diam.
£200–240 / €290–350
$380–450 ⚒ SAS

Pot Lids

Originally these were covers
for shallow pots containing
edible or cosmetic products
that were oily, greasy,
powdery or paste. The lids
were decorated with transfer-
printed pictures such as
buildings, landscapes,
important events such as the
Great Exhibition of 1851,
indoor and outdoor activities,
portraits and bear dancing.
 F. & R. Pratt specialized in
making pot lids from 1846 to
1880. Early examples are flat,
and often in black only, while
later lids are domed and the
designs are more colourful.

▶ 'St. Paul's Cathedral', No. 185,
c1850, 3¾in (9.5cm) diam.
£150–180 / €220–260
$280–330 ⚒ SAS

'Injury', by Bates Eliot & Co, No. 580, 1850–60, 4in (10cm) diam.
£120–140 / €175–210
$220–260 ⚒ BBR

'Napirima, Trinidad', No. 225, c1854, 3¾in (9.5cm) diam.
£180–210 / €260–310
$340–400 ⚒ SAS

'Admiral Sir Charles Napier', the reverse with Feast stamp, No. 167A, c1855, 3½in (9cm) diam.
£700–840 / €1,050–1,250
$1,300–1,600 ⚒ SAS

'Children Sailing Boats in Tub', No. 263, c1855, 3in (7.5cm) diam.
£75–85 / €110–125
$145–165 ⚒ SAS

'New Houses of Parliament', No. 195, c1860, 3½in (9cm) diam.
£440–520 / €650–760
$830–980 ⚒ SAS

Buying advice

When buying, check carefully for damage, especially at the edges and beware of modern reproductions. Fakes, which tend to have a paper image applied to the old lid and then varnished over, can be easily detected by using a finger nail at the edge.

'Wimbledon, July 1860', No. 223, c1860, 4in (10cm) diam.
£100–120 / €145–175
$190–220 ⚒ SAS

▶ **'Walmer Castle with Sentry',** the reverse with Tatnell & Son stamp, c1860, 3¼in (8.5cm) diam.
£460–550 / €680–810
$870–1,050 ⚒ SAS

'The Swallow', the reverse with registration mark, No. 297, c1860, 3¼in (8.5cm) diam.
£260–310 / €380–450
$490–580 ✗ SAS

▶ 'HRH Prince of Wales Visiting the Tomb of Washington', No. 263, c1861, 4in (10cm) diam.
£110–130 / €160–190
$200–240 ✗ SAS

'Rifle Contest Wimbledon 1864', by F. & R. Pratt, c1864, 4in (10cm) diam, in a mahogany frame.
£125–150 / €185–220
$240–280 ✗ GAK

'Rimmels Cherry Tooth Paste', No. 126, 1865, 3in (7.5cm) diam.
£180–210 / €260–310
$340–400 ✗ SAS

'Shells', c1865, 5in (12.5cm) diam.
£20–25 / €30–35
$40–50 ✗ SAS

'Tria Juncta in Uno', c1870, 5¼in (13.5cm) diam.
£700–780 / €1,000–1,150
$1,300–1,450 ⊞ JBL

Pot lid numbers

The numbers in the captions refer to the system used by A. Ball in his reference work *The Price Guide to Pot Lids*, Antique Collectors Club, 1980.

▶ 'The Dentist', c1870, 4in (10cm) diam.
£340–380 / €500–560
$640–710 ⊞ JBL

'Trouchet's Corn Cure', 1880–1920,
2in (5cm) diam.
£50–60 / €75–85
$100–115 ✗ BBR

'Bale's Mushroom Savoury', 1880–1920, 3½in (9cm) diam.
£110–130 / €160–190
$200–240 ✗ BBR

'Genuine Bears Grease', 1890–1900,
2¾in (7cm) diam.
£50–60 / €75–85
$100–115 ✗ BBR

'Whitaker & Grossmith's Genuine Bears
Grease', 1890–1900, 3in (7.5cm) diam.
£460–550 / €680–810
$860–1,000 ✗ BBR

'Patey & Co Genuine Bears Grease',
1890–1900, 3¾in (9.5cm) diam.
£850–1,000 / €1,250–1,450
$1,600–1,900 ✗ BBR

'Regal Cherry Tooth Paste',
1890–1900, 3in (7.5cm) diam.
£190–220 / €280–330
$360–410 ✗ BBR

▶ 'Lorimer & Co Cherry Tooth
Paste', late 19thC, 3¼in (8.5cm) diam.
£35–40 / €50–60
$65–75 ✗ BBR

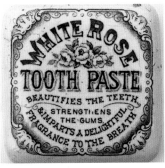

'White Rose Tooth Paste',
late 19thC, 2½in (6.5cm) square.
£25–30 / €40–45
$50–55 ✗ BBR

'James Atkinson's Bears Grease', 1890–1900, 2½in (6.5cm) diam.
£65–75 / €95–105
$125–145 ✗ BBR

▶ 'Thornton's Anthracoline
Deodorizer & Antiseptic', late 19thC,
3½in (9cm) diam.
£120–140 / €175–210
$220–260 ✗ BBR

Sauce Boats & Cream Boats

◀ **A Bow porcelain sauce boat,** painted in the Kakiemon palette, feet damaged, c1747, 8¼in (21cm) wide.
£600–720 / €880–1,050
$1,150–1,350 ⚒ SWO

Sauce or cream boat?

What determines the difference between sauce and cream boats is size. Sauce or gravy boats are larger, whereas cream boats are smaller and daintier. However, some small sauce boats or large cream boats are difficult to classify.

◀ **A Meissen porcelain double-lipped sauce boat,** on four scrolled feet, minor chip to foot, crossed swords mark, German, 1740–45, 10in (25.5cm) wide.
£620–740 / €910–1,100
$1,200–1,400 ⚒ G(L)

A Chelsea porcelain sauce boat, moulded with strawberries, one section repaired, red anchor mark, c1755, 7½in (19cm) long.
£350–420 / €520–620
$660–790 ⚒ WW

◀ **A Bow porcelain sauce boat,** with moulded and painted decoration, c1765, 8¼in (21cm) wide.
£160–190 / €240–280
$300–360 ⚒ G(L)

▶ **A Chelsea porcelain sauce boat,** c1756, 8½in (21.5cm) wide.
£750–850
€1,100–1,250
$1,400–1,600
⊞ AUC

A Leeds Pottery sauce boat, c1770, 6in (15cm) wide.
£260–290 / €380–430
$490–550 ⊞ KEY

A Worcester porcelain cream boat, printed with Obelisk
Fisherman pattern, minor damage, disguised numeral mark,
c1780, 4¼in (11cm) wide.
£700–840 / €1,050–1,250
$1,300–1,550 ✒ WW

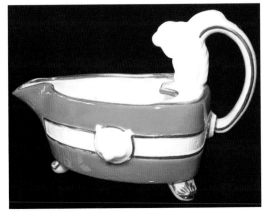

A Minton porcelain cream boat, the handle modelled as
a squirrel, the sides with animal masks, on three raised feet,
printed and impressed marks, registration diamond mark,
19thC, 5in (12.5cm) wide.
£140–165 / €200–240
$260–310 ✒ SJH

A Seth Pennington, Liverpool porcelain cream boat,
c1785, 5in (12.5cm) wide.
£490–550 / €720–810
$920–1,050 ⊞ DSA

A mid-Victorian Staffordshire pottery sauce boat,
transfer-printed with Willow pattern, 6in (15cm) wide.
£60–70 / €85–100
$115–135 ⊞ CoCo

A mid-Victorian Staffordshire pottery sauce boat,
transfer-printed with Willow pattern, 8in (20.5cm) wide.
£35–40 / €50–60
$65–75 ⊞CoCo

◀ **A T. G. Green
pottery Blue
Domino sauce
boat,** early
1950s, 9in
(23cm) wide.
£70–80
€100–115
$135–155
⊞ JWK

Scent Bottles

A pair of porcelain scent bottles, enamel-painted with floral friezes, Continental, 19thC, 6in (15cm) high.
£55–65 / €80–95
$105–125 🔨 BWL

A Spode porcelain scent bottle, stopper associated, red painted mark, c1820, 3¼in (8.5cm) high.
£190–220 / €280–320
$360–410 🔨 WW

A Rockingham porcelain scent bottle, encrusted with flowers, c1835, 4in (10cm) high.
£800–900 / €1,150–1,300
$1,500–1,700 ⊞ TYE

A Coalport porcelain scent bottle, decorated with an enamelled scene, c1881, 4in (10cm) high.
£340–380 / €500–560
$640–710 ⊞ TYE

A Worcester porcelain scent bottle, commemorating Queen Victoria's Golden Jubilee, the screw top modelled as the Royal crown, decorated with Queen Victoria's portrait and names of Commonwealth countries, c1887, 3½in (9cm) high.
£420–500 / €620–740
$790–940 🔨 WW

A porcelain scent bottle, probably Limoges, French, c1860, 4in (10cm) high.
£290–330 / €430–490
$550–620 ⊞ VK

A silver-mounted ceramic scent bottle, hand-painted with lovers in a landscape, mount Birmingham 1903, 2½in (6.5cm) high.
£85–95 / €125–140
$165–185 🔨 GAK

A silver-mounted ceramic scent bottle, modelled as an acorn, mount Birmingham 1904, 2½in (6.5cm) high.
£115–135 / €170–200
$210–250 🔨 GAK

Services

A Caughley porcelain dessert service, comprising 21
pieces, decorated with Weir pattern, minor damage, c1790.
£2,000–2,400 / €2,950–3,500
$3,750–4,500 ⚒ G(L)

A porcelain part tea service, possibly Grainger's Worcester,
comprising 36 pieces, milk jug damaged, early 19thC.
£950–1,100 / €1,400–1,600
$1,800–2,050 ⚒ SWO

A stone china dinner service, comprising 31 pieces,
marked, c1820.
£1,600–1,900 / €2,350–2,800
$3,000–3,550 ⚒ G(L)

A stone china part dinner service, comprising 39 pieces,
some cracks, printed marks, c1820.
£500–600 / €740–880
$940–1,100 ⚒ G(L)

A Coalport porcelain tea service, comprising 17
pieces, c1825.
£250–300 / €370–440
$470–560 ⚒ GAK

A Mason's pottery tea service, comprising 31 pieces,
decorated with Jardinière pattern, 1920–30, teapot 7in
(18cm) high.
£450–500 / €660–740
$850–940 ⊞ ANAn

◄ **A Staffordshire porcelain dessert service,** comprising
11 pieces, painted with flowers, c1835.
£1,200–1,400 / €1,750–2,050
$2,250–2,650 ⚒ G(L)

A Minton bone china part tea service, comprising 33 pieces, painted with flowers, 1830–35.
£180–210 / €260–310
$340–400 ➶ G(L)

A porcelain dessert service, possibly Coalport or Ridgway, comprising 26 pieces, comport damaged, c1835.
£520–620 / €760–910
$980–1,150 ➶ SWO

A Copeland pottery dinner service, decorated with a ruined castle within an acorn border, 1860–80.
£920–1,100 / €1,350–1,600
$1,750–2,050 ➶ BWL

► **A Livesley Powell & Co child's pottery part dinner service,** six pieces damaged, some pieces impressed 'Best L. P. & Co.', mid-19thC.
£150–180 / €220–260
$280–330 ➶ SWO

◄ **A Copeland pottery dinner service,** comprising 10 pieces, damaged, impressed and painted marks, c1880.
£190–220 / €280–320
$360–410 ➶ SWO

Copeland/Spode

Founded in Staffordshire in 1770 by Josiah Spode the factory became famous for its bone china. Josiah Spode II introduced New Stone China around 1805. The company traded as Copeland & Garrett from 1833 to 1848, then Copeland; the name Spode was revived in 1970.

A Meissen-style porcelain tea and coffee service, painted with birds, fruit and foliage, German, late 19thC.
£500–600 / €740–880
$940–880 ➶ CHTR

A Burleigh ware pottery dinner service, comprising 59 pieces, decorated with Haddon pattern, slight damage, printed marks, late 19thC.
£240–280 / €350–410
$450–530 ✗ GAK

Burleigh ware

Burleigh ware is the name given to the pottery produced by the firm of Burgess & Leigh. The factory was founded in Staffordshire in 1851 and specialized in underglaze-decorated earthenware. Their main output was dinner, table, utility and toilet ware.

A Coalport porcelain tea service, comprising five pieces, with 'jewelled' decoration, printed marks, c1900.
£980–1,150 / €1,450–1,700
$1,850–2,150 ✗ SWO

A Limoges porcelain cabaret service, by Haviland & Co, teapot lid missing, milk jug repaired, early 20thC.
£55–65 / €80–95
$105–125 ✗ G(L)

An Aynsley bone china coffee service, comprising 12 pieces, with silver cup holders, Birmingham 1918, in a fitted case.
£180–210 / €260–310
$340–390 ⚲ G(L)

A set of six Shelley bone china coffee cans and saucers, each with pierced silver cup holders, one restored, Birmingham 1923, 2in (5cm) high.
£110–130 / €160–190
$210–240 ⚲ G(L)

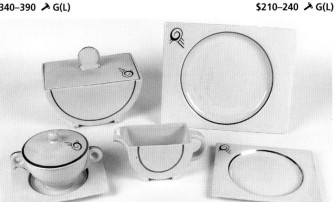

Sets/pairs
Unless otherwise stated, any description which refers to 'a set' or 'a pair' includes a guide price for the entire set or the pair, even though the illustration may show only a single item.

◄ **A Clarice Cliff pottery Biarritz dinner service,** comprising 45 pieces, some damaged, c1930.
£400–480 / €590–710
$750–900 ⚲ FHF

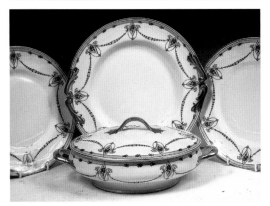

A Limoges porcelain dinner service, comprising 80 pieces, with coloured swag decoration, some damage, French, c1930.
£300–360 / €440–530
$560–670 ⚲ SWO

A Carlton Ware pottery Rita coffee service, comprising 18 pieces, decorated with Sketching Bird pattern, c1937, with six silver spoons, Sheffield 1937, in a fitted case.
£600–720 / €880–1,050
$1,150–1,350 ⚲ G(L)

A Shelley bone china coffee service, comprising 16 pieces, printed marks, 1930s.
£130–150 / €190–220
$240–290 ⚲ SWO

A Susie Cooper pottery part dinner service, comprising 18 pieces, printed marks, 1930s.
£150–180 / €220–260
$280–330 ⚲ SWO

A Shelley bone china Eve tea service, comprising 28 pieces, damaged, one with rim chip, 1930s, teapot 4¾in (12cm) high.
£320–380 / €470–560
$600–710 ➶ SWO

A Susie Cooper pottery dinner service, comprising 25 pieces, slight damage, 1930s.
£110–130 / €160–190
$210–240 ➶ SWO

◀ **A Shelley bone china tea service,** comprising 21 pieces, 1930s.
£170–200 / €250–290
$320–380 ➶ G(L)

A Windsor china coffee service, comprising 16 pieces, c1946, teapot 8in (20.5cm) high.
£110–125 / €160–185
$210–240 ⊞ DEB

A Midwinter pottery Stylecraft dinner service, by Hugh Casson, comprising 43 pieces, enamelled with Cannes pattern, 1950s.
£230–270 / €340–400
$430–510 ➶ G(L)

A Celtic Pottery coffee service, slight damage, 1960s–70s, coffee pot 10in (25.5cm) high.
£260–310 / €380–450
$490–580 ➶ SWO

Tea Canisters

A Meissen porcelain tea canister,
with a metal cover, crossed swords and
incised marks, German, mid-18thC,
4¼in (11cm) high.
£640–760 / €940–1,100
$1,100–1,400 ⚶ WW

A Durlach faïence tea canister,
painted with Oriental flowers in a
fenced garden, the shoulder with two
insects, minor glaze chips, German,
c1770, 4½in (11.5cm) high.
£500–600 / €740–800
$940–1,100 ⚶ S(O)

A pearlware tea canister, with
chinoiserie decoration, cover missing,
c1780, 3¾in (9.5cm) high.
£370–420 / €540–620
$700–790 ⊞ G&G

A Bow porcelain tea canister, cover
damaged, 1755–60, 5½in (14cm) high.
£600–720 / €880–1,050
$1,150–1,350 ⚶ WW

**A pair of Worcester porcelain tea
canisters,** painted with Kylin pattern,
damaged, square seal marks, c1770,
5½in (14cm) high.
£520–620 / €760–910
$980–1,150 ⚶ WW

▶ **A Meissen porcelain tea canister,**
painted with a pastoral scene, cover
missing, crossed swords mark with
star, German, Marcolini period,
1774–1813, 4in (10cm) high.
£300–360 / €440–530
$560–670 ⚶ DORO

A Worcester porcelain tea canister,
printed and painted with Borghese Vase
pattern, c1765, 5in (12.5cm) high.
£630–700 / €930–1,050
$1,150–1,300 ⊞ JUP

A Worcester porcelain tea canister, painted with Wildflower Spray pattern, c1775, 5½in (14cm) high.
£720–800 / €1,050–1,200
$1,350–1,500 ⊞ JUP

A Leeds creamware tea canister, c1780, 3½in (9cm) high.
£250–280 / €370–410
$470–530 ⊞ KEY

◄ **A creamware tea canister,** Dutch-decorated with William V of Orange and his Queen, 1780, 4in (10cm) high.
£360–410 / €530–600
$680–770 ⊞ WAA

A Minton pottery tea caddy, transfer-printed with Basket of Flowers pattern, 1825, 7in (18cm) long.
£800–900 / €1,200–1,350
$1,500–1,700 ⊞ GN

A Prattware tea canister, decorated with Macaroni figures, c1790, 5½in (14cm) high.
£280–320 / €410–470
$530–600 ⊞ KEY

► **A Portmeirion pottery tea canister,** decorated with Tiger Lily pattern, c1962, 4in (10cm) high.
£120–140 / €175–210
$230–260 ⊞ CHI

Teapots & Coffee Pots

A Staffordshire salt-glazed stoneware teapot, with crabstock handle and spout, on three feet, restored, c1750, 6½in (16.5cm) high.
£260–310 / €380–460
$490–580   ↗ WW

A Staffordshire redware teapot, both sides decorated with an Oriental scene, mid-18thC, 4in (10cm) high.
£430–480 / €630–710
$810–900   ⊞ G&G

A salt-glazed stoneware teapot, slipcast with panels of figures and beasts, restored, c1745, 5¼in (13.5cm) high.
£900–1,000 / €1,300–1,450
$1,700–1,900   ↗ WW

A Whieldon-style pottery miniature teapot, with tortoiseshell glaze and branch handle, damaged, mid-18thC, 3in (7.5cm) high.
£165–195 / €240–280
$300–360   ↗ G(L)

Teapots

Always check condition of teapots. Look for staining and crazing and remember that covers and spout tips are particularly vulnerable to damage.

A Worcester porcelain teapot, c1770, 5in (12.5cm) high.
£470–530 / €690–780
$880–1,000   ⊞ DSA

A Worcester porcelain teapot, enamelled with a floral pattern, c1765, 7½in (19cm) long.
£620–740 / €910–1,100
$1,150–1,400   ↗ WW

A Whieldon-style creamware teapot, the handle and spout modelled as twigs, c1770, 4in (10cm) high.
£160–190 / €240–280
$300–360   ↗ SWO

A redware coffee pot, with engine-turned decoration, c1770, 10in (25.5cm) high.
£310–350 / €460–510
$580–660 ⊞ IW

A creamware teapot, decorated with flowers, c1775, 6in (15cm) high.
£800–900 / €1,150–1,300
$1,500–1,700 ⊞ HOW

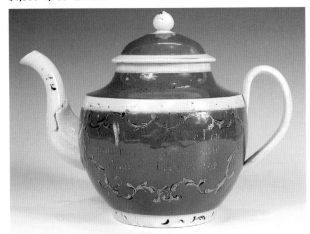

A pearlware tea pot, with rubbed inscription, possibly Yorkshire, dated 1794, 7½in (19cm) high.
£210–250 / €310–370
$390–470 ✗ SWO

A Meissen porcelain coffee pot, the spout modelled as a putto tipping a ewer, the foot with a coiled serpent, restored, impressed marks, German, 1774–1813, 8½in (21.5cm) high.
£1,850–2,200 / €2,700–3,250
$3,500–4,150 ✗ LFA

A pearlware coffee pot, with floral decoration and initials 'SW', c1790, 13in (33cm) high.
£610–680 / €900–1,000
$1,150–1,300 ⊞ AUC

A New Hall porcelain teapot, decorated with flowers, c1800, 10in (25.5cm) wide.
£250–300 / €370–440
$470–560 ✗ WW

New Hall

This Staffordshire factory made very durable 'hybrid hard-paste' porcelain, predominantly for tea and coffee ware. Typical New Hall shapes were often based on silver counterparts, for example the helmet-shaped cream jug.

A feldspathic stoneware Castleford-style teapot, c1800, 6in (15cm) high.
£260–290 / €380–430
$490–550 ⊞ AUC

A feldspathic stoneware Castleford-style teapot, commemorating Admiral Lord Nelson, c1805, 7in (18cm) high.
£760–850 / €1,100–1,250
$1,450–1,600 ⊞ AUC

A Worcester Flight, Barr & Barr porcelain teapot and stand, decorated with flowers, c1815, 8in (20.5cm) high.
£540–600 / €790–880
$1,000–1,150 ⊞ CoS

A Wedgwood smear-glazed stoneware teapot, c1820, 6in (15cm) wide.
£90–100 / €130–145
$170–190 ⊞ IW

Cross Reference
Cups & Saucers see pages 277–230

◀ A pearlware teapot, with transfer-printed decoration, c1820, 5in (12.5cm) high.
£440–490 / €650–720
$830–920 ⊞ CoS

Cadogan teapots

Among the earliest ceramic teapots used in Europe were Chinese wine pourers which, when exported to the West in the 17th century, were packed with tea in order to avoid damage. This lead to the misktaken belief that they were pots used for brewing tea. These items are now known as Cadogan teapots after Earl Cadogan, who according to legend was the first Englishman to own one. Cadogan teapots are lidless pots into which hot water is poured through a hole in the bottom and the pot is then quickly turned the right way up. An interior funnel prevents the water from leaking out through the hole.

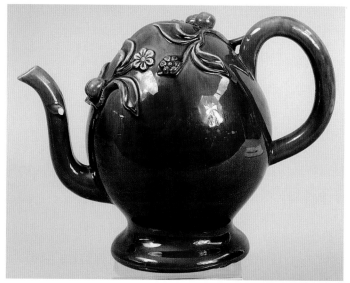

◀ A pottery Cadogan teapot, possibly Swinton Pottery, 1830–40, 7½in (19cm) high.
£60–70 / €85–100
$115–135 ✗ DA

◄ **A Belleek porcelain Bamboo teapot,** Irish, First Period, 1863–90, 5in (14cm) high.
£900–1,000 / €1,300–1,450
$1,700–1,900 ⊞ MLa

A Belleek porcelain teapot, decorated with Thorn pattern, Irish, First Period, 1863–90, 5in (14cm) high.
£720–800 / €1,050–1,200
$1,350–1,500 ⊞ MLa

◄ **A Belleek porcelain teapot,** decorated with Grass pattern, Irish, First Period, 1863–90, 4in (10cm) high.
£280–330 / €410–490
$530–620 ↗ SWO

◄ **A pottery teapot,** decorated in Pratt colours with 'Halt near Ruins' and 'Cows in Stream near Ruins', c1870, 6in (12cm) high.
£40–45 / €60–70
$75–85 ↗ SAS

A Bargeware teapot, cartouche inscribed '1513', c1875, 14in (35.5cm) high.
£540–600 / €790–880
$1,000–1,150 ⊞ JBL

Bargeware

Also known as Measham ware, Bargeware is the name given to earthenware with a treacly-brown glaze. Items are decorated with hand-coloured moulded clay flowers, fruit, animals and birds. A plaque with a stamped message was often added.

◄ **A Bargeware batchelor's teapot,** cartouche inscribed 'W. Thompson, Hyde Park', dated 1875, 4in (10cm) high.
£540–600 / €790–880
$1,000–1,150 ⊞ JBL

A Bargeware teapot, cartouche inscribed 'A Present from the Arley Sewing Guild to Mrs Hazell', handle and finial restored, c1890, 12in (30.5cm) high.
£290–330 / €430–490
$550–620 ⊞ KES

A Minton porcelain teapot, c1895, 3½in (9cm) high.
£240–280 / €350–410
$450–530 ⊞ CoS

▶ **A Royal Worcester porcelain teapot,** painted by Ernest Barker with sheep beneath a flowering fruit tree, handle repaired, signed 'E. Barker', puce mark, 1919, 9in (23cm) wide.
£210–250 / €310–370
$390–470 ⚒ WW

A Carter, Stabler & Adams tin-glazed pottery teapot, by Ruth Pavely, c1920, 8in (20.5cm) wide.
£220–250 / €320–370
$410–470 ⊞ MMc

▶ **A G. Clews & Co pottery novelty teapot,** in the form of an artillery gun, printed Belisha mark, 1930s, 6in (15cm) wide.
£25–30 / €40–45
$50–55 ⚒ G(L)

A Belleek porcelain Hexagon teapot, Irish, Second Period, 1891–1926, 5in (12.5cm) high.
£990–1,100 / €1,450–1,600
$1,850–2,050 ⊞ MLa

A pottery teapot, stand and jug, with moulded scrolled decoration, c1895, jug 8in (20.5cm) high.
£30–35 / €40–45
$55–65 ⚒ G(L)

◄ **A Quimper faïence teapot,** French, c1920, 10in (25.5cm) wide.
£170–200
€250–290
$320–380 ⊞ MLL

A Gray's Pottery teapot, by Susie Cooper, c1928, 8in (20.5cm) wide.
£410–460 / €600–680
$770–860 ⊞ MMc

► **A Crown Ducal pottery coffee pot,** by Charlotte Rhead, decorated with Padua pattern, c1930, 8in (20.5cm) long.
£580–650 / €850–960
$1,100–1,250 ⊞ MMc

Cross Reference
Art Deco see pages 81–86

A Portmeirion pottery coffee pot, decorated with Jupiter pattern, 1964, 12in (30.5cm) high.
£80–90 / €115–130
$155–175 ⊞ CHI

A Portmeirion pottery coffee pot, decorated with Cypher pattern, 1964, 12in (30.5cm) high.
£50–60 / €75–85
$100–115 ⊞ CHI

A Meakin pottery Wayside coffee pot, 1960s, 10in (25.5cm) high.
£35–40 / €40–45
$65–75 ⊞ CHI

Tiles

A pottery stove tile, in the style of Hans Kraut of Villingen, relief-moulded with a figure of Artemesia beneath an archway, German, c1580, 11 x 9¼in (28 x 23.5cm).
£330–390 / €490–570
$620–730 ✗ F&C

A tile, Dutch, c1660, 5in (12.5cm) square.
£90–105 / €130–155
$170–195 ⊞ JHo

A Dutch Delft tile, slightly chipped, c1670, 5¼in (13.5cm) square.
£65–75 / €95–105
$125–145 ⊞ G&G

A collection of 35 Dutch Delft tiles, 1670–90, each 5¼in (13.5cm) square.
£400–480 / €590–710
$750–900 ✗ SWO

A Dutch Delft tile, early 18thC, 5in (12.5cm) square.
£95–110 / €140–160
$175–200 ⊞ JHo

◄ **Four Dutch Delft tiles,** 18thC, 5¼in (13.5cm) square.
£50–55 / €75–85
$100–115 each ⊞ AUC

Two Dutch Delft tiles, 18thC, 5¼in (13.5cm) square.
£50–55 / €75–85
$100–115 each ⊞ AUC

A London delft tile, c1750, 5in (12.5cm) square.
£85–95 / €125–140
$165–185 ⊞ JHo

A set of three delft tiles, printed by Sadler, each depicting an actor in character, c1750, 4¾in (12cm) square, mounted in a damaged and restored ebonized frame.
£480–570 / €710–840
$900–1,050 ⚒ SWO

A Bristol delft tile, c1765, 5in (12.5cm) square.
£95–110 / €140–160
$175–200 ⊞ JHo

A Dutch Delft tile, painted in manganese with a biblical scene, mid-18thC, 5in (12.5cm) square.
£70–80 / €100–115
$135–155 ⊞ KEY

▶ **A set of 12 Minton tiles,** by John Moyr Smith, depicting fables, c1872, 6in (15cm) square.
£480–570 / €710–840
$900–1,050 ⚒ SWO

A Liverpool delft tile, printed with a scene from Aesop's *Fables*, c1770, 5in (12.5cm) square.
£360–400 / €530–590
$680–750 ⊞ RdV

A Minton tile, by John Moyr Smith, Husbandry series, c1876, 6in (15cm) square.
£80–90 / €115–130
$155–175 ⊞ C&W

A pair of earthenware tiles, printed and enamelled with named figures, 'Touchstone, Rosalind, Celia' and 'Ferdinand, Ariel', one cracked and repaired, c1880, 8in (20.5cm) square.
£170–200 / €250–290
$320–380 ⚒ G(L)

A collection of 30 Dutch Delft tiles, depicting children at play, with spider's head corner motifs, late 19thC, 5¼in (13.5cm) square.
£170–200 / €250–290
$320–380 ⚒ SWO

A Maw & Co relief-moulded tile, c1880, 6in (15cm) square.
£90–100 / €130–145
$170–190 ⊞ C&W

A tile, with floral and geometric decoration, c1885, 6in (15cm) square.
£25–30 / €40–45
$50–55 ⊞ C&W

A Minton Hollins & Co tile, from the Bird series, c1885, 6in (15cm) square.
£60–70 / €85–100
$115–135 ⊞ C&W

A Minton tile, by William Wise, from the Animals of the Farm series, c1879, 6in (15cm) square.
£100–120 / €145–175
$190–220 ⊞ C&W

Three William De Morgan tiles, decorated with carnations, impressed marks for Merton Abbey period, 1882–88, 6in (15cm) square.
£240–280 / €350–410
$450–530 ⚒ SWO

An Aesthetic Movement tile, with floral decoration, c1890, 6in (15cm) square.
£20–25 / €30–35
$40–50 ⊞ C&W

A Minton tile, by Leonard Thomas Swetnam, depicting Cardinal Beaton's house, Edinburgh, c1890, 6in (15cm) square.
£80–90 / €115–130
$155–175 ⊞ C&W

A relief-moulded tile, depicting a heron among reeds, c1890, 6in (15cm) square.
£70–80 / €100–115
$135–155 ⊞ C&W

A Sherwin & Cotton Barbotine tile, c1890, 6in (15cm) square.
£30–35 / €45–50
$55–65 ⊞ C&W

A tile, the floral decoration within a central roundel, c1890, 6in (15cm) square.
£30–35 / €45–50
$55–65 ⊞ C&W

A tile plaque, by Craven Dunhill, moulded with a portrait of Joseph Chamberlain, c1895, 4½in (11.5cm) high.
£70–80 / €100–115
$135–155 ↗ SAS

Four William de Morgan tiles, impressed 'Sands End', Fulham Pottery rose mark, c1896, 9in (23cm) square.
£2,300–2,700 / €3,400–3,950
$4,300–5,100 ↗ SWO
These tiles were part of a commission for the P&O ship *India*, one of 12 for which de Morgan supplied tiles. They were used for the companionway frieze and a total of 88 were supplied.

A set of seven Minton tiles, titled with days of the week, and one other tile, late 19thC, 6in (15cm) square.
£390–460 / €570–680
$730–860 ↗ BWL

A Carter & Co tile, decorated with foxgloves, c1902, 11¾ x 6in (30 x 15cm).
£160–180 / €240–270
$300–330 ⊞ DSG

An Art Nouveau floral tile, c1905, 6in (15cm) square.
£40–45 / €60–70
$75–85 ⊞ C&W

A tile, probably by J. C. Edwards, depicting two children, c1905, 8 x 6in (20.5 x 15cm).
£155–175 / €230–260
$290–330 ⊞ C&W

A Sherwin & Cotton Secessionist tile, c1905, 6in (15cm) square.
£45–50 / €65–75
$85–95 ⊞ C&W

◄ **A Sherwin & Cotton tile panel,** entitled 'Winter Gleanings', by George Cartlidge, c1905, 12 x 6in (30.5 x 15cm).
£175–195 / €260–290
$330–37 0 ⊞ C&W

A Dutch Delft tile plaque, moulded with a building, inscribed 'XXIXe Conferentie van de International Law Association, Sept 1914 Sgravenhage', c1914, 7¼in (18.5cm) high.
£15–20 / €22–29
$29–38 ⚒ SAS

◄ **A Minton Hollins & Co quartered tile,** decorated with fruit and foliage, c1920, 6in (15cm) square.
£40–45 / €60–70
$75–85 ⊞ C&W

Toby Jugs

A Wood family pearlware 'Sharp Face' Toby jug, c1780, 9¼in (23.5cm) high.
£8,100–9,700
€11,900–14,300
$15,200–18,200 ⚒ S(O)

A Wood family Toby 'Roman Nose' jug, hat repaired, slight damage, c1780, 9½in (24cm) high.
£1,200–1,400
€1,750–2,050
$2,250–2,650 ⚒ S(O)

▶ **A pearlware Yorkshire Toby jug,** smoking a pipe, c1790, 10in (25.5cm) high.
£1,900–2,200 / €2,800–3,250
$3,550–4,150 ⊞ JBL
A Toby smoking a pipe is particularly rare.

Early Yorkshire Toby jugs
Look for the following typical characteristics:
- A black fringe (even when the hair is brown)
- Dotted eyebrows
- Sponged underglaze colours to base
- Curled pipe on his chest
- Raised octagonal cup

A Wood family creamware Toby jug, damaged and restored, late 18thC, 9½in (24cm) high.
£1,300–1,550
€1,900–2,250
$2,450–2,900 ⚒ S

A Pratt-style Martha Gunn Toby jug, slight damage, c1800, 10¼in (26cm) high.
£1,500–1,800
€2,200–2,650
$2,800–3,350 ⚒ S(O)

▶ **A pearlware Toby jug,** decorated with translucent glazes, c1800, 10in (25.5cm) high.
£810–900 / €1,200–1,350
$1,500–1,700 ⊞ JBL

A pearlware Toby jug, impressed crown mark, possibly Scottish, early 19thC, 9¾in (25cm) high.
£1,350–1,600 / €2,000–2,350
$2,550–3,000 ➢ S(O)

A pearlware Toby jug, with pearlware glaze, c1800, 10in (25.5cm) high.
£1,800–2,000 / €2,650–2,950
$3,400–3,750 ⊞ JBL

A Staffordshire Toby jug, early 19thC, 10in (25.5cm) high.
£300–360 / €440–530
$560–670 ➢ SJH

A North Country pearlware Toby jug, 19thC, 9¾in (25cm) high.
£280–330 / €410–490
$530–620 ➢ SJH

A Staffordshire enamelled pearlware Toby jug, 1820–30, 10in (25.5cm) high.
£320–380 / €470–560
$600–710 ➢ SJH

A Toby jug, his hat forming the cover, hat damaged, c1830, 10¼in (26cm) high.
£300–360 / €440–530
$560–680 ➢ WW

An enamelled pearlware Toby jug,
c1830, 9¾in (25cm) high.
£270–300 / €400–440
$500–560 ⚷ SJH

▶ **A Don Pottery pearlware Hearty Goodfellow Toby jug,** decorated in Pratt colours, maker's mark and date to base, 1830, 10in (25.5cm) high.
£810–900 / €1,200–1,300
$1,500–1,700 ⊞ JBL

A Staffordshire Toby jug, slight damage, 1850–90, 9in (23cm) high.
£105–120 / €155–175
$200–220 ⊞ F&F

▶ **A graduated set of Toby jugs,** complete with measures, c1855, largest 10in (25.5cm) high.
£900–1,000 / €1,300–1,450
$1,700–1,900 ⊞ JBL

How to identify an early Toby

Earthenware jugs in the form of a seated corpulent man wearing 18th-century dress and a tricorn hat were made by Ralph Wood and his son from around 1760 at their Burslem, Staffordshire, pottery and were widely copied by other makers.

The best Toby jugs were made between 1780 and 1825 and are characterized by sharp, well-defined modelling and subtle colours in the glazes. Colours were limited to brown, yellow, green, blue grey and purple; the hat will often appear to be black but is actually very dark brown. The best of the translucent glazes were from the Woods factory. William Pratt (1780–1840) used a different process which obtained very bright yellow, blue, orange, ochre and brown – a palette which became known as Prattware. Tobies with a cream-coloured body visible through the glaze were called creamware and those with a bluish glaze pearlware.

A good early Toby can be identified by the presence of separately applied hollow legs and feet. Check inside the body that the clay is in one piece from face to the base, with no pressed-out shapes of legs. The pressed leg was quicker and therefore cheaper to produce as more moulds were required for applied hollow legs or feet. Look also for moulded teeth and lips – the flat painted-on teeth appeared later, usually on Victorian pieces.

A Staffordshire Toby jug, handle repaired, 1820–40, 9¾in (25cm) high.
£320–380 / €470–560
$600–710 ⚷ SWO

A Landlord Toby jug, with original cover, c1860, 13in (33cm) high.
£850–950 / €1,250–1,400
$1,600–1,800 ⊞ JBL

A Staffordshire Toby jug, c1860, 8½in (21.5cm) high.
£330–370 / €480–540
$620–700 ⊞ RAN

A Staffordshire Mr Punch Toby jug, c1860, 12in (30.5cm) high.
£420–470 / €610–690
$790–880 ⊞ RAN

A Toby jug, his tricorn hat with a measuring cup, repaired, c1870, 9¾in (25cm) high.
£95–110 / €140–165
$175–200 ⚒ SWO

▶ **A Staffordshire Mr Pickwick Toby jug,** late 19thC, 8in (20.5cm) high.
£55–65 / €80–95
$105–125 ⚒ G(L)

A Snuff Taker Toby jug, with treacle glaze, c1870, 10in (25.5cm) high.
£70–80 / €100–115
$135–155 ⊞ IW

A Squire Toby jug, pipe missing, c1875, 10in (25.5cm) high.
£580–650 / €850–960
$1,100–1,250 ⊞ JBL

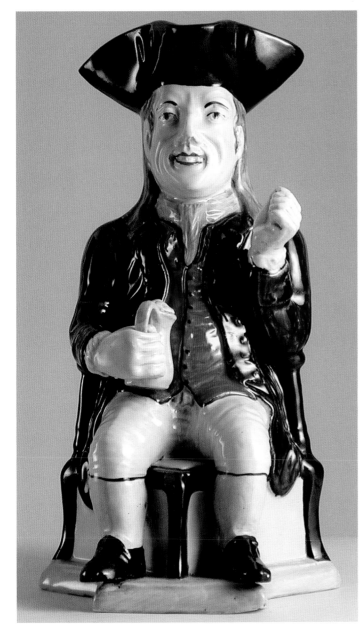

A **Squire Toby jug,** and a pipe, 1875–1925, 9½in (24cm) high.
£180–210 / €260–310
$340–390 ⚲ SJH

◄ A **Squire Toby jug,** 1875–1925, 10¾in (27.5cm) high.
£90–100 / €130–145
$170–190 ⚲ WW

A **Toby jug,** by Allertons, c1900, 6in (15cm) high.
£80–90 / €115–130
$150–170 ⊞ DHA

A **Toby jug,** North Country or Scottish, c1900, 10in (25.5cm) high.
£260–310 / €380–450
$490–580 ⚲ SAS

A majolica *Tit-Bits* **Toby jug,** by William Ault, commemorating WWI, c1917, 10in (25.5cm) high.
£360–400 / €530–590
$680–750 ⊞ JBL

Tureens

A Marieburg faïence tureen and cover, painted with Meadow pattern, the cover with pomegranate knop, damaged and repaired, marked, Swedish, 1758–66, 15¾in (40cm) diam.
£1,300–1,550 / €1,900–2,250
$2,450–2,900 ⚖ BUK

A Stralsund faïence tureen, cover and stand, painted with hops and vines, the cover with a pear knop, marked 'B', German, c1770, 11¾in (30cm) wide.
£2,600–3,100 / €3,800–4,550
$4,900–5,800 ⚖ BUK

▶ **A Leeds Pottery creamware soup tureen and cover,** knop missing, impressed mark, 1775–80, 13¾in (35cm) wide.
£280–330 / €410–480
$530–620 ⚖ WW

A Vienna porcelain tureen and cover, painted with panels of flowers, with a lemon knop, cover restored, shield mark, Austrian, c1780, 5½in (14cm) high.
£260–310 / €380–450
$490–580 ⚖ SWO

▶ **A creamware tureen, cover, stand and ladle,** transfer-printed with birds, c1780, 8in (20.5cm) wide.
£1,450–1,600 / €2,100–2,350
$2,700–3,000 ⊞ HOW

A Bow porcelain tureen and cover, painted with floral sprays, with a bird knop, the handles with female masks, restored, c1760, 9½in (24cm) high.
£200–240 / €290–350
$380–450 ⚖ SWO

A Derby porcelain tureen and cover, painted with panels of fruit, on gilt claw feet, handles repaired, marked, c1815, 7¼in (18.5cm) wide.
£220–260 / €320–380
$410–490 ⚲ **G(L)**

A pottery tureen and cover, probably Herculaneum, transfer-printed with Etruscan bands, c1815, 13¾in (35cm) wide.
£90–105 / €130–150
$170–200 ⚲ **L&E**

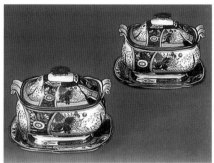

A pair of porcelain tureens, covers and stands, possibly Davenport, decorated in the Imari palette, early 19thC, 4¾in (12cm) high.
£350–420 / €510–610
$660–790 ⚲ **HYD**

A pottery tureen, transfer-printed with The Wine Makers pattern, c1820, 16in (40.5cm) wide.
£1,550–1,750
€2,250–2,600
$2,900–3,300 ⊞ **GN**

◄ **A pair of Grainger's Worcester porcelain dessert tureens, covers and stands,** with swan knops, 1815–20, stands 9in (23cm) diam.
£1,100–1,250
€1,600–1,850
$2,100–2,350 ⊞ **JAK**

LOCATE THE SOURCE
The source of each illustration in Miller's can be found by checking the code letters below each caption with the Key to Illustrations, pages 311–314.

► **A pottery two-handled tureen,** transfer-printed with Holywell Cottage pattern, cover missing, c1825, 14in (35.5cm) wide.
£160–190 / €240–280
$300–360 ⚲ **GAK**

◄ **A pair of Derby porcelain sauce tureens and covers,** painted with roses and gilt bands, one crazed and one stained, c1820, 6¾in (17cm) wide.
£160–190 / €240–280
$300–360 ⚒ SWO

An Enoch Wood pottery tureen, cover and stand, transfer-printed with Sherborne Castle and Cokelthorpe Park, from the Grapevine Border series, c1820, 7in (18cm) wide.
£350–400 / €510–580
$650–750 ⊞ GN

Enoch Wood

Enoch Wood (1759–1840) of Burslem, Staffordshire, is often described as father of the potteries. Between 1783 and 1790 he was in partnership with Ralph Wood, and from 1790 to 1818 he worked with J. Caldwell. Thereafter the firm was known as Enoch Wood & Sons and produced stoneware and earthernware, although it is thought some porcelain may have been made.

A pair of porcelain tureens, covers and stands, c1820, 8in (20.5cm) diam.
£1,000–1,150 / €1,450–1,700
$1,900–2,150 ⊞ DAN

► **An Enoch Wood pottery vegetable tureen and cover,** decorated with Lanercost Priory pattern, with lion knop, 1820, 9in (23cm) wide.
£450–500 / €660–730
$850–940 ⊞ GN

An Enoch Wood pottery vegetable tureen and cover, with lion knop, from the Grapevine Border series, c1820, 11in (28cm) wide.
£570–640 / €840–940
$1,050–1,200 ⊞ GN

► **A pair of H. & R. Daniel porcelain tureens, covers and stands,** painted with roses, the covers with butterfly knops, c1824, 7in (18cm) high.
£2,000–2,250 / €2,900–3,300
$3,750–4,200 ⊞ JOR

◄ **A Staffordshire pottery tureen and cover,** in the form of a hen and chicks, 19thC, 6in (15cm) high.
£610–680 / €890–1,000
$1,150–1,300 ⊞ ReN

A pair of Bloor Derby porcelain sauce tureens, covers and stands, decorated with masks and flowers, printed marks, c1830, 8¾in (22cm) wide.
£520–620 / €760–910
$980–1,150 ↗ WW

A Meissen porcelain soup tureen and cover, painted with flowers, crossed swords mark, German, mid-19thC, (43.5cm) wide.
£360–430 / €530–630
$680–810 ↗ WW

A Victorian pottery child's tureen, cover and stand, decorated with Persia pattern, 6in (15cm) wide.
£25–30 / €40–45
$50–55 ⊞ BAC

A pair of Staffordshire pottery tureens and covers, in the form of pigeons, damaged, late 19thC, 8¾in (22cm) wide.
£660–770 / €970–1,150
$1,250–1,450 ↗ SWO

A Clarice Cliff pottery Bizarre tureen, decorated with Solomon's Seal pattern, 1931, 6in (15cm) wide.
£300–340 / €440–500
$560–640 ⊞ TAC

◄ **A Staffordshire pottery tureen and cover,** in the form of a hen on a nest, late 19thC, 9½in (24cm) wide.
£120–140 / €175–210
$220–260 ↗ SJH

Vases

A Spode porcelain spill vase, painted with a bird in a nest, with gilt decoration, repaired, painted mark, c1815, 4½in (11.5cm) high.
£100–120 / €145–175
$180–210 ✒ G(L)

A pearlware vase, printed in Pratt colours with flowers, late 18thC, 5½in (14cm) high.
£120–140 / €175–210
$220–260 ✒ G(L)

A Spode porcelain spill vase, painted with flowers, with gilt beaded borders, c1820, 6¼in (16cm) high.
£270–320 / €400–470
$500–600 ✒ WW

A Spode porcelain vase, painted with flowers, slight damage, pattern No. 1166, c1820, 6¼in (16cm) high.
£200–240 / €290–350
$370–450 ✒ G(L)

A pair of Worcester Flight, Barr & Barr porcelain spill vases, painted with butterflies and flowers, damaged, c1820, 3½in (9cm) high.
£600–720 / €880–1,050
$1,150–1,350 ✒ G(L)

A Mayer & Newbold porcelain vase, the reserve painted with a flower spray, rim regilded, 1820–25, 5in (12.5cm) high.
£430–490 / €630–720
$810–920 ⊞ CoS

A pair of Worcester Flight, Barr & Barr porcelain miniature vases, painted with exotic birds, slight damage, script marks, c1825, 2in (5cm) high.
£1,300–1,550 / €1,900–2,250
$2,450–2,900 ⚒ G(L)

A Staffordshire porcelain vase, c1840, 8in (20.5cm) high.
£400–450 / €590–660
$750–840 ⊞ DAN

A Meissen porcelain vase, encrusted with flowers and fruit, German, c1860, 10in (25.5cm) high.
£1,650–1,850 / €2,400–2,700
$3,100–3,450 ⊞ MAA

A pair of Pinder, Bourne & Co faïence vases, decorated by Mary M. Arding with daffodils, 1875–82, 9½in (24cm) high.
£160–190 / €240–280
$300–360 ⚒ G(L)

◄ **A Wedgwood pottery amphora-shaped two-handled vase,** painted with a country scene, 1870–80, 7in (18cm) high.
£95–110 / €140–160
$180–210 ⚒ TMA

► **A Belleek porcelain Fish spill vase,** Irish, First Period, 1863–90, 7in (18cm) high.
£580–650 / €850–960
$1,100–1,250 ⊞ MLa

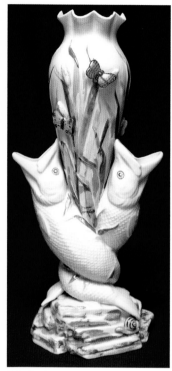

A Belleek porcelain Double Fish vase, Irish, First Period, 1863–90, 8in (20.5cm) high.
£2,600–2,900 / €3,850–4,250
$4,900–5,500 ⊞ MLa

▶ **A Linthorpe Pottery vase,** signed 'H. T.' and Christopher Dresser facsimile signature, c1880, 8in (20.5cm) high.
£670–750 / €980–1,100
$1,250–1,400 ⊞ HUN

A Meissen porcelain vase, German, c1880, 5½in (14cm) high.
£1,150–1,300 / €1,700–1,900
$2,150–2,450 ⊞ MAA

▶ **A pair of Davenport porcelain vases,** painted with insects, butterflies and grasses, with handles in the form of gilt butterflies, c1880, 9½in (24cm) high.
£160–190 / €240–280
$300–360 ➤ DA

A pair of Meissen porcelain vases, German, c1870, 11¾in (30cm) high.
£4,900–5,500 / €7,200–8,100
$9,200–10,300 ⊞ MAA

A pair of Meissen porcelain vases, decorated with pastoral scenes, German, c1880, 11½in (29cm) high.
£6,200–6,900 / €9,000–10,100
$11,700–13,000 ⊞ MAA

An Alexander Lauder pottery vase, decorated with scrolling foliage and flowers, 1891, 16in (40.5cm) high.
£420–470 / €620–690
$790–880 ⊞ MMc

A pair of Derby Crown Porcelain Co vases, decorated and gilt with flowers, dated 1887, 8¾in (22cm) high.
£280–330 / €410–480
$530–620 ⚒ SWO

A pottery vase, attributed to Bretby, c1890, 9in (20.5cm) high.
£145–165 / €210–240
$270–310 ⊞ HUN

◀ **A miniature *pâte-sur-pâte* vase,** probably Limoges, French, c1900, 3in (7.5cm) high.
£200–220 / €290–320
$370–410 ⊞ ANO

A Burmantofts pottery vase, shape No. 94, c1895, 5in (12.5cm) high.
£55–65 / €80–95
$100–120 ⊞ WAC

▶ **A *pâte-sur-pâte* vase,** Continental, c1900, 4¼in (11cm) high.
£310–350
€460–510
$580–660
⊞ ANO

A Locke & Co, Worcester *pâte-sur-pâte* vase, c1900, 7½in (19cm) high.
£360–400 / €530–590
$680–750 ⊞ JUP

A Doulton Lambeth pottery vase, both sides decorated with a girl, early 20thC, 8¾in (22cm) high.
£200–240 / €290–350
$380–450 ✕ G(L)

A Royal Worcester porcelain posy vase, painted by James Stinton, signed, c1910, 3in (7.5cm) high.
£490–550 / €720–810
$920–1,050 ⊞ GRI

A Bretby pottery vase, by Malcolm Haslam, c1906, 12½in (32cm) high.
£260–290 / €380–430
$490–550 ⊞ HUN

Sets/pairs

Unless otherwise stated, any description which refers to 'a set' or 'a pair' includes a guide price for the entire set or the pair, even though the illustration may show only a single item.

A Bretby pottery two-handled vase, c1908, 10in (25.5cm) high.
£260–290 / €380–430
$490–550 ⊞ HUN

A pair of Royal Worcester porcelain vases, with stylized enamel decoration, c1915, 8in (20.5cm) high.
£260–310 / €380–450
$490–580 ✕ SWO

A Quimper faïence vase, c1920, 9in (23cm) high.
£250–280 / €360–410
$460–520 ⊞ MLL

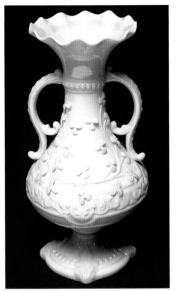

A Belleek porcelain Finner vase, Irish, Third Period, 1926–46, 9in (23cm) high.
£890–990 / €1,300–1,450
$1,650–1,850 ⊞ MLa

A Zsolnay Pecs bronze-metal-mounted vase, Hungarian, 1920s, 4¼in (11cm) high.
£860–1,000 / €1,250–1,450
$1,600–1,800 ⚒ TMA

A Crown Ducal pottery vase, by Charlotte Rhead, decorated with tube-lined flowers, printed marks, c1930, 8¾in (22cm) high.
£170–200 / €250–290
$320–370 ⚒ L&E

A pair of Shelley pottery vases, shape No. 946, c1930, 5in (12.5cm) high.
£30–35 / €45–50
$55–65 ⊞ HeA

A pair of Carlton Ware pottery vases, decorated with stylized hollyhocks, c1930, 9in (23cm) high.
£320–380 / €470–560
$600–710 ⚒ CHTR

A Pilkington's Royal Lancastrian pottery vase, by W. S. Mycock, 1932, 12in (30.5cm) high.
£450–500 / €660–740
$850–940 ⊞ C&W

A Fieldings Crown Devon pottery two-handled vase, painted with spring flowers, 1930s, 5in (12.5cm) high.
£60–70 / €90–105
$110–130 ⚒ TMA

◀ **A pottery vase,** by Alice Teichner, with Chinese-style decoration, signed, c1937, 5in (12.5cm) high.
£75–85 / €110–125
$140–160 ⊞ KES

A Crown Devon pottery vase,
1930s, 8in (20.5cm) high.
£850–950 / €1,250–1,400
$1,600–1,800 ⊞ BEV

A Pilkington's Royal Lancastrian pottery vase, 1948–57,
9½in (24cm) high.
£155–175 / €230–260
$290–330 ⊞ C&W

◄ **A Belleek porcelain Rose Isle vase,** Irish, Fourth Period, 1946–1955,
30in (76cm) high.
£760–850 / €1,100–1,250
$1,450–1,600 ⊞ MLa

A Quimper faïence vase, 1940s,
5½in (14cm) high.
£40–45 / €55–65
$75–85 ⊞ SER

A Poole Pottery vase, No. 542,
inscribed 'X/PY', mid-20thC,
9¼in (23.5cm) wide.
£180–210 / €260–310
$340–390 ⚒ SWO

Prices

The price ranges quoted in
this book reflect the average
price a purchaser might expect
to pay for a similar item. The
price will vary according to
the condition, rarity, size,
popularity, provenance, colour
and restoration of the item,
and this must be taken into
account when assessing
values. Don't forget that if
you are selling it is quite likely
that you will be offered less
than the price range.

A majolica spill vase, decorated with
fish, mid-20thC, 4in (10cm) high.
£60–70 / €90–100
$110–130 ⚒ MUL

A Gambone pottery bottle vase,
1970s, 5¼in (13.5cm) high.
£110–130 / €160–190
$200–240 ⚒ SWO

Index to Advertisers

Antiques Magazine . . . .*front end paper*

Mervyn Carey .147

Chinasearch Ltd 273

Andrew Dando 207

Julian Eade 117

Caren Fine 183

Goss & Crested China Club . . . .

& Museum 63

Hallidays 41

John Howard at Heritage . . . .

. . . .*front end paper*

William R. & . . . .

Teresa F. Kurau . . . .*back end paper*

Lambert & Foster 257

Miller's Publications 305

Gillian Neale . . . . .43, *back jacket*

Potteries Antique Centre 119

Potteries Specialist Auctions 119

Special Auction Services . . .*front end paper*

Tablewhere Ltd 275

Louis Taylor Auctioneers & Valuers 69

Islwyn Watkins 27

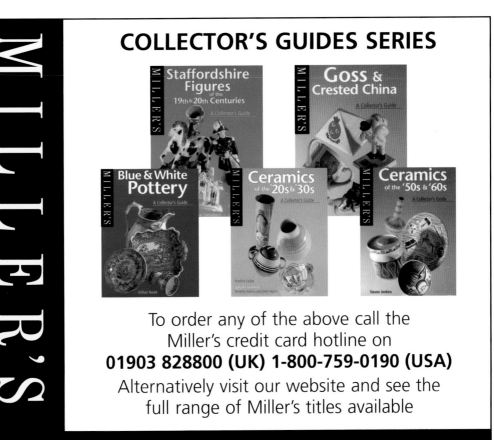

Glossary

Below are explanations of some of the terms you will come across in this book.

acid etching: technique involving treatment of glass with hydrofluoric acid, giving a matt or frosted finish.

agateware: type of pottery resembling agate as a result of the partial blending of different-coloured clays.

applied decoration: surface ornament made separately and applied to the body of an object.

basalt: unglazed, very hard, fine-grained stoneware stained with cobalt and manganese oxides, developed by Wedgwood c1768.

biscuit (bisque): unglazed porcelain or earthenware fired once only. Popular for neoclassical porcelain figures because it suggests classical marble sculptures. Also used for making dolls' heads.

bocage: encrustations of flowers, grass and moss generally used to decorate the supporting plinths of ceramic figures.

body: the material from which a piece of pottery or porcelain is produced, although the term paste is more often used for porcelain. Also refers to the main part of a piece.

bone china: a soft-paste porcelain consisting of petuntse (china stone), kaolin (china clay) and calcined bone.

brownware: salt-glazed brown stoneware, especially that made in Nottingham, Derby and elsewhere in England.

cachepot: ornamental container for flowerpots. A smaller form of jardiniére.

cameo: a design in contrasting low relief, as found in **jasper ware**.

cartouche: decorative frame in the form of a scroll of paper with rolled ends, usually surrounding an inscription or pictorial decoration.

celadon: semi-opaque, green-tinted glaze used first on ware made during the Chinese Sung Dynasty (960–1280).

chinoiserie: decoration consisting of Oriental-style figures and motifs, such as pagodas, pavilions, birds and lotus flowers, that permeated Europe from the Far East; prevalent from the late 17th century.

cloisonné: enamel fired into compartments (cloisons) formed by metal wires.

cobalt: basic blue colouring, originally imported from Saxony, Germany, extremely important in early ceramics as it stood up to the extreme heat of the glazing kiln.

cow creamer: milk jugs modelled to resemble a cow. The tail would be the handle, the mouth the spout, and milk was poured into the body through an opening in its back.

crackleware: (craquelure) deliberate cracked effect achieved by firing ceramics to a precise temperature.

crazing: tiny, undesirable surface cracks caused by shrinking or other technical defects in a glaze.

creamware: cream-coloured earthenware with a transparent lead glaze, developed by Wedgwood c1760.

Delftware: tin-glazed earthenware from Delft, in the Netherlands, refers to British ware when it does not have a capital letter.

enamel: form of decoration involving the application of metallic oxides to metal, ceramics, or glass in paste form or in an oil-based mixture, which is then usually fired for decorative effect.

faïence: tin-glazed earthenware usually applied to France and Germany and also to later Italian ware. The name is derived from Faenza, one of the biggest pottery-making centres in Italy. (Similar to **mailolica** and delftware).

fairings: mementoes of a visit to the fair, they were small porcelain items manufactured mainly in Germany in the last half of the last century and the early part of the 20th for the English market.

famille rose: palette used on 18th-century Chinese porcelain, which includes a dominant opaque pink. Much copied in Europe.

feldspar porcelain: a tough form of bone china which contains pure feldspar. Coalport were the first to sucessfully produce this type of porcelain.

flambé: glaze made from copper, usually deep crimson, flecked with blue or purple, and often faintly crackled.

flatbacks: pottery figures with flat, unmodelled and undecorated backs, designed to be viewed from the front only. They were intended as mantelpiece decorations and produced mainly in the 19thC by Staffordshire Potteries.

flow blue: blurred blue transfer-printed decoration on Staffordshire earthenware.

fluting: a pattern of concave grooves repeated in vertical, parallel lines. The inverse of **gadrooning**.

gadrooning: decorative edging consisting of a series of convex, vertical or spiralling curves.

hard-paste porcelain: pure white, translucent porcelain approximating to oriental 'china'. Has a metallic ring when struck and is immensely strong in spite of its apparent delicacy. It was first made in China using the combination of kaolin (china clay 50%), petuntse (china stone 25%) and quartz (25%). The strength is acquired by ageing the paste, kaolin and china stone before firing at high temperature.

Imari: Japanese porcelain with dense decoration, based on brocade patterns, in a palette that is dominated by underglaze blue, iron-red, green, manganese, yellow and gold.

incised decoration: decoration that is cut into the body of an object with a sharp metal point.

ironstone: tough earthenware made from mineral base.

jasper ware: hard, fine-grained, coloured stoneware developed by Wedgwood in the 1770s.

knop: literally the bud of a flower, a term used to describe the decorative finial on teapot and vase lids.

lead glaze: clear glaze generally composed of siliceous sand, salt, soda and potash mixed with a lead component.

lustre ware: pottery with an irridescent surface produced using metallic pigments, usually silver or copper.

maiolica: tin-glazed earthenware produced in Italy from 15th–18thC.

majolica: corruption of the term maiolica, which refers to a type of 19thC earthenware in elaborate forms with thick, brightly coloured glazes.

moulded: tableware and figures made from pressing the body (stoneware, earthenware, porcelain etc.) between two moulds, allowing great freedom of shape and variety of decoration which could be repeated identically.

Parian: semi-matt porcelain made with **feldspar** and therefore not requiring a separate glaze. Also called statuary porcelain, it became known as Parian because of its similarity to the white marble from the Greek island of Paros.

pâte-sur-pâte: a kind of porcelain decoration involving low-relief designs carved in **slip** and applied in layers to a contrasting body.

redware: stoneware, generally unglazed and often decorated with applied motifs in relief.

reeding: a milled edge, or parallel pattern in the form of reeds.

relief decoration: decoration that stands out from the surface of any object and is usually described, according to its depth, as low-relief or high-relief.

reserve: a self-contained blank area within a pattern, reserved for other decoration.

saltglaze: thin, glassy glaze applied to some stoneware and produced by throwing salt into the kiln at the height of firing. The glaze may show a pitted surface, known as 'orange peel'.

Satsuma: type of Japanese pottery with elaborate decoration, crackle glaze and heavy gilding named after the Japanese port where it was made.

sgraffito: form of ceramic decoration incised through a coloured slip, revealing the ground beneath.

slip: smooth dilution of clay and water used in the making and decoration of pottery.

slipware: type of red-bodied earthenware decorated largely with slip in contrasting colours.

spill vase or jar: wide-mouthed, often straight-sided jar to hold strips of wood, paper, etc. to light pipes from the fire.

terracotta lightly fired red earthenware, usually unglazed.

tin glaze: glassy glaze made opaque by the addition of tin oxide and commonly used on earthenware.

transfer-printing: the process of transferring a single-colour image (a transfer), printed from an engraved copper plate on to tissue paper, on to the unglazed surface of a ceramic object.

tube-lining: type of ceramic decoration in which thin trails of slip are applied as outlines to areas of coloured glaze.

tyg: a drinking pot often with two or more handles.

underglaze: colour or design painted before the application of the glaze on a ceramic object.

Directory of Restorers

UK & IRELAND

Mary Acton Ceramic Restoration & Conservation,
Dorset Tel: 01258 880712/88096

Appleton Antiques,
Harrogate & Middlesburgh Tel: 01642 316417

David Battams,
China Repairs & Restorations Tel: 07956 832375
info@chinarepairsandrestorations.com

Bendall Ceramic Conservation,
Suffolk Tel: 01449 768879

Regina Bogossian,
Ballinmona Park, Waterford, Co Waterford
Tel: (0) 5187 4429

Bouke de Vries Ceramic and Glass Conservation,
41 Wallingford Avenue, London, W10 6PZ
Tel: 0208 960 8010 bouke@btinternet.com

Bradford Conservation & Research,
West Yorkshire Tel: 01274 235210

Ellen L. Breheny,
Edinburgh Tel: 0131 667 2620
ellen@breheny.com

China Restore Studio,
London Tel: 020 7731 3226

The Cliveden Conservation Workshop Ltd,
The Tennis Courts, Cliveden Estate, Taplow, Maidenhead,
Berkshire, SL6 0JA Tel: 01628 604721
cliveden@clivedenconservation.co.uk
www.clivedenconservation.co.uk

Conservation Services: Julia Park,
Suffolk Tel: 01473 832896
julia.park@conservationservices.co.uk
www.conservationservices.co.uk

The Conservation Studio,
Oxfordshire Tel: 01844 214498
sandbill@conservation.fsnet.co.uk

Roger Dunford,
Sunny Inch Crafts, 25 Cotterhill Road, Downpatrick,
Co Down Tel: (0) 28 4461 5571

Glebe Hall Studios,
Old Killermogh Rectory, Rathmakelly Glebe, Ballacoll,
Co Laois Tel: (0) 502 34105/34154

Phillippa Hinde,
The Mill House, Milltown, Rathkenny, Navan, Co Meath
Tel: (0) 4654 686

Jackfield Conservation Studio Ltd,
Jackfield Tile Museum, Ironbridge, Telford, Shropshire,
TF8 7LJ Tel: 01952 883720
lesley@jackfield.fsbusiness.co.uk

Scott Lovering,
Kent Tel: 01233 720550

Manor House Fine Arts,
73 Pontcanna Street, Cardiff, CF11 9HS
Tel: 029 20 227787
services@manorhousefinearts.co.uk

Matilda Mitchell China Conservation,
Wellgate, Morebattle, Kelso, Roxburghshire, TD5 8QV
Tel: 01573 440687 emandee@care4free.net

Valerie McCoy,
Restoration Studio, Seven Churches, Glendalough,
Co Wicklow Tel: (0) 4044 5125

Helen Moody Conservation and Collections Care,
Bristol Tel: 0117 949 3222 helenmoody@casterbridge.net

Sarah Peek Conservation of Ceramics,
Glass and Enamels
Redwins, Rear of 6 Preston Park Avenue, Brighton,
East Sussex, BN1 6HJ Tel: 01273 243 744
conservation@sarahpeek.co.uk

PJD Ceramics Ltd
Vale of Glamorgan Tel: 01446 748153
pete@pjdceramics.fsnet.co.uk

Plowden and Smith Ltd
190 St Ann's Hill, Wandsworth, London, SW18 2RT
Tel: 020 8874 4005 or 07889 828777
info@plowden-smith.com www.plowden-smith.com

The Porcelain Restorers,
West Sussex Tel: 01243 641784
davidcaldwell@supanet.com

QW Conservation,
London Tel: 020 7498 5938 stylish.moves@virgin.net

Rattee and Kett,
Digital Park, Station Road, Longstanton, Cambridge,
CB4 5FB Tel: 01954 262632 rattee&kett@mowlem.com
www.ratteeandkett.com

Ravensdale Studios,
Staffordshire Tel: 01782 836810
restore@ravensdalestudios.co.uk

Restoration Works
Tel: 01865 761033

Restorer of Porcelain,
Hampshire Tel: 023 9282 9863
maryrose@ceramics-restoration.com
www.ceramics-restoration.com

Rogers de Rin,
76 Royal Hospital Road, Paradise Walk, Chelsea, London,
SW3 4HN Tel: 020 7352 9007
rogersderin@rogersderin.co.uk www.rogersderin.co.uk

Desiree Short,
38 North Great George's Street, Dublin 1
Tel: (0) 1872 2285

The Traditional Studio,
Hertfordshire Tel: 01707 332084 or 07748 224287
viki@traditionalstudio.fsnet.co.uk

Helen Warren Restoration,
Kent Tel: 01580 713500
chinarestoration@helenwarren.com www.helenwarren.com

Hannah West,
Oxfordshire Tel: 01993 705709 or 07963 630898

West Dean College,
West Sussex Tel: 01243 811301

USA

Antique & Art Restoration by Wiebold,
413 Terrace Place, Terrace Park, Ohio 45174
Tel: 513 831 2541 wiebold@eos.net www.wiebold.com

Association of Restorers,
8 Medford Pl, New Hartford, NY 13413 Tel: 315 733 1952
www.assoc-restorers.com

Bradshaw & Whelan Restoration and Conservation,
PO Box 18521, Asheville, NC 28814
Toll free tel (in US): 1 877 244 0716
International tel: 828 253 1829 ceramics5@charter.net

Ceramic Restorations of Westchester, Inc.,
8 John Walsh Blvd., Suite 412, Peekskill, New York 10566
Tel: 914 734 8410

CP Restoration,
Christine & Paul Peltier, 6 South 3rd Avenue, Taftville,
CT 06380 Tel: 860 886 1870 cprest@snet.net

Just Enterprises,
679 Santa Ysabel, Los Osos, CA 93402
Tel: 805 441 3991

Keller China Restoration,
Corey and Jo Ann Keller, 4825 Winddsor Drive,
Rapid City, SD 57702 Tel: 605 342 6756
kellerchina@rushmore.com

Precious Pieces by Suzanne,
Henderson, Nevada Tel: 702 451 9489/877 451 9489

Restoration by Heart,
Los Angeles, California Tel: 213 427 4338
kirel@pacbell.net

Restoration Services,
PO Box 104, Webster City, Iowa 50595
Tel: 866 353 1122 or 515 832 2437

Restoration Services,
9 Mystic Street, Arlington, MA 02474
Tel: 781 648 3322

Sidmore Antiques,
PO Box 127, 600 Main St, Dumont, IA 50625

Directory of Specialists

If you require a valuation for an item it is advisable to check whether the dealer or specialist will carry out this service, and whether there is a charge. Please mention Miller's when making an enquiry. Having found a specialist who will carry out your valuation, it is best to send a description and photograph of the item to them, together with a stamped addressed envelope for the reply. A valuation by telephone is not possible. Most dealers are only too happy to help you with your enquiry, however, they are very busy people and consideration of the above points would be welcomed.

UK & IRELAND

Judi Bland Antiques
Tel: 01276 857576 or 01536 724145
18th & 19th century English Toby jugs

Aurea Carter, P.O. Box 44134, London SW6 3YX
Tel: 020 7731 3486
aureacarter@englishceramics.com
www.englishceramics.com
18th and early 19th century English pottery and porcelain

Bac to Basic Antiques Tel: 07787 105609
bcarruthers@waitrose.com
Late 19th and early 20th century porcelain, Doulton and Parian ware. Royal, military and exhibition commemoratives. Goss and Crested china.

Barling Porcelain Tel: 01621 890058
stuart@barling.uk.com www.barling.uk.com
Royal Crown Derby and Royal Worcester porcelain

Bellhouse Antiques
Tel: 01268 710415 bellhouse.antiques@virgin.net
18th & 19th century Meissen

Beth, GO 43-44, Alfies Antique Market,
13-25 Church Street, Marylebone, London, NW8 8DT
Tel: 020 7723 5613 or 0777 613 6003
19th & 20th century ceramics

Beverley, 30 Church Street, Marylebone, London, NW8 8EP
Tel: 020 7262 1576 or 07776136003
19th & 20th century ceramics

David Brower, 113 Kensington Church Street,
London, W8 7LN Tel: 0207 221 4155
David@davidbrower-antiques.com
www.davidbrower-antiques.com
Meissen, KPM, European porcelain and Oriental ceramics

Chinasearch, P.O. Box 1202, Kenilworth, Warwickshire,
CV8 2WW Tel: 01926 512402
info@chinasearch.co.uk www.chinasearch.co.uk
Discontinued dinner, tea and collectable ware

The Crested China Company, Highfield,
Windmill Hill, Driffield, East Yorkshire, YO25 5YP
Tel: 0870 300 1 300
dt@thecrestedchinacompany.com
www.thecrestedchinacompany.com
Goss and Crested china

Andrew Dando, 34 Market Street, Bradford on Avon,
Wiltshire, BA15 1LL Tel: 01225 865444
andrew@andrewdando.co.uk www.andrewdando.co.uk
English, Oriental and Continental porcelain

Sandra D Deas
Tel: 01333 360 214 or 07713 897 482
Scottish ceramics including Wemyss

Delf Stream Gallery Tel: 07974 926137
nic19422000@yahoo.co.uk www.delfstreamgallery.com
19th–20th century Art pottery

Delphi Antiques, Powerscourt Townhouse Centre,
South William Street, Dublin 2, Republic of Ireland
Tel: 1 679 0331
19th century Irish, English and Continental porcelain

Julian Eade Tel: 01865 300349 or 07973 542971
Doulton Lambeth stoneware and signed Burslem wares

Fair Finds Antiques, Rait Village Antiques Centre, Rait,
Perthshire, PH2 7RT, Scotland Tel: 01821 670379
Wemyss ware

Gazelles Ltd, Hampshire Tel: 023 8081 1610
allan@gazelles.co.uk www.gazelles.co.uk
Art Deco ceramics

Glebe Antiques, Robert Rankine
Tel: 01259 214559 or 07050 234577
rrglebe@aol.com
Wemyss ware, Dunmore and related Scottish pottery

The Goss & Crested China Club & Museum,
62 Murray Road, Horndean, Hampshire, PO8 9JL
Tel: (023) 9259 7440 info@gosschinaclub.demon.co.uk
www.gosscrestedchina.co.uk
Goss & Crested china

Guest & Gray, 1-7 Davies Mews, London, W1K 5AB
Tel: 020 7408 1252
info@chinese-porcelain-art.com
www.chinese-porcelain-art.com
Chinese porcelain

Hallidays Tel: 07763 823274
blueandwhite@btinternet.com www.4blueandwhite.com
Blue and white transferware 1780–1840

Muir Hewitt Art Deco Originals, Halifax Antiques Centre,
Queens Road Mills, Queens Road/Gibbet Street, Halifax,
Yorkshire, HX1 4LR Tel: 01422 347377
muir.hewitt@virgin.net www.muirhewitt.com
Art Deco ceramics

Jonathan Horne, 66c Kensington Church Street,
London, W8 4BY Tel: 020 7221 5658
JH@jonathanhorne.co.uk www.jonathanhorne.co.uk
Early English pottery

Tony Horsley Antiques, P.O. Box 3127, Brighton, BN1 5SS
Tel: 01273 550770
Candle extinguishers, Royal Worcester and other fine porcelain

Houghton Antiques
Tel: 01480 461887 or 07803 716842
19th & 20th century ceramics

John Howard, Heritage, 6 Market Place, Woodstock, Oxon
OX20 1TA Tel: 0870 444 0678 or 07831 850544
Howards@antiquepottery.co.uk www.antiquepottery.co.uk
Staffordshire pottery, creamware, lustreware and Gaudy Welsh pottery

Rick Hubbard Art Deco, 3 Tee Court, Bell Street, Romsey,
Hampshire, SO51 8GY Tel: 01794 513133
or 07767 267607
rick@rickhubbard-artdeco.co.uk
www.rickhubbard-artdeco.co.uk
20th century ceramics & collectables

Clive & Lynne Jackson
Tel: 01242 254375 or 07710 239 351
Parian ware

Jupiter Antiques, P.O. Box 609, Rottingdean,
East Sussex, BN2 7FW Tel: 01273 302865
English porcelain from 18th century factories and Royal Worcester and Royal Crown Derby

Marion Langham Tel: 028 895 41247
marion@ladymarion.co.uk www.ladymarion.co.uk
Belleek

Law Fine Art Tel: 01635 860033 info@lawfineart.co.uk
www.lawfineart.co.uk
Ceramic auctions

Lewis & Lewis Deco Tel: 07739 904681
lewis_robin@hotmail.com
Art Deco ceramics

Louis Taylor, Britannia House, 10 Town Road, Hanley,
Stoke-on-Trent, ST1 2QG Tel: 01782 214111
Doulton and Beswick ceramic auctions

Lovers of Blue & White, Steeple Morden, Royston,
Hertfordshire, SG8 0RN Tel: 01763 853 800
china@blueandwhite.com www.blueandwhite.com
Antique English china and pottery, transferware and an antique china replacement service

Marsh-McNamara Tel: 07790 759162
19th & 20th century ceramics

David March, Abbots Leigh, Bristol, Gloucestershire, BS8
Tel: 0117 937 2422
18th century English porcelain figures

Mere Antiques, 13 Fore Street, Topsham, Exeter, Devon,
EX3 0HF Tel: 01392 874224
Oriental porcelain

Millers Antiques Ltd, Netherbrook House,
86 Christchurch Road, Ringwood,
Hampshire, BH24 1DR Tel: 01425 472062
mail@millers-antiques.co.uk
www.millers-antiques.co.uk
Majolica and Quimper

Gillian Neale Antiques, P.O. Box 247, Aylesbury,
Buckinghamshire, HP20 1JZ
Tel: 01296 423754 or 07860 638700
gillianneale@aol.com www.gilliannealeantiques.co.uk
British transfer-printed pottery 1790–1900

Janice Paull, P.O. Box 100, Kenilworth, Warwickshire,
CV8 IJX Tel: 351 282799701 or 07876 284647
janicepaull@yahoo.com www.janicepaull.com
Mason's & other English ironstone china c1790–1890

Potteries Specialist Auctions, 271 Waterloo Road,
Cobridge, Stoke-on-Trent, Staffordshire,
ST6 3HR Tel: 01782 286622
www.potteriesauctions.com
Ceramics and 20th century collectables auctions

Potteries Antique Centre, 271 Waterloo Road,
Cobridge, Stoke-on-Trent, Staffordshire,
ST6 3HR Tel: 01782 201455
sales@potteriesantiquecentre.com
www.potteriesantiquecentre.com
*Wedgwood, Royal Doulton, Beswick, Wade, Moorcroft and
all types of pottery. One of the largest collections of rare
and discontinued pottery in the UK.*

Sylvia Powell Decorative Arts, Suite 400, Ceramic House,
571 Finchley Road, London, NW3 7BN
Tel: 020 8458 4543 or 07802 714998
*Doulton stoneware and other British and Continental
Art pottery*

Pretty Bizarre, 170 High Street, Deal, Kent, CT14 6BQ
Tel: 07973 794537
20th century ceramics

Rogers de Rin Antiques, 76 Royal Hospital Road, London,
SW3 4HN Tel: 029 7352 9007
rogersderin@rogersderin.co.uk www.rogersderin.co.uk
Specialising in Wemyss ware

Peter Scott Tel: 0117 986 8468 or 07850 639770
Blue & White transferware

Serendipity, 125 High Street, Deal, Kent, CT14 6BB
Tel: 01304 369165/01304 366536
dipityantiques@aol.com
Staffordshire pottery

Ian Sharp Antiques, 23 Front Street, Tynemouth,
Tyne & Wear, NE30 4DX Tel: 0191 296 0656
sharp@sharpantiques.com www.sharpantiques.com
*Tyneside & Wearside ceramics, including Sunderland lustre
and Maling ware*

Special Auction Services, Kennetholme, Midgham, Reading,
RG7 5UX Tel: 0118 971 2949
www.antiquestradegazette.com/sas
*Commemoratives auctions including royalty, political,
exhibition and war, pot lids & Prattware, fairings, Goss &
Crested china*

Tablewhere Ltd, 4 Queens Parade Close,
London, N11 3FY Tel: 0845 130 6111
www.tablewhere.co.uk
Tableware matching service

Roger de Ville Antiques
Tel: 01629 812496 or 07798 793857
www.rogerdeville.co.uk
*18th & 19th century British pottery, particularly Prattware,
creamware, saltglaze, Delft, blue & white printed wares,
Masons Ironstone & political & Royal Commemoratives*

Islwyn Watkins, Offa's Dyke Antique Centre, 4 High Street,
Knighton, Powys, LD7 1AT, Wales
Tel: 01547 520145
18th & 19th century pottery and Studio Pottery

Winson Antiques, Unit 11, Langston Priory Workshops,
Kingham, Oxfordshire, OX7 6UR
Tel: 01608 658856 or 07764 476776
www.clivepayne.co.uk
Mason's Ironstone china

USA

Back Alley Antiques, 128 E Kings Hwy, Shreveport,
LA 71104 Tel: 318 219 7440
www.backalleyantiques.com
*Antique pottery including McCoy, Red Wing, Van Briggle,
Hull, Hall, Bauer, Purinton and Maddox. Also Goebel and
Hummel figures*

Bishop and Daughter Antiques, P.O. Box 519,
Newtown Square, PA 19073 Tel: 610 359 1908
www.bishopantiques.com
*Victorian Staffordshire pottery animals, figures and
children's dishes, Royal Winton chintz and cottageware,
Royal Doulton figures, jugs, plates, as well as Clarice Cliff
and Susie Cooper items*

Danish Porcelain Imports, 214 West F Street, Joplin,
MO 64801 Tel: 866 228 9374 or 417 624 1798
sales@danishporcelain.com
www.danishporcelain.com
*Scandinavian ceramics including Royal Copenhagen and
Bing & Grondahl collector plates*

Caren Fine, 11603 Gowrie Court, Potomac,
Maryland 20854 Tel: 301 854 6262
caren4antiques@yahoo.com
20th century ceramics

Hopes Time & Again, Park West Station, P.O. Box 20784,
New York, NY 10025-1516
www.tias.com/stores/hta
19th & 20th century cups and saucers

Hyacinth House, P.O. Box 2261, Winchester, VA 22604
www.tias.com/stores/hyh
Late 19th & 20th century American china

Just Art Pottery, Greg and Lana Myroth,
6606 N Rustic Oak Ct, Peoria, IL 61614
Tel: 309 690 7966
gregmy@justartpottery.com www.justartpottery.com
Antique American Art pottery

William R. & Teresa F. Kurau, P.O. Box 457, Lampeter,
PA 17537 Tel: 717 464 0731
lampeter@epix.net www.historicalchina.com
Historical Staffordshire and collectors items

Limoges Antique Shop, 20 Post Office Avenue, Andover,
MA 01810 Tel: 978 470 8773
dlimoges@flash.net www.limogesantiques.com
Limoges, Paris and American Belleek

MBC Antiques, P.O. Box 200336, Austin,
TX 78720 Tel: 512 250 2621
info@mbcantiques.com www.mbcantiques.com
Staffordshire and other fine English china

The Meissen Shop, By appointment only,
205 Worth Avenue, Suite 311, Palm Beach, FL 33480
Tel: 561 832 2504 themeissenshop@aol.com
18th & 19th century Meissen

One of a Kind Antiques, Warehouse Gallery, Unit D,
36 Plains Road, Essex, CT 06426 Tel: 860 767 2150
www.oneofakindantiques.com
American and continental Art pottery

Pot O' Gold Antiques, P.O. Box 560, Allenwood,
NJ 08720 Tel: 732 528 6648
potogoldantiques@verizon.net
www.potogoldantiques.com
English transfer printed earthenware and pottery

Recollections by Arlene and Barry, 3823 Oceanside Road
East, Oceanside, NY 11572 Tel: 516 678 4652
recollects@usa.net www.recollects.com
Royal Doulton, Lambeth, Moorcroft and Shelley

Staffordshire Stateside Antiques, 118 Partridge Circle,
Winter Springs, FL 32708
www.staffordshirestateside.com
*Direct importer of 19th century English transfer printed
earthenware, ironstone and hand painted china*

Sweet Pea Antiques, 1265 Route 7 South, P.O. Box 468,
Bennington, Vermont 05201 Tel: 802 442 3336
www.sweetpea.net/sweetpea
English china, chintz and Art pottery

Westwood Antiques, 11814 Watercrest Lane,
Boca Raton, FL 33498
www.westwoodantiques.com
*Hand painted antique Limoges as well as American Belleek,
Pickard, Bavaria and Austria*

Key to Illustrations

Each illustration and descriptive caption is accompanied by a letter code. By referring to the following list of Auctioneers (denoted by ⚒) and Dealers (⊞) the source of any item may immediately be determined. Inclusion in this edition in no way constitutes or implies a contract or binding offer on the part of any of our contributors to supply or sell the goods illustrated, or similar articles, at the prices stated. Advertisers are denoted by †.

If you require a valuation for an item, it is advisable to check whether the dealer or specialist will carry out this service and if there is a charge. Please mention Miller's when making an enquiry. Having found a specialist who will carry out your valuation it is best to send a photograph and description of the item to the specialist together with a stamped addressed envelope for the reply. A valuation by telephone is not possible.

Most dealers are only too happy to help with enquiries – however, they are very busy people and consideration of the above points would be welcomed.

AFD ⊞ Afford Decorative Arts Tel: 01827 330042 or 07831 114909 afforddecarts@fsmail.net

AH ⚒ Andrew Hartley, Victoria Hall Salerooms, Little Lane, Ilkley, Yorkshire, LS29 8EA Tel: 01943 816363 info@andrewhartleyfinearts.co.uk www.andrewhartleyfinearts.co.uk

ANAn ⊞ Angel Antiques, Church Street, Petworth, West Sussex, GU28 0AD Tel: 01798 343306 swansonantiques@aol.com www.angel-antiques.com

ANO ⊞ Art Nouveau Originals, The Bindery Gallery, 69 High Street, Broadway, Worcestershire, WR12 7DP Tel: 01386 854645 cathy@artnouveauoriginals.com www.artnouveauoriginals.com

ASP ⊞ Aspidistra Antiques, 51 High Street, Finedon, Wellingborough, Northamptonshire, NN9 9JN Tel: 01933 680196 info@aspidistra-antiques.com www.aspidistra.antiques.com

AU ⊞ Auto Suggestion Tel: 01428 751397

AUC ⊞ Aurea Carter, P.O. Box 44134, London, SW6 3YX Tel: 020 7731 3486 aureacarter@englishceramics.com www.englishceramics.com

BAC ⊞ The Brackley Antique Cellar, Drayman's Walk, Brackley, Northamptonshire, NN13 6BE Tel: 01280 841841

BBR ⚒ BBR, Elsecar Heritage Centre, Elsecar, Barnsley, South Yorkshire, S74 8HJ Tel: 01226 745156 sales@onlinebbr.com www.onlinebbr.com

BD ⊞ Banana Dance Ltd, 155A Northcote Road, Battersea, London, SW11 6QT Tel: 01634 364539 jonathan@bananadance.com www.bananadance.com

Bea ⚒ Bearnes, St Edmund's Court, Okehampton Street, Exeter, Devon, EX4 1DU Tel: 01392 207000 enquiries@bearnes.co.uk www.bearnes.co.uk

BERN ⚒ Bernaerts, Verlatstraat 18-22, 2000 Antwerpen/ Anvers, Belgium Tel: +32 (0)3 248 19 21 edmond.bernaerts@ping.be www.auction-bernaerts.com

BET ⊞ Beth, GO 43-44, Alfies Antique Market, 13-25 Church Street, Marylebone, London, NW8 8DT Tel: 020 7723 5613/0777 613 6003

BEV ⊞ Beverley, 30 Church Street, Marylebone, London, NW8 8EP Tel: 020 7262 1576

BGe ⊞ Bradley Gent Tel: 07711 158005 www.antiques-shop.co.uk

BHa ⊞ Judy & Brian Harden, P.O. Box 14, Bourton on the Water, Cheltenham, Gloucestershire, GL54 2YR Tel: 01451 810684 harden@portraitminiatures.co.uk www.portraitminiatures.co.uk

BP ⊞ Barling Porcelain Tel: 01621 890058 stuart@barling.uk.com www.barling.uk.com

BROW ⊞ David Brower, 113 Kensington Church Street, London, W8 7LN Tel: 020 7221 4155 David@davidbrower-antiques.com www.davidbrower-antiques.com

BRT ⊞ Britannia, Grays Antique Market, Stand 101, 58 Davies Street, London, W1Y 1AR Tel: 020 7629 6772 britannia@grays.clara.net

BtoB ⊞ Bac to Basic Antiques Tel: 07787 105609 bcarruthers@waitrose.com

BUK ⚒ Bukowskis, Arsenalsgatan 4, Stockholm, Sweden Tel: +46 (8) 614 08 00 info@bukowskis.se www.bukowskis.se

BWL ⚒ Brightwells Fine Art, The Fine Art Saleroom, Easters Court, Leominster, Herefordshire, HR6 0DE Tel: 01568 611122 fineart@brightwells.com www.brightwells.com

C&W ⊞ Carroll & Walker Tel: 01877 385618

CaF ⊞†Caren Fine, 11603 Gowrie Court, Maryland 20854, U.S.A. Tel: 301 854 6262 caren4antiques@yahoo.com

CAL ⊞ Cedar Antiques Ltd, High Street, Hartley Wintney, Hampshire, RG27 8NY Tel: 01252 843222 or 01189 326628

CANI ⊞ Caniche Decorative Arts, P.O. Box 350, Watford, Hertfordshire, WD19 4ZX Tel: 01923 251 206

CAu ⚒ The Cotswold Auction Company Ltd, incorporating Short Graham & Co and Hobbs and Chambers Fine Arts, The Coach House, Swan Yard, 9-13 West Market Place, Cirencester, Gloucestershire, GL7 2NH Tel: 01285 642420 info@cotswoldauction.co.uk www.cotswoldauction.co.uk

CCH ⊞ Collectors Choice, P.O. Box 99, Guildford, Surrey, GU1 1GA Tel: 01483 531104 louise@collectors-choice.net www.collectors-choice.net

CCs ⊞ Coco's Corner, Unit 4, Cirencester Antique Centre, Cirencester, Gloucestershire Tel: 01452 556 308 cocos-corner@blueyonder.co.uk

CDC ⚒ Capes Dunn & Co, The Auction Galleries, 38 Charles Street, Off Princess Street, Greater Manchester, M1 7DB Tel: 0161 273 6060/1911 capesdunn@yahoo.co.uk

CHAC ⊞ Church Hill Antiques Centre, 6 Station Street, Lewes, East Sussex, BN7 2DA Tel: 01273 474 842 churchhilllewes@aol.com www.church-hill-antiques.com

CHI ⊞†Chinasearch Ltd, 4 Princes Drive, Kenilworth, Warwickshire, CV8 2FD Tel: 01926 512402 info@chinasearch.co.uk www.chinasearch.co.uk

CHTR ⚒ Charterhouse, The Long Street Salerooms, Sherborne, Dorset, DT9 3BS Tel: 01935 812277 enquiry@charterhouse-auctions.co.uk www.charterhouse-auctions.co.uk

COBB ⚒ The Cobbs Auctioneers LLC, Noone Falls Mill, 50 Jaffrey Rd, Peterborough, NH 03458, U.S.A. Tel: 603 924 6361 info@thecobbs.com www.thecobbs.com

CoCo ⊞ Country Collector, 11-12 Birdgate, Pickering, Yorkshire, YO18 7AL Tel: 01751 477481 www.country-collector.co.uk

CoS ⊞ Corrinne Soffe, Nooky Cottage, Main Street, North Newington, Banbury, OX15 6AJ Tel: 01295 730317 soffe@btinternet.co.uk

DA ⚒ Dee, Atkinson & Harrison, The Exchange Saleroom, Driffield, East Yorkshire, YO25 6LD Tel: 01377 253151 info@dahauctions.com www.dahauctions.com

DAN ⊞†Andrew Dando, 34 Market Street, Bradford on Avon, Wiltshire, BA15 1LL Tel: 01225 865444 andrew@andrewdando.co.uk www.andrewdando.co.uk

DAP ⊞ David Phillips Antiques, Westbank, Pontypridd, Mid Glamorgan, CF37 2HS, Wales Tel: 01443 404646

DAU ⚒ Dickins Auctioneers Ltd, The Claydon Saleroom, Calvert Road, Middle Claydon, Buckinghamshire, MK18 2EZ Tel: 01296 714434 info@dickins-auctioneers.com www.dickins-auctioneers.com

DAV ⊞ Hugh Davies, The Packing Shop, 6-12 Ponton Road, London, SW8 5BA Tel: 020 7498 3255

DD 🗗 David Duggleby, The Vine St Salerooms, Scarborough, Yorkshire, YO11 1XN Tel: 01723 507111 auctions@davidduggleby.com www.davidduggleby.com

DeA ⊞ Delphi Antiques, Powerscourt Townhouse Centre, South William Street, Dublin 2, Republic of Ireland Tel: 1 679 0331

DEB ⊞ Debden Antiques, Elder Street, Debden, Saffron Walden, Essex, CB11 3JY Tel: 01799 543007 info@debden-antiques.co.uk www.debden-antiques.co.uk

DHA ⊞ Durham House Antiques, Sheep Street, Stow-on-the-Wold, Gloucestershire, GL54 1AA Tel: 01451 870404

DIA ⊞ Mark Diamond Tel: 020 8508 4479 mark.diamond@dial.pipex.com

DMa ⊞ David March, Abbots Leigh, Bristol, Gloucestershire, BS8 Tel: 0117 937 2422

DN 🗗 Dreweatt Neate, Donnington Priory, Donnington, Newbury, Berkshire, RG14 2JE Tel: 01635 553553 donnington@dnfa.com www.dnfa.com/donnington

DN(BR) 🗗 Dreweatt Neate, The Auction Hall, The Pantiles, Tunbridge Wells, Kent, TN2 5QL Tel: 01892 544500 tunbridgewells@dnfa.com www.dnfa.com/tunbridgewells

DN(EH) 🗗 Dreweatt Neate, 46-50 South Street, Eastbourne, East Sussex, BN21 4XB Tel: 01323 410419 eastbourne@dnfa.com www.dnfa.com/eastbourne

DN(HAM) 🗗 Dreweatt Neate, Baverstock House, 93 High Street, Godalming, Surrey, GU7 1AL Tel: 01483 423567 godalming@dnfa.com www.dnfa.com/godalming

DORO 🗗 Dorotheum, Palais Dorotheum, A-1010 Wien, Dorotheergasse 17, 1010 Vienna, Austria Tel: 515 60 229 client.services@dorotheum.at

DSA ⊞ David Scriven Antiques, P.O. Box 1962, Leigh-on-Sea, Essex, SS9 2YZ Tel: 07887 716677 david@david-scriven-antiques.fsnet.co.uk

DSG ⊞ Delf Stream Gallery Tel: 07816 781297 nic19422000@yahoo.co.uk www.delfstreamgallery.com

DuM 🗗 Du Mouchelles, 409 East Jefferson, Detroit, Michigan 48226, U.S.A. Tel: 313 963 6255 info@dumouchelles.com

EHCS The European Honeypot Collectors' Society, John Doyle, The Honeypot, 18 Victoria Road, Chislehurst, Kent, BR7 6DF Tel: 020 8289 7725 johnhoneypot@hotmail.com www.geocities.com/tehcsuk

EMH ⊞ Eat My Handbag Bitch, 37 Drury Lane, London, WC2B 5RR Tel: 020 7836 0830 contact@eatmyhandbagbitch.co.uk www.eatmyhandbagbitch.co.uk

EZC ⊞ Easy Chairs, 375 Huron Avenue, Cambridge MA 02138, U.S.A. Tel: 617 491 2131 easychairslee@aol.com www.leejosephauctions.com

F&C 🗗 Finan & Co, The Square, Mere, Wiltshire, BA12 6DJ Tel: 01747 861411 post@finanandco.co.uk www.finanandco.co.uk

F&F ⊞ Fenwick & Fenwick, 88-90 High Street, Broadway, Worcestershire, WR12 7AJ Tel: 01386 853227/841724

FHF 🗗 Fellows & Sons, Augusta House, 19 Augusta Street, Hockley, Birmingham, West Midlands, B18 6JA Tel: 0121 212 2131 info@fellows.co.uk www.fellows.co.uk

FRD ⊞ Fragile Design, 8 The Custard Factory, Digbeth, Birmingham, West Midlands, B9 4AA Tel: 0121 693 1001 info@fragiledesign.com www.fragiledesign.com

G(B) 🗗 Gorringes Auction Galleries, Terminus Road, Bexhill-on-Sea, East Sussex, TN39 3LR Tel: 01424 212994 bexhill@gorringes.co.uk www.gorringes.co.uk

G(L) 🗗 Gorringes inc Julian Dawson, 15 North Street, Lewes, East Sussex, BN7 2PD Tel: 01273 478221 clientservices@gorringes.co.uk www.gorringes.co.uk

G&CC ⊞✝ The Goss & Crested China Club & Museum, incorporating Milestone Publications, 62 Murray Road, Horndean, Hampshire, PO8 9JL Tel: 023 9259 7440 info@gosschinaclub.demon.co.uk www.gosscrestedchina.co.uk

G&G ⊞ Guest & Gray, 1-7 Davies Mews, London, W1K 5AB Tel: 020 7408 1252 info@chinese-porcelain-art.com www.chinese-porcelain-art.com

GAK 🗗 Keys, Off Palmers Lane, Aylsham, Norfolk, NR11 6JA Tel: 01263 733195 www.aylshamsalerooms.co.uk

GaL ⊞ Gazelles Ltd Tel: 023 8081 1610 allan@gazelles.co.uk www.gazelles.co.uk

GAU ⊞ Becca Gauldie Antiques, The Old School, Glendoick, Perthshire, Scotland, PH2 7NR Tel: 01738 860 870 becca@scottishantiques.freeserve.co.uk

GGD ⊞ Great Grooms Antiques Centre, 51/52 West Street, Dorking, Surrey, RH4 1BU Tel: 01306 887076 dorking@greatgrooms.co.uk www.greatgrooms.co.uk

GH 🗗 Gardiner Houlgate, The Bath Auction Rooms, 9 Leafield Way, Corsham, Nr Bath, Somerset, SN13 9SW Tel: 01225 812912 www.invaluable.com/gardiner-houlgate

GIL 🗗 Gilding's Auctioneers and Valuers, 64 Roman Way, Market Harborough, Leicestershire, LE16 7PQ Tel: 01858 410414 sales@gildings.co.uk www.gildings.co.uk

GIR ⊞ Helen Girton Antiques, P.O. Box 2022, Buckingham, MK18 4ZH Tel: 01280 815012

GLB ⊞ Glebe Antiques, Scottish Antique Centre, Doune, Scotland, FK16 6HG Tel: 01259 214559 rrglebe@aol.com

GN ⊞✝ Gillian Neale Antiques, P.O. Box 247, Aylesbury, Buckinghamshire, HP20 1JZ Tel: 01296 423754/ 07860 638700 gillianneale@aol.com www.gillinnealeantiques.co.uk

GOv ⊞ Glazed Over Tel: 0773 2789114

GRe ⊞ Greystoke Antiques, 4 Swan Yard, (off Cheap Street), Sherborne, Dorset, DT9 3AX Tel: 01935 812833

GRI ⊞ Grimes House Antiques, High Street, Moreton-in-Marsh, Gloucestershire, GL56 0AT Tel: 01608 651029 grimes_house@cix.co.uk www.grimeshouse.co.uk www.cranberryglass.co.uk

GRo ⊞ Geoffrey Robinson, GO77-78, GO91-92 (Ground floor), Alfies Antique Market, 13-25 Church Street, Marylebone, London, NW8 8DT Tel: 020 7723 0449 info@alfiesantiques.com www.alfiesantiques.com

H&G ⊞ Hope & Glory, 131A Kensington Church Street, London, W8 7LP Tel: 020 7727 8424

HA ⊞ Hallidays, The Old College, Dorchester-on-Thames, Oxfordshire, OX10 7HL Tel: 01865 340028/68 antiques@hallidays.com www.hallidays.com

HABA ⊞ Hall-Bakker Decorative Arts at Heritage, 6 Market Place, Woodstock, Oxfordshire, OX20 1TA Tel: 01993 811332

Hal 🗗 Halls Fine Art Auctions, Welsh Bridge, Shrewsbury, Shropshire, SY3 8LA Tel: 01743 231212

HarC ⊞ Hardy's Collectables Tel: 07970 613077 www.poolepotteryjohn.com

HeA ⊞ Heanor Antiques Centre, 1–3 Ilkeston Road, Heanor, Derbyshire, DE75 7AE Tel: 01773 531181/762783 sales@heanorantiquescentre.co.uk www.heanorantiques.co.uk

HEI NO LONGER TRADING

HEW ⊞ Muir Hewitt, Art Deco Originals, Halifax Antiques Centre, Queens Road Mills, Queens Road/Gibbet Street, Halifax, Yorkshire, HX1 4LR Tel: 01422 347377 muir.hewitt@virgin.net muir_hewitt@btconnect.com www.muirhewitt.com

HKW ⊞ Hawkswood Antiques, P.O. Box 156, Goole, DN14 7FW Tel: 01757 638630/07971 232602 jenny@hawkswood.fsbusiness.co.uk

HOM ⊞ Home & Colonial, 134 High Street, Berkhamsted, Hertfordshire, HP4 3AT Tel: 01442 877007 homeandcolonial@btinternet.com www.homeandcolonial.co.uk

HOW ⊞✝ John Howard at Heritage, 6 Market Place, Woodstock, Oxfordshire, OX20 1TA Tel: 0870 4440678 john@johnhoward.co.uk www.antiquepottery.co.uk

HTE ⊞ Heritage, 6 Market Place, Woodstock, Oxfordshire, OX20 1TA Tel: 01993 811332/ 0870 4440678 dealers@atheritage.co.uk www.atheritage.co.uk

HUM ⊞ Humbleyard Fine Art, Unit 32 Admiral Vernon Arcade, Portobello Road, London, W11 2DY Tel: 01362 637793 or 07836 349416

HUN ⊞ The Country Seat, Huntercombe Manor Barn, Henley-on-Thames, Oxfordshire, RG9 5RY Tel: 01491 641349 wclegg@thecountryseat.com www.thecountryseat.com

HYD ⚒ Hy Duke & Son, The Dorchester Fine Art Salerooms, Weymouth Avenue, Dorchester, Dorset, DT1 1QS Tel: 01305 265080 www.dukes-auctions.com

IQ ⊞ Cloud Cuckooland, 12 Fore Street, Mevagissey, Cornwall, PL26 6UQ Tel: 01726 842364 Paul@cloudcuckooland.biz www.cloudcuckooland.biz

IW ⊞†Islwyn Watkins, Offa's Dyke Antique Centre, 4 High Street, Knighton, Powys, LD7 1AT, Wales Tel: 01547 520145

JAA ⚒ Jackson's International Auctioneers & Appraisers of Fine Art & Antiques, 2229 Lincoln Street, Cedar Falls, IA 50613, U.S.A. Tel: 319 277 2256/800 665 6743 sandim@jacksonsauctions.com www.jacksonsauction.com

JAK ⊞ Clive & Lynne Jackson Tel: 01242 254375

JAY ⊞ Jaycee Bee Antiques

JBL ⊞ Judi Bland Antiques Tel: 01276 857576 or 01536 724145

JDJ ⚒ James D Julia, Inc., P.O. Box 830, Rte.201, Skowhegan Road, Fairfield, ME 04937, U.S.A. Tel: 207 453 7125 www.juliaauctions.com

JE ⊞†Julian Eade Tel: 01865 300349 or 07973 542971

JFME ⊞ James Ferguson & Mark Evans Tel: 0141 950 2452/077 699 72935 & 01388 768108/07979 0189214 james@dec-art.freeserve.co.uk mark@evanscollectables.co.uk www.evanscollectables.co.uk

JHo ⊞ Jonathan Horne, 66c Kensington Church Street, London, W8 4BY Tel: 020 7221 5658 JH@jonathanhorne.co.uk www.jonathanhorne.co.uk

JIL ⊞ Jillings Antique Clocks, Croft House, 17 Church Street, Newent, Gloucestershire, GL18 1PU Tel: 01531 822100 clocks@jillings.com www.jillings.com

JMC ⊞ J & M Collectables Tel: 01580 891657 or 077135 23573 jandmcollectables@tinyonline.co.uk

JOA ⊞ Joan Gale, Tombland Antiques Centre, 14 Tombland, Norwich, Norfolk, NR3 1HF Tel: 01603 619129 joan.gale@ukgateway.net

JOR ⊞ John Rogers Tel: 01643 863170 or 07710 266136 johnrogers024@btinternet.com

JP ⊞ Janice Paull, P.O. Box 100, Kenilworth, Warwickshire, CV8 1JX Tel: 07876 284647 janicepaull@yahoo.com www.janicepaull.com

JSG ⊞ James Strang Tel: 01334 472 566 or 07950 490088 jameslstrang@hotmail.com www.mod-i.com

JUP ⊞ Jupiter Antiques, P.O. Box 609, Rottingdean, East Sussex, BN2 7FW Tel: 01273 302865

JWK ⊞ Jane Wicks Kitchenalia, Country Ways, Strand Quay, Rye, East Sussex, TN31 7AY Tel: 01424 713635 Janes_kitchen@hotmail.com

K&M ⊞ K & M Antiques, 369-370 Grays Antique Market, 58 Davies Street, London, W1K 5LP Tel: 020 7491 4310 or 07787 565 505 Kandmantiques@aol.com

KES ⊞ Keystones, P.O. Box 387, Stafford, ST16 3FG Tel: 01785 256648 www.keystones.co.uk

KEY ⊞ Key Antiques of Chipping Norton, 11 Horsefair, Chipping Norton, Oxfordshire, OX7 5AL Tel: 01608 644992/643777 info@keyantiques.com www.keyantiques.com

KMG ⊞ Karen Michelle Guido, Karen Michelle Antique Tiles, PMB 243, 1835 US 1 South #119, St Augustine, FL 32084, U.S.A. Tel: 904 471 3226 karen@antiquetiles.com www.antiquetiles.com

KUR ⊞†William R. & Teresa F. Kurau, P.O. Box 457, Lampeter, PA 17537, U.S.A. Tel: 717 464 0731 lampeter@epix.net www.historicalchina.com

L ⚒ Lawrence Fine Art Auctioneers, South Street, Crewkerne, Somerset, TA18 8AB Tel: 01460 73041 www.lawrences.co.uk

L&E ⚒ Locke & England, 18 Guy Street, Leamington Spa, Warwickshire, CV32 4RT Tel: 01926 889100 info@leauction.co.uk www.auctions-online.com/locke

LBr ⊞ Lynda Brine - By appointment only lyndabrine@yahoo.co.uk www.scentbottlesandsmalls.co.uk

LFA ⚒ Law Fine Art Tel: 01635 860033 info@lawfineart.co.uk www.lawfineart.co.uk

LGr ⊞ Langton Green Antiques, Langton Road, Langton Green, Tunbridge Wells, Kent, TN3 0HP Tel: 01892 862004 antiques@langtongreen.fsbusiness.co.uk www.langtongreenantiques.co.uk

LHA ⚒ Leslie Hindman, Inc., 122 North Aberdeen Street, Chicago, Illinois 60607, U.S.A. Tel: 312 280 1212 www.lesliehindman.com

LLD ⊞ Lewis & Lewis Deco Tel: 07739 904681 lewis_robin@hotmail.com

MAA ⊞ Mario's Antiques, 75 Portobello Road, London, W11 2QB Tel: 020 8902 1600 marwan@barazi.screaming.net www.marios_antiques.com

MAR ⚒ Frank R. Marshall & Co, Marshall House, Church Hill, Knutsford, Cheshire, WA16 6DH Tel: 01565 653284

MARK ⊞ 20th Century Marks, Whitegates, Rectory Road, Little Burstead, Near Billericay, Essex, CM12 9TR Tel: 01268 411 000 info@20thcenturymarks.co.uk www.20thcenturymarks.co.uk

MCA ⚒†Mervyn Carey, Twysden Cottage, Scullsgate, Benenden, Cranbrook, Kent, TN17 4LD Tel: 01580 240283

MCC ⊞ M.C. Chapman Antiques, Bell Hill, Finedon, Northamptonshire, NN9 5NB Tel: 01933 681260

MED ⚒ Medway Auctions, Fagins, 23 High Street, Rochester, Kent, ME1 1LN Tel: 01634 847444 medauc@dircon.co.uk www.medwayauctions.co.uk

MER ⊞ Mere Antiques, 13 Fore Street, Topsham, Exeter, Devon, EX3 0HF Tel: 01392 874224

MFB ⊞ Manor Farm Barn Antiques Tel: 01296 658941 or 07720 286607 mfbn@btinternet.com btwebworld.com/mfbantiques

MI ⊞ Mitofsky Antiques, 8 Rathfarnham Road, Terenure, Dublin 6, Republic of Ireland Tel: 492 0033 info@mitofskyantiques.com www.mitofskyantiques.com

Mit ⚒ Mitchells Auction Company, The Furniture Hall, 47 Station Road, Cockermouth, Cumbria, CA13 9PZ Tel: 01900 827800 info@mitchellsfineart.com

MLa ⊞ Marion Langham Tel: 028 895 41247 marion@ladymarion.co.uk www.ladymarion.co.uk

MLL ⊞ Millers Antiques Ltd, Netherbrook House, 86 Christchurch Road, Ringwood, Hampshire, BH24 1DR Tel: 01425 472062 mail@millers-antiques.co.uk www.millers-antiques.co.uk

MMc ⊞ Marsh-McNamara Tel: 07790 759162

MSB ⊞ Marilynn and Sheila Brass, P.O. Box 380503, Cambridge, MA 02238-0503, U.S.A. Tel: 617 491 6064 shelmardesign1@aol.com

MUL ⚒ Mullock & Madeley, The Old Shippon, Wall-under-Heywood, Nr Church Stretton, Shropshire, SY6 7DS Tel: 01694 771771 or 01584 841 428 auctions@mullockmadeley.co.uk www.mullockmadeley.co.uk

NAW ⊞ Newark Antiques Warehouse Ltd, Old Kelham Road, Newark, Nottinghamshire, NG24 1BX Tel: 01636 674869/07974 429185 enquiries@newarkantiques.co.uk www.newarkantiques.co.uk

NSal ⚒ Netherhampton Salerooms, Salisbury Auction Centre, Netherhampton, Salisbury, Wiltshire, SP2 8RH Tel: 01722 340 041

OD ⊞ Offa's Dyke Antique Centre, 4 High Street, Knighton, Powys, Wales, LD7 1AT Tel: 01547 528635/520145

Oli ⚒ Olivers, Olivers Rooms, Burkitts Lane, Sudbury, Suffolk, CO10 1HB Tel: 01787 880305 oliversauctions@btconnect.com

PeN ⊞ Peter Norden Antiques, 61 Long Street, Tetbury, Gloucestershire, GL8 8AA Tel: 01666 503 854 peternorden_antiques@lineone.net www.peter-norden-antiques.co.uk

PFK ✎ Penrith Farmers' & Kidd's plc, Skirsgill
Salerooms, Penrith, Cumbria, CA11 0DN
Tel: 01768 890781 info@pfkauctions.co.uk
www.pfkauctions.co.uk

PGO ⊞ Pamela Goodwin, 11 The Pantiles, Royal
Tunbridge Wells, Kent, TN2 5TD
Tel: 01892 618200
mail@goodwinantiques.co.uk
www.goodwinantiques.co.uk

PICA ⊞ Piccadilly Antiques, 280 High Street, Batheaston,
Bath, Somerset, BA1 7RA Tel: 01225 851494
piccadillyantiques@ukonline.co.uk

Pott ✎† Potteries Specialist Auctions, 271 Waterloo
Road, Cobridge, Stoke on Trent,
Staffordshire, ST6 3HR Tel: 01782 286622
www.potteriesauctions.com

POW ⊞ Sylvia Powell Decorative Arts, Suite 400,
Ceramic House, 571 Finchley Road, London,
NW3 7BN Tel: 020 8458 4543
dpowell909@aol.com

PrB ⊞ Pretty Bizarre, 170 High Street, Deal, Kent,
CT14 6BQ Tel: 07973 794537

PSA ⊞ Pantiles Spa Antiques, 4, 5, 6 Union House,
The Pantiles, Tunbridge Wells, Kent, TN4 8HE
Tel: 01892 541377 psa.wells@btinternet.com
www.antiques-tun-wells-kent.co.uk

RAN ⊞ Ranby Hall Antiques, Barnby Moor, Retford,
Nottinghamshire, DN22 8JQ Tel: 01777 860696
www.ranbyhall.antiques-gb.com

RCA ⊞ Raccoon Creek Antiques, U.S.A.
Tel: 856 224 1282 raccooncreek@msn.com
raccooncreekantiques.com

RdeR ⊞ Rogers de Rin, 76 Royal Hospital Road,
London, SW3 4HN Tel: 020 7352 9007
rogersderin@rogersderin.co.uk
www.rogersderin.co.uk

RdV ⊞ Roger de Ville Antiques, Bakewell Antiques
Centre, King Street, Bakewell, Derbyshire,
DE45 1DZ Tel: 01629 812496
contact@rogerdeville.co.uk
www.rogerdeville.co.uk

ReN ⊞ Rene Nicholls, 56 High Street, Malmesbury,
Wiltshire, SN16 9AT Tel: 01666 823089

RH ⊞ Rick Hubbard Art Deco, 3 Tee Court, Bell Street,
Romsey, Hampshire, SO51 8GY
Tel: 01794 513133
rick@rickhubbard-artdeco.co.uk
www.rickhubbard-artdeco.co.uk

RIT ✎ Ritchies Inc., Auctioneers & Appraisers of
Antiques & Fine Art, 288 King Street East,
Toronto, Ontario, M5A 1K4, Canada
Tel: (416) 364 1864 auction@ritchies.com
www.ritchies.com

ROSc ✎ R. O. Schmitt Fine Art, Box 1941, Salem, New
Hampshire 03079, U.S.A. Tel: 1 603 432 2237
roschmittclocks@yahoo.com
www.antiqueclockauction.com

RTo ✎ Rupert Toovey & Co Ltd, Spring Gardens,
Washington, West Sussex, RH20 3BS
Tel: 01903 891955 auctions@rupert-
toovey.com www.rupert-toovey.com

RUSK ⊞ Ruskin Decorative Arts, 5 Talbot Court, Stow-
on-the-Wold, Cheltenham, Gloucestershire,
GL54 1DP Tel: 01451 832254
william.anne@ruskindecarts.co.uk

S ✎ Sotheby's, 34-35 New Bond Street, London,
W1A 2AA Tel: 020 7293 5000
www.sothebys.com

S(Am) ✎ Sotheby's Amsterdam, De Boelelaan 30,
Amsterdam 1083 HJ, Netherlands
Tel: 31 20 550 2200

S(Mi) ✎ Sotheby's, Palazzo Broggi, Via Broggi, 19,
Milan 20129, Italy Tel: 39 02 295 001

S(NY) ✎ Sotheby's, 1334 York Avenue at 72nd St, New
York, NY 10021, U.S.A. Tel: 212 606 7000

S(O) ✎ Sotheby's Olympia, Hammersmith Road,
London, W14 8UX Tel: 020 7293 5555

SAAC ⊞ Scottish Antique Centre, Abernyte, Perthshire,
PH14 9SJ, Scotland Tel: 01828 686401
sales@scottish-antiques.com
www.scottish-antiques.com

SAS ✎† Special Auction Services, Kennetholme,
Midgham, Reading, Berkshire, RG7 5UX
Tel: 0118 971 2949
www.antiquestradegazette.com/sas

SAT ⊞ The Swan at Tetsworth, High Street,
Tetsworth, Nr Thame, Oxfordshire, OX9 7AB
Tel: 01844 281777 antiques@theswan.co.uk
www.theswan.co.uk

SCH ⊞ Scherazade Tel: 01708 641117 or
07855 383996 scherz1@yahoo.com

SCO ⊞ Peter Scott Tel: 0117 986 8468 or 0850 639770

SDD ⊞ Sandra D Deas
Tel: 01333 360 214 or 07713 897 482

SEA ⊞ Mark Seabrook Antiques, P.O. Box 396,
Huntingdon, Cambridgeshire, PE28 0ZA
Tel: 01480 861935
enquiries@markseabrook.com
www.markseabrook.com

SER ⊞ Serendipity, 125 High Street, Deal, Kent,
CT14 6BB Tel: 01304 369165/01304 366536
dipityantiques@aol.com

SHa ⊞ Shapiro & Co, Stand 380, Gray's Antique
Market, 58 Davies Street, London, W1Y 5LP
Tel: 020 7491 2710

SHER ⊞ Sherwood Golf Antiques Tel: 07968 848448
sherwoodgolf@btinternet.com

SHSY ✎ Shapiro Auctioneers, 162 Queen Street,
Woollahra, Sydney NSW 2025, Australia
Tel: 612 9326 1588

SJH ✎ S.J. Hales, 87 Fore Street, Bovey Tracey,
Devon, TQ13 9AB Tel: 01626 836684

SK ✎ Skinner Inc., The Heritage On The Garden,
63 Park Plaza, Boston, MA 02116, U.S.A.
Tel: 617 350 5400

SPG ✎ Sprague Auctions, Inc., Route 5, Dummerston,
VT 05301, U.S.A. Tel: 802 254 8969
bob@spragueauctions.com
www.spragueauctions.com

STA ⊞ George Stacpoole, Main Street, Adare,
Co. Limerick, Republic of Ireland
Tel: 6139 6409 stacpoole@iol.ie
www.georgestacpooleantiques.com

SWO ✎ Sworders, 14 Cambridge Road, Stansted
Mountfitchet, Essex, CM24 8BZ
Tel: 01279 817778 auctions@sworder.co.uk
www.sworder.co.uk

TAC ⊞ Tenterden Antiques Centre, 66-66A High
Street, Tenterden, Kent, TN30 6AU
Tel: 01580 765655/765885

TDG ⊞ The Design Gallery 1850–1950, 5 The Green,
Westerham, Kent, TN16 1AS Tel: 01959
561234 sales@thedesigngalleryuk.com
www.thedesigngalleryuk.com

TEN ✎ Tennants, The Auction Centre, Harmby Road,
Leyburn, Yorkshire, DL8 5SG
Tel: 01969 623780
enquiry@tennants-ltd.co.uk
www.tennants.co.uk

TH ⊞ Tony Horsley, P.O. Box 3127, Brighton,
East Sussex, BN1 5SS Tel: 01273 550770

TMA ✎ Tring Market Auctions, The Market Premises,
Brook Street, Tring, Hertfordshire, HP23 5EF
Tel: 01442 826446
sales@tringmarketauctions.co.uk
www.tringmarketauctions.co.uk

TREA ✎ Treadway Gallery, Inc., 2029 Madison Road,
Cincinnati, Ohio 45208, U.S.A.
Tel: 513 321 6742
www.treadwaygallery.com

TWO ⊞ Two P'S Tel: 01252 647965 or 07710 277726
twops@ntlworld.com

TYE ⊞ Typically English Antiques Tel: 01249 721721
or 07818 000704 typicallyeng@aol.com

VK ⊞ Vivienne King of Panache Tel: 01934 814759
or 07974 798871 Kingpanache@aol.com

VS ✎ T. Vennett-Smith, 11 Nottingham Road,
Gotham, Nottinghamshire, NG11 0HE
Tel: 0115 983 0541 info@vennett-smith.com
www.vennett-smith.com

WAA ⊞ Woburn Abbey Antiques Centre, Woburn,
Bedfordshire, MK17 9WA Tel: 01525 290666
antiques@woburnabbey.co.uk
www.discoverwoburn.co.uk

WAC ⊞ Worcester Antiques Centre, Reindeer Court,
Mealcheapen Street, Worcester, WR1 4DF
Tel: 01905 610680 WorcsAntiques@aol.com

WeW ⊞ West Wales Antiques, 18 Mansfield Road,
Murton, Swansea, SA3 3AR, Wales
Tel: 01792 234318/01639 644379
info@westwalesantiques.co.uk
www.westwalesantiques.co.uk

WW ✎ Woolley & Wallis, Salisbury Salerooms,
51-61 Castle Street, Salisbury,
Wiltshire, SP1 3SU
Tel: 01722 424500/411854
enquiries@woolleyandwallis.co.uk
www.woolleyandwallis.co.uk

Index

Bold numbers refer to information and pointer boxes

A

Acier, Michel Victor 137–8, 140, 141
Adams 246
Aesthetic Movement tiles 286
agate ware 24, 194
albarellos 22
Aldermaston Pottery 90, 93
Alexandra Porcelain 71
Allertons 293
Aluminia 186
American ceramics 176–83
Amphora 84
Anglo-American pottery 177
animals 55, 206–10
  armorial and crested china 63, 64
  Art Deco 84
  badgers 145
  bears 25, 27, 188, 189, 207, 243
  Belleek 102
  bulls 210
  camels 206
  cats 21, 192, 206, 208
  cows 18, 209
  creamware 27
  deer 206
  delft 18
  Derby 111–13
  dogs 24, 53, 55, 64, 102, 113, 130, 138, 169, 185, 190, 207–10
  elephants 84, 208, 209
  faïence 21
  foxes 59, 209
  gazelles 84
  giraffes 209
  goats 190, 206
  hares 207
  hippopotamuses 188
  leopards 207
  lions 56, 206, 207
  majolica 56, 59
  Meissen 138, 145
  Minton 130
  monkeys 210
  pigs 63, 208, 209
  post-war design 95
  rabbits 210
  Royal Worcester 172, 210
  salt-glazed stoneware 24
  Scandinavian 185, 188, 189
  Scottish 190, 192, 195
  sheep 111, 208
  Staffordshire 25, 53, 55
  water buffalo 25
  Worcester 169
apothecary jars 16, 23
Arabia 188, 189
Arcadian 63–5
Arding, Mary M. 299
armorial china 62–5
Arnhem 70
Art Deco 81–6, 226
Art pottery 66–80
  Brannam Pottery 71, 71
  Martin Brothers 77, 77–8
  Ruskin Pottery 79, 79–80
  William de Morgan 66, 66
Ashstead 82
ashtrays 105, 149
Ashworth 70
Atkins, Elizabeth 115
Ault, William 293
Ault Pottery 71
Australian ceramics 93
Austrian ceramics
  Art Deco 84, 85
  Art pottery 76
  boxes 218
  tureens 294
Aynsley 274
Ayrton, Harry 173

B

baby's bottles 44
Bancroft, Joseph 129

barber's bowls 27
Bargeware 248, 281, 281–2
Barker Bros 90
Barlow, Florence 114, 116, 120
Barlow, Hannah 115, 116
Barlow, Lucy 120
Barr, Flight & Barr 165, 168–9, 236
barrels, delft 19
baskets 211–14
  Art pottery 67
  Belleek 101, 212–14
  Chelsea 36, 211
  creamware 160
  Meissen 211, 212
  Staffordshire 212
  Wedgwood 160, 211
  Worcester 164, 165, 212
Bates Eliot & Co 265
beakers 65, 118
beer mugs 179
Belgian Art pottery 74
Bell, John 131
Belleek 100, 100–2
  animals 102, 208
  baskets 101, 212–14
  biscuit boxes 100
  bowls 101, 102
  busts 102
  cabaret sets 102
  cups 100, 228, 229
  figures 100
  jugs 100–2
  Ott & Brewer Belleek 180, 180
  spill vases 100, 299
  teapots 100, 101, 281, 282
  vases 101, 102, 300, 302, 304
Bengtson, Hertha 186
Berlin porcelain 228, 232, 262
Beswick
  animals 209, 210
  vases 82, 89
Billingsley, William 196, 197
Bing & Grøndahl 185, 185
birds
  Bow 35
  majolica 59, 61, 208
  Martin Brothers 78
  Meissen 138, 143, 144, 208
  Prattware 27
  Staffordshire 207
  Willow Art 209
Birks, Alboin 132
Birks, Lawrence 132
biscuit barrels
  Art pottery 75
  Belleek 100
  Clarice Cliff 108, 110
  Doulton 115, 117
bisque
  animals 209
  busts 233
  clocks 226
  piano babies 234
Bitossi Pottery 89
black basalt 159, 161, 161, 231
Blair, Catherine 86, 195
Blake, Kitty 173
blanc de Chine 31
Bloor Derby 257, 257, 297
blue-printed pottery 39–46, 41, 43
bocage figures 47
Boch Frères 82
Boehm 214
Bohemian ceramics 242
bone china
  cabaret sets 161
  chambersticks 221
  coffee services 274
  cups 228
  dessert services 272
  extinguishers 223
  mugs 251
  plates 95
  tea services 272, 275
  tureens 295

bookends 209
Boston House pattern 39
bottles
  armorial and crested china 63
  blue-printed pottery 44
  scent bottles 153, 159, 270
  wine bottles 12
bough pots 159
Boullemier, Antonin 131, 132
Boullemier, Lucien 171
Bow 34, 35
  baskets 211
  birds 35
  candlesticks 220
  coffee cans 30–2
  dishes 30, 35
  egg cups 31
  figures 34, 35
  fountain groups 30
  mugs 34
  plates 36
  sauce boats 31, 268
  tea canisters 32, 276
  tureens 294
  vases 30, 33
Bowden, Maud 121, 244
Bowditch, Florence 115
bowls 215–16
  armorial and crested china 65
  Art Deco 81, 83, 85
  Art pottery 75, 76
  barber's 27
  Belleek 101, 102
  blue-printed pottery 40–6
  Caughley 38
  Chaffer's Liverpool 34
  Chelsea 30
  Clarice Cliff 103, 105, 106, 108, 109
  delft 18, 19, 215
  earthenware 187
  faïence 21, 189
  Lowestoft 38, 215
  lustre 133, 215–16
  majolica 61
  Meissen 134, 136
  Minton 129, 130, 133
  Moorcroft 146, 149–51, 153
  pearlware 43
  post-war design 87, 88, 90, 92
  Royal Doulton 123, 216
  Royal Winton 216
  Royal Worcester 216
  Ruskin Pottery 80, 216
  Rye Pottery 216
  Scandinavian 186, 187, 189
  Scottish 191, 192, 195
  spongeware 101, 191
  stoneware 88
  Wedgwood 162
  Welsh 197, 199, 200, 202
  Worcester 163, 164, 171, 215
boxes 217–19
  Bristol 217
  Carlton Ware 219
  Chelsea 31, 217
  Clarice Cliff 105
  Dresden 217
  faïence 219
  Meissen 217, 219
  Paris 217
  pearlware 217
  Quimper 219
  Ridgway 217
  Royal Doulton 124
  Scottish 190
Brannam Pottery 70–2, 71, 241, 249
bread dishes 60
bread plates 130
breakfast sets 39
Bretby
  jardinières 241
  pots 69
  spill vases 70
  vases 68, 69, 72, 300, 302
Briglin Pottery 93

Bristol
  boxes 217
  delft 12, 14–17, 215, 285
  saucers 36
Britannia Pottery 194
British delftware 15
Broad, John 116
brooches 80, 124
Brown, Helen Paxton 195
Brown-Westhead, Moore & Co 70, 233, 237
Brownfield, William 248
Brownsword, Harold 209, 223
bulb bowls 192
Burleigh Ware 82, 86, 272
Burmantofts
  jardinières 240, 242
  vases 66, 68, 301
Bursley Ware 82
busts
  Belleek 102
  Chelsea 34
  Copeland 233
  Meissen 234
  Minton 130, 131
  Parian 233
  Robinson & Leadbeater 231
  Wedgwood 231
  Worcester 170
Butler, Frank 115, 116, 120, 222
butter boats 164
butter boxes 135
butter dishes 41

C

cabaret sets 102, 161, 271, 273
cabinet cups 129, 156, 227
cabinet plates 131, 132, 158
Cadogan teapots 280, 280
Caiger-Smith, Alan 90, 93
Caledonia 64
candelabra 143
candlesticks 220–4
  Bow 220
  Carter, Stabler & Adams 223
  Chelsea 35, 220
  Clarice Cliff 223–4
  Derby 220
  Doulton 222
  faïence 223
  Gouda 224
  Meissen 140
  Minton 222
  pearlware 220
  Ridgway 221
  Royal Worcester 221
  Scandinavian 187
  Staffordshire 52, 220, 221
  Wedgwood 160, 222
  Wemyss 223
  Worcester 168, 222
caneware 159
card racks 127
Cardew, Michael 75
Carlton Ware 81
  armorial and crested china 63
  boxes 219
  coffee services 84, 91, 274
  ginger jars 81
  teapots 89
  vases 81, 303
Carter & Co 71, 288
Carter, Stabler & Adams
  animals 209
  candlesticks 223
  teapots 282
  vases 301
Cartlidge, George 75, 76, 288
Casson, Hugh 88, 275
Castelli 22, 23, 255
Castleford 29, 280
Catrice, Nicolas 155
Caughley 36
  armorial and crested china 62
  bowls 38
  dishes 37
  ladles 38

teapots 38
Celtic Pottery 92, 275
centrepieces 73, 197, 211–14
Chaffers, Richard 34, **36**
Challis, Margaret M. 117
chamber pots 126
Chamberlain's Worcester **169**
  baskets 212
  cups 227
  dessert services 168
  inkwells 235, 236
chambersticks 73, 168, 221
character jugs 19
chargers
  Art Deco 82, 86
  Art pottery 70
  delft 12, 14–17
  majolica 61
  post-war design 92
cheese cradles 39
cheese dishes 46, 56–9, 85
Chelsea **31**, **32**
  baskets 36, 211
  bowls 30
  boxes 31, 217
  busts 34
  candlesticks 35, 220
  chocolate cups 37
  dishes 32–4
  figures 35
  knives and forks 32
  plates 33
  sauce boats 31, 268
  saucers 33
  tea bowls 37
  vases 36
Chetham & Woolley 239
children's ceramics
  dinner services 272
  jugs 247
  mugs 251–3
  plates 257
  tureens 297
chinoiserie 13
Chivers, Frederick 171
chocolate cups 37, 168
chocolate pots 104
Christensen, Karri 188
Christian, Philip **36**
Christian's Liverpool 35, 36
cisterns 27, 61
Claesson, Ilse 184
claret jugs 170
Clauss, Eugène 217
Clerici, Felice 23
Clerici, Giuseppe Maria 23
Clews, G. & Co 282
Cliff, Clarice **103**, 103–10
  ashtrays 106
  biscuit barrels 108, 110
  bowls 105, 106, 108, 109
  boxes 105
  candlesticks 223–4
  chocolate pots 104
  coffee services 104
  cruet sets 107
  cups 109, 230
  dinner services 274
  egg cups 103
  honey pots 103, 104, 106
  jardinières 110, 244
  jugs 103–5, 107–10
  plaques 110
  plates 105, 108, 109, 259
  preserve pots 104–6, 108, 110
  sugar sifters 103, 108, 110
  tea services 105, 107, 108
  teapots 106, 107
  toilet sets 103
  tureens 297
  vases 106
clocks 29, **225**, 225–6
Coalport
  cabaret sets 273
  chambersticks 221
  cups 227–9
  inkwells 235, 236
  jardinières 239
  mugs 251
  scent bottles 270
  tea services 271
Cochran & Fleming 194
coffee cups and cans

Bow 30–2
Christian's Liverpool 35
Clarice Cliff 109, 230
Longton Hall 32
Paragon 230
post-war design 94
Wedgwood 161
Worcester 163, 164, 167
coffee pots
  Art pottery 76
  creamware 28
  Crown Ducal 283
  faïence 21
  Leeds Pottery 26
  Meakin 283
  Meissen 142, 279
  pearlware 25
  Portmeirion 283
  post-war design 87, 90–3
  redware 279
  Scandinavian 189
  Sèvres 156
  Staffordshire 24
  Wedgwood 160
  Worcester 166
coffee services
  Art Deco 84, 86
  Aynsley 274
  Carlton Ware 274
  Celtic Pottery 275
  Clarice Cliff 104
  Derby 113
  Meissen 271
  post-war design 90, 91
  Royal Doulton 124
  Royal Worcester 173
  Shelley 274
  Windsor 275
  Worcester 167
Coleman, W.S. 66
Colenbrander, T.A.C. 76
Colledge, Glyn 89, 254
commemorative ware
  bowls 216
  delft 12
  jugs 29, 120, 124, 191, 248
  loving cups 124, 133, 254
  mugs 202, 252, 254
  plates 95, 258, 259
  scent bottles 270
comports 113, 126, 150
Conde, G. 84
contemporary ceramics see
  post-war design
Continental
  boxes 217
  cabaret sets 271
  jugs 246
  plaques 260, 261, 263
  plates 256
  scent bottles 270
  vases 301
coolers 177
Cooper, Susie
  cups 83
  dinner services 274, 275
  jugs 85
  teapots 283
Copeland **271**
  armorial and crested china 63
  blue-printed pottery 46
  busts 233
  cups 229
  dinner services 271
  inkstands 238
  jugs 248
Copeland & Garrett 44
cottages, model 53
cow creamers
  creamware 47
  Staffordshire 55
  Welsh 196, 201, 203
  Whieldon 24
Coyne, Sallie 180
Craven Dunhill 287
cream boats 111, 166, **268**, 269
cream jugs
  Art Deco 83
  Belleek 102
  blue-printed pottery 43
  Clarice Cliff 104
  Lowestoft 37
  Meissen 249

post-war design 88
Rockingham 246
Worcester 245
creamware **26**
  animals 27, 206
  baskets 160
  coffee pots 28
  cow creamers 47
  dishes 24, 26, 29
  inkstands 29
  jugs 25–7, 29, 176
  mugs 27, 28, 250
  nightlight holders 29
  plates 26
  tea canisters 276, 277
  tea services 161
  teapots 24–6, 28, 278, 279
  Toby jugs 289
  tureens 294
  water cisterns 27
crested china 62–5
crocks 179
Crown Devon
  bowls 85
  jardinières 243
  jugs 81
  vases 303, 304
Crown Ducal 83, 85, 283, 303
Crown Staffordshire 224, 238
cruet sets 83, 84, 107, 114
cups and saucers 227–30
  armorial and crested china 62
  Art Deco 83
  Belleek 100, 228, 229
  Berlin 228
  blue-printed pottery 44
  cabinet porcelain **227**
  Clarice Cliff 104, 230
  Coalport 227–9
  Copeland Spode 229
  Derby 113
  faïence 21
  Meissen 136, 143, 229
  Minton 129, 228
  Nantgarw 227
  Paragon 230
  Paris porcelain 228
  post-war design 95
  Quimper 230
  Rathbone 228
  Ridgway 227
  Rosenthal 229
  Royal Crown Derby 230
  Royal Worcester 229
  Scandinavian 185, 188
  Scottish 195
  Sèvres 155–7
  Staffordshire 228
  stoneware 188
  Wedgwood 227
  Welsh 196, 199
  Wemyss 229
  Worcester 164, 167, 170, 227
  see also coffee cups
Curnock, Percy 122

D
Dali, Salvador 87
Daniel, H. & R. 296
Danish ceramics 184–9
Davenport
  blue-printed pottery 42, 44
  mugs 253
  tureens 295
  vases 301
Davis, Harry 172, 263
Davis, Louisa J. 118
De Morgan, William **66**, 66, 286, 287
De Paeuw 13
decanters 83
Delecia 244
delft **12**, 12–19
  animals 18
  apothecary jars 16
  barrels 19
  bottles 12
  bowls 14, 18, 19, 215
  chargers 12, 14–17
  dishes 13–19, 255
  drug jars 13
  flower bricks 15, 18
  jugs 17, 19

pill slabs 19
plaques 263
plates 12–18
posset pots 14, 15
tiles 17, 19, 284–5
Toby jugs 290
vases 13
wall pockets 19
Della Robbia 68, 71
Denby 92–3, **93**
Derby **111**, 111–13
  animals 111–13
  candlesticks 220
  coffee services 113
  comports 113
  cream boats 111
  cups 113
  dishes 111, 112
  figures 231, 232
  ice pails 112
  inkwells 236
  mugs 112, 251
  plates 113
  sauce boats 111
  spill vases 112
  tea bowls 112
  tureens 295–7
  vases 112, 113, 300
Deruta 22
desk sets 144, 237
dessert services 271
  bone china 272
  Minton 129, 132
  Ridgway 272
  Scandinavian 184
  Wedgwood 161
  Worcester 168
Desvres 21
Dewdney, James 249
Dewsbery, David 121
dinner services
  blue-printed pottery 40
  Burleigh Ware 272
  child's 272
  Clarice Cliff 274
  Copeland 271
  Limoges 274
  Mason's Ironstone 127
  Midwinter 275
  stone china 272, 273
  Susie Cooper 274, 275
dishes 255–9
  armorial and crested china 62
  Art Deco 82
  Art pottery 75
  Bloor Derby 257
  blue-printed pottery 39–42, 44–6
  Bow 30, 35
  Caughley 37
  Chelsea 32–4
  creamware 24, 26, 29
  Delft 13–19, 255
  Derby 111, 112
  faïence 20, 255
  Limehouse 30
  Longton Hall 31, 36
  Lowestoft 37
  maiolica 22
  majolica 57–60, 255
  Mason's Ironstone 127
  Moorcroft 152
  New Hall 256
  pearlware 40, 127, 212
  post-war design 91, 94
  Royal Worcester 171, 173
  Scandinavian 187, 189
  slipware 28, 255
  spongeware 258, 259
  Staffordshire 259
  stoneware 189
  Wedgwood 160
  Welsh 198
  Worcester 168, 255
dog bowls 42
Donn Pottery 291
Doulton **114**, 114–24, **115**, **116**
  beakers 118
  biscuit barrels 115, 117
  candlesticks 222
  cruets 114
  ewers 118, 120
  flasks 114, 122

ice cream drums 121
inkwells 237
jardinières 241
jars 114
jugs 114–17, 120, 121
mugs 119
oil lamps 116
pipe stands 118
planters 116
spill vases 115
tankards 118
tea services 115, 120
toilet sets 119
tygs 118
vases 114–21, 302
see also Royal Doulton
Doulton & Watts 114
'drabware' 160
drainers 44, 127
Dresden 217, 226
Dresser, Christopher 67, 75
dressing table boxes 217
drug jars 13, 22, 23
Dubuisson 226
Dunmore Pottery **191**, 191–2
Durlach 276
Durtnall, Beatrice M. 241
Dutch ceramics
  Art Deco 82
  Art pottery 76
  candlesticks 224
  dishes 255
Dutch Delft **12**
  animals 18
  bowls 14
  dishes 13, 15, 16
  jugs 19
  pipkins 12
  plaques 263
  plates 12–14, 18
  tiles 284, 285
  vases 13
Dwight, John **26**

E
early English porcelain 30–8, **36**
early English pottery 24–9
écuelles 158
Edwards, J.C. 288
Edwards, Louisa E. 114
egg cups 31, 103
egg timers 84
Eichwald 242
Elkin Knight & Co 45
Elsmore & Forster 245
Elstrodt, W. 76
English Delft 12–19
English porcelain 30–8, **36**
English pottery 24–9
Epply, Lorinda 182
Esser, Max 145
Ewenny Pottery **202**, 202, 203
ewers
  Doulton 118
  faïence 20
  Goss 248
  Hicks & Meigh 246
  Martin Brothers 77, 78
  Minton 132
  Royal Doulton 120
  Royal Worcester 248
extinguishers 222–4, **223**

F
faïence
  animals 206
  bowls 189
  boxes 219
  candlesticks 223
  dishes 255
  French **20**, 20–1
  inkstands 238
  jardinières 239, 240, 242
  jars 114
  snuff boxes 184
  tea canisters 276
  teapots 283
  tureens 184, 294
  vases 66, 117, 119, 188, 299, 302, 304
Falcon ware 83
famille rose 31, 32
Felton, Miss 115

Fieldings 243, 303
Fife Pottery 191
figures 231–4
  armorial and crested china 64
  Art Deco 82–5
  Art pottery 73
  Belleek 100
  Berlin porcelain 232
  bocage figures **47**
  Bow 34, 35
  Chelsea 35
  Derby 231, 232
  Longton Hall 31
  majolica 57
  Martin Brothers 78
  Meissen 134–45, **139**, 233, 234
  military 54
  Minton 131
  Parian 131
  pearlware 48–51, 232
  piano babies 234
  political **53**
  Royal Doulton 122, 123, 234
  Scandinavian 185
  Scottish 190
  Staffordshire 47–55, 231, 232
  Welsh 200
Finnish ceramics 188, 189
flagons 179
flasks
  Art pottery 72
  blue-printed pottery 45
  delft 12
  Scottish 190, 192
Flight & Barr 62
Flight, Barr & Barr 28, 62, **165**, 169–70, 236, 239, 298
Florenz 88
flower bricks 15, 18–19
Foley 68
footbaths 130
Foresters 56
fork handles 32
Fornasetti, Piero 87–9
Forster, Minnie 121
Forsyth, Gordon 74
Fouillen, P. 230
Francis, Catherine 241
Franciscan 91
Frankfurt 255
French ceramics
  animals 206
  Art Deco 82–4
  Art pottery 73
  boxes 219
  centrepieces 213
  clocks 225, 226
  cups 228, 230
  dinner services 274
  faïence **20**, 20–1
  inkstands 238
  jardinières 239, 240
  jugs 245, 248, 249
  majolica 61
  plaques 263
  scent bottles 270
  Sèvres **155**, 155–8
  teapots 283
  vases 301
Friberg, Berndt 187
Fumez 156

G
Gallé, Emile 21, 206
Gamboni 87, 304
game pie dishes 59, **297**
garden seats 56
Gates, William Day 181
Gaudy Welsh **245**, 245
Gazzard, Marea 93
Gerace 23
German ceramics
  animals 208
  Art Deco 84, 85
  baskets 211, 212
  boxes 217–19
  busts 234
  centrepieces 214
  clocks 225, 226
  coffee pots 279
  cups 229
  dishes 255

figures 82, 232, 233
jugs 245, 249
Meissen 134–45
mirrors 225, 226
plaques 260, 262
post-war design 88, 91
sauce boats 268
tankards 250
tea canisters 276
tea services 271
tiles 284
tureens 294, 295
vases 299, 300
Gien 20
Gilbody, Samuel **36**
Gille, Jean 233
ginger jars
  Art Deco 81, 85
  Art pottery 74
  Mason's Ironstone 127
  Moorcroft 154
  Ruskin Pottery 79
glass coolers 155
Goebel, W. 238
Goldscheider 85
Goss, W.H. 63, 65, 248
Gouda 82, 83, 224
Grainger's Worcester
  bowls 171
  jugs 170
  potpourri bowls 171
  teapots 169
  tureens 295
gravy boats 30
Gray's Pottery 74, 83, 283
Green, T.G. 85, 269
Grueby Pottery **180**, 180
guglets 59, 164
Gustavsberg **184**, 184–8

H
Hackwood 44
Hadley's Worcester 171, 242
Haley, Ruben 182
Hancock, S. & Sons 75, 76
Hannong, Joseph 20
Harradine, Leslie 123
Hart, Clive 67
Haslam, Malcolm 302
Haviland & Co 273
Heath, Joseph 41, 178
Herbst, René 83
Herculaneum 41, 295
Hermann 179
Hicks & Meigh 42, 246
Holdcroft, Joseph 59, 207, 249
Hollinshead & Kirkham 76
Holm, Åke 187
honey pots 103, 104, 106
Hornsea Pottery 89, 91, 94
Höroldt, J.G. 134
Hosel, Eric 208
hot water dishes 169
hot water jugs 180
Huet, C. 135
Huggins, Vera 123
humidors 150
Hungarian ceramics 234, 303
Hurley, E.T. 181

I
ice cream drums 121
ice pails 112
Iden Pottery 87, 90, 92
inkstands
  Copeland 238
  creamware 29
  faïence 238
  Meissen 138
  Scottish 194
inkwells 235–8, **238**
  Coalport 235, 236
  Crown Staffordshire 238
  Derby 236
  Doulton 237
  majolica 58, 237
  Martin Brothers 78
  Royal Crown Derby 238
  Sèvres-style 236
  slipware 28
  Staffordshire 237
  stoneware 235–6

Welsh 198
Wemyss 238
Worcester 235, 236
Ipsen, P. 184
Irish ceramics
  animals 208
  baskets 212–14
  Belleek **100**, 100–1
  cups 228, 229
  spill vases 299
  teapots 281, 282
  vases 300, 302, 304
ironstone **125**, 125–8, 256
Irvine, Sadie 182
Isle of Wight 93
Italian ceramics
  Art pottery 75
  boxes 218
  dishes 255
  maiolica **22**, 22–3
  plaques 261
  post-war design 87, 89, 91

J
Jackfield 250
Jackson 178
jardinières 239–44
  American 182, 183
  Art pottery 67, 68
  Brannam Pottery 241
  Bretby 241
  Burmantofts 240, 242
  Clarice Cliff 110, 244
  Coalport 239
  Crown Devon 243
  Delphin Massier 240
  Doulton 241
  Eichwald 242
  faïence 21, 239, 240, 242
  George Jones 241
  Leeds 242
  Longchamps 243
  majolica 61, 131, 239–40, 242
  Martin Brothers 77
  Minton 131, 133, 239–40
  Moorcroft 244
  Royal Doulton 243, 244
  Sèvres-style 157, 239
  stoneware 239, 244
  Wardle Art Pottery 244
  Wedgwood 242
  Wemyss 240, 241, 243, 244
  Worcester 171, 239, 242
jars
  American 176
  Art Deco 81, 85
  Art pottery 74, 76
  blue-printed pottery 39
  delft 12, 15
  Doulton 114
  drug 13, 22, 23
  faïence 114
  Mason's Ironstone 127
  Moorcroft 154
  redware 176
  Ruskin Pottery 79
  Scottish 193, 195
  tobacco 55
jasper ware **160**
  candlesticks 222
  coffee cans 161
  jardinières 242
  plaques 159
  potpourri vases 160
  scent bottles 159
  vases 160, 161
  Wedgwood **160**
jelly moulds 178, 180, 181
Jensen 185
Jones, Florrie 123
Jones, George 46, 57–60, 241
Joyce, Richard 73
jugs 245–9
  Adams 246
  American 178, 179, 182
  armorial and crested china 62
  Art Deco 81, 83, 85, 86
  Art pottery 67, 73, 74, 76
  Arthur Wood 249
  Bargeware 248
  Belleek 100–2
  blue-printed pottery 41, 43–6
  Brannam Pottery 249

Chaffer's Liverpool 34
character jugs 19
Clarice Cliff 103–5, 107–10
Copeland 248
creamware 25–7, 29, 176
delft 17, 19
Doulton 114–15, 117
Gaudy Welsh 245
Lowestoft 37
lustre 62, 246, 247
majolica 59, 60, 130, 245–9
Mason's Ironstone 125, 126, 128
Meissen 249
Minton 130, 247
Mocha ware 247
Moorcroft 154
pearlware 27, 190
post-war design 88, 93
Prattware 27, 29
puzzle jugs 17, 46, **245**, 245, 247
Rockingham 246
Royal Doulton 120, 121, 123, 124
Royal Worcester 172
Scandinavian 186
Scottish 190, 191, 195
Spode 246
stoneware 73, 116, 117, 121, 245–8
Sunderland 246
SylvaC 249
Toby jugs 289–93
Welsh 196, 199, 201, 202
Worcester 166, 167, 170, 245

K
Kåge, Wilhelm 184
Kaipiainen, Birger 189
Kändler, J.J. 134, 137, 144
Katzhütte 85
Keel St Pottery 254
Keeling 42
Kennon, Roberta 181
Kerr & Binns 170
Kerton, Irene 92
King, Jessie Marion 75, 195
Kirkcaldy Pottery 190
knife handles 32
Konig, A. 145
KPM 262
Kraut, Hans 284
Kyhn, Knud 188, 189

L
ladles 38
Lambeth delft 12, 13
lamp bases
  American 181
  Art Deco 84
  Moorcroft 154
  post-war design 89, 95
  Ruskin Pottery 80
  Troika 96
lanterns 21
Larson, Lisa 188
Lauder, Alex 69, 241, 301
Leach, Bernard **87**
Leach, David 90
Leach Pottery 87
Leclerc 157
Leeds Pottery
  blue-printed pottery 41
  bowls 27
  coffee pots 26
  jardinières 242
  mugs 28
  sauce boats 269
  tea canisters 277
  teapots 28
  tureens 294
  water cisterns 27
lemonade sets 162
Lenoble, Emile 83
letter racks 238
Limehouse 30, **36**
Limoges
  cabaret sets 273
  dinner services 274
  plaques 263
  scent bottles 270
  vases 301

Lindberg, Stig 185–7
Lindner, Doris 210
Linthorpe Pottery 66–7, 300
Liotard, Jean-Etienne 260
lithophane plaques 201
Liverpool
  cream boats 269
  creamware 28, 176
  delft 16–19, 285
Livesley Powell & Co 272
Llanelli Pottery 201–3, **203**
Locke & Co 301
London delft 12, 14–19, 284
Longchamps 243
Longton Hall **36**
  coffee cups 32
  dishes 36
  figures 31
loving cups
  Martin Brothers 77
  Minton 133
  Royal Crown Derby 254
  Royal Doulton 124
Lowestoft **36**
  bowls 38, 215
  gravy boats 30
  jugs 37
  pickle dishes 37
  sauce boats 36
  tea bowls 37
Lucas, Daniel 112
Lupton, Edith 116
lustre ware **251**
  bowls 133, 162, 215–16
  boxes 219
  cow creamers 201
  cups 228
  egg timers 84
  jugs 62, 246, 247
  mugs 251
  plaques 261, 262
  plates 81
  saucers 227
  vases 71, 74, 146, 162

M
Mafra 61
maiolica, Italian **22**, 22–3
majolica **56**, 56–61
  animals 56, 59, 208
  birds 61
  bowls 61
  chargers 61
  cheese dishes 56–9
  cisterns 61
  desk stands 237
  dessert services 161
  dishes 57–60, 255
  figures 57
  garden seats 56
  inkwells 58, 237
  jardinières 61, 131, 239–40, 242
  jugs 59, 60, 130, 245–9
  planters 58
  plaques 261
  plates 56–8, 60, 256
  spill vases 304
  teapots 56–60
  Toby jugs 293
  urns 132
  vases 58
  wall pockets 161
Makeig-Jones, Daisy 81, 162
Mak'Merry **195**, 195
Malty 262
Manzoni, A.C. 69
Marieberg 184, 294
Markmerry 86
Marsh, Jacob 40
Marshall, Mark 118, 121
Martin Brothers **77**, 77–8, 226
Martinez, Maria and Santana 183
Mason's Ironstone **125**, 125–8
Massier, Delphin 240
match strikers 71
Maw & Co 286
Mayer & Newbold 299
Meakin 90, 283
Measham ware see Bargeware
measures 46
meat dishes

American 178
  blue-printed pottery 39, 40, 42, 44
  Mason's Ironstone 127
  Welsh 196
medals, Sèvres 158
Meissen **134**, 134–45, **135**, **136**
  animals 138, 145, 207, 208
  armorial and crested china 62
  baskets 211, 212
  birds 138, 143, 144
  bowls 134, 136
  boxes 135, 217, 219
  busts 234
  candlesticks 140, 143
  centrepieces 212
  clocks 225, 226
  coffee pots 142, 279
  coffee services 271
  cups 136, 143, 229
  desk sets 144
  figures 134–45, **139**, 233, 234
  inkstands 138
  jugs 249
  plaques 260
  potpourri vases 135
  sauce boats 268
  stands 143
  sucriers 134, 135
  tea canisters 276
  tea services 271
  tureens 295
  vases 299, 300
Memphis 95
Methrus of Kirkcaldy 191
Meyer, Joseph 181
Midwinter 88, 94, 275
Midwinter, Eve 94
Milan maiolica 23
military figures 54
milk jugs
  creamware 25
  Welsh 199
  Worcester 166, 167, 245
Minton **129**, 129–33
  animals 130
  bowls 129, 130, 133
  busts 130, 131
  candlesticks 222
  centrepieces 213
  cream boats 269
  cups 129, 228
  dessert services 129, 132
  ewers 132
  figures 131
  footbaths 130
  jardinières 131, 133, 239–40
  jugs 130, 247
  loving cups 133
  majolica 57–61, 130–2
  mugs 133
  plates 130–2, 259
  tea canisters 277
  teapots 282
  tiles 285–8
  vases 131–3
Minton Hollins & Co 286, 288
Minton Studio 66
mirrors 225, 226
Mocha ware 247, **252**, 252
models 29, 63–5, 190
Mondi, Aldo 89
money boxes 51, 191
monteiths 156
Montelupo 22
Moorcroft 146–54, **147**, **148**, 244
Moore, Fred 122
Moore Bros 211, 213
Morris, Henry 198
Morris, R.J. 231
Moyr Smith, John 285–6
muffin dishes 169
mugs 250–4
  American 179
  armorial and crested china 62
  Art Deco 86
  Art pottery 75
  blue-printed pottery 40, 46
  Bow 34
  children's 251–3
  Coalport 251
  commemorative 202, 252, 254

creamware 27, 28, 250
Davenport 253
Derby 112, 251
Keel St Pottery 254
lustre 251
Mason's Ironstone 126, 127
Minton 133
New Hall 250
pearlware 252
post-war design 88
Royal Doulton 119
Scottish 191, 193–4
stoneware 252
Sunderland 252
Vauxhall 32
Welsh 199, 201–3
Wemyss 254
Whieldon 250
Worcester 165, 167, 250
Munch-Khe, Willi 145
Muncie Pottery 182
Murray, Keith **86**, 86, 162
Mycock, William S. 72, 74, 303
Myott 86

N
Nantgarw **196**, 196–200, **200**, 227
Nekola, Karel 192, 241, 254
Nevers 239
New Hall 250, 256, **279**, 279
Newcomb College Pottery **181**, 181–3
nightlight holders 29
Nixon, Harry **122**
Noke, Charles 122, 234
North Country Toby jugs 290
nursery plates 201, 257
Nylund, Gunnar 186
Nymolle 186, 187

O
oil lamps 116
Orchies 61
Ott & Brewer Belleek **180**, 180
Oxshott Pottery 75
oyster dishes 59

P
Palissy 61, 247
pancake dishes 18
panels, tile 288
paperweights 88, 89
Paragon 230
Pardoe, Thomas 200
Parian
  busts 130, 233
  centrepieces 211
  figures 131
  medals 158
Paris porcelain 217, 228
Parkenson 181
Parr, Thomas 54
pastille burners 49, 51, 52, 54, 55
pâte-sur-pâte 132, **241**, 241, 301
Patterson & Co 45
Paveley, Ruth 86, 282
pearlware
  animals 206
  boxes 217
  candlesticks 220
  coffee pots 279
  dishes 40, 127, 212
  figures 48–51, 232
  jugs 27, 190, 196
  models 190
  mugs 252
  soup bowls 43
  Toby jugs 289, 290
  vases 159
pen trays 168
Pennington, James **36**
Pennington, John **36**, 38, 167
Pennington, Seth **36**, 269
pepperpot figures 52
perfume bottles see scent bottles
Pesaro 22
Petit, Jacob 225
piano babies 234
pickle dishes

armorial and crested china
62, 65
blue-printed pottery 39, 42
Caughley 37
Limehouse 30
Longton Hall 31
Lowestoft 37
Worcester 163
pie plates 178
pilgrim flasks 45, 192
Pilkington's Royal Lancastrian
72–4, 303, 304
pill boxes 217
Pill Pottery 200
pill slabs 19
pin trays 65, 193
Pinder, Bourne & Co 299
pipe stands 118
pipkins 12
pitchers 70, 75
planters 58, 97, 116
plaques 260–3
American 182
Art pottery 66
Berlin porcelain 262
Clarice Cliff 110
Dutch Delft 263
Limoges 263
lustre 261, 262
majolica 261
Meissen 260
porcelain **263**
Prattware 29, 260
Royal Doulton 263
Royal Worcester 173, 263
Scandinavian 186
tile 287, 288
Wedgwood 159
Welsh 201
plates 255–9
American 176–8, 183
armorial and crested china
62, 63
Art Deco 81, 83
Art pottery 68, 71, 74
blue-printed pottery 45
Bow 36
Chelsea 33
Clarice Cliff 105, 109, 259
commemorative 95, 258, 259
creamware 26
Delft 12–18
Derby 113
faïence 20
ironstone 128, 256
lustre 81
maiolica 23
majolica 56–8, 60, 256
Martin Brothers 77
Minton 130–2, 259
Moorcroft 150, 151, 154
nursery ware 257
post-war design 87, 89, 93–5
Royal Doulton 122
Royal Worcester 173, 259
salt-glazed stoneware 25
Scandinavian 187, 189
Scottish 194
Sèvres-style 156–8
Spode 256
Staffordshire 177
Welsh 196–201, 203
Worcester 165, 167, 255
platters 177
Plaue 225
Plichta, Jan 195, 209
political figures **53**
Pollard, William 196, 197, 236
Poole Pottery 86, **92**, 92,
94–5, 304
porringers 194
Portmeirion **90**, 90, 277, 283
Portobello 190
Portuguese ceramics
jugs 247
majolica 61
posset pots 14, 15
Post, Wilhelmina 180
post-war design and
contemporary ceramics 87–97
pot lids **264**, 264–7, **266**
potpourri bowls and vases
Meissen 135

Royal Worcester 172
Wedgwood 160
Worcester 171
Potter, Beatrix 226
powder bowls 153, 154
powder boxes 219
Powell, William 173
Pratt, F. & R. 264, 266
Prattware **260**
animals 206
birds 27
jugs 27, 29
models 29
plaques 29, 260
tea canisters 277
Toby jugs 289
preserve pots
Clarice Cliff 104–6, 108, 110
Moorcroft 149
Scottish 192, 194
pudding moulds 176, 179
Pugin, A.W.N. 130
puzzle jugs 17, 46, **245**, 245,
247

Q
quill holders 237
Quimper
bowls 21
boxes 219
cups 230
teapots 283
vases 302, 304

R
Radford 74, 86
Ram 76
Randell, Emily 241
Ranleigh 89
Rathbone 228
Ravilious, Eric 88, 162
redware **178**, 178
coffee pots 279
jars 176
jugs 178
plates 178
pudding moulds 176
teapots 278
Reinicke, P. 135
Reni, Guido 260
Rhead, Charlotte **82**, 82, 283,
303
Ridgway **272**
armorial and crested china 63
blue-printed pottery 41, 44
boxes 217
candlesticks 221
cups 227
dessert services 272
Rie, Lucie 95
Riley 39, 62, 215
Roberts, Frank 173
Robinson & Leadbeater **231**, 231
Robj 83
Rockingham 246, 270
Rogers 39–42, 45
Roman, Desiree 181
Rooke, Bernard 91
Rookwood Pottery 180–2,
181, **182**
Rörstrand **184**, 184, 186, 187,
189
Rosenthal 229
Roseville Pottery 182, 183
Royal Albert 88
Royal Copenhagen 184–5,
185, 187–9
Royal Crown Derby 230, 238,
254
Royal Doulton 119–24
animals 209, 210
bowls 123, 216
boxes 124
brooches 124
coffee services 124
ewers 120
figures 122, 123, 234
ice cream drums 121
jardinières 243, 244
jugs 120, 121, 123, 124
loving cups 124
mugs 119
plaques 263

plates 122
sugar pots 124
tea services 120
vases 120–3
see also Doulton
Royal Winton 83, 216
Royal Worcester **170**
animals 172, 210
bowls 216
candlesticks 221
claret jugs 170
coffee services 173
cups 229
dishes 171, 173
ewers 248
extinguishers 222–4, **223**
jugs 172
plaques 173, 263
plates 173, 259
potpourri bowls 172
teapots 282
tygs 171
vases 81, 170–3, 302
see also Worcester
royalty, Staffordshire figures **52**
Ruskin Pottery **79**, 79–80, 216
Rye Pottery 216

S
Sadler 83, 86, 285
St Ives 75
salad bowls 61
salt-glazed stoneware **26**
animals 24, 25
coolers 177
flagons 179
inkwells 235
plates 25
shop pots 26
spirit flasks 122
sugar sifters 25
teapots 24, 25, 278
salts 156, 234
Salvini Brevettato 75
San Ildefonso 183
Sandart, Jean Baptiste 155
sardine dishes 60
sauce boats **268**, 268–9
American 177
Bow 31, 268
Chelsea 31, 268
Derby 111
Leeds Pottery 269
Lowestoft 36
Meissen 268
Staffordshire 269
T.G. Green 269
Worcester 163, 165
sauce tureens 296, 297
saucers
Bristol 36
Chelsea 33
maiolica 23
New Hall 256
see also cups and saucers
Scandinavian ceramics 88, 184–9
scent bottles 153, 159, 270
Schenck, Frederick 241
Schliepstein 82
Schönheit 136, 140, 141
Scott & Co 216
Scott of Southwick 252
Scottish ceramics 75, 190–5
Seaton 191
services 271–5
Scandinavian 186
see also coffee services;
dessert services; dinner services;
tea services
Sèvres and Sèvres style **155**,
155–8, **156**
centrepieces 213
coffee pots 156, 158
cups 155–7
écuelles 158
glass coolers 155
inkwells 236
jardinières 157, 239
medals 158
monteiths 156
plates 156–8
salts 156
sucriers 155

teapots 158
trays 155
vases 157, 158
Sharpe, James 193
shaving mugs 126
Shelley
armorial and crested china 64
coffee services 274
ginger jars 74
tea services 84, 275
trios 230
vases 84, 303
Sherwin & Cotton 287, 288
shop pots 26
Shufflebotham 203
Sicilian maiolica 23
Siena 23
Simeon, Harry 122
Simmance, Eliza 115–18, 121,
243
Simpson, Anna Frances 183
slipware 28, 255
slop bowls 43
Smith, William 44
snuff boxes 184, 218, 219
soup bowls and plates
blue-printed pottery 43, 45
pearlware 43
Spode 257
spongeware 255, 256
soup tureens 295
spill vases
Art pottery 70
Belleek 100, 299
Derby 112
Doulton 115
majolica 304
Spode 299
Staffordshire 50
Worcester 298
spirit flasks 122
Spode
blue-printed pottery 42, 44
chambersticks 221
jugs 246
plates 95, 256
scent bottles 270
soup plates 257
spill vases 299
vases 298
spongeware **256**
bowls 101, 191
dishes 258, 259
porringers 194
soup plates 255, 256
tankards 253
spoon trays 38
Stabler, Phoebe 82
Staffordshire
animals 25, 206–8
armorial and crested china 63
baskets 212
blue-printed pottery 39, 46
candlesticks 220, 221
coffee pots 24
cow creamers 55
creamware **26**, 26
cups 228
dishes 259
dogs 53, 55
extinguishers 222, 223
figures 47–55, 231, 232
inkwells 237
majolica 59
model cottages 53
money boxes 51
pastille burners 49, 51, 52,
54, 55
plates 177
quill holders 237
royal figures **52**
sauce boats 269
spill vases 50
sugar sifters 25
teapots 25, 278
tobacco jars 55
Toby jugs 290–2
tureens 55, 297
watch stands 51
Stålhane, Carl-Harry 187
stands 20, 143
steins 180
Stevenson 45

Stevenson, Andrew 43
Stevenson, Ralph 45
Stinton, Harry 172
Stinton, J.A.S. 302
Stinton, James 171
Stinton, John 173
stone china 40, 272, 273
stoneware
  American **179**
  bowls 88
  cups 188
  dishes 189
  ewers 77
  inkwells 235–6
  jardinières 239, 244
  jugs 73, 116, 117, 121, 245–8
  mugs 252
  tankards 250
  teapots 278, 280, 281
  vases 78, 93, 95, 114, 115,
    120, 122, 123, 186
  see also salt-glazed
  stoneware
Stony & Co 65
Stralsund 294
Strasbourg 20
Stump Longniddry 195
sucriers
  Meissen 135
  Sèvres 155
  Worcester 167, 169
sugar bowls
  Belleek 102
  blue-printed pottery 45
  Caughley 38
  post-war design 88
  Welsh 198
sugar boxes 134
sugar pots 124
sugar sifters
  Clarice Cliff 103, 108, 110
  Staffordshire 25
Sundell, Britt-Louise 88
Sunderland
  bowls 215–16
  jugs 246
  mugs 252
Swansea **196**, 196–202, **197**,
  200
  creamware **26**
Swedish ceramics 184–9, 294
sweetmeat dishes 32
Swetnam, Leonard Thomas 287
Swinton Pottery 280
SylvaC 249

T
Tait, Jessie 88
tankards
  Doulton 118
  Glyn Colledge 254
  Jackfield 250
  Mocha ware 252
  spongeware 253
  stoneware 250
  Welsh 203
tart plates 178
Taylor, William Howson 80
tea bowls
  blue-printed pottery 43
  Caughley 38
  Chelsea 37
  Derby 112
  Lowestoft 37
  Welsh 196
  Worcester 165, 166
tea canisters 32, 164, 276–7
tea cups see cups and saucers
tea kettles 60, 101
tea services
  Art Deco 84
  bone china 272
  Clarice Cliff 105, 107, 108
  Coalport 271
  Doulton 115
  Meissen 271
  Royal Doulton 120
  Shelley 275
  Wedgwood 161
teapots **278**, 278–83
  Art Deco 83, 86
  Art pottery 76
  Bargeware 281–2

Belleek 100, 281, 282
Cadogan **280**, 280
Carter, Stabler & Adams 282
Caughley 38
Christian's Liverpool 36
Clarice Cliff 105, 107
creamware 24–6, 28, 278,
  279
faïence 283
Gray's Pottery 283
majolica 56–60
Minton 282
New Hall 279
post-war design 89, 90, 95
Quimper 283
redware 278
Royal Worcester 282
salt-glazed stoneware 24, 25
Sèvres-style 158
Staffordshire 278
stoneware 278, 280, 281
Wedgwood 281
Whieldon 24, 278
Worcester 28, 163, 168,
  169, 278
Teco Art Pottery 181
Teichner, Alice 303
terracotta
  jardinières 243
  vases 67
Thorsson, Nils 187, 188
Thun, Mateo 95
tiles 284–8
  Aesthetic Movement 286
  American 180
  Art pottery 66
  Carter & Co 288
  delft 17, 19, 284–5
  Maw & Co 286
  Minton 285–8
  post-war design 87
  Scandinavian 184
  Sherwin & Cotton 287, 288
  William De Morgan 286, 287
tin-glazed earthenware 12–23
  Dutch and English Delft **12**,
    12–19, **15**
  French faïence **20**, 20–1
  Italian maiolica **22**, 22–3
Tinworth, George 115
tobacco jars 55
Toby jugs **289**, 289–93, **291**
Todd, Charles Stewart 182
toilet boxes 218
toilet sets 103, 119
Tower, James 87
transfer-printed pottery 39–46,
  41, **43**
trays
  Scottish 193, 194
  Sèvres 155
  Welsh 203
Trent Tile Co 180
trios 90, 230
Troika **96**, 96–7
tureens 294–7
  Bloor Derby 297
  Bow 294
  child's 295
  Clarice Cliff 297
  creamware 294
  Davenport 295
  Derby 295–7
  Enoch Wood 296
  faïence 184, 294
  H. & R. Daniel 296
  Herculaneum 296
  ironstone 128
  Leeds Pottery 294
  Mason's Ironstone 127
  Meissen 295
  Scandinavian 184
  Staffordshire 55, 297
  Vienna porcelain 294
  Worcester 295
Turner 39, 41
tygs 72, 118, 171

U
umbrella stands 208
Ungerer, Jakob 145
Upchurch 75
urns 132

V
Vallauris 74
vases 298–304
  American 180–3
  Art Deco 81–4, 86
  Art pottery 66–76
  Belleek 101, 102, 300, 302, 304
  Bow 30, 33
  Bretby 300, 302
  Burmantofts 301
  Carlton Ware 303
  Carter, Stabler & Adams 301
  Chelsea 36
  Clarice Cliff 105
  Crown Devon 303, 304
  Crown Ducal 303
  Davenport 301
  Delft 13
  Derby 112, 113, 300
  Doulton 114–20, 302
  faïence 20, 66, 117, 119,
    188, 299, 302
  Limoges 301
  Linthorpe Pottery 300
  lustre 71, 74, 146, 162
  majolica 58
  Martin Brothers 77, 78
  Mason's Ironstone 125–6
  Meissen 299, 300
  Minton 131–3
  Moorcroft 146–52, 154
  pearlware 159
  Pilkington's 303, 304
  Poole Pottery 304
  post-war design 88–95
  Quimper 302, 304
  Royal Doulton 120–3
  Royal Worcester 81, 170–3, 302
  Ruskin Pottery 79, 80
  Scandinavian 184–9
  Scottish 192, 194
  Sèvres and Sèvres-style 157, 158
  Shelley 303
  Spode 298
  stoneware 78, 93, 95, 114,
    115, 120, 122, 123, 186
  terracotta 67
  Troika 96–7
  Vauxhall 33
  Wedgwood 159–62, 298
  Welsh 197
  Worcester 298, 301
  Zsolnay Pecs 303
Vauxhall 32, 33, **36**
vegetable tureens 296
vegetables dishes 41
Vieillard 155
Vienna porcelain 73, 218, 294
Volkstadt 226

W
wall masks 85
wall plaques see plaques
wall pockets
  Art pottery 67
  delft 19
  faïence 21
  Wedgwood 161
Walther, Paul 208
Walton 206
Wardle, J. & Co 258
Wardle Art Pottery **244**, 244
watch stands 51
water jugs 182, 183
Watt, William John 195
Wedgwood **160**
Wedgwood **159**, 159–62
  baskets 160, 211
  black basalt 159, **161**, 161, 231
  bough pots 159
  bowls 162
  busts 231
  cabaret sets 161
  candlesticks 160, 222
  clocks 226
  coffee cans 161
  coffee services 86
  creamware **26**
  cups 227
  dessert services 161
  dishes 160
  jardinières 242
  jasper ware 159–61, **160**

jugs 25
lamp bases 84
lemonade sets 162
majolica 60, 61
mugs 86, 88
plaques 159
plates 81
potpourri vases 160
scent bottles 159
tea services 161
teapots 281
vases 86, 159–62, 298
wall pockets 161
Welsh 196–203
Wemyss **191**, **192**
  bulb bowls 192
  candlesticks 223
  cups 229
  honey boxes 190
  inkstands and inkwells 194, 238
  jardinières 240, 241, 243, 244
  jars 193
  mugs 191, 193–4, 254
  plates 194
  preserve pots 192, 194
  trays 193, 194
wet drug jars 13, 22, 23
Whieldon **24**
  animals 25
  cow creamers 24
  mugs 250
  teapots 24, 278
White, N. & Co 179
White Star Line 65
Wiener Keramik 76
Wiener Werkstätte 73
Wileman & Co 76
Willow Art 63, 209
Wilson 235
Wimblad, Bjorn 186, 187
Windsor 275
wine bottles 12
Wise, William 286
Withnall 243
Wood, Arthur 249
Wood, Enoch 48, 177, **296**, 296
Wood, Ralph 48, 206
Wood family 206
Worcester **163**, 163–73, **164**,
  165, **169**
  animals 169
  armorial and crested china 62
  baskets 164, 165, 212
  bowls 163, 164, 171, 215
  busts 169
  butter boats 164
  candlesticks 168, 222
  chambersticks 168
  chocolate cups 168
  coffee pots 166
  coffee services 167
  cream boats 166, 269
  cups 163, 164, 167, 170, 227
  dessert services 168
  dishes 168, 255
  hot water dishes 169
  inkwells 235, 236
  jardinières 171, 239, 242
  jugs 166, 167, 170, 245
  muffin dishes 169
  mugs 165, 167, 250
  pen trays 168
  pickle dishes 163
  plates 165, 167, 255
  potpourri bowls 171
  sauce boats 163, 165
  scent bottles 270
  sucriers 167, 169
  tea bowls 165, 166
  tea canisters 164, 276, 277
  teapots 28, 163, 168, 169, 278
  tureens 295
  vases 298, 301

Y
yellow ware 178
Yorkshire pottery
  creamware 26, 29
  Toby jugs **289**, 289, 293
Young, William Weston 196

Z
Zsolnay Pecs 234, 303